Cahiers
du
Cinéma

Harvard Film Studies

Cahiers
du
Cinéma

The 1950s: Neo-Realism, Hollywood, New Wave

Edited by
Jim Hillier

Harvard University Press
Cambridge, Massachusetts

English translation and editorial matter

Copyright © 1985 by the British Film Institute

Originally published in French in *Cahiers du Cinéma*, numbers 1–102, April 1951 to December 1959, © Les Editions de l'Etoile

Printed in the United States of America

10 9 8 7 6 5 4 3

Library of Congress Cataloging in Publication Data

Cahiers du cinéma, the 1950s.
 Includes index.
  1. Moving-pictures—Philosophy—Addresses, essays, lectures. 2. Moving-pictures—Aesthetics—Addresses, essays, lectures. 3. Moving-pictures—France—History—Addresses, essays, lectures. 4. Moving-pictures—Italy—History—Addresses, essays, lectures. 5. Moving-pictures—United States—History—Addresses, essays, lectures.
 I. Hillier, Jim. II. Cahiers du cinéma.
 PN1195.C29 1985   791.43'01   84–25215

ISBN 0–674–09060–8 (cloth)
ISBN 0–674–09061–6 (paper)

Contents

Contents

Part Four Polemics

I Criticism

II Dossier – CinemaScope

Preface and Acknowledgments

When this anthology of selections from *Cahiers du Cinéma* was first discussed, it was planned that each volume should be self-contained and coherent within its own terms, should be representative of the period covered (in this case, some nine years and over a hundred issues of the magazine), should contain largely newly translated material rather than material already easily available in English, should be relevant and useful within contemporary film culture and film education, and should be pleasurable and accessible.

I hope that this somewhat tall order has been filled to a large extent, but some of the requirements have worked against each other. If, for example, work by André Bazin, Jean-Luc Godard and François Truffaut is not as fully represented in the volume as their importance to *Cahiers* would merit, this is because a great deal of their critical work is already available in English (and the same goes for work *on* Renoir, for example). At the same time, not to have represented Bazin, Godard and Truffaut by important writings would have been quite wrong. As a result, all three are represented here both by some already available material and by some newly translated contributions. In any case, what could being 'representative' of *Cahiers* mean? It could be taken to mean several rather different things: representative of contributions by quantity, or by importance – at the time or in retrospect – or representative of the magazine's broad range of concerns. The volume is, I think, generally representative in most of these ways, but I am conscious that, among other omissions, some *Cahiers* contributors, often with long and important associations with the magazine between 1951 and 1959, are poorly or not at all represented.

I have in mind, for example, Jacques Doniol-Valcroze, represented here only in discussions; Louis Marcorelles (independently minded in his interest in such areas as Polish cinema and New York American cinema); André Martin (specialist in animation and comedy); Claude Beylie (Renoir specialist); François Mars (comedy specialist); Jean Douchet, Philippe

viii

Demonsablon, André-S. Labarthe, Claude de Givray, Jacques Siclier and, from the early years, Jean-José Richer and Michel Dorsday, as well as many others. There is no intention to underestimate the value of their work. In some cases, their work is likely to be included in future volumes; in some other cases, examples of their work are available elsewhere in translation. Appendix 2, a guide to *Cahiers* articles from the period April 1951 to December 1959 in translation, is designed very precisely to extend the necessarily limited scope of this volume, and hence its usefulness, by pointing to other *Cahiers* (and related) material available in English. No definitive listing of such material exists, and our listing, although the best we have been able to achieve, is almost certainly incomplete; we would be grateful for additions and/or corrections from readers.

It has proved difficult to fix upon an appropriate structure for the book, but attempts to organize it by critics, or chronology, or theoretical issues, for example, seemed less successful than the present structure. Certainly, the major categories which provide the book's structure – French cinema, American cinema, Italian cinema, polemics – were meaningful ones (though certainly not the only ones) for *Cahiers* during the 1950s. I have felt this perspective to be generally important in the sense that I have preferred to work broadly within the critical work's own terms rather than constantly to subject it to a critique whose terms belong to much later debates. On the other hand, I have wanted to make it clear in my introductions, particularly my general introduction, what kinds of relationships exist between the work of *Cahiers* in this period and later work in *Cahiers* and elsewhere, and why. In my introductions to each section I have tried to tease out some of the major critical threads and implications in the material as well as to relate it both to other *Cahiers* material and to its influence on contemporary and later work in English (hence the – I hope, productive and suggestive – profusion of footnote references).

A Note on translations

Translation always poses problems about accurate rendition, especially when, as in this case, several different translators are involved and some of the original writing is quite difficult or dense. In particular, I should point out that the French *auteur* is usually, but not always, retained when 'author' would have been the straight translation, and *mise en scène* when 'direction' would have been the likely translation. Both terms have entered critical discussion in English, but *auteur* in particular did not always have the meanings currently attached to it: we have tried to be sensitive to the varying usage of the two terms

Les Cahiers du Cinéma – literally 'Cinema Exercise (or Note) Books' – are of course plural, and should perhaps be referred to as 'they', but we have preferred to refer to *Cahiers* as if in the singular. *Cahiers* is the normal abbreviation used.

Notes and references

All notes are the editor's except where specifically designated as authors' or translators' notes.

A number of books referred to in notes with some frequency are given in abbreviated form in references. Full details are provided under 'Books Frequently Cited in Text', on pp xii–xiii.

Acknowledgments

My principal debts relate less to this particular volume than to the more general perspective which informs it. First, like any teacher, my greatest debts are to my students, over a period of almost fifteen years, at British Film Institute summer schools, at BFI–University of London extra-mural classes, and at Bulmershe College of Higher Education: their puzzlements and excitements, their understandings and insights, constantly renewed, have always been the most vital stimulus. Second, over the past fifteen years or so I have been fortunate to find myself among colleagues whose ideas, interests and enthusiasms have also been constantly stimulating – my colleagues at BFI Education and on BFI summer schools 1969–79, on the editorial board of *Movie* and in the Film and Drama division at Bulmershe College. To all of them, my continuing thanks; the value I place on some of these colleagues should be clear from my references to their work, but I do not place less value on the less visible or available work of the others. Third, very specific thanks to BFI Library Services, whose help is so fundamental to this book as to so many others, and to my editors, Angela Martin and David Wilson. Behroze Gandhy has been both support and stimulus and she, and my children Joachim and Amy, have suffered from time spent with *Cahiers* which should have been spent with them: my thanks and apologies to them.

In my own formation, the late Paddy Whannel – my first film teacher, later a colleague at BFI Education, and a friend – was probably the most important single influence. The vitality of British film culture – publications, education, exhibition – over the last twenty years owes a great deal to Paddy's work and to the spirit in which he undertook it, more than has been generally acknowledged. I miss him, and this book is dedicated to the memory of him and his work.

Chapters 3, 4, 13 and 14, translated by Tom Milne, are reprinted from *Godard on Godard*, ed. Jean Narboni and Tom Milne (© Martin Secker & Warburg, 1972).

Chapter 16, translated by Russell Campbell and Marvin Pister, originally appeared in *Focus on Howard Hawks*, ed. J. McBride (Prentice-Hall and Spectrum Books, 1972). It is adapted from a translation by Adrian Brine which appeared in *Movie*, December 1962.

Chapters 19 and 26, translated by Tom Milne, are reprinted from *Rivette*, ed. J. Rosenbaum (© British Film Institute 1977).

Chapter 31, translated by Peter Graham, is reprinted from *The New Wave*, ed. Peter Graham (© Martin Secker & Warburg, 1968).

The publishers and the British Film Institute gratefully acknowledge the help of *Cahiers du Cinéma* in the compilation of these volumes.

Books Frequently Cited in Text

Abbreviated forms and full bibliographical details

Bazin, *What is Cinema? Vol. 1*

Bazin, André, *What is Cinema? Volume 1* (Essays selected and translated by Hugh Gray, foreword by Jean Renoir), Berkeley, University of California Press, 1967; selected from Bazin, *Qu'est-ce que le cinéma? tome 1: Ontologie et langage* and *tome 2: Le Cinéma et les autres arts*, Paris, Editions du Cerf, 1958, 1959.

Bazin, *What is Cinema? Vol. 2*

Bazin, André, *What is Cinema? Volume 2* (Essays selected and translated by Hugh Gray, foreword by François Truffaut), Berkeley, University of California Press, 1971; selected from Bazin, *Qu'est-ce que le cinéma? tome 3: Cinéma et sociologie* and *tome 4: Une esthétique de la Réalité: le néo-réalisme*, Paris, Editions du Cerf, 1961, 1962.

Cameron, *Movie Reader*

Cameron, Ian (ed.), *The Movie Reader*, London, November Books; New York, Praeger, 1972.

Caughie, *Theories of Authorship*

Caughie, John (ed.), *Theories of Authorship*, London, Routledge & Kegan Paul, 1981 (BFI Readers in Film Studies series).

Godard on Godard

Godard, Jean-Luc, *Godard on Godard: Critical Writings by Jean-Luc Godard* (edited by Jean Narboni and Tom Milne, with an introduction by Richard Roud), London, Secker & Warburg; New York, Viking, 1972 (Cinema Two series); originally published as *Jean-Luc Godard par Jean-Luc Godard*, Paris, Editions Pierre Belfond, 1968.

Graham, *New Wave*

Graham, Peter (ed.), *The New Wave* (Critical landmarks selected by Peter Graham), London, Secker & Warburg; New York, Doubleday, 1968 (Cinema One series).

Magny, *Age of the American Novel*

Magny, Claude-Edmonde, *The Age of the American Novel: The Film Aesthetic of Fiction between the Two Wars* (translated by Eleanor Hochman), New York, Frederick Ungar, 1972; originally published as *L'Age du roman américain*, Paris, Editions du Seuil, 1948.

Nichols, *Movies and Methods*
Nichols, Bill (ed.), *Movies and Methods: An Anthology*, Berkeley, University of California Press, 1976.

Perkins, *Film as Film*
Perkins, V. F., *Film as Film*, Harmondsworth, Penguin Books, 1972.

Rohmer and Chabrol, *Hitchcock*
Rohmer, Eric, and Chabrol, Claude, *Hitchcock: The First Forty-Four Films* (translated by Stanley Hochman), New York, Frederick Ungar, 1979; originally published as *Hitchcock*, Paris, Editions Universitaires, 1957.

Sarris, *American Cinema*
Sarris, Andrew, *The American Cinema: Directors and Directions 1929–1968*, New York, E. P. Dutton, 1968.

Screen Reader 1
Screen Reader 1: Cinema/Ideology/Politics, London, Society for Education in Film and Television, 1977.

Truffaut, *Films in My Life*
Truffaut, François, *The Films in My Life* (translated by Leonard Mayhew), New York, Simon & Schuster, 1978; London, Allen Lane, 1980; originally published as *Les Films de ma vie*, Paris, Flammarion, 1975.

Wollen, *Signs and Meaning*
Wollen, Peter, *Signs and Meaning in the Cinema*, London, Secker & Warburg; Bloomington, Indiana University Press, 1969; second edition 1972 (Cinema One series).

Wood, *Hitchcock's Films*
Wood, Robin, *Hitchcock's Films*, London, Zwemmer; New York, A. S. Barnes, 1965; second and third editions 1969, 1977.

Wood, *Hawks*
Wood, Robin, *Howard Hawks*, London, Secker & Warburg; New York, Doubleday, 1968; second edition London, British Film Institute, 1981 (originally in the Cinema One series).

Introduction

It is still a pretty widespread, though rather vague, idea that film criticism and theory as we know it today – and even film-making too – owe almost everything to French film criticism in the period since 1945, and particularly to the achievements of the journal *Cahiers du Cinéma*, founded in 1951. Two especially important phases are usually cited: the period of *Cahiers* in the 1950s, which brought forth the films of the *nouvelle vague* and helped set off an important critical debate in Britain and the USA in the late 1950s and early 1960s (effectively the period of *Cahiers* covered by this volume, the first in a planned series of four); and the post-1968 period of theoretical elaboration and politicization of *Cahiers* and subsequently of film theory and criticism in Britain and the USA in the 1970s.[1]

Within the narrower focus of 'the systematic elevation of Hollywood movies to the ranks of great art' (but a focus which incorporates the essential critical-theoretical assumptions about authorship and *mise en scène* which characterized *Cahiers* in the 1950s), Thomas Elsaesser noted that 'Legend has it that the feat was accomplished almost single-handed by motivated and volatile intellectuals from Paris sticking their heads together and pulling off a brilliant public relations stunt that came to be known as *Cahiers du Cinéma* and *nouvelle vague*.'[2] This volume, and the volumes planned to follow, have been designed to make possible a proper examination of that legend, with a view to its modification, while at the same time making clear the real and vital contributions to criticism that *Cahiers* did make.

French film culture and *Cahiers du Cinéma*

Among some common misconceptions is the idea that *Cahiers* was alone in taking American cinema seriously: *Positif*, founded shortly after *Cahiers*, in 1952, for example, also took American cinema seriously, though in a rather different overall perspective.[3] But, more important, neither *Cahiers*

1

nor *Positif* was being particularly radical or original in its interest. The cinema, and the popular culture aspect of it best represented by Hollywood, had long been taken more seriously in France than in Britain, while Britain in turn had often been a good deal more interested than the USA itself: one need think only of the French Surrealists' interest, for example, not only in the 1920s when cinema was more generally a respectable concern for intellectuals,[4] but also consistently since then (*Positif* itself being an important manifestation of this continuing interest), while John Grierson's writings from the 1920s and 1930s on American cinema[5] provide a good example of (rather different) British interest.

In the case of *Cahiers* the relationship to historically well-defined ideas and areas of interest is particularly clear. A great deal of André Bazin's important work had been done well before the inception of *Cahiers* in 1951, much of it in a journal that was very specifically the forerunner of *Cahiers*, the *Revue du Cinéma*, which had been published 1929–31 and 1946–9 under the editorship of Jean-George Auriol. In the hundredth issue of *Cahiers* in 1959 Jacques Doniol-Valcroze, looking back, leaves no doubt about the relationship: 'In the minds of the founders of *Cahiers* it was never a matter of anything other than continuing the work undertaken by Jean-George Auriol.'[6]

Even a cursory examination of the contents of the *Revue du Cinéma* reveals a profile strikingly similar to that of the later *Cahiers*. In the 1929–31 period, more or less equal weight was being given to European 'art cinema' and avant-garde film (Pabst and Lang, Eisenstein and Pudovkin, Man Ray, Ruttmann and Buñuel, Dreyer) and American cinema (articles on Stroheim, Chaplin, of course, but also on Laurel and Hardy, Langdon, King Vidor, Hawks, Borzage, Sternberg, Lubitsch, Dwan), alongside discussions of technology and aesthetics (pre-eminently, at this time, the coming of sound, of course) and of historical origins (Méliès, Emile Cohl, for instance). None of which would have seemed at all out of place in *Cahiers* in the 1950s. It is hardly surprising that the similarities should be even greater between *Cahiers* and the *Revue* in its 1946–9 phase, when both externally (*Cahiers* inheriting its familiar 1950s and early 1960s yellow cover from the *Revue*) and internally (in content) clear continuities exist: a concern with American cinema, in particular *films noirs* and, via Welles, Wyler, Toland and Flaherty, questions of realism; an interest in realism also in relation to Italian cinema, and Rossellini in particular; a special concern with French cinema, with articles on or by Clément, Clair, Cocteau, Rouquier, Renoir, Autant-Lara, Grémillon, Clouzot, Leenhardt, Becker; a continuing interest in the work of film-makers such as Lang, Eisenstein, Dreyer, Lubitsch, Hitchcock; regular critical contributions from subsequent *Cahiers* editors Bazin and Doniol-Valcroze, as well as from later occasional contributors to, and friends of, *Cahiers* (such as Lotte Eisner, Henri Langlois, Herman Weinberg, Georges Sadoul), plus the first articles by Eric Rohmer (then writing under his real name, Maurice Schérer), later also a *Cahiers* editor. If we then glance forward ten years to 1959, at the end of the period covered by this volume, what are the typical contents of *Cahiers*? A continuing concern with American cinema, with many names familiar from the *Revue* in the 1920s (Hawks, Hitchcock, Ford, Lang), as well as, of course, some newer names (Brooks, Fuller, Lumet and Frankenheimer, Ray, Minnelli, Tashlin, Mann, Preminger); a continuing concern with Italian cinema and realism (Zavattini, Visconti, Rossellini) as well as with realism more broadly (the first signs of interest in 'direct cinema'); a continuing attention to Soviet cinema (Eisenstein and Dovzhenko) and 'art cinema' generally (Bergman, Buñuel, Mizoguchi, Wajda); and polemics for French cinema, with articles on or by Cocteau, Becker, Renoir, Vigo as well as newer names more associated with the *nouvelle vague*, such as Franju, Chabrol, Truffaut, Resnais.

Clearly, polemical and influential though *Cahiers* proved to be, it inherited a great deal both generally from French culture and very specifically from a tradition of film cultural concerns and interests well established since the 1920s. More immediately, the central elements of Bazin's theses about realism – generally endorsed by *Cahiers* as a whole in the 1950s – had already been established in the 1940s through articles not only in the *Revue du Cinéma* but also in the Catholic journal *Esprit* and elsewhere[7] well before *Cahiers* began. Bazin and Pierre Kast had also written for the Communist-sponsored journal *Ecran Français*, which also published, for example, Alexandre Astruc's important essay 'The Birth of a New Avant-Garde: *la caméra-stylo*' in 1948,[8] until, apparently, that journal's hostility to American cinema caused them to stop writing for it; Kast's first article for the *Revue* appeared in 1948. As well as Bazin, then, the *Revue* helped to establish Doniol-Valcroze, Kast and Rohmer: Bazin and Rohmer were to be decisive editorial influences on *Cahiers* in its first decade. Almost certainly Jean-George Auriol, editor of the *Revue*, would have become editor of the new journal already being planned before the final demise of the *Revue*. As it was, Auriol's death in a car accident in 1950 gave considerable impetus to the birth of *Cahiers*: the first issue was dedicated to his memory. But there had been other influences at work, linked to the same personalities. In 1948–9, something else was being born, as Doniol-Valcroze put it, which would 'constitute the first link in the chain which is resulting today in what has been called the *nouvelle vague*, the first jolt against a cinema which had become too traditional: "Objectif 49", a ciné-club unlike any other, which under the aegis of Jean Cocteau, Robert Bresson, Roger Leenhardt, René Clément, Alexandre Astruc, Pierre Kast, Raymond Queneau, etc. brought together all those – critics, film-makers and future film-makers – who dreamed of a *cinéma d'auteurs*'.[9]

It was, then, from the background of the *Revue du Cinéma* and 'Objectif 49' that *Cahiers* derived its main contributors and concerns when the first issue was finally published in April 1951, with Lo Duca (who had also been active on the *Revue*), Bazin and Doniol-Valcroze as joint editors (though Bazin was ill and was not officially on the editorial mast-head until the second issue) and Léon Kiegel financing. But by the end of 1953 the tenor of *Cahiers* was already changing: over the period of a year or so in 1952–3 Jean-Luc Godard (initially under the pseudonym Hans Lucas), Jean Domarchi, François Truffaut, Jacques Rivette and Claude Chabrol wrote their first articles for *Cahiers* and became regular contributors, Truffaut coming from a close personal relationship with Bazin, and Godard, Rivette and Chabrol from an involvement during 1950–1 with Rohmer through the Ciné-Club du Quartier Latin and its bulletin, edited by Rohmer, the *Gazette du Cinéma*, which published articles by Rivette and Godard.[10]

Among the early contributions to *Cahiers* which in retrospect he singled out as important, Doniol-Valcroze mentions[11] Bazin on Bresson,[12] Rohmer on Murnau, Flaherty and film space,[13] the special issue on Renoir,[14] the first articles by Godard[15] and Truffaut,[16] articles on Murnau by Astruc and Domarchi[17] and Rivette on Hawks.[18] Thus, in retrospect at least, the so-called 'young Turks' were seen to have made their mark on *Cahiers* very quickly. As if to emphasize the point, Doniol-Valcroze remembers that the publication of Truffaut's article 'Une Certaine Tendance du cinéma français' in January 1954[19] – apparently after some months of hesitation – consciously marked a definitive new departure for the journal:

> the publication of this article marks the real point of departure for what, rightly or wrongly, *Cahiers du Cinéma* represents today. A leap had been made, a trial begun with which we were all in solidarity, something bound us together. From then on, it was known that we were *for* Renoir, Rossellini, Hitchcock, Cocteau, Bresson . . . and against X, Y and Z. From then on there was a doctrine, the *politique des auteurs*, even if it lacked flexibility. From then on, it was quite natural that the series of interviews with the great directors would begin and a real contact be established between them and us. Ever afterwards people could pull the *hitchcocko-hawksiens* to pieces, get indignant about the attacks on 'French quality cinema', declare as dangerous the 'young Turks' of criticism . . . but an 'idea' had got under way which was going to make its obstinate way to its most logical conclusion: the passage of almost all those involved in it to directing films themselves.[20]

With Truffaut's salvo fired, the journal's complexion was now clearer, and everything seemed in place for *Cahiers* to do what its subsequent reputation suggested that it did. Editorially speaking, *Cahiers* was then relatively stable through the 1950s: Bazin, Lo Duca and Doniol-Valcroze continued as joint editors, with Bazin (and perhaps Truffaut) exercising most influence, until early 1957, when Rohmer replaced Lo Duca and began to exert increasing influence, in part just because others were so busy (Truffaut and Godard were also writing for the weekly newspaper *Arts* and other publications[21] while also, like Chabrol, preparing films), in part because of Bazin's illness; Rohmer's position as joint editor with Doniol-Valcroze was then confirmed after Bazin's death in November 1958 and continued until 1963.[22] But it is always wrong to think of the *Cahiers* writers during this period as a really homogeneous group: Bazin and

Rohmer were close in their Catholicism and their theses about the realist vocation of film, but Bazin argued strenuously against Rohmer on Hitchcock and Hawks; Rivette and Godard admired Rossellini for reasons considerably different from those of Rohmer; Godard and Rivette were more inclined, relatively speaking, to 'modernism' than most of their colleagues; Kast stood out in this period as almost the only *Cahiers* writer with clearly left-wing, anti-clerical sympathies, but like Bazin he opposed aspects of the *politique des auteurs*, though for different reasons; Truffaut was personally close to Bazin but proved very often distant from him in his tastes and values, and so on. Yet Doniol-Valcroze is right to talk about 'solidarity' in the sense that despite their differences there were usually broad areas of agreement and shared assumptions on some fundamental questions.

Authorship

Among the broad areas of agreement the most important was probably the idea of 'authorship', implied by Truffaut's discussion of *auteurs* in 'Une Certaine Tendance du cinéma français' but by much that had gone before also, by Rivette's essay on Hawks,[23] for example: it provided a doctrine, a *politique*, though hardly a 'theory'.[24] The concept of authorship, and its essential underpinning, the concept of *mise en scène*, are introduced here, then fleshed out and more fully discussed in relation to the critical writings translated in this volume in the introductions to the individual sections of the book.[25]

The November 1946 issue of the *Revue du Cinéma* had contained an article by the American director Irving Pichel entitled 'La création doit être l'ouvrage d'un seul' ('Creation must be the work of one person'). Truffaut prefaces his collection of his critical writings[26] with a quotation from Orson Welles: 'I believe a work is good to the degree that it expresses the man who created it.' At these levels, authorship was for *Cahiers* a relatively simple concept, essentially the idea that the film *auteur* was to be considered as fully an artist as any of the great novelists, painters or poets. As Eric Rhode summarized their views: 'the director as the ultimate authority and the sole arbiter of a film's meaning . . . they required one consistency only: that the director should have a strong personality and that he should be able to project his convictions'.[27] Thus, for Truffaut in 'Une Certaine Tendance', that the 'enemies' – primarily, for French cinema, screenwriters Jean Aurenche and Pierre Bost – lack authentic and individual personality (or, as Jean-José Richer said of Astruc, 'the thing most important to the artist: a *temperament*',[28]) is 'proved' by the fact that they collaborate with the most diverse directors on a wide diversity of themes. But, as we shall see in relation to the favoured *auteurs* of *Cahiers*, this was not all: it was not *any* world view but rather a *particular* world view that was being privileged. It was not just that Renoir or Bresson had 'a world view at least as valuable as that of Aurenche and Bost',[29] nor that they created their own stories and dialogue; it was also that Truffaut considered the films which Aurenche and Bost had written manifested a distinctly 'negative' view of the world. In two important and acute articles analysing the early years of *Cahiers*,[30] American critic John Hess argues that the films favoured by *Cahiers* tended to tell very much the same kinds of story: 'the most important determinant of an *auteur* was not so much the director's ability to express his personality, as usually has been claimed, but rather his desire and ability to express a certain world view. An *auteur* was a film director who expressed an optimistic image of human potentialities within an utterly corrupt society. By reaching out emotionally and spiritually to other human beings and/or to God, one could transcend the isolation imposed on one by a corrupt world.'[31]

Going further, Hess links this analysis explicitly with the social-political history of post-war France: '*la politique des auteurs* was, in fact, a justification, couched in aesthetic terms, of a culturally conservative, politically reactionary attempt to remove film from the realm of social and political concern, in which the progressive forces of the Resistance had placed all the arts in the years immediately after the war'.[32] If Hess's argument depends on a somewhat selective reading of early *Cahiers*, and if it fails to recognize the diversity of positions and the struggles going on there, there is nevertheless no doubt that he identifies and analyses probably the most important tendencies in *Cahiers* during this period: reading the material in this volume one is reminded time and time again of the trenchant accuracy of his analysis. The tendency Hess describes embodied, of course, an essentially romantic conception of art and the artist which we can find expressed elsewhere in the period, for example in André Malraux, for whom art transcended history, expressing man's freedom over destiny. In a formulation perfectly in accord with the assumptions of *Cahiers* during this period, Malraux argues, for example, that 'we now know that an artist's supreme work is not the one in best accord with any tradition – not even his most complete and "finished" work – but his most personal work, the one from which he has stripped all that is not his own, and in which his style reaches its climax'.[33]

Malraux can also provide a useful reference for the more explicitly political position of *Cahiers*. Militantly Leftist during the Spanish Civil War, Malraux mirrored broader political-cultural currents in moving steadily to the Right in the post-war period (ending up as de Gaulle's Minister for Culture). *Cahiers* (as opposed to *Positif*, which was consistently Leftist in sympathies) was very much part of this context, varying between being more or less overtly anti-Left and simply being silent on political issues of the day such as the Algerian struggle for independence, despite the exceptions of people like Kast who maintained Left positions within *Cahiers*. In a 1962 interview Godard expresses the general situation and attitude of the period rather well while discussing the politics of his film *Le Petit Soldat*: 'I have moral and psychological intentions which are defined through situations born of political events. That's all. These events are confused because that's how it is. My characters don't like it either. My film belongs to the generation which regrets not having been twenty at the time of the Spanish Civil War.'[34]

If the *politique des auteurs* caused ripples, and more, in French film culture and beyond, it was not because of the idea itself but because the idea was used in *Cahiers* with polemical brio to upset established values and reputations. There was nothing new or scandalous in either France or Britain or the USA in discussing, say, Murnau, Buñuel, Dreyer, Eisenstein, Renoir, Cocteau or Bresson or, from the USA, Stroheim or Welles or Chaplin, as the *auteurs* of their films. It was a slightly different matter – but only slightly – to propose, say, Howard Hawks as an *auteur*, mainly because, unlike Stroheim, Welles or Chaplin, Hawks had not been noticeably in conflict with the production system. It was perhaps a significantly different matter when the cultural perspectives brought to bear on the proposal of Hawks as *auteur* of Westerns, gangster movies and comedies derived their terms from classical literature, philosophy or the history of art.[35] It verged on positive outrage when, at the end of the 1950s and the beginning of the 1960s, such perspectives were brought to bear on, say, Vincente Minnelli or Samuel Fuller,[36] not to mention Don Weis or Edward Ludwig.[37] In other words, the closer *Cahiers* moved to what had been traditionally conceived as the 'conveyor belt' end of the cinema spectrum, the more their 'serious' discussion of film-makers seemed outrageously inappropriate. As it happens (even if *Cahiers* did not see it in quite these terms at the time), the more they outraged in this way, the more acutely they raised crucial questions, however unsystematically, about the status and criticism appropriate to film as an art form in which unsystematic divisions were constantly being made between art and commerce.[38] If *Cahiers* came to be associated primarily with American cinema and a revaluation of its status, it was not because they talked about American cinema more than about other cinema – quite simply, they did not – but because American cinema as a whole, so generally ignored, misunderstood or undervalued, provided the most obvious site for engagement with these critical questions.

Although *Cahiers* could be said to have been predisposed towards American cinema because of the perspective on film language opened up by Bazin in the post-war years,[39] a perspective which did away with some of the traditional distinctions in a European/American film, and a silent/ sound film, dichotomy, that predisposition undoubtedly owed most, given the political atmosphere of France in the 1950s described above, to the ways in which American cinema was perceived to relate to American society: it was, often enough, socially 'critical', but critical without being directly 'political'. This relationship was likely to be very appealing to the apolitical nature of much of French intellectual life in the 1950s. Thomas Elsaesser puts it well:

That the dramatic pattern inevitably engineered a 'personalised' solution to social problems and that they distinguished only with difficulty the dividing line between the moral and the political is a matter which affects a lot of social thinking in America . . . Not only is Hollywood ideologically transparent in the way films aim at internalising and psychologising the public and social issues of American history, but their aesthetic and stylistic devices are geared towards locating the value and purpose of that experience in recognisably commonplace situations and everyday contexts, mainly by means of a visual-dramatic rhetoric, a strategy of persuasion as 'classical' and subtly adaptable as any which past civilisations have produced in periods of hegemony. During the apogee of Hollywood, even the most outlandish adventure story or musical extravaganza had to build its dramatic structure and narrative development on a familiar, easily identifiable subsoil of emotional reactions, drawn from the basic psychological dilemmas of the age . . .

What French intellectuals expected from things American were works of fiction that could serve as creative models, representative of their own situation and embodying specifically modern tensions – between intellect and emotion, action and reflection, consciousness and instinct, choice and spontaneity.[40]

Raymond Durgnat expressed it rather differently: 'One can understand why Hawks's films mean so much to French intellectuals. His very simplicity can have a tonic, and a real value, as a corrective to various debilitating concomitants of European culture ("confusionism", snobbery, contempt for decision, action, efficacy, simplicity).'[41] These are very much the perspectives informing Godard's thought in commenting, in 1962, that 'The Americans, who are much more stupid when it comes to analysis, instinctively bring off very complex scripts. They also have a gift for the kind of simplicity which brings depth – in a little Western like *Ride the High Country* [GB title: *Guns in the Afternoon*], for instance. If one tries to do something like that in France, one looks like an intellectual. The Americans are real and natural. But this attitude means something over there. We in France must find something that means something – find the French attitude as they have found the American attitude.'[42]

Mise en scène

However, in terms of *auteurs'* ideas about the world, *Cahiers* conceded, in an important 1960 article by Fereydoun Hoveyda, 'the consistency of the ideas we came across in the films of Lang, Rossellini, Renoir, Welles . . . we realized that our favourite *auteurs* were in fact talking about the same things. The "constants" of their particular universes belonged to everybody: solitude, violence, the absurdity of existence, sin, redemption, love, etc. Each epoch has its own themes, which serve as a backcloth against which individuals, whether artists or not, act out their lives.'[43] But if these themes were more or less constant across different *auteurs*, how were they to be told apart, and what made them original?

The originality of the *auteur* lies not in the subject matter he chooses, but in

8

the technique he employs, i.e. the *mise en scène*, through which everything on the screen is expressed . . . As Sartre said: 'One isn't a writer for having chosen to say certain things, but for having chosen to say them in a certain way'. Why should it be any different for cinema? . . . the thought of a *cinéaste* appears through his *mise en scène*. What matters in a film is the desire for order, composition, harmony, the placing of actors and objects, the movements within the frame, the capturing of a movement or a look; in short, the intellectual operation which has put an initial emotion and a general idea to work. *Mise en scène* is nothing other than the technique invented by each director to express the idea and establish the specific quality of his work . . . The task of the critic thus becomes immense: to discover behind the images the particular 'manner' of the *auteur* and, thanks to this knowledge, to be able to elucidate the meaning of the work in question.[44]

Mise en scène thus establishes itself as a – perhaps *the* – central and essential concept in *Cahiers* and in later criticism influenced by *Cahiers*. There is clear continuity, for example, between Truffaut's comment that 'it is not so much the choice of subject which characterizes [Jacques] Becker as how he chooses to treat this subject'[45] and V. F. Perkins's comment on *Carmen Jones* that 'what matters is less the originality or otherwise of Preminger's theme than the freshness, economy and intelligence of the means by which the theme is presented'.[46]

In origin *mise en scène* is a word drawn from the theatre, neutral in intention, meaning literally 'placing on the stage' or 'staging', that is, the way in which a play-text becomes a staged play. For several reasons, the word's original descriptive neutrality no longer applied to its usage. Firstly, Antonin Artaud, in *The Theatre of Cruelty*, had used the term polemically in relation to theatre in arguing for the supremacy of the director, as the person responsible for visualizing the spectacle, over the writer:

> The typical language of the theatre will be constituted around the *mise en scène* considered not simply as the degree of refraction of a text upon the stage, but as the point of departure for all theatrical creation. And it is in the use and handling of this language that the old duality between author and director will be dissolved, replaced by a sort of unique Creator upon whom will devolve the double responsibility of the spectacle and the plot.[47]

In the 1940s Alexandre Astruc, arguing for the *caméra-stylo* as a 'means of expression, just as all the other arts have been before it, and in particular painting and the novel . . . in which and by which an artist can express his thoughts', had taken a recognizably similar position in relation to the *auteur*-director in cinema (and one similar to Truffaut's in 'Une Certaine Tendance'): 'this of course implies that the scriptwriter directs his own scripts; or rather, that the scriptwriter ceases to exist, for in this kind of film-making the distinction between author and director loses all meaning. Direction is no longer a means of illustrating or presenting a scene, but a true act of writing.'[48]

Secondly, the way *Cahiers* conceived *mise en scène* tended toward an aesthetic which privileged realist, or illusionist, narrative. In this sense *mise en scène* became a sort of counter to theories of montage, privileging the action, movement forward and illusion of narrative against any fore-grounding of the relations between shot and shot, and narrative function against any sense of pictorialism in the individual shot (hence Astruc's 'tyranny of what is visual; the image for its own sake').[49] The body of conventions to which this conception of *mise en scène* was attached was, of course, broadly that of mainstream narrative cinema, particularly American cinema – that cinema characterized so effectively by V. F. Perkins in *Film as Film*. It is a relatively 'conservative' aesthetic, and one broadly adhered to by *Cahiers* in the 1950s. There is a clear enough continuity, for example, between Bazin's pre-*Cahiers* writings on realism[50] and both the aesthetic assumptions of most *Cahiers* critics and the aesthetic practices of the films they themselves made in the late 1950s – see, as an instance, Hoveyda's account of Truffaut's *Les 400 Coups*.[51] Interestingly enough, at the same moment that this aesthetic triumphs with *Les 400 Coups* and the *nouvelle vague*, it is also 'challenged' by the relative modernism of *Hiroshima mon amour*.[52]

Thirdly, *mise en scène* was not a neutral term in the sense that it was the start of an attempt to raise the very important question – fundamental to the critical-theoretical debates which *Cahiers* provoked in Britain and the USA – of *specificity*: 'the specificity of a cinematographic work lies in its form rather than in its content, in the *mise en scène* and not in the scenario or the dialogue'.[53] This concept of specificity was absolutely central to the discussion and validation of American cinema, as Elsaesser points out:

> Given the fact that in Hollywood the director often had no more than token control over choice of subject, the cast, the quality of the dialogue, all the weight of creativity, all the evidence of personal expression and statement had to be found in the *mise en scène*, the visual orchestration of the story, the rhythm of the action, the plasticity and dynamism of the image, the pace and causality introduced through the editing.[54]

Much *Cahiers* discussion of genre, for example, depended on the suppos-edly transcendent qualities of *mise en scène*: 'the strength of the cinema is such that in the hands of a great director, even the most insignificant detective story can be transformed into a work of art'.[55]

It was this question of the cinematographic specificity of *mise en scène* which contributed so decisively to what John Caughie calls the 'radical dislocation' in the development of film theory: *auteurism* 'effected . . . a shift in the way films were conceived and grasped within film criticism. The personality of the director, and the consistency within his films, were not, like the explicit subject matter which tended to preoccupy established criticism, simply there as a "given". They had to be sought out, discovered, by a process of analysis and attention to a number of films.'[56] As Geoffrey Nowell-Smith put it: 'It was in establishing what the film said, rather than reasons for liking or disliking it, that authorship criticism validated itself as an approach.'[57] *Mise en scène* provided the means by which the *auteur* expressed his thought, as Hoveyda put it, and thus also the means by which the *auteur* is critically discovered, analysed.

> In many respects, the attention to *mise en scène*, even to the extent of a certain historically necessary formalism, is probably the most important positive contribution of *auteurism* to the development of a precise and detailed film criticism, engaging with the specific mechanisms of visual discourse, freeing it from literary models, and from the liberal commitments which were prepared to validate films on the basis of their themes alone.[58]

The impact of *Cahiers du Cinéma* and the *nouvelle vague*

Such a view is very much a retrospective one, but its contours were beginning to become clear in the debates opened up in Britain in the early 1960s. In *Sight and Sound* Penelope Houston began a defence of traditional, liberal values in criticism against *Cahiers* and against a British magazine assumed to be mightily influenced by *Cahiers*, *Oxford Opinion*, arguing that 'cinema is about the human situation, not about "spatial relationships" ' and that criticism should examine film primarily in terms of its 'ideas'.[59] Thus began a major revaluation, in Britain and the USA, of both critical assumptions and films themselves, especially American films: the first issue of the British magazine *Movie*, developed from *Oxford Opinion*, appeared in 1962; Andrew Sarris first sketched out his '*auteur* theory' in 1963.[60] By this time the character of *Cahiers* itself was already changing and several of its major critics from the 1950s were already much less involved. Godard, interviewed in 1963, felt that the magazine was in decline: 'I think it is due chiefly to the fact that there is no longer any position to defend. There used always to be something to say. Now that everyone is agreed, there isn't so much to say. The thing that made *Cahiers* was its position in the front line of battle.'[61]

There is little doubt that *Cahiers*, and the various debates it stimulated in Britain and the USA, brought about significant changes in attitudes to film – particularly American film – not only among critics and theorists but also more widely (and not least among film-makers). We can get some sense of these changes, and of Godard's feeling that 'there is no longer a position to defend', from a comparison of reviews in the 'quality' British newspaper the *Guardian* of *Rio Bravo* – a film much venerated by *Cahiers* and *Movie* – on its first appearance in 1959 and its re-release in 1963, that is, before and after the period of critical debate which *Cahiers* provoked:

> *Rio Bravo* is a typical Western of this age of the long-winded, large screen. It lasts for 140 minutes and it contains enough inventiveness to make do for about half that time. It is, in fact, a soporific 'blockbuster'. John Wayne leads its cast. (1959)

Rio Bravo is a gem. For some strange reason (probably the presence of a pop singer, Ricky Nelson, in the cast) it was not too well reviewed in this country when it was first shown, but it was (deservedly) a great popular success and also achieved great prestige on the Continent. Starring John Wayne at his most archetypal, Dean Martin at his coolest, and Angie Dickinson at her hottest, *Rio Bravo* is, however, first and last a Howard Hawks film. For those who know Hawks this should be enough; for those who don't, it means that *Rio Bravo* is an example of the classical, pre-Welles school of American film-making at its most deceptively simple: broad lines, level glances, grand design, elementary emotions. (1963)

If the changes are clear enough, so is their superficiality. John Caughie is right to point out[62] that because *auteurism* was essentially 'romantic' in conception, and because the dominant critical mode in the arts was already romantic, once the scandal died down *auteurism* was relatively easily accommodated in its simplest form, while its deeper implications had very little real impact.

Although many of the ideas in *Cahiers* were not particularly new, and although other journals were working with similar concerns, it was *Cahiers* and not other journals which had most impact and influence, in France as elsewhere. Why? One general reason might be that its relatively apolitical stance responded to broad currents in French, and British, cultural and political life during a period of crisis for liberal values. A certain reason was its polemical edge. As Godard said, 'the *Cahiers* critics were commandos',[63] and they enjoyed polemicizing, busily reversing established tastes and values. Nevertheless, the magazine's circulation remained rather small, though growing steadily through the 1950s, and its ideas and polemics had little impact outside France until the period 1958–60 – in other words, until the period during which the first *nouvelle vague* films burst upon the world. This period, covering the appearance of a number of internationally acclaimed films, and the preparation of others, by Chabrol, Truffaut, Rivette, Godard, Rohmer and Doniol-Valcroze, was precisely the period during which the polemics and positions argued in *Cahiers* throughout the 1950s decisively entered British and American criticism, stimulating new polemics and positions. Reflecting on the appearance of films like Hitchcock's *Vertigo*, Hawks's *Rio Bravo*, Fuller's *Run of the Arrow*, Sirk's *A Time to Love and a Time to Die* or Ray's *Wind Across the Everglades* in *Cahiers* critics' lists of ten best films of the year,[64] Richard Roud conceded, in *Sight and Sound*, that

One's first reaction might be to conclude that these men must be very foolish. And indeed, until a year or two ago, one might have got away with it. But today it would be difficult, I think, to maintain that film-makers like Alain Resnais, François Truffaut, Claude Chabrol, Jean-Luc Godard, Pierre Kast and Jean-Pierre Melville are fools . . . if one admits, as one must, that some of them have made remarkable and even great films, then rather than throwing up one's hands in the air or dismissing them all as mad, one should try to see why and how their judgments of American films differ so substantially from ours.[65]

But if the success of the *Cahiers* critics as film-makers was vital to the wider circulation of their critical values and tastes, particularly outside France, there was nothing accidental for the critics themselves about the relationship between criticism and film-making. As Andrew Sarris noted, 'Truffaut was involved in nothing less than changing the course of the French cinema. His bitterest quarrels were with film-makers, whereas the bitterest quarrels of the New Critics in England and America were with other critics.'[66] The clearest way for them to change French cinema was to make the films themselves, to make different films. Many of the *Cahiers* critics had made short films before 1959, often long before, but probably more important was the very clear relationship they saw between criticism and film-making. Thus Godard: 'All of us at *Cahiers* thought of ourselves as future directors. Frequenting ciné-clubs and the Cinémathèque was already a way of thinking cinema and thinking about cinema. Writing was already a way of making films . . . We were thinking cinema and at a certain moment we felt the need to extend that thought.'[67] The perception of this relationship informed a great deal of *Cahiers* writing about any film, but particularly about French cinema: in their reviews of Becker's *Touchez pas au grisbi* or Vadim's *Sait-on jamais?*,[68] Truffaut and Godard write precisely as if rehearsing the processes of realization. Writing in 1958 about a cheaply made Japanese film, *Juvenile Passion*, Truffaut's intentions, ambitions and position – and indeed his passion – are clear:

One would have to say that the greatest film-makers are over fifty, but it is important to practise the cinema of one's own age and try, if one is twenty-five and admires Dreyer, to emulate *Vampyr* rather than *Ordet*. Youth is in a hurry, it is impatient, it is bursting with all sorts of concrete ideas. Young film-makers must shoot their films in mad haste, movies in which the characters are in a hurry, in which shots jostle each other to get on screen before 'The End', films that contain their ideas. Later on, this succession of ideas will give way to one great, overriding idea, and then the critics will complain about a 'promising' film-maker who has grown old. So what?

M. Tessoneau, the general administrator of the Institut des Hautes Etudes Cinématographiques,[69] should buy a copy of *Juvenile Passion* and show it to his flock on the first Monday of each month to keep them from acquiring the mentality of assistants. And what is the assistant's mentality? It can be summed up: 'I am finally going to make my first film; I am terrified of falling on my face; I have allowed a script and actors to be imposed on me, but there is one thing I won't give in on, and that is time; I demand fourteen weeks of shooting, thirteen of them in the studio, because if I can use time and film as much as I want, I will be able, if not to make a good film, at least to prove that I can make a film'. *Juvenile Passion* was shot in seventeen days.[70]

It seems appropriate, therefore, to begin with material on French cinema, for a clearer sense of what *Cahiers* liked and disliked in it and of what they wanted – and planned – to do about it.

Notes

1 These developments are traced in John Caughie, *Theories of Authorship*, which reprints a number of articles from *Cahiers* in its different phases.

2 Thomas Elsaesser, 'Two Decades in Another Country: Hollywood and the Cinéphiles', in C. W. E. Bigsby, *Superculture*, London, Elek, 1975, p. 199.

3 *Positif* articles by Gérard Gozlan and Robert Benayoun, both written in 1962, attacking *Cahiers* positions and *nouvelle vague* films are translated in Peter Graham, *The New Wave*; Thomas Elsaesser, *op. cit.*, gives a useful account of the differing responses of *Cahiers* and *Positif*.

4 See, for example, Paul Hammond, *The Shadow and Its Shadow: Surrealist Writings on Cinema*, London, British Film Institute, 1978.

5 See, for example, 'The Logic of Comedy' (written 1929–37), 'Directors of the Thirties' (1930–2), 'Hollywood Looks at Life' (1931–8) in Forsyth Hardy, *Grierson on Documentary*, London, Faber, 1946 and 1966; these articles are reprinted in slightly different versions ('Directors of the Thirties' becoming 'The Master Craftsmen') in Forsyth Hardy, *Grierson on the Movies*, London, Faber, 1981, which also includes new material, 'New York 1925–26', 'The Coming of the Talkies' (1929–30) and 'Garbo, Dietrich, Mae West and Co' (1932–8).

6 Jacques Doniol-Valcroze, 'L'Histoire des *Cahiers*', *Cahiers* 100, October 1959, p. 63.

7 See particularly 'William Wyler, ou le janséniste de la mise en scène', originally published in *La Revue du Cinéma*, no. 11, March 1948, translated as 'William Wyler, or the Jansenist of *mise en scène*' in Christopher Williams, *Realism and the Cinema*, London, Routledge & Kegan Paul, 1980, pp. 36–52; 'Le réalisme cinématographique et l'école italienne de la Libération', originally published in *Esprit*, January 1948, translated as 'An Aesthetic of Reality: Neo-Realism (Cinematic Realism and the Italian School of the Liberation)' in André Bazin, *What is Cinema? Vol. 2*; 'Bicycle Thief', originally published in *Esprit*, November 1949, translated in Bazin, *What is Cinema? Vol. 2*. Dudley Andrew (author of *André Bazin*, New York, Oxford University Press, 1978) discusses the beginnings of Bazin's work during the 1940s in a useful article, 'Bazin before *Cahiers*: Cinematic Politics in Post-war France', in *Cineaste*, vol. 12, no. 1, 1982, drawing particularly on André Bazin, *French Cinema of the Occupation and Resistance: The Birth of a Critical Aesthetic* (translated by Stanley Hochman, foreword by François Truffaut, New York, Oxford University Press, 1981), and on Olivier Barrot, *L'Ecran Français, 1943–1953, histoire d'un journal et d'une époque* (Paris, Editions les Editeurs Français Réunis, 1979).

8 Alexandre Astruc, 'The Birth of a New Avant-Garde: *la caméra-stylo*', originally published in *Ecran Français*, no. 144, 1948, translated in Peter Graham, *The New Wave*.

9 Doniol-Valcroze, *op. cit.*, p. 64.

10 Godard's articles for the *Gazette du Cinéma*, nos 2–4, June–October 1950, are translated in *Godard on Godard*.

11 Doniol-Valcroze, *op. cit.*, pp. 67–8.

12 André Bazin, 'La Stylistique de Robert Bresson', *Cahiers* 3, June 1951; for translations, see Appendix 2.

13 Eric Rohmer (the pseudonym of Maurice Schérer), 'Vanité que peinture', *Cahiers* 3, June 1951.

14 *Cahiers* 8, January 1952; for translation of material in this issue by Bazin, Renoir and Rohmer, see Appendix 2.

15 Reviews (under the pseudonym Hans Lucas) of *No Sad Songs for Me*, *Cahiers* 10, March 1952, and *Strangers on a Train*, *Cahiers* 10, March 1952, and article 'Défense et illustration du découpage classique', *Cahiers* 15, September 1952; all translated in *Godard on Godard*.

16 For example, reviews of *Sudden Fear*, *Cahiers* 21, March 1953, and *The Snows of Kilimanjaro*, *Cahiers* 23, May 1953, and article on CinemaScope, 'En avoir plein la vue', *Cahiers* 25, July 1953, translated in this volume (Ch. 34).

17 Alexandre Astruc, 'Le Feu et la glace', *Cahiers* 18, December 1952, and Jean Domarchi, 'Présence de F. W. Murnau', *Cahiers* 21, March 1953.

18 Jacques Rivette, 'Génie de Howard Hawks', *Cahiers* 23, May 1953, translated in this volume (Ch. 16).

19 François Truffaut, 'Une Certaine Tendance du cinéma français', *Cahiers* 31, January 1954, translated as 'A Certain Tendency of the French Cinema' in Bill Nichols, *Movies and Methods*; see discussion of the article in my introduction to the section on French cinema in this volume.

20 Doniol-Valcroze, *op. cit.*, p. 68.

21 Godard's articles for *Arts*, February 1958–May 1959, are translated in *Godard on Godard*; Truffaut wrote for *Arts* and other journals but the material in *The Films in My Life* is unidentified except by date; since much of the material in the book is not from *Cahiers* it can be assumed that a good deal of it is from *Arts* or synthesizes various different articles: see Truffaut's introduction to the book, p. 17.

22 A brief account of the history of *Cahiers* since 1960, and its representation in future volumes of translations, is given in Appendix 3.

23 See note 18 above.

24 The *'auteur' theory* – as opposed to the *politique des auteurs* as conceived by *Cahiers* – is usually associated with Andrew Sarris, whose articles on American cinema in *Film Culture*, Spring 1963, were later elaborated in his book, *The American Cinema*, but Luc Moullet does use the word 'theory' in his article on Fuller, in this volume (Ch 20).

25 See particularly my introductions to Sections 1, 2 and 4 of this volume, on French cinema, American cinema and Polemics, respectively.

26 François Truffaut, *Films in My Life*.

27 Eric Rhode, *A History of the Cinema: From its Origins to 1970*, London, Allen Lane, 1976, p. 530.

28 Jean-José Richer, 'L'Ecran diabolique' (on *Le Rideau cramoisi*), *Cahiers* 21, March 1953.

29 Truffaut, 'Une Certain Tendance', Nichols translation p. 233.

30 John Hess, '*La Politique des auteurs*: Part One: World View as Aesthetic', *Jump Cut*, no. 1, May–June 1974; Part Two: 'Truffaut's Manifesto', *Jump Cut*, no. 2, July–August 1974.

31 Hess, *op. cit.*, Part Two, p. 20.

32 *Ibid.*, Part One, p. 19.

33 André Malraux, *The Voices of Silence*, London, Secker & Warburg, 1954, p. 19, quoted in Rhode, *op. cit.*, p. 532.

34 Interview with Godard in *Cahiers* 138, December 1962, translated in *Godard on Godard*, p. 179.

35 Rivette's article on Hawks, for example, compares him with Molière and Corneille. See Ch. 16.

36 Moullet's article on Fuller compares Welles with Shakespeare and Fuller with Marlowe. See Ch. 20.

37 See, for example, Michel Mourlet, 'Sur un art ignoré', *Cahiers* 98, August 1959.

38 Cf. V. F. Perkins: 'All our critics distinguish, more or less explicitly, between commercial and personal cinema. The distinction is occasionally valid, often silly, and always dangerous', 'The Cinema of Nicholas Ray', *Movie* 9, May 1963, p. 5; reprinted in Cameron, *The Movie Reader*, and Nichols, *Movies and Methods*.

39 See note 7; cf. 'L'Evolution du langage cinématographique', originally published in 1958, but constituted from articles written 1950–5, translated as 'Evolution of the Language of Cinema' in Bazin, *What is Cinema? Vol. 1*.

40 Elsaesser, *op. cit.*, pp. 206, 210.

41 Raymond Durgnat, *Films and Feelings*, London, Faber, 1967, p. 82.

42 Godard, *op. cit.*, p. 193.

43 Fereydoun Hoveyda, 'Les Taches du soleil', *Cahiers* 110, August 1960, p. 41, to be translated in Volume 2. Hoveyda's listing of thematic constants lends considerable credence to Hess's thesis, outlined above.

44 *Ibid.*, pp. 41–2.

45 François Truffaut, 'Les Truands sont fatigués', *Cahiers* 34, April 1954, translated in this volume (Ch 1).

46 V. F. Perkins, *Film as Film*, p. 80.

47 Antonin Artaud, 'The Theatre of Cruelty (First Manifesto)', originally published 1932, in Artaud, *The Theatre and its Double*, London, Calder & Boyars; New York, Grove Press, 1958, pp. 93–4.

48 Astruc in Graham, *The New Wave*, pp. 17–18, 22; cf. discussion in my introduction to the Polemics section of this volume.

49 *Ibid.*, p. 18.

50 Cf. note 7.

51 *Cahiers* 97, July 1959, translated in this volume (Ch. 5).

52 See the editorial discussion, 'Hiroshima, notre amour', *Cahiers* 97, July 1959, translated in this volume (Ch. 6). As it happens, *A bout de souffle* and possibly *Paris nous appartient* may have contained the seeds of more significant challenges to the aesthetic enshrined in *Les 400 Coups*; certainly, Godard's and Rivette's later work proved much more radical formally than Resnais's later work, but it would have been difficult to foresee this in 1959, when Resnais's film looked much more innovative.

53 Hoveyda, 'Les Taches du soleil', p. 37.

54 Elsaesser, *op. cit.*, p. 211.

55 Hoveyda, *op. cit.*, p. 38.

56 Caughie, *Theories of Authorship*, p. 11.

57 Geoffrey Nowell-Smith, Introduction to 'New Hollywood Cinema', *Film Reader* 1, Evanston, Illinois, 1975, p. 58.

58 Caughie, *op. cit.*, p. 13.

59 Penelope Houston, 'The Critical Question', *Sight and Sound*, vol. 29, no. 4, Autumn 1960, p. 163.

60 Cf. note 24.

61 Godard, *op. cit.*, p. 195.

62 Caughie, *op. cit.*, p. 11.
63 Godard, *op. cit.*, p. 195.
64 Cf. Appendix 1.
65 Richard Roud, 'The French Line', *Sight and Sound*, vol. 29, no. 4, Autumn 1960, p. 167.
66 Sarris, *The American Cinema*, p. 29.
67 Godard, *op. cit.*, pp. 171–2.
68 Both in this volume (Chs 1 and 3 respectively).
69 Institut des Hautes Etudes Cinématographiques, Paris, founded 1944, the official French film school, generally scorned at this period for what was taken to be excessive 'academicism' by *Cahiers* and the *nouvelle vague* generally, though Louis Malle, for example, was a graduate; Alain Resnais spent some time there in 1944–5 but found it too theoretical and left. Cf. comments by Rossellini in the interviews translated in this volume (Ch. 28).
70 Truffaut, *Films in My Life*, pp. 246–7.

Part One

French Cinema

Introduction

Although American and Italian cinema often seemed to be the main interests of the *Cahiers* critics, more often than not in their writings on those cinemas what was fundamentally at stake was *French* cinema. When Rohmer and Rivette talk about American cinema as 'efficacious', elegant, contemplative, moral,[1] or when they talk about the combined rigour, improvisation and lucidity of Rossellini,[2] they make it clear that these are precisely the qualities they find lacking in French cinema. In other words, and inevitably given the cinema they had grown up with, French cinema provided the frame or context within which they thought about the cinema itself; and, given their aspirations toward film-making, French cinema was also the field of battle (a battle which, of course, the *nouvelle vague* film-makers were largely to win).

Thus, Jacques Doniol-Valcroze is quite clear[3] about the historical importance of the publication of Truffaut's 'Une Certaine Tendance du cinéma français' in 1954:[4] *Cahiers* identified its enemies, and those enemies identified *Cahiers*. Certainly, Truffaut's essay is vastly polemical – he admits, in concluding, to its being subject to 'a great deal of emotion and taking sides'.[5] The significance of the essay in other than those polemical terms is rather less than its reputation merits: it tends to be diffuse and is significantly blurred in its arguments by Truffaut's rather reactionary ideological assumptions. At the same time, the essay can begin to suggest what *Cahiers* disliked in mainstream French cinema of the time, and why.

Truffaut points to three different elements in the French cinema (although he links them, they are not in fact mutually dependent). First, he takes as chief avatars of the 'tradition of quality' the screenwriters-adapters Jean Aurenche and Pierre Bost,[6] characterizing them as primarily *literary* men, contemptuous of the cinema and its public: 'when they hand in their scenario, the film is done; the *metteur en scène*, in their eyes, is the gentleman who adds the pictures to it'.[7] That such men lack authentic individual personality is self-evident, for Truffaut, from the diversity of both the subjects and the directors they work with. Second, at the level of content, this 'official' cinema is characterized as wishing to be, in moral terms, anti-bourgeois, against family, religion, and so on (despite the bourgeois nature of both its producers and its audiences): 'they give the public its habitual dose of smut, non-conformity and facile audacity'.[8] Lastly, the general literary quality is complemented in visual terms by 'scholarly framing, complicated lighting effects, "polished" photography'.[9]

Truffaut's polemic was not an empty one, of course; it was also a polemic *for* a different French cinema. He considered the dominance of the tradition of quality and of 'psychological realism' (which he opposed to the pre-war 'poetic realism') responsible for public incomprehension of 'such new works as *Le Carrosse d'or, Casque d'or*, not to mention *Les Dames du Bois de Boulogne* and *Orphée'*.[10] The names Truffaut cites in arguing for a French cinema of *auteurs* are Renoir, Bresson, Cocteau, Becker, Gance, Ophuls, Tati, Leenhardt (which more or less exhausts *Cahiers'* French *auteurs* before the *nouvelle vague*, though Guitry was later revalued, particularly by Truffaut; *Cahiers'* interest in the early work of Astruc, Franju and Vadim had much more to do with their own film-making aspirations). Such film-makers, Truffaut argued, have a 'world-view at least as valuable as that of Aurenche and Bost', would be incapable of conceiving characters as 'abject' as Aurenche's and Bost's, and, 'curious coincidence . . . they are *auteurs* who often write their dialogue and some of them themselves create the stories they direct'.[11]

Is this anything more than a pretty conventional plea for authentic personality and freedom to write as well as direct? One significant factor Truffaut points to is the importance not just of a world view, but a *particular kind* of world view – in Truffaut's argument, generosity, optimism and ambiguity (all values one associates very much with André Bazin) are valued above what he takes to be misanthropy, pessimism, non-conformity. Also important is the value placed on audacities of *realization* – Truffaut mentions, for example, 'the gait of Hulot . . . the *mise en scène* of *Le Carrosse d'or*, the direction of actors in *Madame de . . .'*[12] – above audacities of conception or content. In a very important sense, Truffaut (in a passage quoted by Hoveyda in his article on *Les 400 Coups*[13]) manifests a concern with 'realism' as opposed to 'academicism' – 'so careful is the (traditional) school to lock these beings in a closed world, barricaded by formulae, plays on words, maxims, instead of letting us see them for ourselves, with our own eyes'.[14] Louis Marcorelles, a frequent contributor to *Cahiers* from 1956 onwards, is very clear about these tendencies; writing in 1958, he argues that the French cinema in the post-war years, 'missing the turning towards neo-realism which it might have taken, moved instead towards academicism and the great "machine" constructions of directors such as Clément and Clouzot'; Marcorelles, like Truffaut, felt that owing to a lack of the 'generosity of inspiration which animated the pre-war realist school' French cinema risked producing only 'works lacking real creative originality, adaptations of famous novels, imitations of American styles, films whose distinction is a matter of craftsmanship rather than originality, authenticity, the excitement of living'.[15]

The articles translated and printed here all relate very clearly to the broad thrust of Truffaut's polemic (though they need to be supplemented by important writings by Bazin, Truffaut, Godard and others on Renoir, Bresson, Gance, Guitry, Cocteau, Becker, Ophuls, Astruc, Franju, Vadim[16]). Truffaut wrote two years before the appearance of Astruc's *Les Mauvaises Rencontres* (1955), and three years before Vadim's *Et Dieu . . . créa la femme* (1956), both of which were important signposts[17] for a *nouvelle vague* which, after the Cannes Festival triumph of Truffaut's *Les 400 Coups* and Resnais's *Hiroshima mon amour* in 1959, was no longer in doubt.

Meanwhile, *Cahiers* wrote about the French cinema they admired (and Truffaut's distaste for the 'academic' led him along some pretty strange paths, such as Guitry's work) rather than the French cinema they abhorred. Becker's work, as Truffaut says in his review of *Touchez pas au grisbi*, was 'both a lesson and an encouragement'. What Truffaut values in Becker neatly exemplifies his arguments in 'Une Certaine Tendance du cinéma français': Becker's personal mark on the film – a certain autobiographical element[18] and closeness to personal experience; a refusal of the conventional and the vulgar; and 'not so much his choice of subject . . . as how he chooses to treat this subject'. Godard deals similarly with *Sait-on jamais?* (but then this was how Truffaut himself had dealt with *Et Dieu . . . créa la femme*[19]): 'Vadim's great strength is in the fact that he talks only about things he knows well . . . and, above all, as a beginner, he describes himself with all his qualities and defects, through these characters'. Vadim was, of course, the closest in age of the new directors to Godard and Truffaut, and the closest in sensibility, so it was no surprise that 'our only modern film-maker', as *Cahiers* called Vadim,[20] should stimulate the film-maker in Godard. Like Truffaut on Becker, Godard's discussion of *Sait-on jamais?* is concerned with attitudes to subject matter and more particularly with reflecting upon detailed problems of *mise en scène*, very much the concerns of future film-makers.

The *Cahiers* polemic about French cinema did not involve only being for or against certain *auteurs*: there was also a concern with the economics of production and distribution[21] and with the more general conditions – social, political and cultural – of production. As the title of the 1957 editorial discussion – 'Six Characters in Search of *auteurs*' – implies, *Cahiers* was anxious both to understand why, a few rather special *auteurs* apart, French cinema's prospects looked so bleak, and to try to promote a new cinema. One factor which lies just below the surface, in this discussion as elsewhere,[22] is articulated by Marcorelles when he comments, from the vantage point of 1958, that work is being produced 'which may once more restore France to the position of creative eminence which she held in the 1930s'.[23]

If, in the final analysis, the six participants in the discussion do not come up with anything very concrete to explain why there was 'something rotten' in France's 'cinematographic kingdom', much that is very revealing is said en route. The most insistent theme of the discussion, also strongly present in Rohmer's and Rivette's discussions of American cinema,[24] is French cinema's supposed failure to represent contemporary French society, while the strength of both American and Italian cinema is taken to be precisely their social context. Kast, 'doing duty as the Marxist', as he puts it, tries to get some discussion of economics, but without much success. The view expressed several times that French cinema has nothing to say hides the fact that these discussion participants simply do not much like what *is* being said. And just as this picks up from Truffaut, so his complaints about 'academicism' also find clear echoes here, given a new, more urgent, edge by Rivette's plea for 'a spirit of poverty', for taking risks and 'filming with whatever turns up'.[25] But in many ways what is most interesting in the discussion is the light in which it places Truffaut's earlier polemic. Truffaut's apparently obsessive concern with literature and literary adaptation looks less idiosyncratic when, three and a half years later, this group is still so obsessed – a clear enough indication of the degree to which both good and bad French cinema depended on adapting literary works, and of course of the degree to which literature, and particularly the novel, dominated French culture. This was a domination which only began to be shaken off as the *nouvelle vague* emerged. Despite a continuing close relationship between novel and cinema (think of Marguerite Duras, Alain Robbe-Grillet), not the least of the long-term achievements of the *nouvelle vague* was to put cinema into the predominant position in French culture which the novel had occupied.

At Cannes in 1959, Truffaut's *Les 400 Coups* won the Director's Prize and Resnais's *Hiroshima mon amour* won the International Critics' Prize: the renewal of French cinema, signs of which had been seen in Astruc, in Vadim, in Franju, seemed to have come. Truffaut's and Resnais's films were by no means the only ones to mark the arrival of the *nouvelle vague* – Chabrol's *Le Beau Serge*, 1958, preceded them both, for example[26] – but they were particularly important public signs of the new times, and in many ways representative of the (very different) new aesthetic strategies. The ways in which *Cahiers* dealt with the two films are very revealing of the situation *Cahiers* found itself in at the end of the 1950s.

Les 400 Coups was most obviously the kind of film which Truffaut's own polemic had wanted to encourage, and which Rivette's plea for taking risks, etc., would suggest. Given Truffaut's earlier praise for the presence of Becker's personality in *Grisbi*, and his comment on Guitry that 'he experiences the desire to impregnate celluloid, and the films which are born from this intoxicating parallel activity testify lastingly to the nature, character, temperament and gifts of Guitry . . . *It's enough, I believe, that a film resembles its author for it to be impossible to say that it's not cinema'*,[27] it is not surprising that Hoveyda finds every shot of *Les 400 Coups* 'crowded with [Truffaut's] ideas and imagination'. Godard, characteristically gnomic and allusive, 'reads' the film out of Truffaut's critical formation (as

Hoveyda does, quite explicitly). But what is most striking about Hoveyda's account of the film is its remarkably close resemblance to Bazin's account of *Bicycle Thieves*,[28] as if *Les 400 Coups* came along to confirm, just over ten years after De Sica's film, the same realist – and humanist – avocation of cinema, with a renewed set of realist conventions. Hoveyda's choice of language, conscious or not, leaves no doubt about the resemblance: Truffaut has 'systematically drained the story of any too heavy emphases', so that his 'hero acquires an ambiguity that endows him with truth'; 'the tragedy of everyday life'; 'hostile world'; 'phenomenological description'; 'illusion of the "direct" and "untampered with" '; 'a passion for everything that at first seems trivial'; and so on. It is the triumph, in French cinema and in Truffaut (appropriately enough, given the personally close relationship between Bazin and Truffaut), of the realist aesthetic which Bazin elaborated on the basis of Italian neo-realism. And Hoveyda's response to the film was the dominant *Cahiers* response; Rivette, who will speak with a rather different voice when discussing *Hiroshima mon amour*, comparing Truffaut's aesthetic with Rossellini's, talks of the 'purity of the look . . . perhaps it is enough to believe that things are what they are to be able to see them quite simply on the screen just as they are in reality'.[29]

If *Les 400 Coups* seemed to offer, and to be exemplary in offering, that 'direct engagement with reality' which Leenhardt (in the 'Six Characters' discussion) found lacking in French cinema, then *Hiroshima mon amour* seemed to offer what, in the same discussion, Rivette had called for, for cinema to 'go further than literature'. In this perspective *Hiroshima* was seen as a modernist renewal of 'classical' narrative; literary, by all means, but beyond contemporary French literature, and in other senses thoroughly cinematic. While *Hiroshima* inspires the admiration and interest of all those discussing it, it hardly inspires the *affection* that greeted Truffaut's film. Truffaut was, of course, their long-standing colleague, but the difference of response seems to owe most to the very different aesthetic strategies of the two films, and to *Cahiers'* clear and continuing preference for classical narrative. In some very important senses, however, this discussion of *Hiroshima* (which includes critics-film-makers whose own films were to raise, in very different ways, important formal questions – Godard and Rivette in particular, of course) must be seen as markedly and crucially transitional. Here, for example, we find Rohmer, probably the most conservative of those present, apparently ready – faced by a 'totally new film', perhaps 'the most important film since the war, the first modern film of sound cinema' – to abandon a classicism he had been defining and staunchly defending since at least 1947; or Godard, raising 'the famous problem of the text and the image', with no one else quite understanding what he means; or Rivette, reflecting upon the dialectical 'double movement of consciousness' in the representation of cinema within the cinema; or Rivette and Godard pointing out the degree to which Resnais's film returns to the montage concepts of Eisenstein.

At the same time this beginning of an engagement with 'modernism' poses some difficult questions about modernism's political implications and affiliations, here hastily and somewhat confusingly buried in references to an 'aesthetic left' and to Resnais being 'ahead of his time' by 'remaining true to *October*'. And despite the recognition of radical formal renewal in *Hiroshima* and of the relationship to Eisenstein, what finally emerges – as with the formally very different Truffaut film – is a characteristically 'Bazinian' reading. Thus Rivette, on Resnais's view of the modern world: 'not only does he accept it, but he analyses it deeply, with lucidity and with love. Since this is the world in which we live and love, then for Resnais it is this world that is good, just and true.' Bazin was not long dead:[30] fittingly, Bazin's position – aesthetic and ideological – finds itself at once enshrined in and threatened by the modes in which *Cahiers* came to critical terms with the first triumphs of the *nouvelle vague*.

Notes

1 Eric Rohmer, 'Redécouvrir l'Amérique', *Cahiers* 54, Christmas 1955, translated as 'Rediscovering America' in this volume (Ch. 7); Jacques Rivette, 'Notes sur une révolution', *Cahiers* 54, Christmas 1955, translated as 'Notes on a Revolution' in this volume (Ch. 8).

2 Jacques Rivette, 'Lettre sur Rossellini', *Cahiers* 46, April 1955, translated as 'Letter on Rossellini' in this volume (Ch. 26); Eric Rohmer, 'La Terre du Miracle', *Cahiers* 47, May 1955, translated as 'The Land of Miracles' in this volume (Ch. 27).

3 Jacques Doniol-Valcroze, 'L'Histoire des *Cahiers*', *Cahiers* 100, October 1959.

4 François Truffaut, 'Une Certaine Tendance du cinéma français', *Cahiers* 31, January 1954, translated as 'A Certain Tendency of the French Cinema' in Nichols, *Movies and Methods*, pp. 224–37.

5 Truffaut, *op. cit.*, p. 235.

6 Aurenche and Bost are now better known for Truffaut's attack on them than for their significant contributions to French cinema. Among the scripts they collaborated on were *La Symphonie pastorale* (Delannoy, 1946), *Le Diable au corps* (Autant-Lara, 1947), *Au-delà des grilles* (Clément, 1949), *L'Auberge rouge* (Autant-Lara, 1951), *Jeux interdits* (Clément, 1952), *Le Rouge et le noir* (Autant-Lara, 1954), *Le Blé en herbe* (Autant-Lara, 1954), *Gervaise* (Clément, 1956), *La Traversée de Paris* (Autant-Lara, 1956), *En cas de malheur* (Autant-Lara, 1958).

7 Truffaut, *op. cit.*, p. 233.

8 *Ibid.*, p. 230. Cf. Rohmer's description of French cinema's 'naive immoralism, and [the] perpetual drivel about love crossed by some religious or social conformism', in 'Rediscovering America'.

9 *Ibid.*, p. 230. Cf. Rohmer's comment that American cinema 'does not smother itself in as many flourishes as our cinema does. Its film-makers have more confidence in the power of what they show us than the angle they choose to show it from', in 'Rediscovering America'.

10 Truffaut, *op. cit.*, p. 234.

11 *Ibid.*, p. 233.

12 *Ibid.*, p. 234.

13 Fereydoun Hoveyda, 'La Première Personne du pluriel', *Cahiers* 97, July 1959, translated as 'The First Person Plural' in this volume (Ch 5).

14 Truffaut, *op. cit.*, p. 232.
15 Louis Marcorelles, 'French Cinema, The Old and the New', *Sight and Sound*, vol. 27, no. 4, Spring 1958, p. 192.
16 André Bazin, *What is Cinema? Vol. 1* (essay on Bresson); André Bazin, *Jean Renoir*; Jean-Luc Godard, *Godard on Godard* (material on Ophuls, Vadim, Renoir, Becker, Astruc, Franju); François Truffaut, *Films in My Life* (material on Becker, Bresson, Cocteau, Gance, Ophuls, Guitry, Tati, Astruc, Vadim). See Appendix 2 for details of *Cahiers* material from this period reprinted in translation.
17 Cf. Marcorelles, *op. cit.*, pp. 193–4.
18 Cf. Hoveyda, 'The First Person Plural'.
19 François Truffaut, on *Et Dieu . . . créa la femme*, in *Films in My Life*, pp. 311–12.
20 'Soixante metteurs en scène français', *Cahiers* 71, May 1957.
21 See, for example, Jacques Doniol-Valcroze, 'Problèmes et perspectives du cinéma français', *Cahiers* 41, December 1954; André Bazin, Jacques Doniol-Valcroze, 'Entretien avec Jacques Flaud' (Directeur Général du Centre National de la Cinématographe); and Jacques Doniol-Valcroze, 'Problèmes du court métrage', both *Cahiers* 71, May 1957.
22 See, for example, Rohmer's conclusion to his 'Rediscovering America'.
23 Marcorelles, *op. cit.*, p. 195.
24 See note 1.
25 Cf. Rivette's comments on Rossellini, in his 'Letter on Rossellini'.
26 Truffaut called *Le Beau Serge* 'an unusual and courageous film that will raise the level of French cinema this year', *Films in My Life*, p. 313.
27 Truffaut, 'L'impossible rendez-vous', on Guitry's *Si Paris nous était conté*, *Cahiers* 57, March 1956, pp. 52–3.
28 André Bazin, '*Bicycle Thief*' and 'De Sica: Metteur en Scène', originally published in 1949 and 1951, in *What is Cinema? Vol. 2*.
29 Jacques Rivette, 'Du côté de chez Antoine', *Cahiers* 95, May 1959. Cf. interview with Rossellini (conducted, precisely, by Hoveyda and Rivette) in *Cahiers* 94, April 1959, translated in this volume (Ch. 28): 'Things are there . . . why manipulate them?'
30 André Bazin died on 11 November 1958; a special issue of *Cahiers*, no. 91, most of it devoted to Bazin, was published in January 1959.

1 | François Truffaut: 'The Rogues are Weary'

('Les Truands sont fatigués', *Cahiers du Cinéma* 34, April 1954)

There are no theories in circulation about Jacques Becker, no scholarly analyses, no theses. Neither he nor his work encourages commentary, and so much the better for that.

The truth is that Becker has no intention of mystifying or demystifying anyone; his films are neither statements nor indictments, which means that his work is outside the parameters of current fashion, and we could even place him at the opposite pole to every tendency in French cinema.

Every one of Jacques Becker's films is a Jacques Becker film. This is only a small point, but an important one. There is, in fact, little to tell us that the recent *Thérèse Raquin* was not made by Feyder, *Les Orgueilleux* by Pagliero, *Les Amants de Brasmort* by Yves Allégret and *Mam'zelle Nitouche* by Duvivier. Yet we could not conceive of *Edouard et Caroline*, *Casque d'or* and *Grisbi* being signed by Autant-Lara, Grémillon or Delannoy.

While there is unanimous acknowledgment that it is preferable for the writer and director to be one and the same, the reasons given for this opinion are banal, and no less an admiration continues to be expressed for partnerships and collaborative enterprises – admiration that to my mind is wasted. The fact that Renoir, Bresson, Cocteau and Becker are involved in the writing of a script and sign their names to it not only gives them greater freedom on the studio floor, but more radically it means that they replace scenes and dialogue typical of what scriptwriters produce with scenes and dialogue that a scriptwriter could never dream up. Specificity, dear to Claude Mauriac, is nothing more. And are examples required? For that scene in *Edouard et Caroline* where Elina Labourdette plays at making 'doe eyes' to be filmable, it had first to have been witnessed in real life, then *thought through* in terms of *mise en scène*. I do not know whether we owe this scene to Annette Wademant or to Jacques Becker, but I am sure of one thing – any other director would have cut it from the shooting script: it advances the plot not one jot and is there most of all to give a touch, not of realism, but of reality; it is also there out of love for doing things the hard way.

This search for an ever more exact tone is particularly marked in the dialogue. In *Casque d'or* Raymond (Bussières) comes into Manda's (Reggiani) carpentry workshop and says, 'Alors, boulot boulot, menuise menuise?' ('Work work, scrape scrape, eh?'). Not only could a scriptwriter never have written this line, but it is also the kind of line which is only improvised on the set. None the less, this 'boulot boulot, menuise menuise' still has an *intelligence* (in the sense of complicity between friends) which confounds me every time I see it.

It is not so much the choice of subject which characterizes Becker as how he chooses to treat this subject and the scenes to illustrate it. While he will keep only what is essential in the dialogue, or the essential part of what is superfluous (sometimes even onomatopoeias), he will readily make short work of something anyone else would handle with extreme care, so that he can take longer over characters having breakfast, buttering their toast, brushing their teeth, etc. There is a convention whereby lovers are only allowed to kiss in a dissolve. If in a French film you show a couple undressing and walking around in nightclothes in the bedroom, it would be meant as a joke. You could suppose that these unspoken rules are dictated by a concern for elegance. What does Becker do in a situation like this? That taste for doing things the hard way which I have already mentioned will make him handle the scene in a way that breaks the rules. In *Casque d'or* he shows us Reggiani in a nightshirt and Simone Signoret in a nightdress, in *Grisbi* Gabin in pyjamas.

This kind of work is a perpetual challenge to vulgarity, a challenge where Becker is always the winner, for his films are the most elegant I know, and his characters the most dignified.

What happens to Becker's characters is of less importance than the way it happens to them. The plot, no more than a pretext, gets thinner with every film. *Edouard et Caroline* is just the story of an evening, with a telephone and a waistcoat as accessories. *Touchez pas au grisbi* is about nothing more than a demand for the handover of 96 kilos of gold. 'What most interests me is the characters,' Becker tells us; as a matter of fact the real subject of *Grisbi* is growing old and friendship. This is clearly an underlying theme in Simonin's book, but few scriptwriters would have known how to bring it out and foreground it, relegating violent action, along with the picturesque, to the background. Simonin is forty-nine, Becker forty-eight: *Grisbi* is a film about reaching fifty. At the end of the film Max – like Becker – puts on his spectacles 'to read'. Growing old and friendship, we said: when Angelo kidnaps Riton to force Max to hand over the fifty million, he comments on Max's legendary friendship for Riton but also, unwittingly, on Max growing old, for he is allowed to imagine that Max, ten years earlier, would have got things moving to get back both his friend and the money, and settle his score with Angelo too.

Simonin and Becker have kept from the book only what would have done very well for the *Nouvelle Revue Française*.

The beauty of the *Grisbi* characters, even more than those in *Casque d'or*, comes from their muteness, the economy of their gestures. They only speak or act to say or do the essential. Like Monsieur Teste, Becker kills the puppet in them. These killers become no more than tom-cats facing one another. I see *Grisbi* as a kind of settling of scores between big cats – but high-class cats – tired and, if I dare say it, used up.

There is a moment when every true creator makes such a leap forward that his audience is left behind. For Renoir, *La Règle du jeu* was the sign of maturity, a film so new that it looks confusingly as if it might be a failure; one of those failures that leaves you, the morning after, counting your friends on the fingers of one hand.

Today, if *La Règle du jeu* is understood, *Le Carrosse d'or* is not. I like this kind of complicated calculation where criticism certainly has nothing to gain, but they are none the less calculations with something to reveal to those who approach them with some friendship: Becker filmed *Casque d'or* at the very same age at which Renoir was making *La Règle du jeu*. With *Casque d'or* Becker shed the less perspicacious among his admirers (I am tempted to write: got rid of them); now he is taking off in an entirely new direction, and *Grisbi* follows in the footsteps of *Swamp Water*.

The clearest thing about the admiration I bring to *Grisbi* comes from my certainty that, as it exists now, this film was unfilmable four years ago. *Casque d'or* had to come first. I am not saying that *Grisbi* is better than *Casque d'or*, but it is an even more difficult film. It is no mean thing to make films in 1954 that were inconceivable in 1950; and that is already the first advantage *Grisbi* has over *Thérèse Raquin*, *Le Blé en herbe*, *L'Amour d'une femme*, those three films of a distant pre-war era.

For those of us who are twenty or not much older, Becker's example is both a lesson and an encouragement. We have known Renoir only as a genius, but we discovered cinema when Becker was just beginning. We have watched him finding his way, trying things out: we have seen a body of work *in progress*. And the success of Jacques Becker is the success of a young man who could conceive of no other way than the one he has chosen, and whose love for the cinema has been repaid.

Translated by Liz Heron

2 | André Bazin, Jacques Doniol-Valcroze, Pierre Kast, Roger Leenhardt, Jacques Rivette, Eric Rohmer: 'Six Characters in Search of *auteurs*: a Discussion about the French Cinema'

('Six personnages en quête d'auteurs: débat sur le cinéma français', *Cahiers du Cinéma* 71, May 1957 (extracts))

So far Cahiers *has said a lot, and at the same time very little, about French cinema. A lot about the directors we like and very little about the others – out of politeness, a sense of futility, lack of energy . . . This could have resulted in the impression that our only concern is with foreign cinema (either across the Alps or the Atlantic). Yet our writers talk more often about Saint-Maurice or Billancourt than about Cinecittà or Beverly Hills. But the discussions in our editorial offices aren't always quite right for publication.*

So the question came up as we were preparing this issue: who would be responsible, and in what form, for an appraisal of our cinema that would be fair and at the same time refrain from setting up Aunt Sallies? Our film-makers have enough licensed sycophants to permit themselves the luxury of doing without the approval of our humble scribes; and who is there to deny that there is something rotten in our cinematographic kingdom? But why? That's what needs lengthy discussion and argument. The easiest way was simply to reproduce one of those conversations where people say what they think more freely than when they put pen to paper. And that's what we did. So André Bazin, Jacques Doniol-Valcroze, Pierre Kast, Roger Leenhardt, Jacques Rivette and Eric Rohmer got together around a tape-recorder.

André Bazin: 'The present situation of French cinema.' That implies both its evolution and the present conjuncture. In my view Rivette should begin. He's the one with the most radical and decided opinions on the subject.

Jacques Rivette: It's not exactly an opinion, more a way of formulating the subject. I think that French cinema at the moment is unwittingly another version of British cinema, or to put it another way, it's a British cinema not recognized as such, because it's the work of people who are none the less talented. But the films seem no more ambitious and of no more real value than what is exemplified in the British cinema. I imagine we all agree on that.

Bazin: What in your opinion defines the mediocrity of British cinema?

Rivette: British cinema is a *genre* cinema, but one where the genres have no genuine roots. On the one hand there are no self-validating genres as there are in American cinema, like the Western and the thriller (run-of-the-mill Westerns have a value independent of the great Westerns). There are just false, in the sense of imitative, genres. Anyway, most of them are only imitations of American imitations. And on the other hand it isn't an *auteur* cinema either, since none of them have anything to say. It's a cinema that limps along, caught between two stools, a cinema based on supply and demand, and on false notions of supply and demand at that. They believe that that's the kind of thing the public wants and so that's what they get, but in trying to play by all the rules of that game they do it badly, without either honesty or talent.

Pierre Kast: The distinction between genre films and *auteur* films is quite arbitrary. The only thing that one can be sure of is that the state of French cinema is one of total mediocrity. It amounts to the manufacture of a product that is always the same. The distributors really control production and they display a complete lack of imagination. They do the same thing over and over again using an absolutely arbitrary and uniform interpretation of public taste as the pretext.

Roger Leenhardt: We could perhaps throw some light on the debate by drawing an analogy, which may seem pointless but could prove fruitful. Let's imagine that instead of talking about the current state of French cinema, we are literary critics talking about the current state of the novel or literature in France and comparing it with English or American literature. We would perceive that this year or for the years ahead there is very little one can say about French literature, and that wouldn't surprise anyone. What we have to establish is whether we are speaking as literary critics from a position above culture, or from the position of professionals in the industry. They are two very different things. The distinction to be made is much less between *auteur* films and genres and much more between run-of-the-mill cinema and the efforts of those new creators who represent new tendencies. I feel that this is a funda-mental distinction that could be made from the outset.

Kast: Unfortunately, such a distinction is completely useless as far as cinema is concerned, given that the very existence of a cinema that would fit the second category in terms of production depends in reality on the first category. *Auteur* films are produced in exactly the same conditions and for the same reasons as commercial films.

Leenhardt: When Prévert made *L'Affaire est dans le sac* twenty-five years ago everybody could take it as a joke. He's been copied a hundred times over fifteen years and the general spirit of French cinema was his creation. The problem, apart from questions of markets or distributors, is knowing whether we are currently witnessing the birth of a new tendency which in fifteen years' time may be the normal trend in the cinema.

Bazin: I agree with Leenhardt. However, I feel I should point out that the essential characteristic of American cinema is that unexceptional films, those commercial films which are its principal ingredient, are precisely genre films. American cinema thrives financially if the genres thrive. Production can keep going at an average or even above average rate as long as there are good genres. The weakness of the European film industries is that they are incapable of relying on genres for current production. In French pre-war cinema, even if there wasn't exactly a genre there was a style, the realist *film noir*. It's still around but it's diversified, and I'm afraid that one of the problems of French cinema may arise from its inability to sustain good basic genres that thrive, the way they do in America. That's by the way, and of more concern to American than French cinema.

Rivette: By the way perhaps, but I think it opens out on to the fundamental, since in fact I think it's impossible to do anything worthwhile in European cinema (not just French cinema, but English and Italian as well) except from that premise, i.e. the non-existence of basic genres. One then has to resign oneself to exceptions. That means admitting from the outset that there can't be any good European films, far less great ones, unless one decides not to make use of 'genre' subjects, since every genre is essentially doomed to failure.

Kast: Not doomed, since you've just explained very clearly that genre doesn't exist.

Rivette: Not in the profound sense. Unfortunately it does in reality.

Kast: I'm very sorry to have to do duty as the Marxist – like the drunken Helot at the Spartan banquets – but it's certain that one of the issues facing French cinema (one that has to be recognized at the outset, or we risk getting everything the wrong way round) is the question of the conditions in which potential *auteurs* have the chance to express themselves.

Leenhardt: I don't like quoting authority to support an argument, but I remember a conversation I had with the *directeur général de la cinématographie* [Jacques Flaud] who told me (it was his personal opinion, given in what was a private and very free conversation) that, whatever may be argued to the contrary, the financial state of French cinema was relatively remarkably healthy. 'It's quite obvious,' he added, 'that what we are facing is almost solely a crisis on the level of subject matter in films.' My argument is that pre-war French cinema (I mentioned Prévert, and we could add Aurenche, Cocteau and a few others) was decisively influenced, even in terms of quantity, by particular scriptwriters. In the same way, the Italian intelligentsia of the new generation of writers has shaped Italian cinema. And the American cinema itself has taken its direction from the thriller and the great sociological best-sellers.

Jacques Doniol-Valcroze: Yes, but contrary to the phenomenon you describe,

33

i.e. the influence of the scriptwriters, what is recognizable in French cinema since the Liberation is the emergence of a number of directors who are more or less *auteurs* and who could have been the cinema's equivalent of the Paris School in painting. In 1946 or 1947 one might optimistically have thought that Messieurs Bresson, Becker, Clouzot and Clément were going to create, in terms of style, a new school of French cinema. That didn't happen, I think, because there was no agreement on its substance and no shared inspiration.

Rivette: That's indisputable. You could say that in spite of their great successes, Clouzot, Clément and Becker failed because they thought that finding a style was all it took to create a new soul for French cinema. It's quite clear, on the other hand, that Italian neo-realism wasn't first and foremost a search for a style. It became a style; but it was part of a conception of the new world. I defy anyone (and I think everyone would agree) to find any conception of the world in Clouzot's films, or Becker's or Clément's films. At very best it would be a conception of the world that is banal, literary, and twenty or thirty years out of date.

Kast: I agree that the failure to achieve what could have been a post-war school of French cinema is an accurate way of describing it. All the same I want to correct some of the things that you are asserting. Of the major French films that have been made since then there are some that I like and some that I don't like. For instance, I like Clément's work very much. I can see a continuity in it. Of course it's not the continuity of what one might call Clément's *Weltanschauung*, but it's there in a particular style and tone evident in all his work, and in my opinion it makes him our greatest living director (leaving Bresson out of it for the time being). However (and I'm sorry to have to insist on this point), I'd like us first to clear up the problems of the conditions of production. It's undeniable that if you look at how films are made in France you can see that it's relatively easy (assuming that you already have a subject and the desire to film it) to find a producer and a star who'll do the film. The real problems start when you have to deal with the true masters of production, the distributors. The distributor is far from being the odious beast people think: he's someone with a certain amount of capital to manage and he tries to make use of it in conditions that will give a maximum return. But he completely lacks imagination. The big distribution companies always want the follow-up; they won't buy the first *Bread, Love and Dreams*, but they will buy the follow-up; they won't buy the first *Don Camillo* but they'll buy the second one. One of the key problems of production in France is finding a distributor who'll take the first film. The crisis facing subject matter isn't simply an *auteur* crisis, it's also the problem of having subjects accepted.

[. . .]

Rivette: I think we all implicitly agree on the name for the evolution of the great directors: it's called *academicism*. This academicism isn't serious in itself. For example, academicism is less of a serious problem in the

American cinema – when King Vidor made *War and Peace* we were very clear beforehand about the limits imposed on him by Paramount, Dino de Laurentiis and the whole super-production system. What is serious in the latest films of Becker and Clément is that it's an academicism to which the directors acquiesced. And one even wonders whether they aren't actually seeking it out.

[. . .]

Leenhardt: Well, there I'll take up Kast's position, which is the economic point of view. What has characterized the evolution of French cinema over the last four years, in economic terms, that's to say in terms of financing, is that, for reasons which we don't need to go into here, the films that make money are the big productions and co-productions that are described as international – the ones that are essentially aiming at the foreign market. And it's very likely that a certain insipidness, a certain tendency towards what you call academicism, is connected with the fact that the directors concerned dare not throw themselves into a film whose perspective is essentially that of their own culture. In other words a French film. Instead they aim at making an international film. I'll always remember being struck by something said by the producer of Becker's last film but one, *Ali Baba*: 'You see, I told Becker, it doesn't have to be a big money spinner, but it does have to be a film that people will go to see in Berlin, in Peking and in Hollywood!'

Eric Rohmer: That's very important, because it's precisely its universal character that gives American cinema its value. American cinema gives a lead. What should be deplored is not so much that French cinema isn't producing worthwhile work, but that its work is shut off – I mean it doesn't influence work in other countries. There is no French school, at least not any more, while there is an American school and an Italian school.

Kast: I'm sorry to go off the point a little bit. I would like to go on from all that Rohmer has just said, and all that Leenhardt was saying, and try to take a very small step forward. Although I'm not a Christian I think that we can find an explanation for all that in a short parable: he who would save his life loses it, and it is he who does not seek above all to save it who has every chance of winning. In other words, in the search for success there is already the seed of failure, while if you look for something new you begin to have a small chance of real success. The production system has a bad way of looking at things, which is to imagine that because a success has been achieved it's enough to reproduce the same climatic conditions to do it all over again; while the real wisdom would be to say, '*Ali Baba* was successful, well I'm going to do something different now,' and not, '*Ali Baba* was successful, now I'm going to make *Son of Ali Baba*.'

[. . .]

Rivette: The ideal for French cinema would to be to have on the one hand super-productions made by directors like Delannoy or Le Chanois (people who are suited to that kind of thing and who do it well, so that a film that costs 500 million brings in 800 or even more, which is after all what everyone wants), and on the other hand talented directors who would refuse to involve themselves in such deals, which can in no way be profitable for them, and who have the kind of moral integrity to be satisfied with films – let's say costing 100 million – which don't need foreign markets to avoid making a loss, but with which they could really create *auteur* works. These two spheres would have to coexist and would also have to be quite clearly separate. That's exactly what is happening in Italian cinema, which also has its crises but stays in better health because there is never any confusion between *Ulysses*, or all the other super-productions, and the school of Rossellini, Zavattini, De Sica, Antonioni, all of whom, although they disagree on a lot of issues, have never compromised. Never. The only exception is Visconti, in making *Senso*, but it's quite clear that this is a purely formal exception, since Visconti just got as much as he could out of the producer, like Ophuls with *Lola Montès* and Renoir, to some extent, with *Eléna et les hommes*. But at heart Italian cinema has never let itself be taken over, while in France what we've been witnessing over the past two or three years is the disintegration of what we regarded as the core of French cinema. People like Becker, Clément and Clouzot have successively let themselves be swallowed up by the all-devouring super-productions. I don't know why: for love of either money or international fame. And now you might as well say that there is nobody. There's only one film-maker left who hasn't sold out, and that's Bresson. He's the only one. And there are some youngsters,[1] but there hasn't exactly been time yet for temptation to come their way. Perhaps they'll give in too when the time comes? There's no way of knowing.

[. . .]

Rivette: Why such a desire to conquer the world? That's precisely the cause of the disaster. On the contrary, we should be trying above all to maintain French audiences and only conquer the world as an indirect consequence. From the moment we start trying to manufacture international stars, from the moment we aim at making international films, nine times out of ten we'll fall flat on our faces.

Bazin: I think there's some truth in both points of view.[2] I mean that there is a certain kind of film, with a particular cinematic importance, which is based on the star. It's quite obvious that French cinema before the war was built round Gabin. There's an essential and profound connection between the scripts, the style of the films and Gabin. It's indisputable. But on the other hand you could give ten examples where the star is a disaster. You have to judge it in context. I think we're all agreed in assuming that it's not in the direction of the international super-production, where the star has a fundamental role, that French cinema has most chance of progress. This will happen by rediscovering a way of capturing the inspiration of talented people, and that ought not to happen independently of acting but with acting at a level beyond that of the star.

Rivette: In fact, Gabin wasn't an actor, he was something else. He wasn't an actor, he was someone who brought a character into French cinema, and it wasn't only scripts that he influenced but *mise en scène* as well. I think that Gabin could be regarded as almost more of a director than Duvivier or Grémillon, to the extent that the French style of *mise en scène* was constructed to a large extent on Gabin's style of acting, on his walk, his way of speaking or of looking at a girl. It's also what gives the great American actors their dynamism, actors like Cary Grant, Gary Cooper or James Stewart. For instance, Anthony Mann's *mise en scène* is definitely influenced by James Stewart's style of acting. Now, I can't see any actor in France at the moment who has that power of his own to go beyond just acting.

[. . .]

Bazin: I'm wondering whether pre-war cinema, which did in fact demonstrate quite exceptional thematic and inspirational unity, whichever directors were involved, could be linked up with the up-and-coming literature of that time. It's normal for there to be a time-lag between a literary generation and its passage into cinema. For instance existentialism, which is out of date in literature, could have brought us (I don't think it will now) the equivalent of the pre-war *film noir*, whose relationship to surrealism Leenhardt has clearly shown.[3]

[. . .]

Leenhardt: I started this conversation by saying that the literary parallel was interesting. If the Italian cinema is interesting it's because I read Pavese. If American cinema is interesting it's because I read not only Caldwell but several other new American novelists. If French cinema isn't interesting it's because at the moment there is nothing interesting happening in the French novel.

[. . .]

Kast: . . . When you look at what we're reading in France every year, you can see that, while you may not like the vast majority of the films that come out during the year, there aren't many worthwhile novels either. Which are the two or three outstanding books that I've read this year? First there's Claude Lévi-Strauss's *Tristes tropiques*, which I can't envisage transferred to the screen, at least for the time being, considering the direction exotic films are taking. Then I'd say Carpentier's *Le Partage des eaux*, which has no connection with French literature. This year there haven't been any French novels that I've really liked. I'm sorry, but that's how it is. There are several simultaneous reasons for that. First, one which seems very clear to me: a lot of people who might write novels have turned to the idea of making films. There's no doubt that in Astruc's case, for instance, it explains both his qualities and his defects. He makes films without the slightest conception of film-making as a technical craft, something one does with one's hands, but exactly in the way that he would write the books he doesn't write. That does away at a stroke with the distinction between scriptwriter and director, which is a long-standing, traditional distinction in French cinema, and now on its way out. Professional scriptwriters were necessary when you had old-style directors whose role was technical. There had to be someone to write the story for them since they were only capable of doing the *mise en scène* – in fact, nothing! (*Laughter*.) When Vadim makes a film or when Astruc makes a film, whatever the film is like or whatever reservations you may have about it, it's something quite different from a film made by two people – a scriptwriter and a director.

Rivette: It's what we call an *auteur* film!

Doniol-Valcroze: We're falling back on our old 'Objectif 49' theories,[4] which are outdated in principle but still correct. We've reached a point where the cinema is a medium of expression for saying something. And the staggering thing is that the cinema in France has nothing to say, and that French film says nothing.

Leenhardt: The notion of the total *auteur* is a myth all the same, because the director's craft requires specific capabilities which are not the same as those of a writer. It's possible that one man could have both, but the fact that at the moment directors who have no apparent talent for scriptwriting, like Becker for example, are doing it and risking disaster, means the degeneration of what is a major profession. It still exists in Italy (where there are usually five scriptwriters, not just one) and in the USA.

Kast: But it's obvious that however many people work on a Fellini scenario the film is Fellini's, including its subject.

Rivette: I think that what you're saying about Fellini could apply just as well to the American film-makers, in spite of the credits, for as we now know for sure there isn't a single one of the great American directors who doesn't work on the scenario himself right from the beginning, in collaboration with a scriptwriter who writes the screenplay for him and does the purely literary work that he himself couldn't do with the same formal skill but which is nevertheless in accordance with his own directives (not simply under his supervision but following the direction he gives to it). And that's why in *Cahiers* we've chosen to defend directors like Hitchcock rather than Wyler, and Mann rather than Zinnemann, because they are directors who actually work on their scenarios. And that's precisely the new element that they've introduced over these last ten years. So I agree with Kast in thinking that the question of the pure scriptwriter is out of date.

Bazin: It's out of date in psychological terms. It's possible that the evolution of the cinema (I know nothing about it, which I readily admit) is moving in the direction of the director-*auteur* working on the scenario with the scriptwriter or scriptwriters. But it matters very little to me whether there are scriptwriters as such – what does matter is that the scriptwriter should exist as a function. [. . .] What we come back to in fact isn't the problem of people, but the problem of inspiration and themes. American cinema is just about inexhaustible in the richness of its themes; that's just not the case in France. Before the war there were thematic continuities. Now we have to ask ourselves what they are. The great unity there was before the war has split in all sorts of directions. But one characteristic remains – of context though not of subject-matter: that is, beyond psychology, a particular novelistic vision of the world. Films like Becker's *Casque d'or* or *Edouard et Caroline* are films which, without any specific literary origins, to me seem very French and very 'post-war'. *Les Dernières Vacances* is also a very post-war film. Similarly Clément's *Jeux interdits* or Bresson's *Journal d'un curé de campagne*. While they vary widely in style, atmosphere and theme, they have in common a sharper sense of humanity than anything in pre-war cinema, as well as a capacity for analysis which is close to literature. I'm afraid we're losing this, and it's the only capital we've got.

Doniol-Valcroze: [. . .] Why have adaptations from fiction failed? Because apart from a few isolated instances like Bresson, there is no adequate sociological or social *context* in the films to support them. The strength of American cinema is that it has this context. That's also the strength of the Italian cinema. When Antonioni made that extraordinary film *Le Amiche*, adapted from Pavese, he was able to keep the same context as Pavese's book. I think French cinema missed out for several reasons: the *auteurs* lacked confidence, but there were also financial prohibitions. I'm going to mention a word that applies very generally: censorship. I don't only mean the Board of Censors, but also pre-censorship, the censorship of the industry, individual censorship.

Rivette: That's right. There's no point in looking to comedy, which will always be a limited sphere; nor to films adapted from the novel, which was hopeful seven or eight years ago but is now out of date. The only possibility left for French cinema would be in films which although not social (I'm not happy with that word) at least take up a position, analogous to Italian post-war cinema. But why have people failed to recognize this possibility until now? I think it's too easy to blame it on censorship and the producers. It's only because the few French directors who have made statements to the press like 'I'd like to make social films' are, in reality, people who have been corrupted. I think that Autant-Lara, Clément and Clouzot are all sickening, to the extent that they could have made those films if they had been willing to work in the same conditions as Rossellini, Fellini or Antonioni, with 30 or 40 million francs, perhaps having to film in the street and being pushed for time. Only they don't want to. What they want, on the one hand, is to go on making money, and on the other to go on making prestige films. It's quite obvious that Clouzot, when he says that he wants to make a film about Indochina and a 300 million franc film, at one and the same time, will never manage either, and anyway has probably never really wanted to. All he did was strut about in front of journalists and acquire a good reputation for himself as a film-maker with courage. Then he makes *Les Diaboliques*. But if Clouzot had really wanted to make that film he could certainly have found 30 million. He wouldn't have had to worry about advance censorship and his film would probably have passed anyway. After all, the Italian film-makers also have censorship and producers and distributors. They have still found a way of saying quite a lot. We haven't seen Lizzani's films in France. But I imagine that Lizzani didn't say straight out, 'I am a Communist and I want the revolution to come.' He implied it, but in a way clear enough for him to say what he wanted to say. Yet Clouzot, Clément and Autant-Lara (I keep coming back to these three names because they are the three who are most guilty) didn't want to take that risk. Because they are cowards, because – I repeat – they are corrupted, corrupted by money. In a word I think that what is most lacking in French cinema is a *spirit of poverty*.[5] Its only hope now lies in other directors – not those three any more (for if they once had the opportunity to say something they let it go by), but new directors taking those risks making films with 20 or 30 million, perhaps even less, and filming with whatever turns up, without putting their scripts forward for approval by the censors and perhaps without even putting them to the producers and the distributors. I think *that* is the only hope for French cinema.

Leenhardt: The true character of pre-war French cinema (which, rightly or wrongly, was important) is that its fundamental non-conformism was positive in relation to humanity, in social and revolutionary terms. Now, following on from it today, this degeneration you're talking about has only kept its negative characteristics.[6] For instance with Clouzot the *film noir* lost that positivity, that poetic transcendence, that revolutionary meaning. And *La Traversée de Paris* is almost a right-wing film. It's the American and Italian cinema that's positive and invigorating. In France we are locked into reactionary values pure and simple, which make an art film a film about destiny, where everything is ill-fated and in the most stupid way imaginable. What constitutes success for Jeanson is to impose an unhappy ending where an inconclusive one or a happy one would have been good aesthetically. There's a kind of inverted censorship which means that nobody dares to attempt a positive film. The only ones that are positive are perhaps Bresson's films.

[. . .]

Kast: What's a positive film, what's a negative film? We would need to engage in a whole discussion which we'd never finish.

Rivette: A negative film is a cowardly film. And I think that the great problem of French cinema now is cowardice.

Kast: If you substitute the word 'complacency' for the word 'cowardice' I entirely agree with you. However, there are some novels that say something that's perhaps not new, but better at any rate. For instance I like Pierre Boulle's novels very much. They would make excellent films, like Henry James and Conrad. That points to something, the complacency of some of the people who run the film industry which has prevented this tendency from materializing. Even Astruc, who's not involved in issues of this kind, and deals with things that are very much outside them, was tempted by Pierre Boulle's *La Face*.

Rivette: Perhaps I'm going to clash quite violently with Pierre Kast, but I think that if Pierre Boulle's novels had been adapted for the cinema it wouldn't have been much of a step forward, because they are literature whose inspiration goes back some fifty years. If you stop at that point you're not going very far. It would be a new type of academicism but it would still be academicism – left academicism, anarchist academicism, academicism of the absurd. But while Huston has had his moments, I can't see why in France we should start by taking him as an example. We need to go further.

Kast: As usual, Rivette's assertions are perfect tautologies. To dismiss Pierre Boulle with the stroke of a pen by saying that his work is fifty years old is ridiculous in my view. Just as his way of saying, *a priori*, 'Huston is finished!' is absolutely disgraceful and quite amazing. I wish Huston did have followers in France.

Rivette: Huston is finished in the way that you can say Conrad's novels date from fifty years ago. To do now in the cinema what people were doing elsewhere fifty years ago is pointless. The only possibility that the cinema has of doing something important (and this is where I part company with Leenhardt) is in *not* following literature, whether it's the literature of fifty or fifteen years ago (as pre-war French cinema did – while Mac Orlan or Carco was being adapted it was the novels of Malraux, Bernanos and the early novels of Sartre that were most important in France). But it's not a question of following the literature of a few years ago. It's perhaps not even a question of trying to keep up with new literature: the real function of the cinema should be to go further than literature.

[. . .]

Rohmer: Rivette was saying that the cinema should be ahead of literature. Whether ahead or behind it's in any case on quite different territory. I wonder whether it's really the aim of the cinema to be in harmony with what Leenhardt calls 'the most contemporary literature', particularly in France where that literature seems to be going in quite a different direction. Cinema and literature are looking for different things. It's possible that this harmony could be achieved in some oblique way, but for the moment I can't easily see how. I find Bresson's latest film a very good example since it was taken from a non-literary work.

Kast: For once I find myself in agreement with Rohmer. I find the relationships between literature and the cinema extremely obscure and difficult to disentangle. They're two quite different areas. The field of literature is one where freedom of expression can be exercised with far fewer internal constraints. The writer is a bit like the painter. The painter

41

works his canvas and tells the world to go to hell. And nobody can say a thing.

Rohmer: What you are saying seems to postulate the inferiority of the film-maker in relation to the writer. You think that the writer can say what he wants while the film-maker can't. And yet what the best – American and other – cinema is saying is as modern and as interesting as what the most free French literature is saying, if not more so.

Kast: I probably didn't express myself clearly enough. It isn't my intention at all to say that I consider cinema inferior to literature as a medium of expression. I simply want to say that the conditions in which it is practised are very different and that, so far, in reality the film-maker's freedom of expression is limited in every area.

Rivette: Leenhardt was saying a little while ago that American cinema had drawn its essential strength from the American novel. But what I see is that the adaptations of the great contemporary novelists by American film-makers have with rare exceptions only produced mediocre films. Quite the contrary, American cinema has developed, alongside American literature, personal themes and a personal vision of the world which are not particularly close to those of Faulkner and Hemingway and are even in certain respects very distant. What precisely constitutes the greatness of the American film is that it has drawn a parallel with the American novel, but these are two lines that do not intersect; they advance side by side.

[. . .]

Bazin: I think that's digressing quite a bit from the specific problem of French cinema. It's not absolutely necessary to establish whether French film-makers should or shouldn't derive the inspiration for their themes from the literary patrimony. Both methods could be useful. If they aren't it's because American cinema actually has themes outside literature. It is perhaps greater because it has in itself enough sociological inspiration to draw on. It is very possible that for historical reasons French cinema has none, and perhaps the novel offers a greater source of inspiration, but it isn't really important. The problem is to find out whether there is material or not.

Rohmer: French cinema doesn't depict French society, while American cinema, like Italian cinema, is able to raise society to a level of aesthetic dignity. Perhaps in conclusion we could try to find out, if not why, at any rate in what way French cinema fails to represent contemporary France.

Doniol-Valcroze: I find it interesting to observe that in two films that have already been mentioned here several times, *Les Mauvaises Rencontres* and *Et Dieu . . . créa la femme*, two talented young film-makers have done exactly the opposite of what other dedicated film-makers would have done. Taking a very debatable novel, *Une Sacrée Salade*, as his source, Astruc has elevated his subject to a kind of personal meditation on youth, on a milieu that he knew, on ambition, etc. Vadim too has done a very good essay on his conceptions of love and relationships with women. I observe with pleasure that two young film-makers of obvious talent are showing an inclination to put their current and future work entirely into a specific historical and social context. I think that this is apparent in all great literary or cinematic works. Stendhal writes about his own time, Flaubert and Balzac of theirs. I am not denying that tomorrow a young film-maker could emerge who would express what he had to say within an evocation of ancient Rome, but that would be an exception. The greatest possibility of doing good work that is open to young film-makers is to continue in the manner of Astruc and Vadim.

Rivette: Whereas the great weakness of *La Traversée de Paris* is that although it does in fact bear witness to a particular society it is not contemporary society. Neither is it 1943, which is when Marcel Aymé's short story was set. It seems to me more like 1930. The very specifically Montmartre relationship of the artist and the bourgeois is a 1930s theme, set in 1943 and filmed in 1956.

Doniol-Valcroze: Yes, but it is of its director's own time. *Marguerite de la nuit* and *La Traversée de Paris* are films that Autant-Lara had been wanting to make for a long time but he was only recently able to do so.

Bazin: There's no inevitability about a direct relationship between a given society and the cinema, although that's the case in America and in Italy. I don't think either that there's any direct relationship between the French novel and French society. It goes beyond just cinema. It's perhaps because at this stage in the development of society and of French art the connection can't be made. Should one seek themes related to contemporary reality at any price? That's what Le Chanois and Cayatte did. We can see the outcome of that. It isn't exemplary.

Doniol-Valcroze: I'm not saying that it's the golden rule. But it happens that in two films that we like there was this connection.

Kast: You'll have to excuse me. I have a lot of respect for Astruc's film. But to say that these two films have any connection with contemporary reality is one of those charming jokes so typical of *Cahiers du Cinéma* in its present form. It's one of those amusing paradoxes. It has to make you laugh but it has no connection with reality. You don't really expect us to believe that there is the slightest relationship, other than the superficial relationship to the world of magazines, between the world of these two films and the real world? If I value Astruc's film it's for other reasons.

Doniol-Valcroze: I think there's a misunderstanding here. I don't mean that either Astruc's film or Vadim's actually expresses the condition of a particular society in a particular year and a particular place. I'm saying that the makers of these films drew their framework and their inspiration from a lived experience. If they betray it, if they represent it in a way that differs from our view, that is something else. But there is a certain sincerity of inspiration that's more genuine than what we hear from some 'social' directors who say that they want to 'do the housing shortage or the problem of abortion'.

Kast: I agree with Doniol in some respects. As far as I'm concerned a film with a pretence to being social is already on the road to failure. There are hundreds of films of the French social-realist-optimist school and I can't stand them. In my opinion they might as well be about the dark side of the moon. They're taken out of different magazines from Vadim's. But even though I don't like Vadim's film I prefer it to those others, because it uses a language that I hear in the street every day. But saying that Vadim was skilful in the way he used the particular mannerisms of speech that are part of the world of the bistros doesn't make his film directly related to contemporary reality.

Rohmer: There's another factor. In twenty years the face of France has changed very little, while America and even Italy have evolved a lot. Nothing new has altered the French way of life since, let's say, 1930, except what reaches us from America.

Kast: For the second time I entirely agree with you. For the moment there's nothing happening in France that's sufficiently decisive to provide the material for a narrative cinema based on a change in society. The only thing I can see is a series of impenetrable illusions created by the dominant mythology: the mythology of success, superiority, and the equation of worth with social function, all of which I see as the pillars of the bourgeoisie. For example monogamy and the family unit, as they exist in the *code civile*, no longer correspond to reality.

Bazin: Ninety-nine per cent of French drama, literature and cinema is based on it.

Rohmer: They are stereotypes as old as the world itself. French film-makers only know how to make endless versions of *La Garçonne*. If there are contradictions in modern society that's not where to look for them. If there's anything new it's that today's generation is not so much looking for freedom (at any rate a theoretical freedom which there's no shortage of) but for morality, whatever it might be.

Bazin: What's more, it's not enough just to have a good rich sociological foundation. There must be extremes. In Italy, unemployment fulfils the role of fate and destiny. Three-quarters of Italian neo-realism is founded on *fear*, social fear. American society is polarized by two things that figure importantly: money and luck. In France it's not material that's lacking, but the possibility of drama inherent in it. That doesn't mean that in France there aren't numerous problems: wars in Indochina or in Algeria, the housing shortage, etc.

Rivette: You certainly can't take up the housing shortage or racism or the war without relating them to a wider context. And you won't be able to do it so long as you go on believing (as Rohmer and Kast do, to my great amazement) that French society hasn't evolved in the last twenty years, which I think is absurd. The first duty of a French film-maker should be to try to see what are the most fundamental new elements in society over the last few years. And then he could handle any one of those issues, because he would have the key. Why haven't we found the key? Because we haven't even looked for it.

Bazin: For each individual the key will be political or moral, while it should in fact be beyond politics and morality.

Leenhardt: While the Italian cinema takes up the same subjects as Italian literature, and the American cinema likewise those of American literature, why the devil do you expect French cinema to take up anything other than what concerns French literature, namely themes that are psychological or have metaphysical resonances? What's more, that's just what Bresson is doing. In the cinema he has exactly the same position as a French writer. Instead of grabbing hold of reality and expressing it in a sensational way he gives it a literary synthesis, freezing it, perfecting it, fashioning a work of art from it. That is what French literature is doing, quite the opposite of the direct engagement with reality of the Americans and the Italians. I can't see what phenomenon would allow French cinema to escape the law which is fundamental to French literature.

Rivette: That's quite true. Bresson corresponds to a literary reality in France. But that is his reactionary aspect. There have been very great reactionary writers, but there have also been, and not so long ago, Bernanos and Malraux. While we have the equivalent of Chardonne, for instance, in French cinema, why don't we have the equivalent of Bernanos or Malraux? . . .

We started this debate without any expectation of reaching positive conclusions, but simply to raise certain problems and stir up every possible and imaginable issue. We do not hide from ourselves the fact that the impression people may finally take from it is that it's 'a lot of wind' – but the wind bloweth where it listeth; and maybe a few specks of dust will have stuck in your eye? We could not wish for more.

Translated by Liz Heron

Notes

1 The 'youngsters' referred to here would be, in particular, Alexandre Astruc and Roger Vadim, whose *Les Mauvaises Rencontres* (1955) and *Et Dieu . . . créa la femme* (1956), respectively, both important precursors of the *nouvelle vague*, have already been mentioned in sections of the discussion omitted here. On Vadim, cf. Godard on *Sait-on jamais?*, Ch. 3 below.

2 'Both points of view': the discussion, in passages omitted here, has touched upon distinctions between a cinema based on stars and a cinema rejecting conventional attitudes to acting, the two kinds of cinema seen to coexist in, for example, Italian cinema.

3 In a passage omitted here, Leenhardt posited the foundation of pre-war French cinema as coming out of 'a union between a French literary movement symbol-

45

ized by Dabit (post-1914 populism) and a movement close to it, bordering on Surrealism, represented by Prévert and Aurenche'.

4 'Objectif 49': a polemical cine-club formed in 1948–9 from film-makers and film critics, generally opposing 'official' French cinema; the group included people like Jean Cocteau, Robert Bresson, Alexandre Astruc, Pierre Kast. 'Objectif 49' exerted significant influence on the formation of *Cahiers du Cinéma*; for further comment, see the Introduction to this volume.

5 Cf. certain aspects of Rivette's discussion of Rossellini, in 'Letter on Rossellini', Ch. 26 in this volume.

6 Leenhardt's comments here are very close in spirit to Truffaut's views in his *Cahiers* 31, January 1954, article 'Une Certaine Tendance du cinéma français', translated as 'A Certain Tendency of the French Cinema' in Nichols, *Movies and Methods*, pp. 224–37, and discussed in the Introduction to the articles on French cinema in this volume.

3 | Jean-Luc Godard: 'Sufficient Evidence'

('Des preuves suffisantes', *Cahiers du Cinéma* 73, July 1957)

It would be a mistake to commend *Sait-on jamais?* simply because this French film is as resolutely modern as *Et Dieu . . . créa la femme*. Roger Vadim is 'with it'. Agreed. His colleagues, for the most part, are still missing the point. Also agreed. But one shouldn't admire Vadim simply because he does naturally what should long ago have been the ABC of the French cinema. What could be more natural, really, than to 'breathe the air of today'? We no longer admire a Maserati or the Leduc 022 for the same reasons that our grandparents admired a de Dion-Bouton or Clément Ader's 'chauve-souris'. So it is pointless to compliment Vadim on being ahead of his time, because all that has happened is that everyone else is behind while he is up to date. An excellent reason, you may say, for proving the theorem which proposes Vadim as the best of the young French directors working today.[1] Reason necessary, I would reply, but not sufficient. So let us look for sufficient evidence to prove this theorem. Where to find it? In *Sait-on jamais?* Is it there? It is.

Let's look at the scenario first. The idea is taken from an unpublished novel[2] written by Vadim about ten years ago. On the suggestion of his producer Raoul Lévy, Vadim transposed the action from Paris to Venice. He also threw in a detective story in order to use up a novel whose rights Lévy had acquired. This sort of thing is common practice in the film industry: difficult to know whether to laugh or cry.

So we are in Venice in 1957, a Venice admirably enhanced by Armand Thirard's photography and in which three men embark on a metaphorical poker-game with a young French girl at stake. Sophie (Françoise Arnoul) is about twenty-five. It's the awkward age when a pretty woman is still desperately anxious to be thought of as a naughty girl.[3] Sophie is mean only because she is naïve, cruel because she is weak. Her favourite lover, Sforzi (Robert Hossein), has passed her on as an expression of his gratitude to Baron von Bergen, whose strong-arm man he had been in the biggest fraud of the Second World War: the circulation of forged sterling banknotes by the government of the Third Reich. Von Bergen (O. E. Hasse), a world-weary sexagenarian, wants to finish his life in peace and quiet. Like all old Germans, he has become a moralist with age. He now prefers the contemplation of crime to crime itself. He takes up with Sophie, but almost paternally. The pleasure he derives from her is disinterested. To caress the girl or surprise her in the bath means little to him. Von Bergen simply needs to know that she is on hand, and that's all. She can make love with anybody and everybody she likes, provided she comes to say goodnight before going out. All would be well that ended well but for Michel (Christian Marquand), a rather drab journalist who becomes enamoured of Sophie at a fleapit showing a Gerald McBoing-Boing cartoon. The affair between Michel and Sophie, in fact, gallops along all the faster because 'when he kisses her, she feels as though she had been running'. In so doing she runs up against the fury of the Baron, who tolerates passing fancies but not liaisons which may be dangerous. And as there is something of Laclos[4] in him, von Bergen encourages Sforzi to put this charming cut-price Cleopatra (to whom he has secretly left the two thousand million lire deposited, in her name, in the coffers of a Swiss bank) back on the leash again. But villainy breeds bigger villainy. Sforzi's plan is soon laid: to betray the Baron and get Sophie back, so as to marry her and lay his hands on the money. Our blackguard soon wins back poor Sophie's heart. Then he kills von Bergen and prevents Michel from going to the police by threatening to frame him for the crime. Sophie's eyes are finally opened by this wickedness, and she forces Michel to take action. With the aid of a friend from Interpol, they frustrate Sforzi's plot. In the end our two pigeons can no doubt live and love each other tenderly. The last shot of the film shows Françoise Arnoul squaring her shoulders as she stands in a police-launch in the Grand Canal under a Titian grey sky.

Here, admittedly, is a very conventional scenario, no better and no worse, *a priori*, than that for Maurice Labro's *Action immédiate*,[5] for example.

Its only value lies in the extent to which the director has probed the stereotyped characters to turn them into living beings. And Michel, Sophie, von Bergen and Sforzi are alive as no French thriller heroes have ever been (with the exception of those in Jean Renoir's *La Nuit du carrefour*). Vadim's great strength is in fact that he talks only about things he knows well, he deals with characters he sees fifty times a day every day, and above all, as a beginner, he describes himself with all his qualities and defects through these characters. Hence the air of extreme novelty about the dialogue and the incisiveness of a *mise en scène* untroubled by complexes or prejudices.

No doubt this was more true of *Et Dieu . . . créa la femme* than of *Sait-on jamais?* The first was the film of an *auteur*, the second only of a director. As a character, Juliette may have been more exact than Sophie, and Curt Jurgens's character more probable than O. E. Hasse's; but over and above the fact that Brigitte Bardot is a more engaging actress than Françoise Arnoul, and that Curt Jurgens is more at ease in the role of a smooth Côte d'Azur operator than O. E. Hasse as a world-weary forger (Stroheim style), one might retort that the characters played by Christian Marquand and Robert Hossein are infinitely more intriguing and subtle than those portrayed by Trintignant and the same Christian Marquand.[6] And if one absolutely had to pinpoint the Orson Welles in *Sait-on jamais?*, I would see it less in the compositions or certain deep-focus effects (justified purely by the use of colour) than in the fact that Vadim, like the director of *Mr Arkadin*, pays as much attention to his male as his female characters.

Unlike so many beginners with five years of Cinémathèque viewing behind them, Vadim does not say to himself, 'I'm going to move the camera thus, and frame the characters so. Now, what are they going to do and say?' Instead, more sensibly, he reasons this way: Michel pulls the curtain and hides Sophie as she lies on the bed, increasing his pleasure at knowing she is there by his displeasure at being unable to see her. How to film this scene? Nothing easier. A shot of Michel pulling the curtain: Sophie can no longer be seen. Change of shot with the camera now in Sophie's place, no longer able to see Michel. Michel opens the curtain. They are together again. It is easy to see from this example that once the characters' motivations are clearly established, *mise en scène* becomes a simple matter of logic. Vadim will become a great director because his scenes are never occasioned by a purely abstract or theoretical idea for a shot; rather it is the *idea of a scene*, in other words a dramatic idea, which occasions the *idea of a shot*.

Another example: the now celebrated shot from the pigeons' point of view. While Sforzi philosophizes with Michel and Sophie in St Mark's Square amid the hellish noise of pigeon wings, the camera suddenly shifts without warning to the rooftops and looks down on the square from, if I may venture to say so, the viewpoint of Sirius. I would bet that Vadim had not planned this shot, and got the idea for it when he was preparing to shoot the scene.[7] It is an arbitrary shot, admittedly, but arbitrary *a posteriori*. Its violent beauty redeems its purpose.

This said, I absolutely agree that Vadim's second film is less personal than his first, more sophisticated, but maybe more successful, more secret too. The characters in *Sait-on jamais?* are filmed after and not before love-making. Cynicism is not the reason why Françoise Arnoul's bath scene is cut off just as she stands up in the bath; it is because the whole of this scene and the next are constructed, not on the fact that Michel is looking at Sophie in her bath, but on the fact that he already has looked at her and so is less interested in her body than her thoughts. In *Et Dieu . . . créa la femme*, tenderness was muffled in eroticism. In *Sait-on jamais?*, it is the reverse.

There remains, for anyone not yet convinced of Vadim's talent, what I would call the photographic proof. I have often noticed that French cameramen – unlike Italians and Americans, who are always consistent – turn out to be brilliant with good directors and disappointing with the rest. Julliard has never done better work than on *Germany Year Zero*,

Alékan than on *La Belle et la Bête,* Claude Renoir than with his uncle, Christian Matras than with Max Ophuls. Armand Thirard does not disprove this rule. The camerawork in *Et Dieu . . . créa la femme* and *Sait-on jamais?* is in a different league from all those Clouzot films photographed by the same Thirard.

Translated by Tom Milne

Notes

1 As translator Tom Milne points out, Vadim's first two films were welcomed by *Cahiers* and were important precursors (aesthetically and industrially) of the *nouvelle vague,* but Vadim himself soon passed from favour. A year later, in *Arts,* 30 July 1958, in a review of Bergman's *Summer with Monika,* Godard already pointed to a relative reassessment of Vadim:

> *Summer with Monika,* five years before its time, brought to a peak that renaissance in modern cinema whose high priests were Fellini in Italy, Aldrich in Hollywood, and (so we believed, wrongly perhaps) Vadim in France.
>
> *Summer with Monika,* in fact, already is *Et Dieu . . . créa la femme,* but brought off brilliantly, without a single flaw, without a single hesitation, with total lucidity in both dramatic and moral construction and in its development, in other words its *mise en scène.* (From *Godard on Godard,* p. 84)

2 No 'novel' is mentioned among the film's credits. (Translator's note.)
3 'A naughty girl': referring to the Bardot film *Cette sacrée gamine,* which was scripted by Vadim. (Translator's note.)
4 'Laclos': Vadim was to film Choderlos de Laclos's novel, *Les Liaisons dangereuses,* in 1959. (Translator's note.)
5 '*Action immédiate*': a routine spy thriller in the 'Coplan' series, made in 1956 and starring Henri Vidal, Barbara Laage and Nicole Maurey. (Translator's note.)
6 It is worth noting that in *Sait-on jamais?* Vadim has given Marquand the role played by Trintignant in *Et Dieu . . . créa la femme,* while Hossein takes over the role played by Marquand in the earlier film. (Author's note.)
7 In *La Mort en ce jardin,* Buñuel slips in a similar shot – the Champs-Elysées at night – into the heart of the jungle. (Author's note.) How similar the two shots Godard compares here are is open to some dispute, since Buñuel's inserted shot is so much closer to being extra-diegetic.

4 | Jean-Luc Godard: *Les 400 Coups*

('La Photo du Mois', *Cahiers du Cinéma* 92, February 1959)

With *Les 400 Coups*, François Truffaut enters both modern cinema and the classrooms of our childhood. Bernanos's humiliated children.[1] Vitrac's children in power. Melville-Cocteau's *enfants terribles*. Vigo's children, Rossellini's children, in a word, Truffaut's children – a phrase which will become common usage as soon as the film comes out. Soon people will say Truffaut's children as they say Bengal Lancers, spoil-sports, Mafia chiefs, road-hogs, or again in a word, cinema-addicts. In *Les 400 Coups*, the director of *Les Mistons* will again have his camera, not up there with the men like Old Man Hawks, but down among the children. If a certain arrogance is implied in talking about 'up there' for the over-thirties, 'down there' should also be taken as implying pride in the under-sixteens: *Les 400 Coups* will be the proudest, stubbornest, most obstinate, in other words most free, film in the world. Morally speaking. Aesthetically, too. Henri Decae's Dyaliscope images will dazzle us like those of *Tarnished Angels*. The scenario will be fresh and airy like that of *Juvenile Passion*. The dialogue and gestures as caustic as those in *Baby Face Nelson*. The editing as delicate as that of *The Goddess*. Precocity will reveal its cloven hoof as in *The Left-handed Gun*. These titles do not spring at random from the keys of my electric typewriter. They come from François Truffaut's list of the ten best films of 1958. A charming and handsome family into which *Les 400 Coups* fits beautifully. To sum up, what shall I say? This: *Les 400 Coups* will be a film signed Frankness. Rapidity. Art. Novelty. Cinematograph. Originality. Impertinence. Seriousness. Tragedy. Renovation. Ubu-Roi. Fantasy. Ferocity. Affection. Universality. Tenderness.

Translated by Tom Milne

Note

1 'Bernanos's humiliated children': there are several 'humiliated children' in Bernanos's novels, e.g. the mutinous schoolgirl suicide of *Nouvelle histoire de*

Mouchette (filmed by Bresson as *Mouchette*), but one of them is entitled *Les Enfants humiliés*. 'Vitrac's children in power' refers to Roger Vitrac's Surrealist play, *Victor ou les enfants au pouvoir*, in which the nine-year-old hero, seven feet tall and endowed with adult intelligence, and his six-year-old girl-friend, are the only sane beings in an insane adult world. Jean-Pierre Melville filmed Cocteau's *Les Enfants terribles* in 1949. Children, of course, loom large in both of Jean Vigo's feature films: the rebel schoolboys in *Zéro de conduite*, and the cabin-boy in *L'Atalante*. 'Rossellini's children' probably refers in particular to *Germany Year Zero*. (Translator's note.)

5 | Fereydoun Hoveyda: 'The First Person Plural'

('La Première Personne du pluriel', *Cahiers du Cinéma* 97, July 1959)

Les 400 Coups is not a masterpiece. So much the better for François Truffaut! In the first place the word has been so debased that it finally becomes meaningless. Next, and above all, with a masterpiece in his pocket at twenty-seven Truffaut would really have something to worry about – he would have to spend his life trying to shed the burden. *Les 400 Coups* is better than a masterpiece. Together with *Hiroshima mon amour*, it is one of the two most original films made in France since the war.

Unafraid to mix genres, Truffaut begins in the usual narrative vein, then, without warning, moves on to reportage, goes back to what appears to be the story and on to a portrait of manners, with a bit of comedy and tragedy inserted here and there. He tells us a complete story just as it should be told, makes his presence felt as a scrupulous observer of reality, turns investigator, then poet, and completes his film on a very beautiful image which is also a first-rate director's idea.

Every time one sees *Les 400 Coups* one wonders how Truffaut manages so miraculously to avoid confusion and chaos and end up with a work that is moving and coherent. The miracle lies in Truffaut's talent; every shot in the film is crowded with his ideas and imagination. Already in *Les Mistons* the threads of the narrative were caught up in the whirlwind, and what we tasted was the enchantment that attended the work and which before our eyes gave cohesion to a formless mass, turning it into a unique and engaging whole.

Truffaut's films make me think of the magician who says 'Look! Nothing in my hands, nothing in my pockets!' Dazzling tricks follow one after the other, and out of the hat pops the unexpected. But while he is a conjurer, Truffaut abhors illusionism. He does not create out of thin air. The material he uses is taken from what is richest and most solid – the real. There lies his secret. Resolutely turning his back on that 'certain tendency' that he had virulently denounced because it destroyed realism 'by locking human beings in a closed world, barricaded by formulae, plays on words, maxims', Truffaut allows his characters 'to reveal themselves as they are before our eyes'.[1] In this, as in many other things, he remains true to himself.

It is interesting to observe the extent to which his conceptions of the script, the editing and the direction were already present in his critical writing. Everyone knows the little series which aims to introduce great writers 'in their own words'.[2] Nothing is easier than to introduce Truffaut 'in his own words', by reference to his writing in *Cahiers* or *Arts*.

Go back and read his proclamation on the subject of the first Cinema-Scope films in *Cahiers* no. 25, and you will understand why he has chosen a similar process.[3]

Are you shocked by the dislocated construction of *Les 400 Coups*? Go back to *Cahiers* no. 83 and re-read the article that he dedicated to *Juvenile Passion*[4] where to him each shot seemed rich and interesting because it had the same value as all the others, and none had the function of preparing for the following shot.

You judge his film imperfect? And what if he wished it to be so? You doubt this? Consult *Cahiers* no. 47[5] and learn from the words of Robert Lachenay,[6] a loyal friend and follower of Truffaut, that perfection does not exist without an element of baseness, that all the great films in the history of cinema were failures, that from the moment you acknowledge that the cinema is more than just spectacle, notions of failure and success lose their meaning.

Do you think that Truffaut the film-maker has short-changed his ideas as a critic? Take another look at his output in *Cahiers* or *Arts* and you will see – not without a few surprises – that Truffaut the critic has shaped the director of the same name.

What is Truffaut's purpose? To describe one of the most difficult periods in our lives, which adults with a short memory frequently endow with an aura of hypocritical beauty. *Les 400 Coups* is an episode in life's problems, the confusion of the individual thrown into the world without being asked first, and refused any means of adjusting. It is a faithful account of the incomprehension which parents and teachers often experience when faced with the problems of children waking up to adult life. A second birth, but no one will assume responsibility for the birth pangs. The child has no alternative but to forge an acceptable world for himself with the means at his disposal. But how can he escape the tragedy of everyday life, as long as he is torn between his parents – fallen idols – and an indifferent, if not hostile world?

To appreciate the accuracy of the film it is enough to take any manual of psychology or psychoanalysis and consult the chapter on the phenomenological description of 'the adolescent's difficult period of adjustment'. All the characteristic features of adolescence are evidenced in the personality and the situation of little Antoine Doinel.

But Truffaut, with a restraint that is all to his credit, finds it distasteful to go into too much personal detail, to take the 'case' of his hero to excess.

To secure the tears of his audience all the more easily, he could have made his Antoine an 'extreme case'. His film would have gained in violence and facility. But there it is: with a kind of artistic masochism Truffaut refuses anything easy. He and Marcel Moussy have systematically drained the story of any too heavy emphasis. Antoine is neither too spoiled nor too unhappy; just an adolescent like so many others. It is indifference he comes up against, not ill-treatment. An unwanted child, he feels in the way, the intruder on a couple locked in the problems of existence. In a perpetual state of anguish he leaves behind one complicated situation only to fall into another, in a web of lies that is as stupid as it is inevitable. Who is to blame? Everyone, and no one. The film brings out a combination of circumstances as the apparent root of the boy's fate – socio-economic (financial situation of the parents, the cramped flat), family (relationship between the parents and with the child) and individual (Antoine's masochistic attitude in relation to his parents).

And so Truffaut's hero acquires an ambiguity that endows him with truth, for which the writers of the script and the dialogue must be congratulated. Antoine is a victim who at the same time colludes in his oppression. Compare his swaggering demeanour outside with his submissive attitude at home. *Les 400 Coups* has a note of authenticity and a deep truth that cannot fail to move the viewer.

It has been said that the film was autobiographical. Truffaut disclaims this completely. I am inclined to think that, after the fashion of one of his masters, Hitchcock, he is laying false trails for his audience. He muddles the clues as it takes his fancy. But lacking as yet the practised hand of the celebrated Hollywood Englishman, he doesn't quite manage to conceal what he is up to. Anyway, every film is in some sense autobiographical. For better or worse, the film absorbs and reflects the personality of the *auteur*. *Les 400 Coups* is what you might call an imaginary autobiography, a genre just as valid as the autobiography and in any case more artistic, since it allows a freer transposition. One could try, as certain literary critics do, to distinguish between the lived and the invented. A futile exercise, for yet again, what does Truffaut the individual matter here? Let's be content with saying that the subject matter of *Les 400 Coups* is the experiences of Truffaut and Moussy as children, reflected upon and transposed by Truffaut and Moussy as adults.

What should be emphasized are the qualities of the script and the *mise en scène*: a phenomenological description of adolescence with the characters and the action clearly situated right from the beginning, the complete freedom of the little hero as we watch. This idea of 'freedom' calls for an important comment: the impression is often that a hidden camera is following Antoine, that he has no idea that he is being filmed. And it is precisely this illusion of the 'direct' and 'untampered with' that gives the film that emotive quality which counterbalances the shock and disorder that might be generated by the film's beginning. The adoption of the television style for the psychology scene by no means constitutes a stylistic hiatus, but ultimately confirms the general impression of the 'direct'.

In this way Truffaut achieves a sense of the real that is rare in the cinema and is underlined by his unfailing concern to refer to authentic details. There is not a single shot where Truffaut does not use some element of the setting to send the profound truth of his subject shattering through the screen. He has an innate sense of inanimate objects and their relationship to human beings. As in the works of the great novelists, these characters also find themselves exposed to objects which oppose them with a form of resistance. From this derives a sense of duration to which we have been unaccustomed in the cinema. Truffaut has a passion for everything that at first sight seems trivial: the papers to be burned, the dustbin to be emptied, the curtains the boy uses to dry his hands, the sideboard from which he takes the cutlery, the banana skin he cuts up, etc. Things thus assume an importance and help to explain the hero's character.

I am also struck by the way the film moves from the particular to the general. The description of adolescence, as I said before, fits those given in specialist manuals. Antoine is simultaneously Truffaut and Moussy, you and me. Sartre said: 'You must know how to say *we* before you can say *I*.' To talk to us Truffaut has chosen to begin with the first person plural. In fact his film sometimes seems too general and not particular enough. But what does it matter, since Truffaut progresses consistently: in *Les Mistons* 'we' was a group of children, here it is one. Not bad going. Perhaps he will be reproached for some carelessness in the film's construction, a touch of rawness in the story. But is there really a story here? Isn't it rather as he has said himself, a *chronicle* of the thirteenth year?

The ending is very beautiful, stopping the film with the hero's gesture as he turns, leaving the door open to the future. But it still leaves us unsatisfied: what will Antoine be like when he gets through adolescence? No doubt Truffaut will deal with this other subject some day.[7] Here his purpose was only descriptive.

As in *Les Mistons*, Truffaut's infinite tenderness towards his characters does not fail. He seeks to express it even better by referring to the film-makers he admires: Vigo, Renoir, Rossellini. Sometimes he likes to pay them direct homage with those 'lavish quotations' he himself talked about in an article.[8] It is of little importance. For the moment Truffaut is not yet alone. He is going through his 'adolescence' as a director. He is still with the 'we' as a means of expression. By necessity, but most of all because of modesty (which is not the least of his qualities). And since I have taken the liberty of explaining our friend in his own words, I shall quote yet another of his articles: 'It must be acknowledged, clearly, that the greatest film-makers in the world are over fifty; but it is important to practise the cinema of one's own age and, if you are twenty-five and admire Dreyer, to aim to equal *Vampyr* rather than *Ordet*. Youth is full of small ideas, young film-makers have to make films that are absurdly fast, with characters in a hurry or shots piled on, vying for the last word; films full of small ideas. Later the small ideas will disappear and give way to a single, big idea.'[9]

It only remains for me to wish that Truffaut may make many films, so that it will take as little time as possible before he addresses us in the first person singular.

Translated by Liz Heron

Notes

1 François Truffaut, 'Une Certaine Tendance du cinéma français', *Cahiers* 31, January 1954, translated as 'A Certain Tendency of the French Cinema' in Nichols, *Movies and Methods*, pp. 224–37.
2 A reference to the series 'Collection Ecrivains de Toujours', e.g. *Baudelaire par lui-même*, published by Editions du Seuil, Paris. (Translator's note.)
3 François Truffaut, 'En avoir plein la vue', *Cahiers* 25, July 1953, translated as 'A Full View' in this volume (Ch. 34).
4 François Truffaut, 'Si jeunes et des Japonais', *Cahiers* 83, May 1958, translated as 'Juvenile Passion' in Truffaut, *Films in My Life*, pp. 244–7.
5 François Truffaut (under the pseudonym Robert Lachenay), 'Abel Gance, désordre et génie', *Cahiers* 47, May 1955, translated as 'La Tour de Nesle' in Truffaut, *Films in My Life*, pp. 33–5. In the course of this review of Gance's *La Tour de Nesle*, Gance's reputation as being 'failed' leads Truffaut into an arresting discussion of genius and failure/success and imperfection/perfection:

> The question now is whether one can be both a genius and a failure. I believe, on the contrary, that failure is talent. To succeed is to fail. I wish to defend the proposition that Abel Gance is the failed *auteur* of failed films. I am convinced that there is no great film-maker who does not sacrifice something. Renoir will sacrifice anything – plot, dialogue, technique – to get a better performance from an actor. Hitchcock sacrifices believability in order to present an extreme situation that he has chosen in advance. Rossellini sacrifices the connection between movement and light to achieve greater warmth in his interpreters. Murnau, Hawks, Lang sacrifice realism in their settings and atmosphere. Nicholas Ray and Griffith sacrifice sobriety. But a film that succeeds, according to the common wisdom, is one in which all the elements are *equally* balanced in a *whole* that merits the adjective 'perfect'. Still, I assert that perfection and success are mean, indecent, immoral and obscene. In this regard, the most hateful film is unarguably *La Kermesse héroique* because everything in it is incomplete, its boldness is attenuated; it is reasonable, measured, its doors are half-open, the paths are sketched and only sketched; everything in it is pleasant and perfect. All great films are 'failed'. They were called so at the time, and some are still so labelled: *Zéro de conduite*, *L'Atalante*, *Faust*, *True Heart Susie*, *Intolerance*, *La Chienne*, *Metropolis*, *Liliom*, *Sunrise*, *Queen Kelly*, *Un Grand Amour de Beethoven* (Gance), *Abraham Lincoln* (Griffith), *Vénus aveugle* (Gance), *La Règle du jeu*, *Le Carrosse d'or*, *I Confess*, *Stromboli* – I cite them in no particular order and I'm sure I'm leaving out others that are just

as good. Compare these with a list of successful films and you will have before your eyes an example of the perennial argument about official art . . .

6 Robert Lachenay: between 1953 and 1956 Truffaut wrote quite often in *Cahiers* under this pseudonym: the choice of name would seem to derive from the main character in Renoir's *La Règle du jeu*, Robert de la Chesnaye.

7 Truffaut did of course return to the continuing story of Antoine Doinel, as . played by Jean-Pierre Léaud, in *Antoine et Colette* (episode in the film *L'Amour à vingt ans*, 1962), *Baisers volés* (1968), *Domicile conjugale* (1970), *L'Amour en fuite* (1979).

8 François Truffaut, 'La Main de Marilyn', *Cahiers* 57, March 1956, translated as 'The Seven Year Itch' in Truffaut, *Films in My Life*, pp. 159–61.

9 Truffaut, *Cahiers* 83, *op. cit.*

Jean Domarchi, Jacques Doniol-Valcroze, Jean-Luc Godard, Pierre Kast, Jacques Rivette, Eric Rohmer: 'Hiroshima, notre amour'

('Hiroshima, notre amour', *Cahiers du Cinéma* 97, July 1959 (extracts))

In Cahiers no. 71 *some of our editorial board held the first round-table discussion on the then critical question of French cinema. Today the release of* Hiroshima mon amour *is an event which seems important enough to warrant a new discussion.*

Rohmer: I think everyone will agree with me if I start by saying that *Hiroshima* is a film about which you can say everything.

Godard: So let's start by saying that it's literature.

Rohmer: And a kind of literature that is a little dubious, in so far as it imitates the American school that was so fashionable in Paris after 1945.

Kast: The relationship between literature and cinema is neither good nor clear. I think all that one can say is that literary people have a kind of confused contempt for the cinema, and film people suffer from a confused feeling of inferiority. The uniqueness of *Hiroshima* is that the Marguerite Duras–Alain Resnais collaboration is an exception to the rule I have just stated.

Godard: Then we can say that the very first thing that strikes you about this film is that it is totally devoid of any cinematic references. You can describe *Hiroshima* as Faulkner plus Stravinsky, but you can't identify it as such and such a film-maker plus such and such another.

Rivette: Maybe Resnais's film doesn't have any specific cinematic references, but I think you can find references that are oblique and more profound, because it's a film that recalls Eisenstein, in the sense that you can see some of Eisenstein's ideas put into practice and, moreover, in a very new way.

Godard: When I said there were no cinematic references, I meant that seeing *Hiroshima* gave one the impression of watching a film that would have been quite inconceivable in terms of what one was already familiar with in the cinema. For instance, when you see *India* you know that you'll be surprised, but you are more or less anticipating that surprise.

Similarly, I know that *Le Testament du docteur Cordelier* will surprise me, just as *Eléna et les hommes* did. However, with *Hiroshima* I feel as if I am seeing something that I didn't expect at all.

[. . .]

Rohmer: Suppose we talk a bit about *Toute la mémoire du monde*. As far as I'm concerned it is a film that is still rather unclear. *Hiroshima* has made certain aspects of it clearer for me, but not all.

Rivette: It's without doubt the most mysterious of all Resnais's short films. Through its subject, which is both very modern and very disturbing, it echoes what Renoir said in his interviews with us, that the most crucial thing that's happening to our civilization is that it is in the process of becoming a civilization of specialists. Each one of us is more and more locked into his own little domain, and incapable of leaving it. There is no one nowadays who has the capacity to decipher both an ancient inscription and a modern scientific formula. Culture and the common treasure of mankind have become the prey of the specialists. I think that was what Resnais had in mind when he made *Toute la mémoire du monde*. He wanted to show that the only task necessary for mankind in the search for that unity of culture was, through the work of every individual, to try to reassemble the scattered fragments of the universal culture that is being lost. And I think that is why *Toute la mémoire du monde* ended with those higher and higher shots of the central hall, where you can see each reader, each researcher in his place, bent over his manuscript, yet all of them side by side, all in the process of trying to assemble the scattered pieces of the mosaic, to find the lost secret of humanity; a secret that is perhaps called happiness.

Domarchi: When all is said and done, it is a theme not so far from the theme of *Hiroshima*. You've been saying that on the level of form Resnais comes close to Eisenstein, but it's just as much on the level of content too, since both attempt to unify opposites, or in other words their art is dialectical.

Rivette: Resnais's great obsession, if I may use that word, is the sense of the splitting of primary unity – the world is broken up, fragmented into a series of tiny pieces, and it has to be put back together again like a jigsaw. I think that for Resnais this reconstitution of the pieces operates on two levels. First on the level of content, of dramatization. Then, I think even more importantly, on the level of the idea of cinema itself. I have the impression that for Alain Resnais the cinema consists in attempting to create a whole with fragments that are *a priori* dissimilar. For example, in one of Resnais's films two concrete phenomena which have no logical or dramatic connection are linked solely because they are both filmed in tracking shots at the same speed.

Godard: You can see all that is Eisensteinian about *Hiroshima* because it is in fact the very idea of montage, its definition even.

Rivette: Yes. Montage, for Eisenstein as for Resnais, consists in redis-covering unity from a basis of fragmentation, but without concealing the fragmentation in doing so; on the contrary, emphasizing it by emphasizing the autonomy of the shot.

It's a double movement – emphasizing the autonomy of the shot and simultaneously seeking within that shot a strength that will enable it to enter into a relationship with another or several other shots, and in this way eventually form a unity. But don't forget, this unity is no longer that of classic continuity. It is a unity of contrasts, a dialectical unity as Hegel and Domarchi would say. (*Laughter*.)

Doniol-Valcroze: A reduction of the disparate.

Rohmer: To sum up, Alain Resnais is a cubist. I mean that he is the first modern film-maker of the sound film. There were many modern film-makers in silent films: Eisenstein, the Expressionists, and Dreyer too. But I think that sound films have perhaps been more classical than silents. There has not yet been any profoundly modern cinema that attempts to do what cubism did in painting and the American novel in literature, in other words a kind of reconstitution of reality out of a kind of splintering which could have seemed quite arbitrary to the uninitiated. And on this basis one could explain Resnais's interest in *Guernica*, which is one of Picasso's cubist paintings for all that it isn't true cubism but more like a return to cubism – and also the fact that Faulkner or Dos Passos may have been the inspiration, even if it was by way of Marguerite Duras.

Kast: From what we can see, Resnais didn't ask Marguerite Duras for a piece of second-rate literary work meant to be 'turned into a film', and conversely she didn't suppose for a second that what she had to say, to write, might be beyond the scope of the cinema. You have to go very far back in the history of the cinema, to the era of great naïveté and great ambitions – relatively rarely put into practice – to someone like a Delluc, in order to find such a will to make no distinction between the literary purpose and the process of cinematic creation.

Rohmer: From that point of view the objection that I made to begin with would vanish – one could have reproached some film-makers with taking the American novel as their inspiration – on the grounds of its superficiality. But since here it's more a question of a profound equivalence, perhaps *Hiroshima* really is a totally new film. That calls into question a thesis which I confess was mine until now and which I can just as soon abandon without any difficulty (*laughter*), and that is the classicism of the cinema in relation to the other arts. There is no doubt that the cinema also could just as soon leave behind its classical period to enter a modern period. I think that in a few years, in ten, twenty or thirty years, we shall know whether *Hiroshima* was the most important film since the war, the first modern film of sound cinema, or whether it was possibly less important than we thought. In any case it is an extremely important film, but it could be that it will even gain stature with the years. It could be, too, that it will lose a little.

Godard: Like *La Règle du jeu* on the one hand and films like *Quai des brumes* or *Le Jour se lève* on the other. Both of Carné's films are very, very important, but nowadays they are a tiny bit less important than Renoir's film.

Rohmer: Yes. And on the grounds that I found some elements in *Hiroshima* less seductive than others, I reserve judgment. There was something in the first few frames that irritated me. Then the film very soon made me lose this feeling of irritation. But I can understand how one could like and admire *Hiroshima* and at the same time find it quite jarring in places.

Doniol-Valcroze: Morally or aesthetically?

Godard: It's the same thing. Tracking shots are a question of morality.[1]

Kast: It's indisputable that *Hiroshima* is a literary film. Now, the epithet 'literary' is the supreme insult in the everyday vocabulary of the cinema. What is so shattering about *Hiroshima* is its negation of this connotation of the word. It's as if Resnais had assumed that the greatest cinematic ambition had to coincide with the greatest literary ambition. By substituting pretension for ambition you can beautifully sum up the reviews that have appeared in several newspapers since the film came out. Resnais's initiative was intended to displease all those men of letters – whether they're that by profession or aspiration – who have no love for anything in the cinema that fails to justify the unformulated contempt in which they already hold it. The total fusion of the film with its script is so obvious that its enemies instantly understood that it was precisely at this point that the attack had to be made: granted, the film is beautiful, but the text is so literary, so uncinematic, etc., etc. In reality I can't see at all how one can even conceive of separating the two.

Godard: Sacha Guitry would be very pleased with all that.

Doniol-Valcroze: No one sees the connection.

Godard: But it's there. The text, the famous false problem of the text and the image. Fortunately we have finally reached the point where even the literary people, who used to be of one accord with the provincial exhibitors, are no longer of the opinion that the important thing is the image. And that is what Sacha Guitry proved a long time ago. I say 'proved' advisedly. Because Pagnol, for example, wasn't able to prove it. Since Truffaut isn't with us I am very happy to take his place by incidentally making the point that *Hiroshima* is an indictment of all those who did not go and see the Sacha Guitry retrospective at the Cinémathèque.[2]

Doniol-Valcroze: If that's what Rohmer meant by the irritating side of the film, I acknowledge that Guitry's films have an irritating side.

[. . .]

Essentially, more than the feeling of watching a really adult woman in a film for the first time, I think that the strength of the Emmanuelle Riva character is that she is a woman who isn't aiming at an adult's psychology, just as in *Les 400 Coups* little Jean-Pierre Léaud wasn't aiming at a child's psychology, a style of behaviour prefabricated by professional scriptwriters. Emmanuelle Riva is a modern adult woman because she is not an adult woman. Quite the contrary, she is very childish, motivated solely by her impulses and not by her ideas. Antonioni was the first to show us this kind of woman.

Rohmer: Have there already been adult women in the cinema?

Domarchi: Madame Bovary.

Godard: Renoir's or Minnelli's?

Domarchi: It goes without saying. (*Laughter.*) Let's say Eléna, then.

Rivette: Eléna is an adult woman in the sense that the female character played by Ingrid Bergman[3] is not a classic character, but of a classic modernism, like Renoir's or Rossellini's. Eléna is a woman to whom sensitivity matters, instinct and all the deep mechanisms matter, but they are contradicted by reason, the intellect. And that derives from classic psychology in terms of the interplay of the mind and the senses. While the Emmanuelle Riva character is that of a woman who is not irrational, but is not-rational. She doesn't understand herself. She doesn't analyse herself. Anyway, it is a bit like what Rossellini tried to do in *Stromboli*. But in *Stromboli* the Bergman character was clearly delineated, an exact curve. She was a 'moral' character. Instead of which the Emmanuelle Riva character remains voluntarily blurred and ambiguous. Moreover, that is the theme of *Hiroshima*: a woman who no longer knows where she stands, who no longer knows who she is, who tries desperately to redefine herself in relation to Hiroshima, in relation to this Japanese man, and in relation to the memories of Nevers that come back to her. In the end she is a woman who is starting all over again, going right back to the beginning, trying to define herself in existential terms before the world and before her past, as if she were once more unformed matter in the process of being born.

Godard: So you could say that *Hiroshima* is Simone de Beauvoir that works.

Domarchi: Yes. Resnais is illustrating an existentialist conception of psychology.

Doniol-Valcroze: As in *Journey into Autumn* or *So Close to Life*,[4] but elaborated and done more systematically.

[. . .]

Domarchi: In fact, in a sense *Hiroshima* is a documentary on Emmanuelle Riva. I would be interested to know what she thinks of the film.

Rivette: Her acting takes the same direction as the film. It is a tremendous effort of *composition*. I think that we are again locating the schema I was trying to draw out just now: an endeavour to fit the pieces together again; within the consciousness of the heroine, an effort on her part to regroup the various elements of her persona and her consciousness in order to build a whole out of these fragments, or at least what have become interior fragments through the shock of that meeting at Hiroshima. One would be right in thinking that the film has a double beginning after the bomb; on the one hand, on the plastic level and the intellectual level, since the film's first image is the abstract image of the couple on whom the shower of ashes falls, and the entire beginning is simply a meditation on Hiroshima after the explosion of the bomb. But you can say too that, on another level, the film begins after the explosion *for Emmanuelle Riva*, since it begins after the shock which has resulted in her disintegration, dispersed her social and psychological personality, and which means that it is only later that we guess, through what is implied, that she is married, has children in France, and is an actress – in short, that she has a structured life. At Hiroshima she experiences a shock, she is hit by a 'bomb' which explodes her consciousness, and for her from that moment it becomes a question of finding herself again, re-composing herself. In the same way that Hiroshima had to be rebuilt after atomic destruction, Emmanuelle Riva in Hiroshima is going to try to reconstruct *her* reality. She can only achieve this through using the synthesis of the present and the past, what she herself has discovered at Hiroshima and what she has experienced in the past at Nevers.

Doniol-Valcroze: What is the meaning of the line that keeps being repeated by the Japanese man at the beginning of the film: 'No, you saw nothing at Hiroshima'?

Godard: It has to be taken in the simplest sense. She saw nothing because she wasn't there. Nor was he. However, he also tells her that she has seen nothing of Paris, yet she is a Parisian. The point of departure is the moment of awareness, or at the very least the desire to become aware. I think Resnais has filmed the novel that the young French novelists are all trying to write, people like Butor, Robbe-Grillet, Bastide and of course Marguerite Duras. I can remember a radio programme where Régis Bastide was talking about *Wild Strawberries* and he suddenly realized that the cinema had managed to express what he thought belonged exclusively in the domain of literature, and that the problems which he, as a novelist, was setting himself had already been solved by the cinema without its even needing to pose them for itself. I think it's a very significant point.

Kast: We've already seen a lot of films that parallel the novel's rules of construction. *Hiroshima* goes further. We are at the very core of a reflection on the narrative form itself. The passage from the present to the past, the persistence of the past in the present, are here no longer determined by the subject, the plot, but by pure lyrical movements. In reality, *Hiroshima* evokes the essential conflict between the plot and the novel. Nowadays there is a gradual tendency for the novel to get rid of the psychological plot. Alain Resnais's film is completely bound up with this modification of the structures of the novel. The reason for this is simple. There is no action, only a kind of double endeavour to understand what a love story can mean. First at the level of individuals, in a kind of long struggle between love and its own erosion through the passage of time. As if love, at the very instant it happens, were already threatened with being forgotten and destroyed. Then, also, at the level of the connections between an individual experience and an objective historical and social situation. The love of these anonymous characters is not located on the desert island usually reserved for games of passion. It takes place in a specific context, which only accentuates and underlines the horror of contemporary society. 'Enmeshing a love story in a context which takes into account knowledge of the unhappiness of others,' Resnais says somewhere. His film is not made up of a documentary on Hiroshima stuck on to a plot, as has been said by those who don't take the time to look at things properly. For Titus and Bérénice in the ruins of Hiroshima are inescapably no longer Titus and Bérénice.

Rohmer: To sum up, it is no longer a reproach to say that this film is literary, since it happens that *Hiroshima* moves not in the wake of literature but well in advance of it.[5] There are certainly specific influences: Proust, Joyce, the Americans, but they are assimilated as they would be by a young novelist writing his first novel, a first novel that would be an event, a date to be accorded significance, because it would mark a step forward.

Godard: The profoundly literary aspect perhaps also explains the fact that people who are usually irritated by the cinema within the cinema, while the theatre within the theatre or the novel within the novel don't affect them in the same way, are not irritated by the fact that in *Hiroshima* Emmanuelle Riva plays the part of a film actress who is in fact involved in making a film.

Doniol-Valcroze: I think it is a device of the script, and on Resnais's part there are deliberate devices in the handling of the subject. In my opinion Resnais was very much afraid that his film might be seen as nothing more than a propaganda film. He didn't want it to be potentially useful for any specific political ends. This may be marginally the reason why he neutralized a possible 'fighter for peace' element through the girl having her head shaved after the Liberation. In any case he thereby gave a political message its deep meaning instead of its superficial meaning.

Domarchi: It is for this same reason that the girl is a film actress. It allows Resnais to raise the question of the anti-atomic struggle at a secondary level, and, for example, instead of showing a real march with people carrying placards, he shows a filmed reconstruction of a march during which, at regular intervals, an image comes up to remind the viewers that it is a film they are watching.

Rivette: It is the same intellectual strategy as Pierre Klossowski used in his first novel, *La Vocation suspendue*. He presented his story as the review of a book that had been published earlier. Both are a double movement of consciousness, and so we come back again to that key word, which is at the same time a vogue word: dialectic – a movement which consists in presenting the thing and at the same time an act of distancing in relation to that thing, in order to be critical – in other words, denying it and affirming it. To return to the same example, the march, instead of being a creation of the director, becomes an objective fact that is filmed twice over by the director. For Klossowski and for Resnais the problem is to give the readers or the viewers the sensation that what they are going to read or to see is not an author's creation but an element of the real world. Objectivity, rather than authenticity, is the right word to characterize this intellectual strategy, since the film-maker and the novelist look from the same vantage-point as the eventual reader or viewer.

[. . .]

Since we are in the realm of aesthetics, as well as the reference to Faulkner I think it just as pertinent to mention a name that in my opinion has an indisputable connection with the narrative technique of *Hiroshima*: Stravinsky. The problems which Resnais sets himself in film are parallel to those that Stravinsky sets himself in music. For example, the definition of music given by Stravinsky – an alternating succession of exaltation and repose – seems to me to fit Alain Resnais's film perfectly. What does it mean? The search for an equilibrium superior to all the individual elements of creativity. Stravinsky systematically uses contrasts and simultaneously, at the very point where they are used, he brings into relief what it is that unites them. The principle of Stravinsky's music is the perpetual rupture of the rhythm. The great novelty of *The Rite of Spring* was its being the first musical work where the rhythm was systematically varied. Within the field of rhythm, not tone, it was already almost serial music, made up of rhythmical oppositions, structures and series. And I get the impression that this is what Resnais is aiming at when he cuts together four tracking shots, then suddenly a static shot, two static shots and back to a tracking shot. Within the juxtaposition of static and tracking shots he tries to find what unites them. In other words he is seeking simultaneously an effect of opposition and an effect of profound unity.

Godard: It's what Rohmer was saying before. It's Picasso, but it isn't Matisse.

Domarchi: Matisse – that's Rossellini.[6] (*Laughter*.)

Rivette: I find it is even more Braque than Picasso, in the sense that Braque's entire *œuvre* is devoted to that particular reflection, while Picasso's is tremendously diverse. Orson Welles would be more like Picasso, while Alain Resnais is close to Braque to the degree that the work of art is primarily a reflection in a particular direction.

Godard: When I said Picasso I was thinking mainly of the colours.

Rivette: Yes, but Braque too. He is a painter who wants both to soften strident colours and make soft colours violent. Braque wants bright yellow to be soft and Manet grey to be sharp. Well now, we've mentioned quite a few 'names', so you can see just how cultured we are. *Cahiers du Cinéma* is true to form, as always. (*Laughter*.)

Godard: There is one film that must have given Alain Resnais something to think about, and what's more, he edited it: *La Pointe courte*.

Rivette: Obviously. But I don't think it's being false to Agnès Varda to say that by virtue of the fact that Resnais edited *La Pointe courte* his editing itself contained a reflection on what Agnès Varda had intended. To a certain degree *Agnèsvarda* becomes a fragment of Alain Resnais, and *Chrismarker* too.[7]

Doniol-Valcroze: Now's the time to bring up Alain Resnais's 'terrible tenderness' which makes him devour his own friends by turning them into moments in his personal creativity. Resnais is Saturn. And that's why we all feel quite weak when we are confronted with him.

Rohmer: We have no wish to be devoured. It's lucky that he stays on the Left Bank of the Seine and we keep to the Right Bank.[8]

Godard: When Resnais shouts 'Action', his sound engineer replies 'Saturn' ['ça tourne', i.e. 'it's rolling']. (*Laughter*.) Another thing – I'm thinking of an article by Roland Barthes on *Les Cousins* where he more or less said that these days talent had taken refuge in the right. Is *Hiroshima* a left-wing film or a right-wing film?

Rivette: Let's say that there has always been an aesthetic left, the one Cocteau talked about and which, furthermore, according to Radiguet, had to be contradicted, so that in its turn that contradiction could be contradicted, and so on. As far as I'm concerned, if *Hiroshima* is a left-wing film it doesn't bother me in the slightest.

Rohmer: From the aesthetic point of view modern art has always been positioned to the left. But just the same, there's nothing to stop one thinking that it's possible to be modern without necessarily being left-wing. In other words, it is possible, for example, to reject a particular conception of modern art and regard it as out of date, not in the same but, if you like, in the opposite sense to dialectics. With regard to the cinema one shouldn't consider its evolution solely in terms of chronology. For example, the history of the sound film is very unclear in comparison with the history of the silent film. That's why even if Resnais has made a film that's ten years ahead of its time, it's wrong to assume that in ten years' time there will be a Resnais period that will follow on from the present one.

Rivette: Obviously, since if Resnais is ahead of his time he does it by remaining true to *October*, in the same way that Picasso's *Las Meninas* is true to Velazquez.

Rohmer: Yes. *Hiroshima* is a film that plunges at the same time into the past, the present and the future. It has a very strong sense of the future, particularly the anguish of the future.

Rivette: It's right to talk about the science-fiction element in Resnais. But it's also wrong, because he is the only film-maker to convey the feeling that he has already reached a world which in other people's eyes is still futuristic. In other words he is the only one to know that we are already in the age where science-fiction has become reality. In short, Alain Resnais is the only one of us who truly lives in 1959. With him the word 'science-fiction' loses all its pejorative and childish associations because Resnais is able to see the modern world as it is. Like the science-fiction writers he is able to show us all that is frightening in it, but also all that is human. Unlike the Fritz Lang of *Metropolis* or the Jules Verne of *Cinq cents millions de la Bégum*, unlike the classic notion of science-fiction as expressed by a Bradbury or a Lovecraft or even a Van Vogt – all reactionaries in the end – it is very obvious that Resnais possesses the great originality of not *reacting* inside science-fiction. Not only does he opt for this modern and futuristic world, not only does he accept it, but he analyses it deeply, with lucidity and with love. Since this is the world in which we live and love, then for Resnais it is this world that is good, just and true.

Domarchi: That brings us back to this idea of *terrible tenderness* that is at the centre of Resnais's reflection. Essentially it is explained by the fact that for him society is characterized by a kind of anonymity. The wretchedness of the world derives from the fact of being struck down without knowing who is the aggressor. In *Nuit et brouillard* the commentary points out that some guy born in Carpentras or Brest has no idea that he is going to end up in a concentration camp, that already his fate is sealed. What impresses Resnais is that the world presents itself like an anonymous and abstract force that strikes where it likes, anywhere, and whose will cannot be determined in advance. It is out of this conflict between individuals and a totally anonymous universe that is born a tragic vision of the world. That is the first stage of Resnais's thought. Then there comes a second stage which consists in channelling this first movement. Resnais has gone back to the romantic theme of the conflict between the individual and society, so dear to Goethe and his imitators, as it was to the nineteenth-century English novelists. But in their works it was the conflict between a man and palpable social forms that was clearly defined, while in Resnais there is none of that. The conflict is represented in a completely abstract way; it is between man and the universe. One can then react in an extremely *tender* way towards this state of affairs. I mean that it is no longer necessary to be indignant, to protest or even to explain. It is enough to show things without any emphasis, very subtly. And subtlety has always characterized Alain Resnais.

Rivette: Resnais is sensitive to the current abstract nature of the world. The first movement of his films is to state this abstraction. The second is to overcome this abstraction by reducing it through itself, if I may put it that way; by juxtaposing with each abstraction another abstraction in order to rediscover a concrete reality through the very act of setting them in relation to one another.

Godard: That's the exact opposite of Rossellini's procedure – he was outraged because abstract art had become official art.[9] So Resnais's tenderness is metaphysical, it isn't Christian. There is no notion of charity in his films.

Rivette: Obviously not. Resnais is an agnostic. If there is a God he believes in, it's worse than St Thomas Aquinas's. His attitude is this: perhaps

God exists, perhaps there is an explanation for everything, but there's nothing that allows us to be sure of it.

Godard: Like Dostoevsky's Stavrogin, who, if he believes, doesn't believe that he believes, and if he doesn't believe, doesn't believe that he doesn't believe. Besides, at the end of the film does Emmanuelle Riva leave, or does she stay? One can ask the same question about her as about Agnès in *Les Dames du Bois de Boulogne*, when you ask yourself whether she lives or dies.

Rivette: That doesn't matter. It's fine if half the audience thinks that Emmanuelle Riva stays with the Japanese man and the other half thinks that she goes back to France.

Domarchi: Marguerite Duras and Resnais say that she leaves, and leaves for good.

Godard: I'll believe them when they make another film that proves it to me.

Rivette: I don't think it really matters at all, for *Hiroshima* is a circular film. At the end of the last reel you can easily move back to the first, and so on. *Hiroshima* is a parenthesis in time. It is a film about reflection, on the past and on the present. Now, in reflection, the passage of time is effaced because it is a parenthesis within duration. And it is within this duration that *Hiroshima* is inserted. In this sense Resnais is close to a writer like Borges, who has always tried to write stories in such a way that on reaching the last line the reader has to turn back and re-read the story right from the first line to understand what it is about – and so it goes on, relentlessly. With Resnais it is the same notion of the infinitesimal achieved by material means, mirrors face to face, series of labyrinths. It is an idea of the infinite but contained within a very short interval, since ultimately the 'time' of *Hiroshima* can just as well last twenty-four hours as one second.

[. . .]

Translated by Liz Heron

Notes

1 'Tracking shots are a question of morality': Godard's dictum, intentionally provocative in its time for its refusal to distinguish form from content (see, for example, Richard Roud on this issue, 'The French Line', *Sight and Sound*, vol. 29, no. 4, Autumn 1960), has achieved a certain notoriety; but Luc Moullet, in an article on Samuel Fuller in *Cahiers* 93, March 1959, had already pronounced that 'morality is a question of tracking shots': see Luc Moullet, 'Sam Fuller: In Marlowe's Footsteps', Ch. 20 in this volume.

2 François Truffaut had been writing very enthusiastically about Sacha Guitry's work, much to the astonishment of some of his *Cahiers* colleagues, who tended to find it theatrical; Guitry was re-rediscovered, as it were, by *Cahiers* in the

1960s. See Truffaut, *Films in my Life*, pp. 214–16 (on Guitry's *Assassins et voleurs*, originally published as 'Du cinéma pur' in *Cahiers* 70, April 1957) and pp. 216–19 ('Sacha Guitry the Villain', also 1957, probably from *Arts*).

3 For clarity, Ingrid Bergman plays Eléna, the title role in Jean Renoir's 1956 film *Eléna et les hommes*.

4 *Journey into Autumn* (*Kvinnodröm*, also known as *Dreams*, Ingmar Bergman, 1955), *So Close to Life* (*Nära livet*, also known as *Brink of Life*, Bergman, 1957). Bergman was at this time one of *Cahiers'* most favoured *auteurs* (see my Introduction to the section on Italian cinema, in this volume): a Cinémathèque retrospective in 1958 was followed by the phased release of almost all Bergman's films and in 1958–9 hardly an issue of *Cahiers* went by without a review, interview or article on Bergman; see, for example, Godard, 'Bergmanorama', *Cahiers* 85, July 1958, reprinted in *Godard on Godard*, pp. 75–80.

5 Cf. the discussion about literature and film towards the end of the discussion 'Six Characters in Search of *auteurs*', Ch. 2 in this volume. Evidently, part of the value placed on *Hiroshima mon amour* comes from the literary context made very clear in that discussion.

6 The reference is to Rivette's 'Letter on Rossellini', Ch. 26 in this volume.

7 As indicated in the text, Resnais had edited Agnès Varda's 1955 feature, *La Pointe courte*; Resnais and Chris Marker had shared direction, script and commentary credits on *Les Statues meurent aussi* (1950–3), a short film about the decline of black African art brought about by contact with Western civilization (banned by the French censor until 1965); Marker had also collaborated on Resnais's and André Heinrich's short film *Le Mystère de l'Atelier 15* (1957), contributing the film's commentary.

8 Together, Resnais, Varda and Marker and their associates formed what came to be known sometimes as the 'Left Bank' group within the *nouvelle vague*, in contradistinction to the 'Right Bank' group associated primarily with *Cahiers* (Godard, Truffaut, Rivette, Rohmer, Chabrol, Doniol-Valcroze). The distinction is no longer as clear as it seemed in 1959–60, but the 'Left Bank' group (who did live on the Left Bank) marked itself off from the 'Right Bank' group in sharing a significantly more left-wing political stance (hence the aesthetics-politics discussion which follows) and a more active social concern, as well as having a closer relationship to modernist tendencies in the arts, and especially in literature (novelists Marguerite Duras and Alain Robbe-Grillet collaborating on Resnais's first two features), and hence a more pronounced concern (at this time, anyway) with formal innovation.

9 The reference is to the interview with Rossellini in *Cahiers* 94, April 1959, reprinted as Ch. 28(ii) in this volume.

Part Two

American Cinema

Introduction

What *Cahiers* felt much American cinema (and much Italian cinema) offered, and French cinema did not, was what Roger Leenhardt called a 'direct engagement with reality'.[1] Since this was the precise opposite of the conventional Anglo-Saxon view of American cinema at the time (and even now) – a view in which American cinema was seen to be largely 'escapist', removed from contemporary reality – the *Cahiers* view needs some explanation. Among the explanations offered by Anglo-Saxon critics at the time were that the French critics were misled by their lack of knowledge of English, or were taken in by the exoticism of American cinema.[2] Whatever the truth of those views, the primary concerns evident in the critical writing which follows point elsewhere.

As I have argued in introducing the material on French cinema, a constant perspective in discussion of *all* cinema in *Cahiers* was *French cinema* – the contrasts which could be made, the lessons which could be learned. Although American cinema often appeared to be of paramount importance to *Cahiers*, it was not the best model for French cinema, and partly because of this *Cahiers'* greatest *auteurs* were not American. Rivette concludes his 'Notes on a Revolution' with pride of place accorded to Rossellini, and Rohmer, in 'Rediscovering America', is explicit about his 'dearest masters: Murnau, Dreyer, Eisenstein, Renoir, Rossellini'. At some level there was always an acknowledgment that one reason for this was to be found in the industrial nature of 'Hollywood' as a system. Rivette's essay appears to reject any consideration of either economics or conventions of genre – both seen to be irrelevant – and to retain as important only some few names of *auteurs*, but some recognition of production conditions creeps back into his argument. Rohmer is a little more cautious: acknowledging the economic power of Hollywood, he is nevertheless inclined to see it as a favourable creative climate, taking a position similar to Bazin's in 'On the *politique des auteurs*', that 'the cinema is an art which

73

is both popular and industrial' and that Hollywood in particular is supported by the 'vitality and . . . excellence of a tradition'.[3]

At one level the differences between Rohmer and Rivette derive from the *kind* of American cinema they were describing and promoting. Thus, while Rohmer has in mind a 'classicism of form and inspiration', an art making a universal appeal with 'a certain idea of man' – a cinema represented quintessentially for Rohmer by Hawks[4] – Rivette has in mind a 'modern', even 'revolutionary', American cinema best represented by Nicholas Ray, formally more at odds with narrative conventions, with an apparent 'clumsiness' and naïveté. At the same time, Rivette and Rohmer agree on cinema as 'the art of action'. In some ways this is close to the aesthetic promoted by V. F. Perkins in *Film as Film*,[5] but for *Cahiers* 'action' was both a very specifically non-discursive or non-literary quality *and* action in the sense of 'all-action adventure', the vehicle by means of which cinema was also 'the art of the moralist', morality being created through action.[6] Action also meant violence, particularly for Rivette's 'modern' American cinema, both as a subject matter – a rejection of social conventions, balanced by contemplation – and as a style, a violent confrontation with narrative conventions. The continuing concern with action and violence in American cinema – partly a reaction against European gentility and intellectualism, partly an expression of a certain male perspective – though evidently necessary, given its predominance in American cinema, always proved difficult, as we shall see.

Rohmer's 'classicism' (though also 'modern' in its response to the 'natural or social environment') emphasizes universal themes such as 'power and the law, will and destiny, individual freedom and the common good', while Rivette's 'revolutionary' cinema stresses the desire of *auteurs* to 'produce work that is modern . . . [to] draw the most striking picture of the contemporary world'. Hence also the distinction between the 'serenity' of the themes and style of a Hawks and the 'modern bitterness and disenchantment' of a Ray, a distinction obviously akin to the one which Bazin makes between the classically heroic persona of Gary Cooper and the persona of Bogart, modern in its ambiguity and interiority, its 'moral contradictions' (even if Bogart was also Hawksian in his stoicism).

Just as Bazin insisted more emphatically than his colleagues on the constraints of industry and genre conventions,[7] so his characteristically thoughtful and provocative Bogart obituary essay pointed to the star as a source of meaning independent of the designs of the *auteur*: 'the permanence of the character . . . lies beyond his roles'. Stars were examined in *Cahiers* from time to time with some seriousness: Bazin refers to Lachenay (i.e. Truffaut) on Bogart,[8] and there were also analyses of stars such as Rita Hayworth,[9] Marilyn Monroe[10] and Ava Gardner,[11] although the evident emphasis on the erotic aspect of female star images bears witness to a degree of sexism readily apparent in the opening paragraph of Bazin's Bogart essay.

But despite stars, despite industrial factors, despite genre, authorship –

the *politique des auteurs* – was the undisputed system on which almost all *Cahiers* writing was based; even Bazin's critique of the *politique* lent it fundamental support in essentials. This was as true of *Cahiers* writing about other cinemas as of their writing on American cinema – Truffaut's seminal essay being precisely concerned with *French* cinema[12] – but because of its more evidently industrial nature American cinema was taken to be more prone to obstruct individual expression and thus became the privileged site for *auteur* discussion (though rather less in *Cahiers* than in subsequent Anglo-Saxon work). As John Caughie rightly points out (not just of *Cahiers* but of *auteurism* in general), '*auteurism* is more clearly a critical practice than a theory',[13] a point Bazin had perceived quite clearly back in 1957: 'Our finest writers on *Cahiers* have been practising [the *politique des auteurs*] for three or four years now and have yet to produce the main corpus of its theory.'[14] There was no theory as such, and Bazin's objections to certain ways of practising the *politique*, particularly in relation to American cinema, represented the most theoretical stance taken by *Cahiers* in this period. In the early days of *Cahiers* there was some confusion as to what the term *auteur* meant precisely, and certainly Truffaut[15] used it in both the 'technical' sense of the director who wrote his own scripts and in the broader sense of the creator whose authentic personality is felt in the work. Since these two senses were seen to be related (it was important for *Cahiers*, for example, that Hollywood directors kept telling them that they worked, uncredited, on their scripts), it is not surprising to see them both still in use in Moullet's article on Fuller. But since the basic concept in the *politique* was the director's control of, and hence responsibility for, his work, despite collaboration with others and despite industrial constraints, primarily through the process of directing itself, through the *mise en scène*, the two senses did not need to go together. This concept did not apply to *most* film-makers, who were simply not *auteurs*, but since there was no theoretical base to the concept, the distinction between *auteurs* and non-*auteurs* was always problematic, as Bazin saw quite clearly. Whether a director was or was not an *auteur* depended on the works, and no proof other than the works was necessary. Thus, Rivette's 'Notes on a Revolution' is clear about 'not putting forward scholarly theories; just four names' and his Hawks essay, its title *assuming* Hawks's genius, begins: 'The evidence on the screen is the proof of Hawks's genius: you only have to watch *Monkey Business* to know that it is a brilliant film.'

Some distinctions can be made about the ways *Cahiers* writers thought *auteurs* worked, particularly between an earlier generation of directors like Hawks, Hitchcock and Lang and younger American film-makers like Ray. Rivette's thesis was that the latter owed much to Welles's 'egocentric conception of the director' and, 'without paying much attention to . . . rules and conventions', aimed to produce works that were 'personal'. The more classical, pre-Welles directors communicated less directly, perhaps, though ultimately no less personally: more at ease and in accord with

generic conventions and commercial expectations, they retained individuality and personal vision by conforming to, yet transcending, genre and
commerce, finally perhaps less great for remaining traditional.

Rohmer's belief that no one could truly love any film if they did not
love the films of Hawks[16] is picked up by Truffaut's review of *Johnny Guitar*
which, contrasting Hawks (mind) and Ray (heart), tells anyone who rejects
both Ray and Hawks to 'stop going to the cinema' because they will never
know what inspiration in the cinema really is. From the mid-1950s to the
early 1960s, despite the polemics about Hawks and Hitchcock, Nicholas
Ray was probably the most important *auteur* in the American cinema for
Cahiers, embodying a particular conception of the film-maker working
within the system, always rebellious, often doomed, and a particular
response to the modern world, as well as a particularly affecting style. If
the classicism of Hawks, relatively adjusted to commercial constraints, is
often mentioned by contrast, the idiosyncratic and improvisatory Rossellini
as often provides a comparison:[17] closer to the *Cahiers* writers in age and
sensibility, Ray and Rossellini offered a cinema akin to the one which
future film-makers in France could aspire to. We can take a definition of
the *Cahiers* conception of authorship from the accounts of Ray's films
collected here: Rohmer talks of Ray being 'one of the few to possess his
own style, his own vision of the world, his own poetry; he is an *auteur*,
a great *auteur*', while for Truffaut, as for Rivette, 'all his films tell the same
story'. As Fereydoun Hoveyda later pointed out,[18] this did not take them
very far, since they 'realized that our favourite *auteurs* were in fact talking
about the same things . . . solitude, violence, the absurdity of existence,
sin, redemption, love, etc.',[19] a thematic set which could have been drawn
from the articles on Ray but which Hoveyda argues are the themes of a
whole generation of artists. So Ray's greatness could not only depend on
his themes, broadly speaking 'the heroism of modern life', and Hoveyda
goes on to argue that 'the originality of the *auteur* lies not in the subject
matter he chooses, but in the technique he employs . . . the thought of a
cinéaste appears through his *mise en scène* . . . in short, the intellectual
operation which has put an initial emotion and a general idea to work'.[20]
As Truffaut and Rivette describe it, the lack of artifice and the clumsiness
of Ray's technique are seen not as a fault but as a necessary sacrifice to
expression, to sincerity, providing direct access to Ray's imagination, to
the way his ideas find form. John Caughie's general characterization of
auteurist critical practice – 'uniqueness of personality, brash individuality,
persistence of obsession and originality were given an evaluative power
above that of stylistic smoothness or social seriousness'[21] – fits these *Cahiers*
articles on Ray perfectly. Later British work on Ray, such as that of V. F.
Perkins,[22] takes a very different view of the function of Ray's style.

Ray was by no means a *Cahiers* 'discovery': their enthusiasm was shared,
from time to time, with *Sight and Sound*, for example, in the 1950s. But
Sight and Sound reserved its interest for Ray's 'serious' works – whereas
Cahiers writers made few distinctions between, say, *Rebel Without a Cause*

and *Johnny Guitar* – and that interest was grounded in rather different assumptions and language. Thus, the *Sight and Sound* identification of Ray's subjects – 'social maladjustment',[23] 'adolescence as a particular age of anxiety' and 'the responsibility of parents for the sins of their children'[24] – and style ('admirably real and convincing'[25]), as well as its worries (about violence[26] and about Ray's apparent lack of perspective on his subjects [27]), was markedly different from the *Cahiers* responses represented here.

Truffaut argues that 'a director should be able to recognize himself in the portrait that we draw of him and his films', and interviews with film-makers were an absolutely central feature of *Cahiers*, often the occasion for a sort of 'testing out' of critical theses with the *auteurs* themselves.[28] Part of the interest of the Ray interview here comes from this testing out, but it can also represent (along with the interview with Rossellini[29]) the rather different style of interviewing which *Cahiers* writers developed. Their detailed questions about *mise en scène* very much reflect both their detailed knowledge of the films and their view that elucidation of the forms gave access to the ideas – and are a further reminder, perhaps, of the extent to which they saw themselves always as future film-makers.

Ray's most creative period, roughly 1949–59, almost exactly parallels this volume of *Cahiers*. Though, as Andrew Sarris puts it, Ray was very much the *'cause célèbre* of the *auteur* theory',[30] Ray is remarkable among major American film-makers for the scarcity of critical work on his films: not one good, serious, full-length study exists, for example. It is appropriate therefore to exemplify *Cahiers'* enthusiasm for Ray at some length in the brief dossier of materials collected here.

As the title of one of Bazin's earlier confrontations with his colleagues over the *politique des auteurs* ('How can one be a Hitchcocko-Hawksian?'[31]) indicates, Hawks and Hitchcock were from the beginning of *Cahiers* major *auteurs* of a more classical Hollywood cinema, and almost articles of faith in the journal's (polemical) conception of cinema. That both directors are now so highly regarded in Britain and the USA owes a good deal to their having been championed by *Cahiers*, doubtless an important stimulus for two of the best *auteur* studies in English in the 1960s, Robin Wood's *Hitchcock's Films* and *Howard Hawks*[32] (though Wood's work is very different from *Cahiers* in its assumptions and emphases).

Rivette's pioneering analysis of Hawks ('an interpretation of Hawks's films that is still definitive, and has been largely confirmed by the director's later work', as *Movie* put it[33]) has hardly been bettered: Wood's full-length study, Perkins's brief but concise article on the comedies,[34] Wollen's structural analysis[35] all evidently owe much to Rivette's insights on the relationship between the comedies and the adventure films, the importance of the themes of responsibility and the lure of the instinctual, the idea of pragmatic intelligence, and so on. Here, we need only place Rivette's essay firmly within the *auteurist* methodology and the account of American cinema offered above. Thus, Hawks is validated, partly, for the 'unified and coherent world' he creates, through a similarity of themes or concerns across different kinds of movie, discovered critically by the elaboration of master concepts or polarities which unify apparently disparate works. But it is not only a question of thematics: as Bazin put it, 'every technique relates to a metaphysic',[36] and the 'honesty' of Hawks's 'use of time and space', the 'functional beauty' of his aesthetic, are integral to his vision. At the same time Rohmer had argued that *what* Hawks showed was more important than how he showed it: 'I know not one director with more disregard for plasticity and more banality in his editing, but balanced by a greater sensitivity to the precise delineation of the gesture and its duration.'[37] Evidently, Hawks exemplifies the classical American cinema which Rohmer had tried to define in 'Rediscovering America' (and which Sarris was later to describe as 'good, clean, direct, functional cinema, perhaps the most distinctively American cinema of all'[38]), particularly in what Rivette praises as Hawks's 'marvellous blend of action and morality'.

Hitchcock was also, essentially, a (Christian) moralist in Chabrol's review of *Rear Window* (as in Truffaut's contemporaneous review[39]). There is some truth in Robin Wood's complaint that the accounts of Hitchcock's films by Chabrol and Rohmer in their book,[40] including that of *Rear Window*, where they draw extensively on Chabrol's *Cahiers* review, tend to 'deprive the films of flesh and blood, reducing them to theoretical skeletons'.[41] As Wood says, part of this comes from *Cahiers*' 'sense of the need to make Hitchcock seem "respectable" '[42] – hence, perhaps, Chabrol's title, 'Serious Things'. As Chabrol makes clear, *Rear Window* was an important film in the struggle to get Hitchcock taken seriously: two years later *The Wrong Man* was perhaps even more important, and taken by *Cahiers* almost as a personal vindication of their theses about Hitchcock.[43] We should remember that *Cahiers* critics very rarely tried to recreate or reconstruct the films they reviewed (a methodology more associated with Robin Wood and *Movie*); rather, they tried to construct the conceptual key that would unlock the work, and the *œuvre*.[44] As basic to Chabrol's analysis of *Rear Window* as to Rivette's analysis of Hawks is the assumption that meaning was to be looked for in formal structure; Rohmer and Chabrol conclude their Hitchcock book: 'In Hitchcock's work, form does not embellish content, it creates it.'[45] Five years later, in Britain, Richard Roud is to be found proposing to *Sight and Sound* readers, though with the utmost circumspection, that 'the one thing [*Cahiers* critics] all have in common, I think, and that we would gain most by adopting, is the firm belief that form is at least as important as content.'[46]

For *Cahiers*, one important function of films was to provoke reflection upon the nature of cinema itself. Chabrol's *Rear Window* piece hovers round, without quite landing on, an idea central to his and Rohmer's account of the film when they came to write their book – *Rear Window* as metaphor for 'the very essence of cinema . . . *seeing, spectacle*'.[47] Reflection upon cinema is absolutely central to Rivette's articles on *Angel Face* and *Beyond a Reasonable Doubt*, as it was later to be central to Rivette's (and

Godard's) film practice, and a good deal of the critical and theoretical productivity of the work of *Cahiers* in this period lies precisely in this process of reflection. Thus the starkness, the stripped-down quality of both films provokes reflection in which Preminger's art, reduced to the 'essential', is seen to relate to specific qualities of cinema beyond plot, having to do with 'the creation of a precise complex of sets and characters, a network of relationships, an architecture of connections . . . If ever a film was the expression of the practice of *mise en scène* for its own sake, it is this. What is cinema, if not the *play* of actor and actress, of hero and set, of word and face, of hand and object?' At the same time, Rivette makes clear his preference for 'the old school, more naive perhaps, of Hawks, Hitchcock, Lang, who first believe in their themes and then build the strength of their art upon this conviction. Preminger believes first in *mise en scène* . . .'. Thus Preminger is less an *auteur* than a *metteur en scène*, while Lang, '*cinéaste* of the concept', creates a 'world of necessity' not for its own sake but integrally 'derived from the real movement of the concept' – the concept, as it were, predicates the form which Lang's film will take.[48] Lang's 'diagrammatic', conceptual cinema – posing an experimental relationship between viewer and film – is valorized above its own superficial seriousness of theme ('the usual indictment of the death penalty') and above the 'brilliant touches' of a Lumet or a Kubrick: as with Hawks, it is not the ideas *per se* which are interesting, but rather the uses to which they are put and the reflection they provoke.

Luc Moullet's essay on Fuller represents an important tendency in *Cahiers* around 1958–9, important not least for being so provocative. Undoubtedly, Moullet's style and tone owe much to Godard's allusive, provocative and epigrammatic reviews (such as those of *Hot Blood* and *Bitter Victory*), but the broad context for Moullet's polemic had been set long before. Rivette's 'Notes on a Revolution', for example, had emphasized Ray's primitive or clumsy technique in confrontation with orthodox narrative conventions, and action and violence and their relationship to morality, while his comments on *Angel Face* valorized *mise en scène* as a possible end in itself. Moullet's description of Fuller's 'rough sketches' is thus close to the way Ray had been discussed earlier, and he echoes most other *Cahiers* critics in his lack of generosity towards overtly stated 'serious' themes or messages – hence his 'aversion to philosophers who get into making films in spite of *what film is*'. Yet, despite these similarities and continuities, Moullet goes provocatively much further, from a concern with specificity to the valorization of 'gratuitous' camera movements, from a moral conception of violence primarily as action to *necessary* and *violent* action (and towards sadism), from the intuition of the creator to an idea of 'instinctive' *mise en scène* 'correcting' conscious intentions. While the purely polemical in Moullet (as in Godard and others) should not be underestimated, we are already a long way, with 'fascism is beautiful', from Bazin's humanism,[49] although there was still some distance to travel to Michel Mourlet's more overtly reactionary 'apology for violence'.[50] In the meantime, of course, *Cahiers* was exposing, without resolving or even taking very far, some of the problems about politics and form: could Fuller's style be separated from his politics, could content and form be distinct? These questions significantly informed discussion of Fuller in Britain where, ten years later, Fuller was one of the most discussed *auteurs*.[51] It is worth noting that later British accounts of Fuller bear little relation to Moullet's: Victor Perkins, for example, while admitting the importance of visual and emotional shock in the Fuller aesthetic, argues (as one would expect from the author of *Film as Film*) that he 'sacrifices neither clarity nor credibility in order to create his effects'.[52]

The predominantly *auteurist* emphases in discussion of American cinema in *Cahiers*, in the material collected here, so far, might seem to have been balanced by the space devoted to the evolution of the major genres in the *Cahiers* Christmas 1955 special issue on American cinema.[53] In fact, certainly during the 1950s, but for long after also, this was not the case, I think, and genre was not a crucial concept for *Cahiers* in making sense of American movies. What we find is a great deal of critical confusion on the issue and an unresolved – sometimes unrecognized – conflict between the *auteur* principle and the concept of genre. Rohmer, for example, opens his 1953 review of *The Big Sky* thus:

> I am not mad about Westerns. The genre has its requirements and conventions, just like any other, but in this case they are less liberal. The plains, the herds, the awful wooden towns, the mandolins, the chases, the perennial good guys and their homespun gallantry, the stale Scots and Irish jokes, are all cause enough for boredom with any of those in the Old World who can hark back to a more distant and noteworthy past. All the same, the greatest masters, the Fords and the Wylers, have been able to affirm their mastery in this domain, while at the same time losing nothing of themselves.[54]

Rivette's comments in 'Notes on a Revolution' are in much the same vein. In this view genre was little more than an unwelcome constraint, a threat to the *auteur*'s individuality or his ability to express it. In many ways, genre was treated similarly to the larger question of cinema as an industry. At the same time, there was a (relatively unformulated) recognition that the American cinema provided, in its total output, a greater percentage of works that were interesting or valuable than other national cinemas, and further that this might in some way be ascribed to the existence of genres. Thus, for example, at the start of the editorial discussion of French cinema, Rivette argues that American cinema's genres like the Western and thriller are 'self-validating' and that 'run-of-the-mill Westerns have a value independent of the great Westerns'.[55] And, some five years after his *Big Sky* piece, Rohmer's position (in a reflective article prompted by Cukor's, *Les Girls* and called 'The Quintessence of the Genre') has modified:

> Bresson, Renoir, Rossellini and Ophuls all have a very exalted notion of their art, and they are repaid with interest. Walsh, Dwan, Minnelli, Kelly or Donen

openly display a much more modest one and art gives them a small return too, smaller in absolute value, but greater, proportionately, than what the others receive. To account for the higher percentage rate we have to invoke – to use one of André Bazin's expressions – some *genie of the genre*, a notion that is still obscure, but of whose reality there can be no doubt.[56]

These somewhat contradictory assumptions and perceptions are vividly present in Chabrol's attempt to trace the 'Evolution of the Thriller'. Thus, Chabrol recognizes a richness in the genre which cannot be explained solely in terms of *auteurs*, yet argues that the genre constrains by its 'strict rules' and needs to be liberated by a shattering of its formulae. Finally, for Chabrol, genres do not matter, only the works, and they matter because they are '*sincere* expressions of the preoccupations and ideas of their authors'. If *The Big Sleep* is superior, it's because Hawks has managed to retain his 'individuality' against the demands of the genre, producing a work interesting not for its relationship to the genre but because it has 'deep roots and firm connections [which] link it to the body of Hawks's work'. Nevertheless, precisely because the dominant *Cahiers* perspective on genre *was* a confused and contradictory one, Chabrol's essay manages to be both provocative and productive, joining Rohmer's 'Rediscovering America' and Bazin's 'Death of Bogart' in locating the post-war renewal of narrative around the moral ambiguity of *film noir*,[57] for example, and pointing to questions about the relationships between Welles, Lang and Hitchcock, and then Ray, Losey and Dassin, to the thriller genre. Although Chabrol seems to want consistently to argue for the importance of *auteurs* over genres, generic considerations keep coming back as he concerns himself with the way the films exist in a relationship to the genre, and are understood, to some degree, through that relationship.

On genre as on authorship – necessarily, given the relationship between the two in the context of American cinema – Bazin took a rather different view from most of his *Cahiers* colleagues. The *concept* of genre as a body of conventions with an active life is much more central to Bazin's essay on 'The Evolution of the Western'[58] than to Chabrol's on the thriller or Domarchi's on the musical (the latter being largely a eulogy to Minnelli's transcendence of the musical). In his later essay on the *politique des auteurs*[59] Bazin argues that the vigour and richness of the genres derive from American popular culture, 'resulting as they do from an artistic evolution that has always been in wonderfully close harmony with its public'; Bazin is then (rhetorically) astonished that 'one can read a review in *Cahiers* of a Western by Anthony Mann . . . as if it were not above all a Western. i.e. a whole collection of conventions in the script, the acting, and the direction'. In 'Evolution of the Western' Bazin is concerned, therefore, to argue first of all about the genre, his thesis being that *Stagecoach* represented a point of classical perfection which had suffered degradation in the post-war period from the growth of a sense of the supposed inferiority of the popular generic form *per se*, and hence of a supposed need to renew, and/

or make respectable, the genre. The result of an increasing self-consciousness of both thematic content and formal elaboration – epitomized for Bazin by *Shane* – he called the *sur-western*, or 'superwestern'.

At a certain point, Bazin concedes, like his colleagues, that his attempt to 'explain the evolution of the Western genre by the Western genre itself' will be inadequate and that instead he 'must take the authors into greater account as a determining factor'.[60] However, what Bazin then goes on to argue takes significantly more account of his theses about genre traditions, and the specific contributions these can make, in interaction with authorial designs, than other *Cahiers* critics did. For example, despite the superwestern tendency, Bazin sees in both veteran and newer *auteurs*, in Hawks as well as in Ray, the possibility of a continuing 'sincerity' in relation to the Western form. Thus, *Red River* and *The Big Sky* are 'genuine' Westerns 'based on the old dramatic and spectacular themes, without distracting our attention with some social thesis or, what would amount to the same thing, by the form given the production'.[61] Similarly, Nicholas Ray, with *Johnny Guitar*, 'is no less aware of the rhetoric of the genre than the George Stevens of *Shane* . . . but not once does Ray adopt a condescending or paternalist attitude towards his film . . . He does not feel restricted in what he has to say by the limits of the Western.'[62] Bazin called this tendency 'novelistic', by which he meant that 'without departing from the traditional themes [the film-makers] enrich them from within',[63] and the chief exemplar of this tendency was Anthony Mann: 'Each of Mann's films reveals a touching frankness of attitude toward the Western, an effortless sincerity to get inside its themes and there bring to life appealing characters and invent captivating situations.'[64]

Bazin's reviews of Mann's *The Man from Laramie* and Boetticher's *Seven Men from Now* effectively resume and elaborate his argument in 'Evolution of the Western'. Thus, *The Man from Laramie* is not 'better than a Western', because the genre's 'themes and devices' are a necessary base, on which Mann builds, rather than a pretext. Similarly, although Bazin is clear about Boetticher's intelligence he refuses to ascribe the film's qualities (and he praises it very highly indeed: 'perhaps the best Western I have seen since the war') to Boetticher being an *auteur*: *Seven Men* succeeds because Boetticher and his writer (Burt Kennedy) 'did not choose to dominate their subject with paternalism or to enrich it with a psychological veneer, but simply to push it to its logical limit'.

Bazin's insistence upon 'the anonymous virtues of the tradition itself which can blossom freely when the conditions of production do not deny them', and his awareness of the positive potential of generic themes and structures, bring us nearer than any other *Cahiers* writer did to some of the later British formulations about genre, for which Bazin's work on the Western was an important stimulus. Jim Kitses's idea, working from the Western, that 'Rather than an empty vessel breathed into by the film-maker, the genre is a vital structure through which flow a myriad of themes and concepts. As such the form can provide a director with a range of possible connections and the space in which to experiment, to shape and refine the kinds of effects and meanings he is working towards',[65] clarifies and refines some of Bazin's ideas, while rejecting others, for example the idea of an 'essence'. Similarly, Colin McArthur's argument, working from the gangster film, that the genres are 'animating rather than neutral, that they carry intrinsic charges of meaning independently of whatever is brought to them by particular directors',[66] carried the discussion about genre a significant step forward. In practice, both Kitses and McArthur give absolutely crucial roles to *auteurs* and, significantly, two of the *auteurs* studied in detail by Kitses are Mann and Boetticher.

Notes

1 Roger Leenhardt, in the discussion 'Six Characters in Search of *auteurs*', Ch. 2 in this volume.
2 See, for example, Richard Roud, 'The French Line', *Sight and Sound*, vol. 29, no. 4, Autumn 1960, and Geoffrey Nowell-Smith, 'Movie and Myth', *Sight and Sound*, vol. 32, no. 2, Spring 1963.
3 André Bazin, 'On the *politique des auteurs*', Ch. 31 in this volume.
4 Eric Rohmer (under his real name, Maurice Schérer), 'Les Maîtres de l'aventure' (on *The Big Sky*), *Cahiers* 29, December 1953.
5 V. F. Perkins, *Film as Film*, e.g., p. 69: 'Movies are not distinguished from other forms of narrative by the fact that they isolate and mould aspects of experience in order to intensify our perception. But films are peculiar in performing this work primarily in the sphere of action and appearance rather than of reflection and debate.'
6 Rohmer, *op. cit.*, p. 44.
7 Bazin, *op. cit.*
8 François Truffaut (under the pseudonym Robert Lachenay), 'Portrait d'Humphrey Bogart', *Cahiers* 52, November 1955, translated (in revised version) in Truffaut, *Films in My Life*, as 'Portrait of Humphrey Bogart'.
9 Jacques Siclier, 'Rita assassinée ou comment on détruit les mythes',*Cahiers* 59, May 1956.
10 Barthélemy Amengual, 'Marilyn chérie', *Cahiers* 73, Juy 1957.
11 Claude Gauteur, 'Portrait d'Ava Gardner', *Cahiers* 88, October 1958.
12 François Truffaut, 'Une Certaine Tendance du cinéma français', *Cahiers* 31, January 1954, translated as 'A Certain Tendency of the French Cinema', in Nichols, *Movies and Methods*.
13 John Caughie, *Theories of Authorship*, p. 4.
14 Bazin, *op. cit.*
15 Truffaut, 'Une Certaine Tendance'.
16 Rohmer, *op. cit.*, p. 45.
17 Cf. Jacques Rivette, 'Letter on Rossellini', Ch. 26 in this volume.
18 Fereydoun Hoveyda, 'Les Taches du soleil', *Cahiers* 110, August 1960.
19 *Ibid.*, p. 41.
20 *Ibid.*, pp. 41–2.
21 Caughie, *op. cit.*, p. 11.

22 V. F. Perkins, 'The Cinema of Nicholas Ray', *Movie* 9, May 1963, reprinted in Ian Cameron, *Movie Reader*, and in Nichols, *Movies and Methods*.
23 Derek Prouse, 'Rebel Without a Cause', *Sight and Sound*, vol. 25, no. 3, Winter 1955–6, p. 161.
24 Penelope Houston, 'Rebels without Causes', *Sight and Sound*, vol. 25, no. 4, Spring 1956, p. 180.
25 *Ibid.*, p. 181.
26 *Ibid.*
27 Lindsay Anderson, 'Ten Feet Tall', *Sight and Sound*, vol. 27, no. 1, Summer 1957.
28 Some of Bazin's problems with Hitchcock as *auteur* in 'Hitchcock contre Hitchcock', *Cahiers* 39, October 1954 (translated in *Cahiers du Cinéma in English*, no. 2, 1966, and reprinted in Albert J. LaValley, *Focus on Hitchcock*, Englewood Cliffs, NJ, Prentice-Hall, 1972) bridged precisely the gap between the account of Hitchcock offered by his *Cahiers* colleagues and what Bazin could discern from talking with Hitchcock himself.
29 Eric Rohmer and François Truffaut, Fereydoun Hoveyda and Jacques Rivette, Interviews with Roberto Rossellini, Ch. 28 in this volume.
30 Andrew Sarris, *The American Cinema*, p. 107.
31 André Bazin, 'Comment peut-on être Hitchcocko-Hawksien?', *Cahiers* 44, February 1955.
32 Robin Wood, *Hitchcock's Films* and *Howard Hawks*.
33 *Movie* 5, December 1962, p. 19.
34 V. F. Perkins, 'Comedies', *Movie* 5, December 1962.
35 Peter Wollen, *Signs and Meaning*.
36 Bazin, 'Comment peut-on être Hitchcocko-Hawksien?', p. 18.
37 Rohmer, 'Les Maîtres de l'aventure', p. 44.
38 Sarris, *op. cit.*, p. 55.
39 François Truffaut, *Films in My Life*, pp. 77–9.
40 Eric Rohmer and Claude Chabrol, *Hitchcock*.
41 Robin Wood, *Hitchcock's Films*, p. 17.
42 *Ibid.*, p. 17.
43 See, for example, Jean-Luc Godard, 'Le Cinéma et son double', *Cahiers* 72, June 1957, translated in *Godard on Godard*, pp. 48–55, and François Truffaut, 'The Wrong Man' (originally 1957) in Truffaut, *Films in My Life*, pp. 83–6. As far as Anglo-Saxon criticism was concerned, the process of getting Hitchcock taken seriously was very much consecrated by Robin Wood's *Hitchcock's Films*, despite the rearguard action fought by Penelope Houston in her 'The Figure in the Carpet', *Sight and Sound*, vol. 32, no. 4, Autumn 1963.
44 Truffaut's contribution to the *Cahiers* Hitchcock issue, *Cahiers* 39, October 1954, was entitled 'Un Trousseau de fausses clés', translated as 'Skeleton Keys' in *Film Culture*, no. 32, Spring 1964, reprinted in *Cahiers du Cinéma in English*, no. 2, 1966.
45 Rohmer and Chabrol, *op. cit.*, p. 152 (translation).
46 Roud, *op. cit.*, p. 171.
47 Rohmer and Chabrol, *op. cit.*, p. 124 (translation).
48 Concept and necessity remain crucial terms in Philippe Demonsablon's analysis of Lang, 'La Hautaine Dialectique de Fritz Lang', *Cahiers* 99, September 1959, translated as 'The Imperious Dialectic of Fritz Lang' in Stephen Jenkins (ed.), *Fritz Lang: The Image and the Look*, London, British Film Institute, 1981.

49 Cf. Luc Moullet, André Bazin, Jacques Rivette, 'Exchanges about Kurosawa and Mizoguchi', Ch. 32 in this volume.
50 See, for example, Michel Mourlet, 'Sur un art ignoré', *Cahiers* 98, August 1959, and especially 'Apologie de la violence', *Cahiers* 107, May 1960; cf. the discussion in my introduction to Polemics, in this volume.
51 Cf. David Will and Peter Wollen, *Samuel Fuller*, Edinburgh, Edinburgh Film Festival, 1969; Phil Hardy, *Samuel Fuller*, London, Studio Vista; New York, Praeger, 1970; Nicholas Garnham, *Samuel Fuller*, London, Secker & Warburg; New York, Viking, 1971.
52 V. F. Perkins, 'Merrill's Marauders', *Movie* 2, September 1962, p. 32, reprinted in Will and Wollen, *op. cit.*
53 André Bazin, 'Evolution du Western', Claude Chabrol, 'Evolution du film policier', Jean Domarchi, 'Evolution du film musical', in *Cahiers* 54, Christmas 1955.
54 Rohmer, 'Les Maîtres de l'aventure', p. 43.
55 Rivette, in the discussion 'Six Characters in Search of *auteurs*', Ch. 2 in this volume.
56 Rohmer, *Cahiers* 83, May 1958, p. 46.
57 Cf. later English and American work on *film noir* such as E. Ann Kaplan, *Women in Film Noir*, London, British Film Institute, 1978, revised edition 1980.
58 Translated in Bazin, *What is Cinema? Vol. 2*, and Nichols, *Movies and Methods*.
59 Bazin, 'On the *politique des auteurs*', Ch. 31 in this volume.
60 Bazin, 'Evolution of the Western', *What is Cinema? Vol. 2*, p. 153.
61 *Ibid.*, p. 154.
62 *Ibid.*, p. 155.
63 *Ibid.*, p. 155.
64 *Ibid.*, p. 156.
65 Jim Kitses, *Horizons West*, London, Secker & Warburg; Bloomington, Indiana, Indiana University Press, 1970, p. 26.
66 Colin McArthur, *Underworld USA*, London, Secker & Warburg; New York, Viking, 1972, p. 19.

I | Perspectives

7 | Eric Rohmer: 'Rediscovering America'

('Redécouvrir l'Amérique', *Cahiers du Cinéma* 54, Christmas 1955)

I am willing to forgive my fellow-countrymen for the mistrust with which they view American cinema; a mistrust I myself once shared. But not for long! – to be precise, the three months between my seeing *Quai des brumes* for the first time and a re-run of *It Happened One Night* at Studio 28 (this was some time in 1938 or 1939). To the new filmgoer that I was (until then my entire experience consisted of a few Pathé-Baby Chaplin films, *L'Aiglon* and a few other *Tartarin de Tarascons*) Marcel Carné's film unveiled the brilliance of a poetry which I had not known to be within the powers of the seventh art. The 'Studio des Ursulines' gained a patron: *A nous la liberté* and *The Threepenny Opera* lived up well to my expectations without, however, surpassing them . . . And then came the day when, in the shape of Claudette Colbert and Clark Gable, the cinema held up to me, under the most favourable lighting, a face without artifice, unpolished but not rough. It spoke to me in a language that was open, yet without a hint of coarseness in its tone. It behaved like the most civilized of creatures, yet without diminishing any of its naturalness. It touched, not my schoolboy's heart with its ardour for Gide or Breton, but that innate taste that we French never lose for a moment – beyond all changes of fashion – for the art of the *moralist*.

It goes without saying that since then I have been led to modify my judgment considerably. America is protean: one moment astonishingly familiar, the next incomprehensibly opaque to our European eyes. But in front of the screen my impulse has always been to stay as close as I could to that first perspective. The specifically 'Yankee' character of numerous Hollywood productions has never captured more than my superficial interest; it has excited my curiosity and stimulated my mind, but it has never completely won my heart. The finest American films which it has been my lot to see have more than anything else made me fiercely envious and sorry that France should have abandoned the pursuit of a claim to universality that it once – not long ago – affirmed so strongly, and that we should have let the flame of a certain idea of man be extinguished in order to be re-lit across the ocean, in short that we must admit defeat on ground to which we have a rightful claim.

If the American film enjoys so much popularity on the world market, it is not only by virtue of the economic power that its producers and distributors hold, it is not because it panders to the masses, or that by means of its noisy publicity it has been able to impose, the world over, an unvarying bad taste to whose assaults even the most immune have succumbed in the end. I acknowledge that there is some truth in all this: Hollywood's popularity owes more to the devil than to the Almighty, which is irritating, even if I have decided to keep only the Almighty's portion for myself. But in the midst of an output that, like any other, numbers both masterpieces and disasters, to see a film by Griffith, Hawks, Cukor, Hitchcock, Mankiewicz, or even a comedy, a thriller or a Western by a lesser-known signatory, has always been enough to reassure me and convince me that for the talented and dedicated film-maker the California coast is not that den of iniquity that some would have us believe. It is rather that chosen land, that haven which Florence was for painters of the Quattrocento or Vienna for musicians in the nineteenth century.[1] It is not talents that I propose to discuss with you, however many and varied they have proved to be; it is the air you breathe there, which in my opinion is not only healthy but has a certain fragrance that is far from being a shock to European nostrils. If America does no more than repay us what we lent, then it repays us amply; that is what is important.

I mentioned a particular idea of man; allow me first to stress some points which are more superficial but which will at the same time provide me with a starting point. If I had to characterize the American style of cinema, I would put forward the two words *efficacy* and *elegance*. I know that Hollywood has its share of the precious, but as a rule it does not smother itself in as many flourishes as our cinema does. Its film-makers have more confidence in the power of what they show us than the angle they choose to show it from.[2] For them ellipsis is no more than a narrative process, not, as all too often with us, a convenient way of avoiding any problem of acting or *mise en scène*. The actor is more restrained with the bravura set-pieces in the theatrical style, but, in recompense, he never gives less than his all. In his eyes the word 'style' takes on a significance akin to its meaning in the sporting world: he delivers his punches in accordance with the rules of the ring, not the traditions of Grand Guignol. The merit of a Griffith, a Hawks, and more recently a Nicholas Ray, is that above all they have relied on this elegant restraint to confer on human gesture a grandeur that is not inflated, to envelop it in the kind of mantle with which, for example, the baton of a Furtwängler could enrich a Beethoven symphony. Just as a great conductor has the 'feel' of his score and, unlike so many provincial virtuosos, does not concern himself with studying every note and finds the right tempo instantly without worrying about the composer's intentions, so, as we watch *True Heart Susie* or *Only Angels Have Wings*, we are given a sense of such security that the idea of a possible flaw in the acting cannot cross our minds even for a moment.

While these are minor qualities in the eyes of the critics, they are the ones that impress the masses the world over, and I for one could not put them down to some virtue particular to the Anglo-Saxon race as more sparing of gesture than our own. For British cinema has never failed to disappoint me, notwithstanding the high standard of some English actors whom Hollywood has taken over anyway (the Laughtons, the Nivens, the Sanders) and regardless of the respect it enjoys with a certain audience – an audience that mistrusts the cinema from start to finish. So we should say rather that America has a talent for finding hidden treasures everywhere, and there is not a single actor – Latin, Germanic or Slav – whom it has failed to make something of. This science of efficacity, purity of line, economy of means – hang it all, were these classical characteristics not our prerogative all through French history?

But let us come to the point: we find this characteristic of universality again in the *themes* dear to American cinema. Of course, you will say, most of them are no more than platitudes. But I prefer ideas that are as old as the hills, and unashamedly so, to the flat echo of the turn-of-the-century writing that Europe is wont to take as its inspiration. There is certainly a touch of pedantry in evoking the *Iliad* while discussing a Western, but apart from the fact that certain commentators have had no qualms about comparing Chaplin or some Capra hero to the Percival of Arthurian legend, the obsession with antiquity is so flagrant in some masters of the American novel – Melville, James, Faulkner – that a parallel between the first colonizers of the Mediterranean and the pioneers of Arizona is no mere artifice of rhetoric. The Greek idea has lived on into the most adventurous branches of contemporary art; yet even when it is knowingly a return to sources, as in Picasso, it is still a deliberate cultural act, not a spontaneous efflorescence, even if not entirely unconscious. There is nothing strange for a race of conquerors, which opens up the land, founds cities, is in love with action and adventure, and in spite of or perhaps because of this is more determined to preserve its religious or moral tradition, to have loved as the themes for its works of fiction the relations between power and the law, will and destiny, individual freedom and the common good. What matters is not so much that these serious questions, which are eternal problems, should have been asked, but from what perspective they are to be illuminated for us. For instance, I do not think that there exists in any corner of the world any work of fiction or drama to which the idea of *destiny* is foreign. But it usually remains at the theological, indeed fetishistic level, unless it is no more than a pure poetic sham. In some of the finest American films it is instead posed, as in the fifth-century tragedians, in terms of *morality*: or by reference to religion which, be it a Protestant sect or Irish Catholicism, is sparing of both external ceremony and flights of mysticism, and is above all the promulgation of a moral code for living. Nor is it strange that such a conception of man should have found an ideal voice in the cinema, the art of action, capable of depicting violence of the most physical kind – five or six times a year you are given the opportunity to be convinced of its extraordinary fecundity. And what do we find in our films? Perpetual drivel about love crossed by some religious or social conformism. A thousand leagues from this naive immoralism, which on reflection is only the reverse of a senti- mental holy picture, the Hollywood scriptwriters have been able to paint for us the image of a world where if Good and Evil exist, the boundaries between them are, just as Aristotle wanted, no more than unexpected bends and undulations. Against the clichés and the sometimes irritating convention of the happy ending, measure the variety and complexity of the situations offered by the Western genre alone! Don't films like Hawks's *Red River*, Lang's *Rancho Notorious* and Nicholas Ray's *Lusty Men* throw an entirely new light on those motifs – the clash between generations, the conflict between the individual and the social – which our film-makers reduce to their pedestrian and monotonous essentials? If we have aban- doned some themes that were once so profound and courageous to let them flounder around in the trashy women's magazines or the boys' comics, the responsibility is all ours. Incapable as we are of depicting friendship between two men or making a 'violent' character convincing without lapsing into clichés, what right have we to censor a source of inspiration that the works I have just mentioned find so fertile?

It is indeed a fact that the adventure story, which is a typically Anglo- Saxon speciality, has yet to acquire the seal of literary approval in France. That is how I would explain the current prejudice against all 'action' fiction – on the part of readers whose only knowledge of *Robinson Crusoe* is through adaptations for children, and who, if around the age of twelve they read Robert Louis Stevenson's *Treasure Island*, have never heard of the same author's extraordinary *Ebb Tide*.[3]

I began at the difficult end. A plea for an America that is guilty gives me the chance of a better hearing. Our immediate predilection tends to be for faces marked with the brand of vice and the neon lights of bars rather than the ones which glow with wholesome sentiments and prairie air. One kind of literature, already quite at home here, illustrates this perfectly: '*Sanctuary* is the intrusion of Greek tragedy into the thriller,' said André Malraux. But for us the charm of these works lies more in the delirious romanticism of their heroes and the modernism of their tech- nique. Hollywood, shy of them for so long, suddenly noticed their exist- ence, and a breath of the avant-garde made the studios tremble. What came of it? There is now enough distance for us to judge: the answer is very little, if anything. This 'behaviourist' literature could give back to the cinema no more than it had borrowed:[4] the taste for the elliptical, the clear line, the visual, and then our art went on its peaceful way along the road that led it, far from the sophistry of a 'philosophy of behaviour', towards the search for what I shall rather pompously call 'interiority'[5] or, if you prefer, a greater psychological subtlety. The issue is, in fact, rather more complex, but lack of space condemns me to schematism: so let us just say, after we have thrown the awful 'avant-gardist' Broadway melodramas out of the running, that it is to the thriller genre that the American cinema owes the best of its inspiration, which is not to say that you can make 'good films from bad books', nor, to go to the other extreme, that Dashiell Hammett, that undisputed and undervalued master of the modern thriller, should rank higher than Faulkner, but that ten years ago we allowed ourselves to be seduced by the brilliance of a form that is too knowingly aggressive to avoid paying the price of its past favour today. I know that the script Howard Hawks made from *To Have and Have Not* is only a very glossed-over reflection of the novel. So how do I explain why for me the film has retained all its charm while Hemingway's prose irritates me now? But ultimately that is not the point; parallels of this kind never lead you anywhere. Long live Hemingway, Dos Passos or Caldwell, if need be! The libretto of *The Marriage of Figaro* is not worth as much as the text of [Beaumarchais'] *Marriage*, and yet if I had to choose between them I would go to the opera, not the theatre.

Finally, the last but not the least of its virtues. Notwithstanding its classicism of form and inspiration, American cinema is more modern, in a certain sense, than American literature, which is too turned in on itself to open its eyes to the evolution of the natural or the social environment. It is a platitude to say that we live in the machine age, but the machine itself is being transformed by leaps and bounds. It is natural that it should fall to the most materially developed country to pose, most felicitously, the problems of its time. Of course our scriptwriters have the laudable concern to depict the issues of the moment, but even here I fear that we may be 'one war behind'. If there is one genre where America has shone with an incomparable brilliance, to a point no one else can even approach, it is comedy, ever since the days of Mack Sennett. And what is it that makes its satire so virulent? The denunciation of a bourgeois conformity caving in on itself? Much more that of new constraints which are more topical and more acute. Hawks's *Monkey Business* mocks naive scientism, not obscurantism. George Cukor does not dramatize the woman reduced to the rank of cook or courtesan, but the woman lawyer or the inane social climber.[6] We French have kept the viewpoint of Labiche without being able to pride ourselves on the same verve. With a curious obstinacy we continue to deride the uniform that is no longer being worn, or the slipper that our modern bourgeois has, alas, no time to put on. This slave to speed, to the machine, indeed to the myth of a comfortable and universal happiness that is our 'middle-class man', has numerous failings which, if they escape us, have enormously inspired our neighbours on the other shore. So we should be grateful to America for having made our 'respectable' laughter ring out in unfamiliar tones, for giving us a caricature which stretches our grins to their limits without ever producing embarrassment, and for opposing our boring and antiquated buffoonery with an entirely new kind of comedy that is sharp and full of elegance.

I am making no claim that American cinema is the only one. My dearest masters – Murnau, Dreyer, Eisenstein, Renoir, Rossellini[7] – in all or most cases have laboured far from the sunshine of Hollywood. But Griffith's homeland gives us an unfailing example which is not to be scorned. It is not faultless, its influence when misunderstood is often pernicious. We should reject the bad without as a result despising the good. To be hard on French cinema is not to condemn France, only that section of our elite which is cosily asleep in the present and has no longer an eye for the future or an ear for the past.[8] We should love America; and may I add, lest I be reproached with bias, we should love that Italy which partisan passion foolishly sets up in opposition: the Italy of the Roman and the Florentine legacy, respectful of its monuments and beliefs, but also the capital of futurist architecture and motor-racing. It is perhaps because of its amicable if not harmonious juxtaposition of the most modern and the most ancient that Italy ought to have had the high reputation in European cinema which French cinema has enjoyed since the demise of the silent film. It is only a matter of knowing, now, how to take over.

Translated by Liz Heron

Notes

1 Cf. Bazin's comments on the vitality of Hollywood tradition in 'On the *politique des auteurs*', Ch. 31 in this volume; Robin Wood makes similar points in his introduction to *Howard Hawks*.

2 Cf. V. F. Perkins's elaboration of the aesthetic of illusionist film, based predominantly on American cinema, in *Film as Film*, p. 74: 'The primary appeal of the movies depends on what we see rather than on the way we see it.'

3 In his review of *The Big Sky*, 'Les Maîtres de l'aventure', *Cahiers* 29, December 1953, Rohmer discusses Stevenson and the adventure story form at some length, comparing them with Hawks and saying of *Ebb Tide*, 'What a script for Hawks!'

4 The reference is to *The Age of the American Novel*, Claude-Edmonde Magny's study of the influence of film on the aesthetic strategies of the novel.

5 Cf. Bazin's discussion of Bogart in 'Death of Humphrey Bogart', Ch. 9 in this volume.

6 Rohmer has in mind Katharine Hepburn's lawyer in Cukor's *Adam's Rib* (1949) and probably Judy Holliday in *It Should Happen to You* (1954); Holliday's roles in *Born Yesterday* (1950) and *The Marrying Kind* (1952) might also fit the 'inane social climber' description.

7 Cf. Appendix 1, and particularly the All-Time Best Films list. In listing his 'pantheon' American directors in *Signs and Meaning in the Cinema* (first edition only), Wollen comments similarly: 'For the record I think that the best work of Renoir, Rossellini and Mizoguchi is probably better than anything produced in America.'

8 Much of Rohmer's comparison of American and French cinema echoes the criticisms of French cinema in Truffaut's 'Une Certaine Tendance du cinéma français', translated as 'A Certain Tendency of the French Cinema' in Nichols, *Movies and Methods*, discussed in my introduction to the section on French cinema.

8 | Jacques Rivette: 'Notes on a Revolution'

('Notes sur une révolution', *Cahiers du Cinéma* 54, Christmas 1955)

There are two American cinemas: Hollywood, and Hollywood. But there are no doubt two Hollywoods, the Hollywood of sums and the Hollywood of individuals. Among the second (we can leave the first to the economists) we can at once dismiss the cynics, those who are old in spirit, disillusioned, and without principles. They may as well be nameless – they are the names that appear on each week's billboards, so assiduously publicized by those big companies to whom they have sold their souls. Their cinema is no more American than the one known to you is French.

It was still the rule until recently to talk about American cinema in terms of genres; but where does this approach lead, when we see the majority of young film-makers passing with equal facility from one genre to another, without paying much attention to their particular rules and conventions, and dealing with strangely analogous themes of their own choosing? It is still better simply to trust the credits to know where you are.

After Griffith's existential assault, the first age of the American cinema belonged to its actors; this was followed by the age of the producers. To claim that the age of the *auteurs*[1] is here at last is, I am well aware, to invite smiles of scepticism. I am not putting forward any scholarly theories – just four names. They belong to film-makers – Nicholas Ray, Richard Brooks, Anthony Mann, Robert Aldrich – whom critics had either simply not heard of or, if they had, had given hardly any serious attention to. Why four? I would like to add others (for example Edgar Ulmer, Joseph Losey, Richard Fleischer, Samuel Fuller, and even others who are as yet no more than the promise of things to come: Josh Logan, Gerd Oswald, Dan Taradash), but *at the moment* these four are the indisputable front-rankers.

It is always ridiculous to assemble arbitrarily under the same label creators with different concerns. But at least there is one undeniable feature they have in common: youth (for directors, that is around forty), because they possess its virtues.

Violence is their first virtue; not that facile brutality that made Dmytryk or Benedek successful, but a virile anger that comes from the heart, and is to be found less in the script and the plotting than in the cadences of the narrative and in the very technique of the *mise en scène*. Violence is never an end, but the most effective of the means of access, and those punches, weapons, dynamite explosions have no other purpose than to blast away the accumulated debris of habit, to create a breach – in brief, to open up the shortest roads. And the frequent recourse to a discontinuous, abrupt technique which refuses the conventions of classical editing and continuity is a form of the 'superior clumsiness' which Cocteau talks about, born of the need for an immediacy of expression that can yield up, and allow the viewer to share in, the original emotions of the *auteur*.

Violence is still a weapon, and a double-edged one – making physical contact with an audience insensitive to anything new, imposing oneself as an individual, insubordinate if not rebellious. Above all else, for all of them it's a question of more or less unequivocally refusing the dictatorship of the producers and trying to create a work that is personal. They are all *liberal* film-makers, some openly left-wing. The repudiation of the traditional rhetoric of the script and *mise en scène*, that flabby and anonymous formula imposed by the company executives since the first talkies as a symbol of submission, has first and foremost the value of a manifesto.

In short, violence is the external sign of rupture. Here the truth is inescapable: they are all the sons of Orson Welles, who was the first to dare to reassert clearly an egocentric concept of the director.[2] We are hardly beginning to assess the extent of the repercussions of that Wellesian *coup d'état*, which cracked to its very foundations the whole edifice of Hollywood production and which by its example had already engendered a first generation of revolutionaries – Mankiewicz, Dassin, Preminger.

Violence cannot continue to exist alone without self-annihilation; the other pole of creativity for these directors is *reflection*. Violence has no other purpose, once the ruins of conventions are reduced to dust, than to establish a state of grace, a void, in the midst of which the heroes, completely unfettered by any arbitrary constraints, are free to pursue a process of self-interrogation, and to delve deep into their destiny. That is what generates those long pauses, those turns that are at the centre of Ray's films, as they are in the films of Mann, Aldrich and Brooks. Violence is thus justified by meditation, each so subtly linked to the other that it would be impossible to separate them without annihilating the very soul of the film. This dialectic of themes reappears in terms of the *mise en scène* as the dialectic of efficacity and contemplation.

Like every revolution this one brings together men who are more linked by what they are fighting against than by their profound ambitions. It is justification enough for their struggle that all four are motivated by the same desire to produce work that is modern. Even though it is with different emphases, all four at the same time draw the most striking picture of the contemporary world; they touch us by their immediacy, the physical feeling of the accuracy of what they have drawn.

Of them all, Nicholas Ray is without doubt the greatest and the most secret; without doubt the most spontaneously poetic. All his films are traversed by the same obsession with twilight, with the solitude of living creatures, the difficulty of human relationships (and that is not the only thing he has in common with Rossellini). Unadapted to a hostile world, disturbed by the resurgence of primordial violence, his characters are all more or less marked with the stamp of a new *mal de siècle* which it would be difficult for us to disown.

Richard Brooks, on the contrary, recalls his reporter's background. He lives at the level of the everyday civilized world. All his heroes wage the same battle to save other men from cowardice and fear, to make of them – in spite of themselves if necessary – real men. In the same way Anthony Mann, within the traditional context of the Western, revives the eulogy of will and endeavour that made early American cinema so great. Both are worthy descendants of Hawks, without his serenity. Modern bitterness and disenchantment crack the classical cement.

Robert Aldrich achieves harmony through a precise dissonance, the lucid and lyrical description of a world in decay, aseptic, steely, closed in; the chronicle of the final convulsions of what remains human in man in the midst of a purely artificial universe from which nature – once celebrated in *Apache* – has been almost systematically eliminated (only the purifying presence of water remains), and of which the artificial worlds of the theatre or the degenerate thriller offer the most suffocating image – an account of moral suffocation, whose only way out must be some fabulous destruction. In opposition to the traditional morality of action, exemplified in Ray, Brooks and Mann, Aldrich offers a negative morality, not contradicting it but proving it by the absurd. The real subject of *The Big Knife*, as of *Kiss Me Deadly*, is precisely the destruction of morality, and its consequences.

And so, what is the meaning of this revolution? To pass beyond the long period of submission to the manufactured product and openly renew links with the tradition of 1915, Griffith and Triangle,[3] whose vitality moreover still secretly nourished the work of the old Hollywood directors – Walsh, Vidor, Dwan, and of course Hawks; a return to lyricism, powerful feelings, melodrama (the audiences in the smart halls sneer at Ray's films as they did at Allan Dwan's); the rediscovery of a certain breadth of gesture, an externalizing of the roughest and most spontaneous emotions; in short, the rediscovery of naïveté.

Such, without doubt, is the future of the cinema, in the sense that naïveté, synonymous with perspicacity, is set in opposition to the wiles and tricks of the professional scriptwriters. Ray, Brooks, Mann and Aldrich are, in different ways, all naïfs: Ray in the childlike clarity of his look, the provocative humility of his narratives; Brooks and Mann in the anachronistic honesty of their *mise en scène*; Aldrich, finally, in the candour of the acting and the unsophisticated use of effects.

For years the cinema has been dying from intelligence and subtlety. Now Rossellini is breaking down the door; but you can also breathe in that gust of fresh air reaching us from across the ocean.

Translated by Liz Heron

Notes

1 Cf. Rivette's 'The Age of *metteurs en scène*', Ch. 35 in this volume.
2 Cf. the quotation by Orson Welles with which François Truffaut prefaces his book, *Films in My Life*: 'I believe a work is good to the degree that it expresses the man who created it.'
3 Triangle was the film corporation formed in 1915 to produce the work of the three major film-makers of the time, D. W. Griffith, Thomas Ince and Mack Sennett; the corporation was dissolved in 1918 after Griffith and Sennett left and Triangle was suffering from the losses incurred by *Intolerance*.

9 | André Bazin: 'The Death of Humphrey Bogart'

('Mort d'Humphrey Bogart', *Cahiers du Cinéma* 68, February 1957)

Who does not mourn this month for Humphrey Bogart, who died at fifty-six of stomach cancer and half a million whiskeys? The passing of James Dean principally affected members of the female sex below the age of twenty; Bogey's affects their parents or at least their elder brothers, and above all it is men who mourn. Beguiling rather than attractive, Bogey delighted the women *in* his films; no fear of him leaving millions of widows, like Valentino or James Dean; for the spectator he seems to me to have been more the hero with whom one identifies than the hero one loves. The popularity of Bogart is virile. Women may miss him, but I know of men who would weep for him were not the unseemliness of emotion written all over this tough guy's tomb. No flowers, no wreaths.

I arrive a little late to launch into my funeral oration. Much has already been written about Bogart, his persona and his myth. But none put it better, perhaps, than Robert Lachenay more than a year ago,[1] from whom I cannot help but quote the following prophetic lines:[2] 'Each time he began a sentence he revealed a wayward set of teeth. The set of his jaw irresistibly evoked the rictus of a spirited cadaver, the final expression of a melancholy man who would fade away with a smile. That is indeed the smile of death.

It now seems clear indeed that none more so than Bogart, if I may speak thus, epitomized the immanence of death, its imminence as well. Not so much, moreover, of that which one gives or receives as of the corpse on reprieve which is within each of us. And if his death touches us so closely, so intimately, it is because the *raison d'être* of his existence was in some sense to survive. Thus in his case death's victory is twofold, since it is victorious less over life than over resistance to dying.

I will perhaps make myself better understood by contrasting his character with that of Gabin[3] (to whom one could compare him in so many ways). Both men are heroes of modern cinematographic tragedy, but with Gabin (I am of course speaking of the Gabin of *Le Jour se lève* and *Pépé le*

Moko) death is, after all, at the end of the adventure, implacably awaiting its appointment. The fate of Gabin is precisely to be duped by life. But Bogart is man *defined by* fate. When he enters the film it is already the pale dawn of the following day; absurdly victorious from the macabre combat with the angel, his face marked by what he has seen and his bearing heavy with all he knows, having ten times triumphed over his own death he will doubtless survive for us a further time.

The Face of Death

Not the least admirable feature of the character of Bogart is that he improved, became sharper, as he progressively wasted away. This tough guy never dazzled on the screen by dint of physical force or acrobatic agility. He was neither a Gary Cooper nor a Douglas Fairbanks! His successes as a gangster or as a detective are due first to his ability to take a punch, then to his perspicacity. The effectiveness of his punch testifies less to his strength than to his sense of repartee. He places it well, true, but above all at the right moment. He strikes little, but always when his opponent is wrong-footed. And then there is the revolver which becomes in his hands an almost intellectual weapon, the argument that dumbfounds.

But what I mean is that the visible stigmata marking the character more and more over the last ten years or so only helped accentuate a congenital weakness. In more and more resembling his own death, it was his own portrait Bogart was completing. Doubtless the genius of this actor who knew how to make us love and admire in him the very image of our decomposition will never be sufficiently admired. As though bruised a little more each time by all the bad blows he had taken in the preceding films, he had become, with colour, the extraordinary creature with the belching stomach, sallow, spitting out teeth, just good enough for the swamp leeches, and yet the man who will steer the *African Queen* safely to port. And recall that decaying face testifying at the trial of the officers of the *Caine*. It was clear to see that death had for a long time been unable to conquer from without the being who for a long time had so internalized death.

The 'modern' character of the Bogart myth has been rightly stressed, and J.-P. Vivet is doubly correct in taking the adjective in the Baudelairean sense, since in the hero of *The Barefoot Contessa* we admire precisely the eminence and dignity of our decay. But I would none the less like to comment that to this far-reaching modernity which guarantees the profound poetry of the Bogart character and indisputably justifies his entry into legend, there corresponds a more precise modernity within the compass of our generation. Bogart is, without doubt, typically the actor/myth of the war and post-war period. I mean the period between 1940 and 1955. True, his filmography signals some seventy-five films since 1930, of which forty or so predate *High Sierra* and *The Maltese Falcon* (1941). But these were only supporting roles, and it is beyond question that his character emerged with what is commonly called the *noir* crime film whose ambiguous hero he was to epitomize. In any case for us it was after the war and especially through the films of Huston that Bogart won such popularity. Now one is aware that the years 1940–1 mark precisely the second major stage in the evolution of the American talking picture. 1941 is also the year of *Citizen Kane*. It must be the case, therefore, that there is some secret harmony in the coincidence of these events: the end of the pre-war period, the arrival of a certain novelistic style in cinematographic *écriture*, and, through Bogart, the triumph of interiorization and of ambiguity.[4]

One can in any case easily see in what respect Bogart differs from those pre-war heroes for whom Gary Cooper might be the prototype: handsome, strong, noble, expressing much more the optimism and efficiency of a civilization than its anxiety. Even the gangsters are the conquering and active type, Western heroes who have gone astray, the negative version of industrious audacity. In this period only perhaps George Raft shows signs of that introversion, a source of ambiguity which the hero of *The Big Sleep* will exploit to a sublime degree. In *Key Largo* Bogart overcomes, in the person of Robinson, the last of the pre-war gangsters; with this victory something of American literature probably makes its way into Hollywood. Not at all through the deceptive intermediary of the scenarios but through the human style of the character. Bogart is perhaps, in the cinema, the first illustration of 'the age of the American novel'.[5]

Bogey is a Stoic

One must certainly not confuse the interiority of Bogart's acting style with that developed by the Kazan school and made fashionable by Marlon Brando prior to James Dean. All they have in common is their reaction against psychological-type performance; but taciturn, like Brando, or exuberant, like Dean, the Kazan style is postulated upon anti-intellectual spontaneity. The behaviour of the actors is intended to be unforeseeable, since it no longer translates the profound logic of the feelings but externalizes immediate impulses whose link with the inner life cannot be read directly. Bogart's secret is different. It is of course a case of Conrad's prudent silence, the phlegm of one who knows the perils of inopportune revelations but above all the unfathomable vanity of these skin-deep sincerities. Distrust and weariness, wisdom and scepticism: Bogey is a Stoic.

I particularly admire in his success the fact that he never in the final analysis depended in any respect on the character of the roles he embodied. They all fall short, indeed, of being sympathetic. Let us even admit that the moral ambiguity of Sam Spade in *The Maltese Falcon* or of Philip Marlowe in *The Big Sleep* redound to their advantage, in our estimation – but how to defend the miserable scoundrels in *The Treasure of the Sierra Madre* or the baleful commander of *The Caine Mutiny*? For a few roles as redressor of wrongs or as phlegmatic knight in a noble cause, there are doubtless as many less commendable if not frankly odious exploits. The permanence of the character thus lies beyond his roles, which is not the case with a Gabin, for example, nor could be with James Dean. One can hardly see, too, Gary Cooper claiming to play scoundrels. The special ambiguity of the roles which first brought Bogart success in the *noir* crime film is thus to be found again in his filmography. Moral contradictions meet as much within the roles as in the paradoxical permanence of the character caught between two apparently incompatible occupations.

But is not this precisely the proof that our sympathy went out, beyond even the imaginary biographies and moral virtues or their absence, to some profounder wisdom, to a certain way of accepting the human condition which may be shared by the rogue and by the honourable man, by the failure as well as by the hero. The Bogart man is not defined by his accidental respect, or his contempt, for bourgeois virtues, by his courage or his cowardice, but above all by this existential maturity which gradually transforms life into a stubborn irony at the expense of death.

Translated by Phillip Drummond

Notes

1 François Truffaut (under the pseudonym Robert Lachenay), 'Portrait d'Humphrey Bogart', *Cahiers* 52, November 1955, translated (in revised version) as 'Portrait of Humphrey Bogart' in Truffaut, *Films in My Life*, pp. 292–5.

2 Bogart died on 14 January 1957.

3 Cf. André Bazin, 'Jean Gabin et son destin', originally published in *Radio-Cinéma-Télévision*, October 1950, translated as 'The Destiny of Jean Gabin' in Bazin, *What is Cinema? Vol. 2*.

4 Bazin refers here to the complex of theses about realism in the cinema developed by him in different instances but particularly in the essays 'L'Evolution du langage cinématographique', originally published in 1958, but made up from articles written in 1950, 1952 and 1955, in *Qu'est-ce que le cinéma? tome 1*, translated as 'The Evolution of the Language of Cinema' in Bazin, *What is Cinema? Vol. 1*; 'William Wyler, ou le janséniste de la mise en scène', originally published in *La Revue du Cinéma*, no. 11, March 1948, translated as 'William Wyler, or the Jansenist of *mise en scène*' in Christopher Williams, *Realism and the Cinema*, London, Routledge & Kegan Paul, 1980, pp. 36–52; 'Le Réalisme cinématographique et l'école italienne de la Libération', originally published in *Esprit*, January 1948, translated as 'An Aesthetic of Reality: Neo-Realism (Cinematic Realism and the Italian School of the Liberation)' in Bazin, *What is Cinema? Vol. 2*. As regards interiority and ambiguity, cf. Rohmer, 'Rediscovering America', and Chabrol, 'Evolution of the Thriller', both in this volume (Chs 7 and 21 respectively).

5 The reference is to Claude-Edmonde Magny's *Age of the American Novel*: see Rohmer, 'Rediscovering America', note 4.

II | Dossier – Nicholas Ray

10 | Jacques Rivette: 'On Imagination'

('De l'invention', *Cahiers du Cinéma* 27,
October 1953)

Without any doubt, the most constant privilege of the masters is that of seeing everything, including the most simple mistakes, turn out to their advantage rather than diminishing their stature. If you are now surprised to see me give the benefit of this law to Nicholas Ray's latest film it means you are ill-prepared to appreciate a work which is disconcerting and asks for, not indulgence, but a little love. Far from wishing to excuse it, you must love this lack of artifice, this very pleasing indifference to décors, plasticity, evenness of light, the rightness of a supporting role, and you must recognize even in the clumsiness of this verve, not the caricature, but the youthful exaggeration of a cinema that is dear to us, where all is sacrificed to expression, to efficacity, to the sharpness of a reflex or a look. I find no fault with exaggerations of this kind, and the *auteur*'s own enjoyment, which I feel coming through some of the time, is consolation for many films which only communicate the director's boredom.

But I now want to talk about the real seriousness of this business: a work of verve it may be, but because Nicholas Ray is lavish with *ideas* – which are sometimes channelled into a single great theme, and I am not forgetting the wonderful progression of *On Dangerous Ground* – ideas which in this film are scattered everywhere by the accidents of imagination. But it is precisely this imagination which strikes me with its constant surprises. Certainly Ray is not someone who is unaware of the aesthetic value of surprise, nor is he unaware that beauty has a duty to astonish; but if the imagination is sovereign over all the other faculties, its kingdom certainly seems to be shrinking daily everywhere; and saying that imagination should first consist in the simple pleasure of filming, just like the creative freedom of the brush on the canvas, has not the slightest chance of being taken seriously here. And when I talk about ideas, I really mean ideas of *mise en scène* or – if I were to be shocking about it – of framing or the way shots are put together, which these days are the only ideas whose profundity I wish to recognize, and the only ones which can reach the secret form which is the goal of every work of art. When François Truffaut compares Nicholas Ray with Bresson, I really do see two film-makers who are obsessed with the abstract and whose sole concern is always to reach this ideal countenance by the shortest road, and let clumsiness be the road if it is the shortest one. In *The Lusty Men* you can see how the idea of a role, or a scene, hurriedly sketched,[1] can sometimes prevail over its realization, whether good or bad (but will you understand how much I admire Nicholas Ray if I call him a *metteur en scène*, not a director?[2]), how the imagination of each moment is only the concern to reveal, with each fresh blow of the chisel, the one and only hidden statue.

Perhaps it is clear that beauty is not without importance for him. But where does he seek it (a fundamental question, after all)? I observe a certain dilation of expressive detail, which ceases to be detail so that it may become part of the plot – hence the taste for dramatic close-ups, unexpected within the movement of the scene – and especially the search for a certain breadth of modern gesture and an anxiety about *life*, a perpetual disquiet that is paralleled in the characters; and lastly his taste for paroxysm, which imparts something of the feverish and impermanent to the most tranquil of moments.

A few more words. Nicholas Ray is one of those who fight it out to the finish, and can exhaust the possibilities of a development. Everything always proceeds from a simple situation where two or three people encounter some elementary and fundamental concepts of life. And the real struggle takes place in only one of them, against the interior demon of violence, or of a more secret sin, which seems linked to man and his solitude. It may happen sometimes that a woman saves him; it even seems that she alone can have the power to do so; we are a long way from misogyny.

Nicholas Ray has always offered us the story of a moral dilemma where man emerges as either victor or vanquished, but ultimately lucid: the futility of violence, of all that is not happiness and which diverts man from his innermost purpose.

If art must reveal 'the heroism of modern life', there are few works that better accomplish this purpose. We note, however, that the characters quickly withdraw, that, when all is said and done, the world hardly interferes at all, or if it does, it is only to harm them. Salvation is a private affair. Perhaps we will be sorry to see these heroes withdraw to their tents with so little ceremony;[3] we can also suppose that it is not without bequeathing their fate to the world, or sometimes prolonging the ordeal unnecessarily. But for modern society is not solitude, if not scorn, often the most fitting homage?

Translated by Liz Heron

Notes

1 Cf. Rivette's account of Rossellini's manner in 'Letter on Rossellini', Ch. 26 in this volume.
2 The French word here is *réalisateur*, thus implying the separation of ideas from their *réalisation*.
3 Cf. Eric Rohmer's discussion of *Rebel Without a Cause* as tragedy, in 'Ajax or the Cid?', Ch. 12 below.

11 | François Truffaut: 'A Wonderful Certainty'

('L'Admirable Certitude', *Cahiers du Cinéma* 46, April 1955, written under the pseudonym Robert Lachenay)

We made our discovery of Nicholas Ray seven or eight years ago with *Knock on Any Door*. Then at the 'Biarritz Rendez-vous'[1] we had a dazzling confirmation in *They Live By Night*, which is still unmistakably his best film. Later *In a Lonely Place, On Dangerous Ground* and *The Lusty Men* were released in Paris at one time or another – and went virtually unnoticed by all but the most discerning – and then finally *Johnny Guitar*.[2]

A young American film-maker – of the Wise, Dassin and Losey generation – Nicholas Raymond Kienzle is somewhat, in fact very much, the passionate discovery of the 'young critics'. Nick Ray is an *auteur* in our sense of the word. All his films tell the same story, the story of a violent man who wants to stop being violent, and his relationship with a woman who has more moral strength than himself. For Ray's hero is invariably a man lashing out, weak, a child-man when he is not simply a child. There is always moral solitude, there are always hunters, sometimes lynchers.[3] Those who have seen the films I have just mentioned could multiply and enrich the parallels by themselves; the others will just have to trust me, and that will be their little punishment.

Johnny Guitar is by no means its *auteur*'s best film. Generally, Ray's films bore the public, irritated as they are by the films' slowness, their seriousness, indeed their realism,[4] which shocks them by its extravagance. *Johnny Guitar* is not really a Western, nor is it an 'intellectual Western'. It is a Western that is dream-like, magical, unreal to a degree, delirious. It was but a step from the dream to Freudianism, a step our Anglo-Saxon colleagues have taken by talking about the 'psychoanalytical Western'. But the qualities of this film, Ray's qualities, are not those; they cannot possibly be seen by anyone who has never ventured a look through a camera eyepiece. We flatter ourselves – and it is in this that we are opposed to another form of criticism – that we are able to retrace the origins of cinematic creativity. Contrary to André Bazin[5] I think it is important that a director should be able to recognize himself in the portrait that we draw of him and his films. Otherwise we have failed. The hallmark of Ray's very great talent resides in his absolute sincerity, his acute sensitivity.[6] He is not of great stature as a technician. All his films are very disjointed, but it is obvious that Ray is aiming less for the traditional and all-round success of a film than at giving each shot a certain emotional quality. *Johnny Guitar* is 'composed', rather hurriedly, of very long takes divided into four. The editing is deplorable. But the interest lies elsewhere: for instance in the very beautiful positioning of figures within the frame. (The posse at Vienna's is formed and moves in a V-shape, like migratory birds.)

Nicholas Ray is to some extent the Rossellini of Hollywood;[7] in the kingdom of mechanization he is the craftsman, lovingly fashioning small objects out of holly wood. Hence a hue and cry against the amateur! There is not one of Ray's films without nightfall. He is the poet of nightfall, and in Hollywood everything is permissible, except poetry. Hawks, for example, keeps it at arm's length, and Hitchcock cautiously ventures four or five shots each time, in small doses. While a Hawks settles down in Hollywood – in reality he spends most of the year in Switzerland – and takes things easy, flirting with tradition all the better to flout it, and always winning, Ray is incapable of 'doing a deal' with the devil and turning the arrangement to his advantage – he is picked on and loses the battle even before he starts fighting.

Hawks and Ray form an opposition rather like Castellani and Rossellini. With Hawks we witness a triumph of the mind, with Nick Ray it is a triumph of the heart. You can refute Hawks in the name of Ray (or vice versa), or admit them both, but to anyone who would reject them both I make so bold as to say this: *Stop going to the cinema, don't watch any more films, for you will never know the meaning of inspiration, of a view-finder, of poetic intuition, a frame, a shot, an idea, a good film, the cinema.* An insufferable pretension? No: a wonderful certainty.

Translated by Liz Heron

Notes

1 'Biarritz Rendez-vous': 'During the next year [1949], Objectif 49 [see "Six Characters in search of *auteurs*", Ch. 2, note 4] successfully broadened out and organized in Biarritz, with Cocteau as president, the "Festival du Film Maudit" ' (Jacques Doniol-Valcroze, 'L'Histoire des *Cahiers*', *Cahiers* 100, October 1959). *Maudit* literally means 'cursed', but a more accurate translation here might be 'unjustly neglected'. Ray's *They Live By Night* was an important film at this festival.

2 I am deliberately omitting *Flying Leathernecks*, *A Woman's Secret* and *Born to be Bad*, which are acknowledged as 'assignments' (only the first came out in France). (Author's note.)

3 In *Johnny Guitar* as in *On Dangerous Ground* the lynch-mob is led by Ward Bond:

Johnny: I've got a hunch the posse will be dropping in on you before night.

Same people that paid you a visit yesterday. But they won't be the same. A posse isn't people. I've ridden with them and I've ridden against them. A posse is an animal; it moves like one and thinks like one . . .
Vienna: They're men with itchy fingers and a coil of rope around their saddle-horns looking for somebody to hang. And after riding a few hours they don't care much *who* they hang. You haven't told me a thing I don't know.
Johnny: I haven't finished.
Vienna: Finish, but be brief.
Johnny: A posse feels safe because it's big. They only make a big target. I can ride around and pick off a few; the rest of them will lose their guts, turn tail, break up and go home.

And later:

MacIvers: My men are not killers. They've gotta be cold, tired and hungry before they get mad.
Emma: How long does that take?
MacIvers: You've got five years of mad in you. You can give them another five hours. (Author's note.)

4 Ray's realism is a realism of words and poetic accidents 'à la Cocteau'. A series of larger than life affectations. All the cowboys in *Johnny Guitar* deliver insults by calling each other 'mister':

The Kid: All of a sudden, I don't like you, mister.
Johnny: Now that makes me real sad. I always hate to lose a friend.
Vienna (attributed to The Kid in Truffaut's original): That's the way it goes. Lose one, find one. Play something for me Mister Guitar.

Further on:

The Kid: Heads, I'm gonna kill you, mister. Tails, you can play her a tune.

And finally:

Bart: He ain't all right with me.
Corey: Who is?
Bart: Me. I like *me*, and I'm taking good care of me.

(Not sequential in the film.) (Author's note.)

5 Truffaut seems to be referring here in particular to Bazin's 'Hitchcock contre Hitchcock', *Cahiers 39*, October 1954, in which Bazin is troubled by the distance between his *Cahiers* colleagues' views of Hitchcock's work and Hitchcock's own professed views.
6 For those who need more proofs than those offered on the screen: it is not our custom in *Cahiers* to pay any attention to the tittle-tattle circulated in the Holly-wood gossip columns, but it is important to bear in mind – Bazin agrees with me here – how much Ray's life resembles his films. First a long idyll with Joan Crawford whom he meets again several years later to film *Johnny Guitar*, which

is the story of a couple who come together again! Nicholas Ray was married to Gloria Grahame. After numerous quarrels and reconciliations they got divorced; Gloria accused her husband of violence and brutality. *In a Lonely Place*, whose heroine is Gloria Grahame, tells the story of a scriptwriter who is sick of Hollywood, but because he is in love with a young woman is persuaded to work there again. He hits people who disagree with him, falls out with his friends, and gets drunk. One evening he almost strangles his mistress. She leaves him. It all ends very badly, which is quite surprising for a little studio production film. One can imagine our lovers meeting again six years later. He has become a guitarist, she runs a gambling-joint out West, and here is the end of *In a Lonely Place* running neatly into the beginning of *Johnny Guitar*, with Crawford replacing Gloria.

Johnny: How many men have you forgotten?
Vienna: As many women as you've remembered.
Johnny: Don't go away.
Vienna: I haven't moved.
Johnny: Tell me something nice.
Vienna: Sure, what do you want to hear?
Johnny: Lie to me. Tell me all these years you've waited. Tell me.
Vienna: All these years I've waited.
Johnny: Tell me you'd have died if I hadn't come back.
Vienna: I would have died if you hadn't come back.
Johnny: Tell me you still love me like I love you.
Vienna: I still love you like you love me.
Johnny: Thanks. Thanks a lot. (Author's note.)

7 Like Rossellini, Ray knows the paltriness of speech. He never explains, he never emphasizes. He makes schemas of films, rather than films (cf. Rivette's article on R.R.). There's something else they have in common: Ray is shocked by children's deaths (*They Live By Night*, *Knock on Any Door*, *On Dangerous Ground*, *Johnny Guitar*). The comparison that has been made between *High Noon* and *Johnny Guitar* is like comparing a sardine to Jonah, or to be more precise, Poujade to Bonaparte. Furthermore, I would point out that the American cinema is closer to Gide than ours is, in that understatement is its favourite rhetorical device. For example: 'Sam wasn't a bad guy' or 'Jeff, I've known officers worse than you', or else 'She's not a bad looking doll'. (Author's note.)

  'Rivette's article on R.R.' refers to Jacques Rivette's 'Letter on Rossellini', Ch. 26 in this volume.

  Pierre Poujade, b. 1920, led a much publicized political protest movement in France during the 1950s, reaching its height in 1956 (i.e. shortly after Truffaut's reference here), when elections to the National Assembly brought 'Poujadists' 52 out of a total 595 seats. Initially a petit-bourgeois protest against government taxation and interference, the movement also combined fascistic and anti-semitic elements. 'Poujadisme' survives Poujade himself as a term for right-wing, petit-bourgeois, anti-government tendencies.

12 | Eric Rohmer: 'Ajax or the Cid?'

('Ajax ou le Cid?', *Cahiers du Cinéma* 59, May 1956)

It is to be deplored that the French distributors should have thought fit to wrap up the latest Nicholas Ray film in this non-sense, this grammatically monstrous hodge-podge (I wouldn't call it an expression), by way of a title – *La Fureur de vivre* (The Rage to Live). It is ugly, it is vulgar, and what is more it means absolutely nothing. And yet the American title is restrained and apposite; if it does not yield up the key to the work, it none the less aptly illuminates the author's purpose: *Rebel Without a Cause*, the cause for which one fights.

Cahiers readers know that we deem Nicholas Ray to be one of the greatest – Rivette would say *the* greatest, and I would willingly endorse that – of the new generation of American film-makers, the generation which only came on the scene after the war. In spite of his obvious lack of pretensions, he is one of the few to possess his own style, his own vision of the world, his own poetry; he is an *auteur*, a great *auteur*. A discernible constant factor running all the way through someone's work is a double-edged weapon: it is proof of personality but also, in some cases, of meagreness. Yet the constraints exercised by the production companies on film-makers are such, the manpower, the managers and the good foremen so numerous, that the presence of a leitmotiv is *a priori* an auspicious sign. The diversity of themes handled by Nicholas Ray, and the richness of the variations which he adds to the beauty of the three or four great themes dearest to him, tend to make his originality somewhat less easy to pinpoint than that of any of his rivals. It is impossible to attach any convenient label to his position, as one can with John Huston. It isn't problems that interest him, in the manner of a Brooks, but human beings. There is not a trace of the psychological subtleties so dear to Mankiewicz. None of those instantly dazzling flashes of lyricism, as in Aldrich. His tempo is slow, his melody usually monochord, but its delineation is so precise, its progress so compulsive, that we cannot allow our attention to stray for a moment. The bravura set-pieces, brilliant as they are, only

111

assume prominence after a slow crescendo. It is more an art of 'connections' than of 'brilliancies'.

The spirit of this film is similar to that of the earlier ones, but the situations themselves offer very specific analogies. The youth of the heroes, their stubborn intensity, is that of the characters in *Knock on Any Door* and *They Live By Night*. We have already encountered the theme of violence in *On Dangerous Ground* and *In a Lonely Place*. James Dean's futile heroism is Mitchum's in *The Lusty Men* or Cagney's in *Run for Cover*. The character personified by Natalie Wood is not so dissimilar to the Joan Crawford character in *Johnny Guitar*, despite the age difference. I'll go even further: without exception, all the heroines in his films – Cathy O'Donnell, Gloria Grahame, Susan Hayward, Ida Lupino, Viveca Lindfors, and the two already mentioned – under his direction take on a rather surprising air of physical resemblance. Just as he is the poet of violence, Nicholas Ray is perhaps the only poet of love; it is the fascination peculiar to both feelings that obsesses him, more than the study of their origins and their close or distant repercussions. Neither fury nor cruelty, but that special intoxication into which we are plunged by a violent physical act, situation or passion. Not desire, like the majority of his compatriots in the cinema, but the mysterious affinity that locks two human beings together. To all this I would add a feeling for nature, discernible in the background – in both the literal and the figurative sense – that is in harmony with his temperament as more of a colourist, even in his black and white films, than a plastic artist.

And then no other director knows how to give his characters so clearly the air of having a common genealogy. They are marked with the seal of the same fate, the same moral or physical disease that is not quite taint or decay. Look at the women's faces with their soft cheeks, but the eyes ringed with shadows and the heavy lips; those athletic male silhouettes, the Ryans, the Dereks, the Mitchums, flattened, or rather drawn back into themselves. James Dean takes this even further; he is like a chrysalis badly folded out of its cocoon. Turned in on himself? A solitude that is suffered rather than willed, a tortured quest for affection, for love or friendship. I spoke just now of a linear development, but not as one of those fine straight lines which Hawks would trace, the wide epic road, the calm progressions, the noble bearing. Here everything is circular, from the gestures of love to the movement of the stars, from those devouring looks that envelop you in their intensity while they strive to avoid your eyes, to those wandering pursuits, those deaths that come full circle and return the heroes to their original state of innocence. Yes, that's it: what these men-children lack is the kind of virginity with which the adventure writer usually endows his characters. They do not have the resigned complacency, nor the will to self-abasement that belongs to the man of the modern novel. Nor are they entirely guilty. . . .

Nicholas Ray is a poet, of that there is no doubt, but it is not only the lyrical character of his latest film I want to emphasize but its tragic character. First through its form, which may appear superficial but is not unimportant. *Rebel Without a Cause* is a genuine drama in five acts. *Act One*: exposition. Two youths and a young girl have just been picked up by the police. The parents intervene. The subject is immediately placed on the moral plane where it is to remain throughout the film: why the rebellion? It does not even have that depth proper to the intentionally absurd. Nor is it just the sudden leap of a restive young animal. It is the honour of these boys and girls which is at stake, an honour ill-conceived but which cannot be otherwise because its milieu and its circumstances leave it no more noble terrain. Certainly an excess of naive psychoanalysis weighs down the argument. But I don't think it has to be seen as an explanation or an excuse: it is part of the setting of American life. At any rate that is my opinion, having seen the film. The confusion did irritate me momentarily, as did a certain insolence, apathy, I'd even say stupidity, in the characters. That is how they are, a dramatic necessity. Let us pursue it no further and turn to *Act Two*. Our main hero, personified by James Dean, has promised to behave, and goes back to school. His classmates make fun of his pretensions to 'toughness'. The first lyrical interlude, with the lesson in the planetarium, that apocalyptic evocation which barely succeeds in veiling with anxiety or feigned indifference the empty eyes of our high school kids. An idea that is over-simple on paper, but it has strength and depth in its execution, charged as it is with both gravity and derision, like everything that is to follow. As they leave, fresh provocations. Dean tries not to get involved, but his honour is at stake – not his honour as a small-town tough guy but, we feel, his honour in every sense – in not giving way. A knife fight, where the harshness and the beauty of the landscape against which it is projected make us forget that it is only a children's game. There is more: the second hand must be played that very evening in an even more absurd and dangerous exercise. This is *Act Three*. Don't forget that so far the will of the characters has been the principal mechanism of the plot; and so it will be until the end. The hero withdraws momentarily to his tent – namely, the family – to meditate. Then he presents himself for battle. A new set-piece, but this time it is at night. A peripeteia which makes the action resurge: the game is driving cars into the sea and jumping out at the last moment. The adversary is killed. Everyone takes to their heels. *Act Four*. Dean has saved his honour and won the love of the victim's girl-friend, the girl he met in the police station, played by Natalie Wood. He goes home and announces to his parents his intention of giving himself up to the police. They dissuade him. Their cowardice arouses his indignation. The father's weakness doesn't just 'explain' the presence of the honour 'complex' in the son, and his unhealthy notoriety, it justifies it, in the moral sense of the word, it calls out for it, demands it. Violence, unpleasant scenes handled with unusual candour. He goes to the police station but the police won't see him. Meanwhile his classmates, suspecting betrayal, search for him. His only friend, a little dark-haired kid strangely named 'Plato' (Sal Mineo), manages to join him after several incidents. This is the *Last Act*, at night, in a deserted house that recalls *On Dangerous Ground* or *Johnny Guitar*. The second lyrical interlude, when Natalie Wood joins the two boys. A love scene by candlelight in the empty room; torment and peace in the night; beyond childish cynicism comes the first uneasiness, the first shame – the beauty of kisses and caresses. Before Woman, our erstwhile hero becomes the little boy that he could not be with his parents, but simultaneously he discovers his responsibility as a man. Ray's eroticism is, if it matters, as uneasy and equivocal as one could wish. There too the psychoanalyst will have plenty of scope. But he certainly won't be able to appreciate how much we, the audience, feel as we see the high school kids of that afternoon prepare for a physical and moral battle worthy of the name. . . . And we *move*. Not just with events (which come thick and fast: the arrival of the other kids, the fight with Mineo, who gets scared and shoots, the police on the scene, the chase in the copse); nor with the theatrical grandeur, in the right sense of the term, of the *mise en scène* (the cars with their brilliant headlights encircling the planetarium, the police demands, the dialogue in the shadows with Dean trying to make his friend see reason); nor with the tragedy of the conclusion (when a policeman shoots 'Plato' as he appears at the top of the steps, nervously gripping the revolver that Dean had unloaded without his knowledge). We make an *absolute* move forward: we have eliminated that distance which we had so cautiously kept between the characters and ourselves. Their reasons are our reasons, their honour our honour, their madness ours. They have, to use a modern turn of phrase, emerged from inauthenticity. By merit they have acquired the dignity of tragic heroes, which we could not quite discern in them at first.

May I be forgiven my favourite vice, of evoking the memory of the ancient Greeks. I don't think, in all good faith, that in this case such a parallel would be artificial. The idea of fate is deep-rooted, in the works of every period and every nation. It alone is not enough for the foundation of tragedy; it needs the support of some great dissension between the forces present at every moment, in man and around him, between the individual's own pride and the society – or nature – that cannot allow it, and victimizes it, punishes it. A tragic hero is always in some sense a warrior awoken from the intoxication of battle, suddenly perceiving that he is a god no longer. Anyone who re-reads Greek tragedy for enjoyment, with schooldays over, will be struck by the presence of a theme which the commentators have hardly touched on and which, unhappily, has never inspired our classics – the theme of *violence* (that is how *hubris* and *orgia* should be understood), a violence that is dangerous, to be condemned but exhilarating and beautiful. The modern image of fate is no banal, stupid accident, like the one James Dean, the actor, died in at the height of his career. It is not the absurdity of chance, but of our condition or our will. It is the disproportion that exists between the measure of man – always a noble one – and the futility of the task that

114

he often sets himself. It is not that earlier ages have been wiser than ours, or given more of themselves in the battle, they too without a cause; but more rigidly defined codes of honour always offered some pretext for the most absurd conduct. What I like about this film is that the word 'honour', out of the mouths of these apathetic, petit-bourgeois juveniles, is unchanged and loses none of its pure, dazzling brilliance, kept ablaze by these kids, these rodeo specialists, these outlaws of the prairie, even though their vanity and their foolish obstinacy are condemned by society, by morality, by whatever it is, in short by fate. They are not quite guilty, but not completely innocent either, only blighted by the defect of their century. It is the task of the politicians and the philosophers to show mankind horizons which are clearer than the ones it has chosen, but it is the poet's mission to doubt that optimism, to extract from the lees of his time the precious stone, to teach us to love without forbidding us to judge, to keep always alive in us the sense of *tragedy*. These thoughts came to me one day in a local cinema where they were showing *In a Lonely Place*. Each time I see a new Nicholas Ray film they come to mind again, and particularly with this one, his masterpiece.

Translated by Liz Heron

13 | Jean-Luc Godard: 'Nothing but Cinema'

('Rien que le cinéma', *Cahiers du Cinéma* 68, February 1957)

If the cinema no longer existed, Nicholas Ray alone gives the impression of being capable of reinventing it, and what is more, of wanting to. While it is easy to imagine John Ford as an admiral, Robert Aldrich on Wall Street, Anthony Mann on the trail of Belliou la Fumée or Raoul Walsh as a latter-day Henry Morgan under Caribbean skies, it is difficult to see the director of *Run for Cover* doing anything but make films. A Logan or a Tashlin, for instance, might make good in the theatre or music-hall, Preminger as a novelist, Brooks as a schoolteacher, Fuller as a politician, Cukor a press agent – but not Nicholas Ray. Were the cinema suddenly to cease to exist, most directors would be in no way at a loss; Nicholas Ray would. After seeing *Johnny Guitar* or *Rebel Without a Cause*, one cannot but feel that here is something which exists only in the cinema, which would be nothing in a novel, the stage or anywhere else, but which becomes fantastically beautiful on the screen. Nicholas Ray is *morally* a director, first and foremost. This explains the fact that in spite of his innate talent and obvious sincerity, a script which he does not take seriously will remain superficial.

At first glance this seems to be the case with *Hot Blood*, which is treated very casually, however, for the basic situation is not without promise. Taken literally, it is the situation of *The Lusty Men* in reverse, or Cukor's *Bhowani Junction* if you like: weary of adventure, someone returns to the people to whom he belongs. No one who shares my opinion that D. H. Lawrence's *The Plumed Serpent* is the most important novel of the twentieth century will be surprised when I say that here, had he so chosen, Nicholas Ray could have found a subject even more modern in its overtones than the ones he prefers. It seems he felt differently, however, and saw *Hot Blood* merely as a diversion between two *a priori* more ambitious films. Should one hold this against him? Renoir has just demonstrated with *Eléna* that taking it easy is a very serious thing, and even if he was amusing himself by taking it easy, or vice versa, I would therefore take Nicholas Ray to task for having on this occasion taken his fun too lightly.

But, I can hear people say, the film is just a commercial chore about gipsies, with Cornel Wilde forced to marry Jane Russell while she quits the tribe of which he is Dauphin and then realizes how much she needs them. Perhaps, but it isn't so simple, because I like to think that Nicholas Ray is honest enough to become involved only in something that involves him, and this was the case here. *Hot Blood* offered a chance to tackle a subject which on his own admission is dear to him – the ethnic minority – to depict a race through an individual, and so follow the path opened up by Rossellini while still going his own way.

Each shot of this film (slightly angled since he has been shooting in CinemaScope) proves, moreover, that the director is not totally uninterested, and that he was not replaced by Raoul Walsh as one might have been led to believe by the Jane Russell character, whose mannerisms are exactly those of Mamie in *The Revolt of Mamie Stover*. The plot itself, although badly handled, carries Ray's stamp, and the Cornel Wilde character is very close to those played by Sterling Hayden, Arthur Kennedy and James Cagney in his earlier films. Always, in a Ray film, the leading character returns to something he once abandoned or scorned. For him it is not a question of conquering but – more difficult – of reconquering a position lost through immaturity, inertia or discontent.

So one may well regret that Nicholas Ray did not feel called upon to deal more trenchantly with a situation and characters which might have made *Hot Blood* a less anodyne work. No reservations are necessary, however, in praising the deliberate and systematic use of the gaudiest colours to be seen in the cinema: barley-sugar orange shirts, acid-green dresses, violet cars, blue and pink carpets. The whole thing is a little like Van Dongen (at his best), and puts paid once and for all to those who still believe that colour in the cinema is more suited to soft than violent tones. For a purely technical reason, moreover, depth of focus in Cinema-Scope (which will not permit the use of a lens with a focal length shorter than 50 mm) is obtained by accentuating contrasts (cf. films shot by Joe MacDonald and John Alton).

Hot Blood, in short, is a semi-successful film to the extent that Ray was semi-uninterested in it. A success almost in spite of its director, I should add; or better, brought off by Nicholas Ray's innate sense of cinema: in an almost automatic manner, therefore, but less naively than that writing beloved of the early Surrealists. The whole cinema and nothing but the cinema, I was saying of Nicholas Ray. This eulogy entails a reservation. Nothing but cinema may not be the whole cinema.

Translated by Tom Milne

14 | Jean-Luc Godard: 'Beyond the Stars'

('Au delà des étoiles', *Cahiers du Cinéma* 79, January 1958)

There was theatre (Griffith), poetry (Murnau), painting (Rossellini), dance (Eisenstein), music (Renoir).[1] Henceforth there is cinema. And the cinema is Nicholas Ray.

Why does one remain unmoved by stills from *Bitter Victory* when one knows that it is the most beautiful of films? Because they express nothing. And for good reason. Whereas a single still of Lillian Gish is sufficient to conjure up *Broken Blossoms*, or of Charles Chaplin for *A King in New York*, Rita Hayworth for *Lady from Shanghai*, even Ingrid Bergman for *Eléna*, a still of Curt Jurgens lost in the Tripolitan desert or of Richard Burton wearing a white burnous bears no relation to Curt Jurgens or Richard Burton on the screen. A gulf yawns between the still and the film itself. A gulf which is a whole world. Which? The world of the modern cinema.

It is in this sense that *Bitter Victory* is an abnormal film. One is no longer interested in objects, but in what lies between the objects and becomes an object in its turn. Nicholas Ray forces us to consider as real something one did not even consider as unreal, something one did not consider at all. *Bitter Victory* is rather like one of those drawings in which children are asked to find the hunter and which at first seem to be a meaningless mass of lines.

Not that one should say 'behind the British Commando raid on Rommel's HQ lies a symbol of our time', because there is no behind and no before. *Bitter Victory* is what it is. One does not find reality on the one hand – the conflict between Lieutenant Keith and Captain Brand – and fiction on the other – the conflict between courage and cowardice, fear and lucidity, morality and liberty, or what have you. No. It is no longer a question of either reality or fiction, or of one transcending the other. It is a question of something quite different. What? The stars, maybe, and men who like to look at them and dream.

Magnificently edited, *Bitter Victory* is exceptionally well acted by Curt Jurgens and Richard Burton. With *Et Dieu . . . créa la femme*, this makes twice one can believe in a character created by Jurgens. As for Richard Burton, who has acquitted himself well enough in all his previous films, good or bad, when directed by Nicholas Ray he is absolutely sensational. A kind of Wilhelm Meister 1958? No matter. It would mean little enough to say that *Bitter Victory* is the most Goethian of films. What is the point of redoing Goethe, or of doing anything again – *Don Quixote* or *Bouvard et Pécuchet*, *J'accuse* or *Voyage au bout de la nuit* – since it has already been done? What is love, fear, contempt, danger, adventure, despair, bitterness, victory? What does it matter compared to the stars?

Never before have the characters in a film seemed so close and yet so far away. Faced by the deserted streets of Benghazi or the sand-dunes, we suddenly think for the space of a second of something else – the snack-bars on the Champs-Elysées, a girl one liked, everything and anything, lies, the treachery of women, the shallowness of men, playing the slot-machines. For *Bitter Victory* is not a reflection of life, it is life itself turned into film, seen from behind the mirror[2] where the cinema intercepts it. It is at once the most direct and the most secret of films, the most subtle and the crudest. It is not cinema, it is more than cinema.

How can one talk of such a film? What is the point of saying that the meeting between Richard Burton and Ruth Roman while Curt Jurgens watches is edited with fantastic brio? Maybe this was a scene during which we had closed our eyes. For *Bitter Victory*, like the sun, makes you close your eyes. Truth is blinding.

Translated by Tom Milne

Notes

1 This classification may seem arbitrary, and above all, paradoxical. But it isn't so. Certainly Griffith was the sworn enemy of the theatre, but the theatre of his time. The aesthetic of *Birth of a Nation* or *One Exciting Night* is the same as that of *Richard III* or *As You Like It*. If Griffith invented cinema, he invented it with the same ideas that Shakespeare brought to the theatre. He invented 'suspense' with the same ideas that Corneille brought to 'suspension'.

Similarly, to say that Renoir is close to music and Rossellini to painting, when it is well known that the former adores the boards and the latter hates canvases, is simply to say that the man who made *The River* has an affinity with Mozart, and the man who made *Europa 51*, with Velasquez. To make a crude simplification: one attempts to portray the soul; the other, character.

This, of course, is an attempt to define film-makers by what is deepest inside them, by the 'quality' of their 'invention'. In a Renoir film, for instance, the figure three corresponds to a 'tempo', whereas with Eisenstein the same figure corresponds to a spatial obsession. Eisenstein is dance because, like it, he seeks within the heart of people and things the immobility within movement. (Author's note.)

2 'Behind the mirror': the French title of Ray's film *Bigger than Life* is *Derrière le miroir* (i.e. Behind the Mirror). (Translator's note.)

15 | Charles Bitsch: Interview with Nicholas Ray

('Entretien avec Nicholas Ray', *Cahiers du Cinéma* 89, November 1958 (extracts))

There is an underlying theme which can be seen in all your films: that evil exists in every human being.

That's right. I believe it comes from the feeling – mixed, I hope, with a little insight – that no human being, male or female, is all good or all bad. The essential thing in every portrayal of life, be it fiction based on reality, or strict realism, is that the spectator looking on feels that he or she, under the same circumstances, would act in exactly the same way, be it right or wrong; the character's weaknesses should be human, because if they are, the spectators can recognize their own in them, so that, when the character acts as a hero they feel capable of doing the same thing and so identify with him. Nobody is, or ever has been, a pure and simple hero; I don't know if you've ever had the opportunity, but I've met a few exceptional heroes and, when I said to them, 'You were incredible, you were great,' they didn't understand who it was I was talking about, because they had done their great deed by simply obeying their instinct, an innate grandeur, their education, or something deeply rooted in the recesses of their souls. They may not have been high up on the social scale, they may have been very ordinary, even less than ordinary people; but having acted in this way, they proved that there was something great in them, that when the time came to decide, to act, although they weren't prepared for it, they behaved like great men; and this marked them for the rest of their lives. Some became heroes and this led to their downfall, because after acting so heroically and establishing the reputation of a hero, they expected everything they did afterwards was going to be just as heroic or thought they'd got rid of all the faults they might have had before. The mistakes that criminals make are for the same reasons.

The characters of In a Lonely Place, On Dangerous Ground, Rebel Without a Cause, *all have something in common: they are violent.*

Absolutely, there is violence inside them. There is in each of us: it is there in potential. The bank cashier leading a peaceful life counts his wads of notes and begins to hate everybody: he counts his notes until, one day, suddenly, he seizes the gun he keeps to guard his till, goes out into the street and shoots a dozen people. That's why I like non-conformists: the non-conformist is much saner than the person who, all his life, carries on in his everyday way, because he's the one most likely, at the most unexpected moment, to explode and kill the first person who comes along. In America, standard criminal or anti-social acts can already be seen in eleven- or twelve-year-old children, but most acts of atrocious violence, the ones that make the headlines in the papers, are perpetrated by individuals who have never committed crimes before: it's not the first criminal act they've thought about, but it is the first they have committed.

In your films this theme of violence is always closely linked to that of solitude.
For everything I have written and was closely involved in, my . . . personal trademark has always been 'I'm a stranger here myself.'[1] The first piece of poetry I wrote when I was young was already on that topic. The quest for a fulfilled life is, I think, paradoxically, solitary. I also believe that solitude is very important for man, so long as it does not harm him, if he knows how to use it originally as . . . This is a very personal feeling: it's too difficult to talk about.[. . .]

How did you come to work with Frank Lloyd Wright?
At the age of sixteen I wrote and produced a series of programmes for the radio and they won me a grant for any university of my choice. But there wasn't in fact a university which taught anything about the radio, or drama actually. So I went to the University of Chicago because Hutchins was there and was going to try out a new educational system. But then I became a sort of refugee from higher education in as much as I felt that all I was going to learn with classical university teaching would have to be unlearned in order for me to make my way in drama, in the field that I had chosen, and I found out afterwards that I was right. Architecture is the backbone of all the arts, you know: if it is real architecture it encompasses every domain. The simple word 'architecture' can just as well apply to a play, a score of music or a way of life. Frank Lloyd Wright gave all young people in the world the opportunity to meet, to practise architecture, to lead a communal life, and exchange experiences and points of view. There weren't many Americans among the thirty-five young people who were the first to join Frank Lloyd Wright, but there were Nicaraguans, Japanese, French, Danes, Swiss and Chinese, some of them sculptors like Naguchi, musicians like Brooks, and others painters.

Can't one detect Frank Lloyd Wright's influence in the architecture of the houses in On Dangerous Ground *and* Johnny Guitar?
No. I'd say that the most obvious influence Wright had on me, apart from a kind of philosophic leaning . . . no, not a philosophic leaning, rather a certain way of looking at things, is my liking for CinemaScope; I like the horizontal line, and the horizontal was essential for Wright. I like the CinemaScope format very much; and when I am free to use it as I please, as in *Rebel*, I get great satisfaction from doing so. But in the two films you

121

have mentioned, the architecture was so determined by the time and place that it wasn't at all like Frank Lloyd Wright and owed nothing to the influence he had on me. I used objects, like the tree-trunk for Ida [Lupino], which are, it's true, the kind of props one might find in the living-room of a Frank Lloyd Wright villa, but in the structure, in the architecture itself, Frank Lloyd Wright's influence is non-existent. However, in *Johnny Guitar* . . . it's difficult to say. I needed an almost arbitrarily dramatic moment, so to speak, to place the whiteness of Vienna's dress against the red rocks; but I think you can rarely determine the exact influence you've undergone, where your taste for something comes from, or what that taste was subjected to as it evolved. I would be absolutely incapable of telling you why I wanted to make my life in the theatre, or in music. Did it come from a feeling of revolt, from a particularly pressing influence, from a need to attract attention, or from something else? I don't know.[. . .]
You were telling us that not one of your films has fully satisfied you. Can you say what your 'ideal film' would be?
I don't know. It has always been my aim, even when I was making what I would call 'films to order', at the time I was under contract. You can only refuse a certain number of offers and you're sometimes forced to choose from an often discouraging list of projects, but, on the other hand, the rent has to be paid, the children educated, etc. At last I've got past that stage, but I had to go through it like everyone else. I've had, I think, more luck than most directors, since, two or three exceptions apart, I have never been forced to make a film without having my say. In more than 75 per cent of cases I've been allowed to work on the screenplay, to put forward my ideas and to make changes or improvise on the set. I keep looking, I put my camera on my back and I go hunting.
Do you improvise a lot while you are filming?
The entire ending of *In a Lonely Place*, for example, was improvised. In *Rebel Without a Cause* I improvised, one evening at home, the whole scene where Jimmy returns home to his parents after the tragedy. The scene had been bothering me a lot: according to the script it should have taken place in the mother's bedroom, but it seemed static to me. So one evening when Jimmy dropped by to see me, I began to discuss the scene with him; I asked him to go into the yard while I played the part of the father in the living-room. I gave Jimmy two contradictory instructions: first to go upstairs without being heard, and then, at the same time, to feel the irresistible need to talk to somebody. I then turned on the television to a channel where the programmes had finished, and pretended to be asleep. So Jimmy comes in and walks past me to go upstairs and it's then that the contradictory movement gets the better of him: he falls heavily on to the sofa, with a bottle of milk, and waits for me to wake up; at that very moment I exclaimed, 'Now your mother comes down the stairs!' And I knew that I'd found the dynamics of my scene. I got the designer to come to my place, and the set we used in *Rebel* was copied from my own living-room where we had improvised the scene. It's a very satisfying way to

work; it was also from this that we got the idea of showing the mother coming downstairs from Jimmy's point of view. The planetarium, the kids in the car, and several other scenes were also improvised.

There's a curious thing about the shot of the mother coming downstairs. You used it in Rebel Without a Cause *and in* Hot Blood. *In the former it is taken from Jimmy's point of view, but in* Hot Blood, *when the camera comes back to the horizontal, the two characters are in frame so that it is no longer taken from Cornel Wilde's point of view.*

That's right, and it was a mistake to reframe the two characters. To be honest, what I always try to do, whenever it's possible, is to put the camera in an actor's place, to make it act for him and let it become the point of view of somebody for whom I feel sympathy or antipathy. This shot is the 'point of view' principle exploited to its extreme and comes from the way I treat the camera, making it look for the truth by letting it play for me, like an actor.

Are you as interested in the camera as you are in the screenplay or the actors?

I am interested in the story and the characters. The camera is an instrument, it's the microscope which allows you to detect the 'melody of the look'. It's a wonderful instrument because its microscopic power is for me the equivalent of introspection in a writer, and the unrolling of the film in the camera corresponds, in my opinion, to the train of thought of the writer. But if the character on whom I am working has nothing to photograph, then the camera becomes useless; all you are doing then is playing with the most expensive electric train set in the world.[2]

One often gets the impression that to shoot a scene you work in the following way: you start by filming it in long shot and then you make cutaways.

I can't reply definitively to that question, because it varies. I make them rehearse the scene first; I sometimes start by filming it in long shot in order to give the actors the mood in which they should play it – I even, occasionally, shoot for as long as there is film in the camera. In *Bigger Than Life* I had shot the staircase scene in a single shot of nine minutes and when we looked at the rushes everyone exclaimed, 'Don't make any cutaways, don't do any, it's the most suffocating scene we've ever seen!' Prior to this, a playwright had read that scene and said to me, 'I really can't see how you could get that across.' Had I listened to those who advised me not to make any cutaways, the dynamics of the scene would have been reduced to nothing. I believe, in fact, that they let themselves be impressed by the technical performance, whereas the actors, after rehearsing, were only just beginning to get to grips with the scene and we needed to go even further. But sometimes I start in a completely different way, with a close-up. This can also depend on the actor, the atmosphere or a technical necessity that the actor has to face, and I have to help him to prepare for it. I have no hard and fast rules.

Doesn't your method of filming depend on the style that you give to your film? One would be tempted to divide your work into two categories: some, like Rebel Without a Cause, Bigger Than Life *or* Johnny Guitar *have a theatrical style, and others, like* On Dangerous Ground *or* They Live By Night *a novelistic style.*

No, I don't think so, since I myself adapted *They Live By Night* and *On Dangerous Ground*, and I also wrote the original story of *Rebel*: so there is no reason why one should be related to a novel and the other to a play. Earlier, when I was talking about the camera, I brought up the writer. In fact a film can be related to a novel in as much as sentences are scenes and chapters sequences, but when you're working on a screenplay you readily give it a play form: three acts or, as in *Bitter Victory*, a prologue, two acts and an epilogue. So cinema stands on the borderline between the novel and the theatre. Once again, the only method I can claim to have is to work on the actor. I attach great importance to the actor. Casting a film, to fill a dozen parts I see nearly three hundred actors, I chat with them . . . and sometimes I make the wrong choice. But even in this domain I don't follow any precise rules, for you have to adapt yourself to the actor since each has a different essence. I don't think that any director can assert that his style is the long shot, the medium shot or the close-up, unless he has the mind of a civil servant. One thing is certain, time and space play no role at all in the construction of a film, the cinema is unaware of them; a scene can carry you into another world, another age. One simply tries to capture, in flight, moments of truth, as much by thought as by intuition, instinct, or . . . too rarely . . . by flashes of inspiration. And those moments of truth can be either comic or tragic if one is dealing with kings great enough to fall. That is how a film is made, the rest is simply a question of looking at life and people.

Translated by Liz Heron

Notes

1 'I've a great respect for a gun, and besides I'm a stranger here myself': the line is spoken by Sterling Hayden in the title role of *Johnny Guitar* (1953). *I'm a Stranger Here Myself* is also the title of an American documentary film about Ray (director David M. Halpern, 1974).

2 The reference is to Orson Welles, who is reputed to have said to Richard Wilson, while being shown the RKO studio machinery in 1940: 'This is the biggest electric train set any boy ever had!' See, for example, Joseph McBride, *Orson Welles*, London, Secker & Warburg; New York, Viking, 1972, p. 31.

III | Auteurs

16 | Jacques Rivette: 'The Genius of Howard Hawks'

('Génie de Howard Hawks', *Cahiers du Cinéma* 23, May 1953)

The evidence on the screen is the proof of Hawks's genius: you only have to watch *Monkey Business* to know that it is a brilliant film. Some people refuse to admit this, however; they refuse to be satisfied by proof. There can't be any other reason why they don't recognize it.

Hawks's *œuvre* is equally divided between comedies and dramas – a remarkable ambivalence. More remarkable still is his frequent fusing of the two elements so that each, rather than damaging the other, seems to underscore their reciprocal relation: the one sharpens the other. Comedy is never long absent from his most dramatic plots, and far from compromising the feeling of tragedy, it removes the comfort of fatalistic indulgence and keeps the events in a perilous kind of equilibrium, a stimulating uncertainty which only adds to the strength of the drama. Scarface's secretary speaks comically garbled English, but that doesn't prevent his getting shot; our laughter all the way through *The Big Sleep* is inextricable from our foreboding of danger; the climax of *Red River*, in which we are no longer sure of our own feelings, wondering whose side to take and whether we should be amused or afraid, sets our every nerve quivering with panic and gives us a dizzy, giddy feeling like that of a tightrope walker whose foot falters without quite slipping, a feeling as unbearable as the ending of a nightmare.

While it is the comedy which gives Hawks's tragedy its effectiveness, the comedy cannot quite dispel (not the tragedy, let's not spoil our best arguments by going too far) the harsh feeling of an existence in which no action can undo itself from the web of responsibility. Could we be offered a more bitter view of life than this? I have to confess that I am quite unable to join in the laughter of a packed theatre when I am riveted by the calculated twists of a fable (*Monkey Business*) which sets out – gaily, logically, and with an unholy abandon – to chronicle the fatal stages in the degradation of a superior mind.

It is no accident that similar groups of intellectuals turn up in both *Ball of Fire* and *The Thing from Another World*. But Hawks is not so much concerned with the subjection of the world to the jaded, glacial vision of the scientific mind as he is with retracing the comic misfortunes of the intelligence. Hawks is not concerned with satire or psychology; societies mean no more to him than sentiments do; unlike Capra or McCarey, he is solely preoccupied with the adventure of the intellect. Whether he opposes the old to the new, the sum of the world's knowledge of the past to one of the degraded forms of modern life (*Ball of Fire, A Song is Born*), or man to beast (*Bringing Up Baby*), he sticks to the same story – the intrusion of the inhuman, or the crudest avatar of humanity, into a highly civilized society. In *The Thing*, the mask is finally off: in the confined space of the universe, some men of science are at grips with a creature worse than inhuman, a creature *from another world*; and their efforts are directed towards fitting it into the logical framework of human knowledge.

But in *Monkey Business* the enemy has crept into man himself: the subtle poison of the Fountain of Youth, the temptation of infantilism. This we have long known to be one of the less subtle wiles of the Evil One – now in the form of a hound, now in the form of a monkey – when he comes up against a man of rare intelligence. And it is the most unfortunate of illusions which Hawks rather cruelly attacks: the notion that adolescence and childhood are barbarous states from which we are rescued by education. The child is scarcely distinguishable from the savage he imitates in his games: and a most distinguished old man, after he has drunk the precious fluid, takes delight in imitating a chimp. One can find in this a classical conception of man, as a creature whose only path to greatness lies through experience and maturity; at the end of his journey, it is his old age which will be his judge.

Still worse than infantilism, degradation, or decadence, however, is the fascination these tendencies exert on the same mind which perceives them as evil; the film is not only a story about this fascination, it offers itself to the spectator as a demonstration of the power of the fascination. Likewise, anyone who criticizes this tendency must first submit himself to it. The monkeys, the Indians, the goldfish are no more than the guise worn by Hawks's obsession with primitivism, which also finds expression in the savage rhythms of the tom-tom music, the sweet stupidity of Marilyn Monroe (that monster of femininity whom the costume designer nearly deformed), or the ageing bacchante Ginger Rogers becomes when she reverts to adolescence and her wrinkles seem to shrink away. The instinctive euphoria of the characters' actions gives a lyric quality to the ugliness and foulness, a denseness of expression which heightens everything into abstraction: the fascination of all this gives *beauty* to the metamorphoses in retrospect. One could apply the word 'expressionistic' to the artfulness with which Cary Grant twists his gestures into symbols; watching the scene in which he makes himself up as an Indian, it is impossible not to be reminded of the famous shot in *The Blue Angel* in which Jannings stares at *his* distorted face. It is by no means facile to compare these two similar tales of ruin: we recall how the themes of damnation and malediction in the German cinema had imposed the same rigorous progression from the likeable to the hideous.

From the close-up of the chimpanzee to the moment when the diaper slips off the baby Cary Grant, the viewer's head swims with the constant whirl of immodesty and impropriety; and what is this feeling if not a mixture of fear, censure – and fascination? The allure of the instinctual, the abandonment to primitive earthly forces, evil, ugliness, stupidity – all of the Devil's attributes are, in these comedies in which the soul itself is tempted to bestiality, deviously combined with logic *in extremis*; the sharpest point of the intelligence is turned back on itself. *I Was a Male War Bride* takes as its subject simply the impossibility of finding a place to sleep, and then prolongs it to the extremes of debasement and demoralization.

Hawks knows better than anyone else that art has to go to extremes, even the extremes of squalor, because that is the source of comedy. He is never afraid to use bizarre narrative twists, once he has established that they are possible. He doesn't try to confound the spectator's vulgar tendencies; he sates them by taking them a step further. This is also Molière's genius: his mad fits of logic are apt to make the laughter stick in your throat. It is also Murnau's genius – the famous scene with Dame Martha in his excellent *Tartuffe* and several sequences of *Der letzte Mann* are still models of Molièresque cinema.

Hawks is a director of intelligence and precision, but he is also a bundle of dark forces and strange fascinations; his is a Teutonic spirit, attracted by bouts of ordered madness which give birth to an infinite chain of consequences. The very fact of their continuity is a manifestation of Fate. His heroes demonstrate this not so much in their feelings as in their actions, which he observes meticulously and with passion. It is *actions* that he films, meditating on the power of appearance alone. We are not concerned with John Wayne's thoughts as he walks toward Montgomery Clift at the end of *Red River*, or Bogart's thoughts as he beats somebody up: our attention is directed solely to the precision of each step – the exact rhythm of the walk – of each blow – and to the gradual collapse of the battered body.

But at the same time, Hawks epitomizes the highest qualities of the American cinema: he is the only American director who knows how to draw a *moral*. His marvellous blend of action and morality is probably the secret of his genius. It is not an idea that is fascinating in a Hawks film, but its effectiveness. A deed holds our attention not so much for its intrinsic beauty as for its effect on the inner works of his universe.

Such art demands a basic honesty, and Hawks's use of time and space bears witness to this – no flashback, no ellipsis; the rule is continuity. No character disappears without us following him, and nothing surprises the hero which doesn't surprise us at the same time. There seems to be a law behind Hawks's action and editing, but it is a *biological* law like that governing any living being: each shot has a functional beauty, like a neck or an ankle. The smooth, orderly succession of shots has a rhythm like the pulsing of blood, and the whole film is like a beautiful body, kept alive by deep, resilient breathing.

This obsession with continuity imposes a feeling of monotony on Hawks's films, the kind often associated with the idea of a journey to be made or a course to be run (*Air Force, Red River*), because everything is felt to be connected to everything else, time to space and space to time. So in films which are mostly comic (*To Have and Have Not, The Big Sleep*), the characters are confined to a few settings, and they move around rather helplessly in them. We begin to feel the gravity of each movement they make, and we are unable to escape from their presence. But Hawksian drama is always expressed in spatial terms, and variations in setting are parallel with temporal variations: whether it is the drama of Scarface, whose kingdom shrinks from the city he once ruled to the room in which he is finally trapped, or of the scientists who cannot dare leave their hut for fear of The Thing; of the fliers in *Only Angels Have Wings*, trapped in their station by the fog and managing to escape to the mountains from time to time, just as Bogart (in *To Have and Have Not*) escapes to the sea from the hotel which he prowls impotently, between the cellar and his room; and even when these themes are burlesqued in *Ball of Fire*, with the grammarian moving out of his hermetic library to face the perils of the city, or in *Monkey Business*, in which the characters' jaunts are an indication of their reversion to infancy (*I Was a Male War Bride* plays on the motif of the journey in another way). Always the heroes' movements are along the path of their destiny.

The monotony is only a façade. Beneath it, feelings are slowly ripening, developing step by step towards a violent climax. Hawks uses lassitude as a dramatic device – to convey the exasperation of men who have to restrain themselves for two hours, patiently containing their anger, hatred, or love before our eyes and then suddenly releasing it, like slowly satu rated batteries which eventually give off a spark. Their anger is heightened by their habitual *sangfroid*; their calm façade is pregnant with emotion, with the secret trembling of their nerves and of their soul – until the cup overflows. A Hawks film often has the same feeling as the agonizing wait for the fall of a drop of water.

The comedies show another side of this principle of monotony. Forward action is replaced by repetition, like the rhetoric of Raymond Roussel replacing Péguy's; the same actions, endlessly recurring, which Hawks builds up with the persistence of a maniac and the patience of a man obsessed, suddenly whirl madly about, as if at the mercy of a capricious maelstrom.

What other man of genius, even if he were more obsessed with conti-nuity, could be more passionately concerned with the consequences of men's actions, or with these actions' relationship to each other? The way they influence, repel, or attract one another makes up a unified and coherent world, a Newtonian universe whose ruling principles are the universal law of gravity and a deep conviction of the gravity of existence. Human actions are weighed and measured by a master director preoccupied with man's responsibilities.

The measure of Hawks's films is intelligence, but a *pragmatic* intelligence, applied directly to the physical world, an intelligence which takes its efficacity from the precise viewpoint of a profession or from some form of human activity at grips with the universe and anxious for conquest. Marlowe in *The Big Sleep* practises a profession just as a scientist or a flier does; and when Bogart hires out his boat in *To Have and Have Not*, he hardly looks at the sea: he is more interested in the beauty of his passengers than in the beauty of the waves. Every river is made to be crossed, every herd is made to be fattened and sold at the highest price. And women, however seductive, however much the hero cares for them, must join them in the struggle.

It is impossible adequately to evoke *To Have and Have Not* without immediately recalling the struggle with the fish at the beginning of the film. The universe cannot be conquered without a fight, and fighting is natural to Hawks's heroes: hand-to-hand fighting. What closer grasp of another being could be hoped for than a vigorous struggle like this? So love exists even where there is perpetual opposition; it is a bitter duel whose constant dangers are ignored by men intoxicated with passion (*The Big Sleep*, *Red River*). Out of the contest comes esteem – that admirable word encompassing knowledge, appreciation and sympathy: the opponent becomes a partner. The hero feels a great sense of disgust if he has to face an enemy who refuses to fight; Marlowe, seized with a sudden bitterness, precipitates events in order to hasten the climax of his case.

Maturity is the hallmark of these reflective men, heroes of an adult, often exclusively masculine world, where tragedy is found in personal relationships; comedy comes from the intrusion and admixture of alien elements, or in mechanical objects which take away their free will – that freedom of decision by which a man can express himself and affirm his existence as a creator does in the act of creation.

I don't want to seem as if I'm praising Hawks for being 'a genius estranged from his time', but it is the obviousness of his modernity which lets me avoid belabouring it. I'd prefer, instead, to point out how, even if he is occasionally drawn to the ridiculous or the absurd, Hawks first of all concentrates on the smell and feel of reality, giving reality an unusual and indeed long-hidden grandeur and nobility; how Hawks gives the modern sensibility a classical conscience. The father of *Red River* and *Only Angels Have Wings* is none other than Corneille; ambiguity and complexity are compatible only with the noblest feelings, which some still consider 'dull', even though it is not these feelings which are soonest exhausted but rather the barbaric, mutable natures of crude souls – that is why modern novels are so boring.

Finally, how could I omit mentioning those wonderful Hawksian opening scenes in which the hero settles smoothly and solidly in for the duration? No preliminaries, no expository devices: a door opens, and there he is in the first shot. The conversation gets going and quietly familiarizes us with his personal rhythm; after bumping into him like this, we can no longer leave his side. We are his companions all through the journey as it unwinds as surely and regularly as the film going through the projector. The hero moves with the litheness and constancy of a mountaineer who starts out with a steady gait and maintains it along the roughest trails, even to the end of the longest day's march.

From these first stirrings, we are not only sure that the heroes will never leave us, we also know that they will stick by their promises *to a fault*, and will never hesitate or quit: no one can put a stop to their marvellous stubbornness and tenacity. Once they have set out, they will go on to the end of their tether and carry the promises they have made to their logical conclusions, come what may. What is started must be finished. It doesn't matter that the heroes are often involved against their wills: by proving themselves, by achieving their ends, they win the right to be free and the honour of calling themselves men. To them, logic is not some cold intellectual activity, but proof that the body is a coherent whole, harmoniously following the consequences of an action out of loyalty to itself. The strength of the heroes' willpower is an assurance of the unity of the man and the spirit, tied together on behalf of that which both justifies their existence and gives it the highest meaning.

If it is true that we are fascinated by extremes, by everything which is bold and excessive, and that we find grandeur in a lack of moderation – then it follows that we should be intrigued by the clash of extremes, because they bring together the intellectual precision of abstractions with the elemental magic of the great earthly impulses, linking thunderstorms with equations in an affirmation of life. The beauty of a Hawks film comes from this kind of affirmation, staunch and serene, remorseless and resilient. It is a beauty which demonstrates existence by breathing and movement by walking. That which is, is.

Translated by Russell Campbell and
Marvin Pister, adapted from a
translation by Adrian Brine

17 | Jacques Rivette: 'The Essential'

('L'Essentiel', *Cahiers du Cinéma* 32, February 1954)

The cardinal virtue of this film [*Angel Face*], like *The Moon is Blue*, which follows it chronologically, is that it frees us from certain preconceptions about its director. Our increasing familiarity with the clever ambiguity of his themes and the extraordinary fluidity and subtlety of his camera movements would soon have brought us to the point where we would be unable to see beyond them and would run the risk of reducing the great talent of Otto Preminger to what are, it should be said, modest dimensions. First of all let us be grateful for these two films for proving to us, by their lack of pretension, the starkness of the sets and the improvised quality of the photography that – if it was ever in doubt – there is more to Preminger than the mere ability to get the best out of skilful scripts, excellent actors and the technical resources of a well-equipped studio.

So we should compose our eulogy to poverty,[1] even were its sole advantage the necessity of ingenuity to conceal it and so stimulate creativity. Would it not be a good thing to subject every established film-maker to it just once? It is well known that wealth dulls sensibility; what other test is left for the talent that has no self-doubt?

With equipment that, compared with the technical resources of Twentieth Century-Fox, resembles that of the amateur film-maker, Preminger reduces his art to the essential, to the skeleton that not so long ago was artfully fleshed out by the charms of the image and the opaque architecture of script and *mise en scène*. Here the elements of cinema are almost stripped bare. In contrast to the heavy-handed treatment so beloved of the Selznick or Metro productions, *Angel Face* and *The Moon is Blue* are to Preminger what *Two People* is to Dreyer, what *The Big Heat* is to Lang and *Woman on the Beach* to Renoir: the most conclusive proof of the talent, or the genius, of a director. Let me make myself clear: I am not saying that these two films are his best – they are the ones that give us the best means of approaching the others and the secret of their director's talent, the ones

132

that confirm what we could already suspect: that this talent is first and foremost the function of a specific *idea* of cinema.

But what is this idea? And why should I be so mysterious about it? I no longer know what I think of Preminger; to put it in a nutshell, he intrigues rather than excites me. But I want right away to make this the first, and not the least, of my praises: the number of film-makers who have the merit of intriguing us is not, after all, so great.

I can see very well that this would be the right moment for a predictable elaboration of the theme or the characters. For instance, Jean Simmons's role, and its analogies with or divergences from some of our director's other heroines etc. . . . I can see that very well, but the devil is whispering in my ear, 'Is it really important; is that false and criminal purity not the very site of convention and artifice?' This banal character, for I shall indeed proclaim her as such, is also fresh and surprising. How does this come about, if not by some mystery that is not contained in the script?

Furthermore let us take care not to overvalue the often debased wonders of mystery. But this utterly enigmatic film makes no pretence of being otherwise: it should be pointed out at once that the really quite simple initial enigma is reinforced by a second which is impenetrable. If half the action remains a mystery, it is rather that the solution offered by the logic of the narrative has no correspondence with the emotions aroused: an interest outside that of the plot continually rivets our attention on the gestures of characters whose images at the same time prove to us the lack of any real depth. Yet it is depth they aspire to, depth of the most artificial kind, since it does not come from the suspect, questionable subtlety of human beings, but from art itself, from the use of every means that the cinema offers the film-maker.

I would never lay it down that a director should choose as a pretext the script that will allow him one more opportunity to film, to direct actors, to be creative. Did I say script as pretext? I do not think that this really applies here, but that nevertheless Preminger does see in the script primarily an opportunity to create certain characters, studying them with painstaking attention, observing their reactions to one another, and finally drawing from them particular gestures, attitudes and reflexes – which are the *raison d'être* of his film, and its real subject.

It is not that the theme is a matter of indifference to him. I am now going to offer praise indeed: Preminger is not one of those who can turn their hand to anything; it is easy to see what he is interested in here, through the alternation of successful passages with others of unruffled awkwardness. It is difficult to imagine an exegesis of Preminger based on a comparative study of the anecdotes, easier to see it working through a study of certain constants which would be not so much narrative elements as the obsessions of the *auteur* who knows which themes suit him best.[2]

One can ask what he brings by way of conviction to the story: does he believe it? Does he even try to make us believe it? Its improbabilities are certainly not unconvincing: it is often the very moment when the improbable erupts – Laura brought back to life, Doctor Korvo's self-hypnosis in the mirror – that one can least refuse it credibility. But in this film where formal spells like those of *Laura* or *Whirlpool* are forbidden, the real problem is not so much to make an unbelievable story believable, as to find, beyond dramatic or narrative verisimilitude, a truth that is purely cinematic. I enjoy a different idea of the cinema more, but I also ask that what Preminger is trying to do be clearly understood, and it is subtle enough to hold attention. I prefer the possibly more naive conception of the old school, of Hawks, Hitchcock or Lang, who first believe in their themes and then build the strength of their art upon this conviction. Preminger believes first in *mise en scène*, the creation of a precise complex of sets and characters, a network of relationships, an architecture of connections, an animated complex that seems suspended in space. What tempts him, if not the fashioning of a piece of crystal for transparency with ambiguous reflections and clear, sharp lines or the rendering audible of particular chords unheard and rare, in which the inexplicable beauty of the modulation suddenly justifies the ensemble of the phrase? This is probably the definition of a certain kind of preciosity, but its supreme and most secret form, since it does not come from the use of artifice, but from the determined and hazardous search for a note previously unheard; one can neither tire of hearing it, nor claim by deepening it to exhaust its enigma – the door to something beyond intellect, opening out on to the unknown.

Such are the contingencies of *mise en scène*, and such the example that Preminger seems to offer, of a faith in the very practice of his art which enables him in another way to uncover its greatest depth. For I would not want you to imagine that his is some abstract aesthete's experiment. 'I love work more than anything,' he told me. I do believe that for Preminger a film is in the first place an opportunity for work, for questioning, for encouraging and solving such problems.[3] The film is not so much an end as a means. Its unpredictability attracts him, the chance discoveries that mean things cannot go according to plan, on-the-spot improvisation that is born of a fortunate moment and dedicated to the fleeting essence of a place or a person. If Preminger had to be defined in one word it would really best be *metteur en scène*, even though here his stage directing background seems to have influenced him little. In the midst of a dramatic space created by human encounters he would instead exploit to its limit the cinema's ability to capture the fortuitous (but a fortuity that is willed), to record the accidental (but the accidental that is created) through the closeness and sharpness of the look; the relationships of the characters create a closed circuit of exchanges, where nothing makes an appeal to the viewer.

What is *mise en scène*?[4] My apologies for asking such a hazardous question with neither preparation nor preamble, particularly when I have no intention of answering it. Only, should this question not always inform our deliberations? An example would be better: the heroine's nocturnal stroll among the traces of the past, kin to Dana Andrews's stroll among the dead Laura's possessions, is, in theory, the unmistakable classic temptation of the mediocre. But Preminger is more than author of this idea, he is the one who invents Jean Simmons's uncertain footfall, her huddled figure in the armchair. What could have been banal or facile is saved by a striking absence of complaisance, the hardness of the passage of time and lucidity of the look; or rather, there is no longer either theme or treatment, facility or luck, but the stark, heart-rending, obvious presence of a cinema that is sensitive to its core.

Thus *The Moon is Blue* was less the brilliant execution of a witty comedy by a skilful director of actors than – through the constant inventiveness of word and gesture, through the precision with which the characters' absolute freedom is encircled – the clear affirmation of a power that is more moving than any fable. If ever a film was the expression of the practice of *mise en scène* for its own sake, it is this. What is cinema, if not the *play* of actor and actress, of hero and set, of word and face, of hand and object?

The starkness of these films, far from endangering the essential, accentuates it to the point of provocation. And what could compromise it – the taste for appearances, for the *natural*, the clever surprise of the accidental, the search for the chance gesture – all this nevertheless meets up with that secret side of the cinema, or of man, which keeps them from nothingness. I can ask no more.

Translated by Liz Heron

Notes

1 Rivette's 'eulogy to poverty' is a recurrent theme in his writings in the 1950s; see, for example, in this volume, his 'Letter on Rossellini' (1955) and particularly his contributions to the 'Six Characters in Search of *auteurs*' discussion (1957), Chs 26 and 2 respectively.

2 Thus fascination (*Laura, Whirlpool, Angel Face*), cross-examinations (*Laura, Fallen Angel, Whirlpool, Where the Sidewalk Ends, Angel Face*), rivalry in love (*Laura, Fallen Angel, Daisy Kenyon, Angel Face, The Moon is Blue*). (Author's note.)

3 Cf. Jean-Luc Godard, 'Bergmanorama', *Cahiers* 85, July 1958, translated as 'Bergmanorama' in *Godard on Godard*: 'One is always alone; on the set as before the blank page. And for Bergman, to be alone means to ask questions. And to make films means to answer them.'

4 Cf. Alexandre Astruc, 'What is *mise en scène*?', Ch. 33 in this volume.

18 | Claude Chabrol: 'Serious Things'

('Les Choses sérieuses', Cahiers du Cinéma 46, April 1955)

. . .[1] Whatever happens, I think the release of *Rear Window* will tend to create a united front in film criticism. Even the Anglo-Saxon critics themselves, who had shied away from some of Hitchcock's films for a while, regarded *Rear Window* with seriousness and sympathy. Indeed, right from its opening, *Rear Window* does present an immediate focus of interest that puts it on a higher plane than the majority of the earlier works, enough to warrant its entry into the category of serious films, beyond the mere entertainment thriller.

In fact, in this review, I do not want to concentrate on an element that is all too clear already: the culpability of the central character, a voyeur in the worst sense of the word. Rather I want to engage in drawing out certain elements that are less obvious, but even more interesting, which enrich the work with very specific resonances and make it possible to brush aside the objections and the criticisms that ensued after a superficial viewing of *Rear Window* at the last Venice Biennale.

In its first few minutes *Rear Window* presents us with an assembly of rabbit hutches, each of them completely separate and observed from another closed, incommunicable, rabbit hutch. From there it is obviously just a step, made with no difficulty, to the conclusion that the behaviour of the rabbits is, or should be, the object of attention, since in fact there is nothing to contradict this interpretation of the elements before us. We merely have to acknowledge that the study of this behaviour is carried out by a rabbit essentially no different from the others. Which leads to the notion of a perpetual shift between the real behaviour of the rabbits and the interpretation that the observer-rabbit gives of it, ultimately the only one communicated to us, since any break or choice in the continuity of this behaviour, a continuity multiplied by the number of hutches observed, is imposed on us. While the observer-rabbit is himself observed with a total objectivity, for example that of a camera which restricts itself to the observer's hutch, we are obliged to acknowledge that all the other hutches and all the rabbits in them are the sum of a multiple distortion produced from the hutch and by the rabbit which is objectively, or directly, presented.

So in *Rear Window* the other side of the courtyard must be regarded as a multiple projection of James Stewart's amorous fixation.

The constitutive elements of this multiple projection are in fact a range of possible emotional relationships between two people of the opposite sex, from the absence of an emotional relationship, via the respective solitude of two people who are close neighbours, to a hate which ultimately turns to murder, by way of the sexual hunger of the first few days of love.

Once this is posited, another, essential element should be added: what might be called the position of the author, which, combined with the artistic factors imposed by the very nature of the enterprise, is developed through the characters directly presented and openly avowed by the strength of the evidence and the testimony of three biblical quotations, as Christian.

With these premises duly established, I leave to the reader the conclusion of that syllogism which definitively fixes the moral climate of the work, to pass on to what would properly be called its meaning.

The window which overlooks the courtyard consists of three sections, as stressed in the credit sequence. This trinity demands scrutiny. The work is in fact composed of three elements, three themes one could say, which are synchronic and in the end unified.

The first is a romantic plot, which by turns opposes and reunites James Stewart and Grace Kelly. Both are in search of an area of mutual understanding, for though each is in love with the other, their respective egos, only minimally divergent, constitute an obstacle.

The second theme is on the plane of the thriller. It is located on the other side of the courtyard, and consequently is of a rather complex, semi-obsessional character. Moreover it is very skilfully combined with a theme of indiscretion which runs through the whole work and confers on it a part of its unity. What is more, this thriller element presents all the stock characters of Hitchcock's earlier works, taken to their most extreme limits, since in the end one no longer knows whether the crime may not have been made a *reality* simply by Stewart's *willing* it.

The last theme reaches a complexity that cannot be defined in a single word: it is presented as a kind of realist painting of the courtyard, although 'realist' is a term that in the circumstances is a particularly bad choice, since the painting depicts beings which are, *a priori*, mental entities and projections. The aim is to illuminate, validate and affirm the fundamental conception of the work, its postulate: the egocentric structure of the world as it exists, a structure which the interlinking of themes seeks to represent faithfully. Thus the individual is the split atom, the couple is the molecule, the building is the body composed of x number of molecules, and itself split from the rest of the world. The two external characters have the double role of intelligent confidants, one totally lucid, the other totally mechanized, and of witnesses themselves incriminated. Thus generalizing the exposé.

Risking a musical comparison to illuminate the relationship between the themes, one might say that all three are composed with the same notes, but elaborated in a different order, and in different tonalities, each vying with the other and functioning in counterpoint. What is more, there is nothing presumptuous in such a comparison, since, within the rhythm of the work, it would be easy to determine four different constituent forms definable in musical jargon.

As one would expect in a work as structured as this one, there is in *Rear Window* a moment which crystallizes the themes into a single lesson, an enormous, perfect harmony: the death of the little dog. This sequence, the only one treated peripherally to the position of the narrator as articulated above (the only one where the camera goes into the courtyard without the presence of the hero), though grounded in an incident that in itself is relatively undramatic, is of a tragic and overwhelming intensity. I can well understand how such vehemence and such gravity could seem rather inappropriate in the circumstances; a dog is only a dog and the death of a dog would seem an event whose tragic import bears no relation to the words spoken by the animal's owner. And these words themselves – 'You don't know the meaning of the word "neighbour" ' – which encapsulate the film's moral significance, seem all too clumsy and too naive to justify such a solemn style. But the displacement itself is destroyed, for the tone leaves no room for doubt and gives things and feelings their real intensity and their invective: in reality this is the massacre of an innocent, and a mother who bemoans her child.[2]

From then on the implications of this scene become vertiginous: responsibilities press upon one another at every imaginable level, to condemn a monstrously egocentric world, whose every element on every scale is immured in an ungodly solitude.

On the dramatic level, the scene presents the dual interest of a thriller plot development, aggravating suspicion, and an illustration of a theme dear to its author – the materialization of a criminal act that is indirectly willed (in this particular case, this death *confirms* Stewart's *hopes*).

From this point of view the confrontation scene between the murderer and the 'voyeur' is extremely interesting. The communication sought by the former – 'What do you want from me?' – whether blackmail or confession, involves the latter, who refuses from a recognition of its baseness, and in some way authenticates his responsibility. Stewart's refusal in this way illuminates the profound reason for the loneliness of the world, which is established as the absence of communication between human beings, in a word, the absence of love.

Other works of Hitchcock, like *Rebecca*, *Under Capricorn* or *Notorious*, have demonstrated the corollary of the problem: to know what the power of love can be. What is more, this aspect is not absent from *Rear Window*, where the embodiment of the Grace Kelly character draws her precious ambiguity from the opposition between her 'possible' and her 'being'. The possible is in fact the perceptible irradiation of her beauty and her charm, powerful enough to transform the oppressive and lonely atmosphere of the invalid's room into a flower garden with, in an unforgettable shot, James Stewart's head in repose. Simultaneously, with her appearance on the scene comes the inexpressible poetry which is the love of two human beings: more than justified by the knowing coquetry of the author in the work's construction, this poetry brings into the stifling atmosphere of *Rear Window*, which is the atmosphere of the sewers themselves, a fleeting vision of our lost earthly paradise.[3]

Since I don't want to go through the evidence yet again, I shall just leave it up to the spectator to appreciate the technical perfection of this film and the extraordinary quality of its colour.

Rear Window affords me the satisfaction of greeting the piteous blindness of the sceptics with a gentle and compassionate hilarity.

Translated by Liz Heron

Notes

1 That *Cahiers du Cinéma* directs itself with regularity to the Hitchcock 'case' is no secret, nor are the sarcasms of our colleagues on the subject. From Georges Sadoul to Denis Marion, from Jean Quéval to Georges Charensol, we have been spared no ironies. They've tried to pick quarrels on the shakiest of grounds – even to the point of trying to make believe that on one occasion I translated 'larger than life' into French as *metaphysique* (metaphysical), when anyone who knows me knows I could not possibly have done anything of the kind (Author's note.)

2 In addition the couple with the dog represent the sterile marriage, in Stewart's mind; which explains why it is a dog and not a child. Ever since *Sabotage*, Hitchcock is very wary of children's deaths, which a person of average sensitivity has some difficulty in tolerating. (Author's note.)

3 The final sequence of *Rear Window* is characteristic of the cosmetic transformation of a scene into its opposite, at which Hitchcock is a past-master. Order is re-established, and two amusing notations turn into a 'happy ending'; in reality what is involved is purely and simply a terrible observation – people and things have stayed blindly the same. (Author's note.)

19 | Jacques Rivette: 'The Hand'

('La Main', *Cahiers du Cinéma* 76, November 1957; on *Beyond a Reasonable Doubt*)

The first point that strikes the unsuspecting spectator, a few minutes into the film, is the diagrammatic, or rather expository aspect instantly assumed by the unfolding of the images: as though what we were watching were less the *mise en scène* of a script than simply the reading of this script, presented to us just as it is, without embellishment. Without personal comment of any kind on the part of the storyteller either. So one might be tempted to talk about a purely objective *mise en scène*, if such a thing were *possible*: more prudent, therefore, to suppose this to be some stratagem, and wait and see what happens.

The second point at first seems to confirm this impression: this is the proliferation of denials underlying the very conception of the film, and possibly constituting it. The denial, ostentatiously, of reasonableness,[1] both in the elaboration of the plot as well as in that other, more factitious reasonableness in setting up situations, in preparation, in atmosphere, which usually enables scriptwriters the world over to put across plot points ten times more capricious than the ones here without any difficulty at all. No concession is made here to the everyday, to detail: no remarks about the weather, the cut of a dress, the graciousness of a gesture; if one does become aware of a brand of make-up, it is for purposes of plot. We are plunged into a world of necessity, all the more apparent in that it coexists so harmoniously with the arbitrariness of the premises; Lang, as is well known, always seeks the truth beyond the reasonable, and here seeks it from the threshold of the unreasonable. Another denial, on a par with the first, is of the picturesque: connoisseurs will find none of those amusingly sketched silhouettes, the sparkling repartee, or the brilliant touches due more to surprise than to invention, which are currently making the reputations, after so many others, of film-makers like Lumet or Kubrick. All these denials, moreover, are conducted with a sort of disdain which some have been tempted to see as the film-maker's contempt for the undertaking; why not, rather, for this kind of spectator?

140

Then, as the film continues on its way, these first impressions find their justification. The expository tone proves to be the right one, since all the data for a problem – two problems, actually – are being propounded to us: the first derives from the script, and being quite clear, need not be dwelt on for the moment; the other, more subterranean, might reasonably be formulated as follows: given certain conditions of temperature and pressure (here of a transcendental order of experience), can anything human subsist in such an atmosphere? Or, more unassumingly, what part of life, even inhuman, can subsist in a quasi-abstract universe which is nevertheless within the range of possible universes? In other words, a science fiction problem. (For anyone doubting this assumption, I would suggest a comparison between this film and *Woman in the Moon*, where the plot served Lang primarily as a pretext for his first attempt at a *totally closed* world.)

At this point the *coup de théâtre* intervenes: five minutes before the dénouement, the terms of the problem are suddenly reversed, much to the dismay of Cartesian spirits, who scarcely acknowledge the technique of dialectical inversion. Although the solutions may also seem to be modified, however, it only seems so. *The proportions remain unchanged*, and, all the conditions thus being fulfilled, poetry makes its entry. Q.E.D.

The word 'poetry' may astonish here, doubtless being hardly the term one would have expected. I shall let it stand provisionally, however, since I know no other that better expresses this sudden fusion into a single vibration of all the elements hitherto kept separate by the abstract and discursive purpose. So let us proceed to the most immediate consequences.

One of these I have already alluded to: the reactions of the audience. A film like this is obviously the absolute antithesis of the idea of 'an entertaining evening', and by comparison *Un Condamné à mort s'est échappé* or *The Wrong Man* are jolly Saturday nights out. Here one breathes, if I may venture to say so, the rarefied air of the summits, but at risk of asphyxiation; one should have expected no less from the ultimate in overstepping bounds by one of the most intransigent spirits of today, whose recent films had already prepared us for this *coup d'état* of absolute understanding.

Another objection I take more to heart: that this film is purely negative, and so effective in its destructive aspects that it ends ultimately by destroying itself. This is not unreasonable. In talking just now of denials, I was too tentative: 'destruction' is in fact the word I should have used. Destruction of the scene: since no scene is treated for its own sake, all that subsists is a series of pure moments, of which all that is retained is the mediatory aspect; anything that might determine or actualize them more concretely is not abstracted or suppressed – Lang is not Bresson – but devalued and reduced to the condition of pure spatio-temporal reference, devoid of embodiment. Destruction, even, of the characters: each of them here is really no more than what he says and what he does. Who *are* Dana

Andrews, Joan Fontaine, her father? Questions like this no longer have any meaning, for the characters have lost all individual quality, are no more than human *concepts*. But in consequence they are all the more human for being the less individual. Here we find the first answer: what remains of humanity? There is now only pure humanity, whereas Fellini's exhibitionists instantly reduce it by compromising it with their lies and buffoonery (lies obligatory when one attempts to *reconstitute* some extraordinary situation, buffoonery all the more offensive in that it purports to be 'realistic' and not simply pulling faces). Anyone who fails to be more moved by this film than by such appeals for sympathy knows nothing, not only of cinema but of man.

Strange, this destroyer, leading us to this conclusion while obliging us to resume the objection in reverse: if this film is negative, it can only be so in the mode of *the pure negative*, which is of course also the Hegelian definition of intelligence.[2]

It is difficult to find a precise formula to define the personality of Fritz Lang (best forgotten are the notions someone like Clouzot might have): an 'expressionist' film-maker, meticulous about décor and lighting? Rather too summary. Supreme architect? This seems less and less true. Brilliant director of actors? Of course, but what else? What I propose is this: Lang is the *cinéaste* of the concept, which suggests that one cannot talk of abstraction or stylization in connection with him without falling into error, but of necessity (necessity which must be able to contradict itself without losing its reality); moreover it is not an exterior necessity – the film-maker's, for instance – but derived from the real movement of the concept. It is up to the spectator to assume responsibility not only for the thoughts and 'motives' of the characters, but for this movement from the Interior, grasping the phenomenon solely on its appearances; it is up to him to know how to transform its contradictory moments into the concept. What, then, is this film really? Fable, parable, equation, blueprint? None of these things, but simply the description of an *experiment*.

I realize I have not yet mentioned the subject of this experiment; it isn't without interest, either. The starting point is merely a new, actually quite subtle variation on the usual indictment of the death penalty: a series of damning circumstances may send an innocent man to the electric chair; furthermore, though the innocent is finally found really to be guilty, it is only by his own confession just at the point where his innocence had in fact been recognized; hence, vanity of human justice, judge not, and so forth. But this soon begins to seem too facile: the dénouement resists such easy reduction, and immediately leads in to a second movement: there can be no 'wrong man'; all men are guilty *a priori*; and the one who has just been mistakenly reprieved cannot prevent himself from immediately incriminating himself. This same movement takes us into a pitiless world where everything denies grace, where sin and penalty are irremediably bound together, and where the only possible attitude of the creator must be one of *absolute contempt*. But an attitude like this is difficult to sustain:

142

whereas magnanimity leaves itself open to the inevitable loss of its illusions, to disappointment and bitterness, contempt can encounter only pleasant surprises and realize eventually, not that man is not contemptible (he remains so), but that he perhaps isn't quite so much so as might have been supposed.

So all this obliges us to pass this second stage as well, and finally attempt to reach, *beyond*, that of truth. But of what order can this be?

I think I see a solution: which is that it may be pointless to attempt to contrast this latest film of Fritz Lang's with earlier ones like *Fury* or *You Only Live Once*. What in fact do we see in each case? In the earlier films, innocence with all the appearances of guilt; here, guilt with all the appearances of innocence. Can anyone fail to see that they're about the same thing, or at least about the same question? Beyond appearances, what are guilt and innocence? Is one ever in fact innocent or guilty? If, in the absolute, there is an answer, it can probably only be negative; to each, then, to create for himself his own truth, however unreasonable it may be. In the final shot, the hero finally *conceives himself* innocent or guilty. Rightly or wrongly, what matter to him?

Remembering the last lines of *Les Voix du silence* [Malraux], 'Humanism does not mean saying: what I have done, etc. . . .', let us salute that scarcely wrinkled hand in the penultimate shot, ineluctably at rest *near* to pardon, and which does not cause even a tremor in this most secret form of the power and the glory of being man.

Translated by Tom Milne

Notes

1 'Reasonableness': the French title of *Beyond a Reasonable Doubt* is *Invraisemblable vérité*, i.e. 'implausible truth', or 'improbable truth', though in further meanings *le vraisemblable* also translates as 'verisimilitude'. Here the translator has rendered *vraisemblable* as 'reasonable' to conform with Rivette's play of words on the French title.

2 I know the objection that will undoubtedly be raised: that what we are concerned with here is merely a classic device of the detective novel, particularly the second-rate variety characterized by a sudden dramatic revelation in which the basic premises are turned upside down or altered. But the fact that we find this notion of the *coup de théâtre* reappearing in the scripts of *all* recent important films may mean that what seemed at first to be in the order of arbitrary dramatics is in fact necessity, and that all these films, despite their diversity of theme, no doubt assume precisely the same inner process which Lang makes his immediate subject. Just as the pact which binds Von Stratten to Arkadin [in *Mr Arkadin*, British title: *Confidential Report*] takes on its full reality only when it proves to be negated in its original form, or Irene's fear of blackmail [in Rossellini's *La Paura*, or *Fear*] only when we know it to be devised by her husband, so the necessity of the dialectical movement alone renders credible the resurrection in *Ordet*, the surrender of *Le Carrosse d'or*, the conversion in *Stromboli*, Rossellini, Renoir and Dreyer having openly disdained any justification outside this ultimate reversal. On the other hand, it is clearly the absence of this movement that is the most

serious deficiency in the scripts of films like *Oeil pour œil* [Cayatte, 1957] or *Les Espions* [Clouzot, 1957]; and that the sense of dissatisfaction left by films in other respects as accomplished as *Un Condamné à mort s'est échappé* or *The Wrong Man* probably has no other cause. Not that a movement like this, whose process comprises the element of contradiction, is foreign to Hitchcock or Bresson (one need only think, for instance, of *Suspicion* or *Les Dames du Bois de Boulogne*), nor totally absent from their most recent films, though it is there rather by implication and never dependent on the rigour of the concept: there is an element of wager in Fontaine's escape, but more particularly the logical consequence of his persistence; its success never seems anything other than the parity achieved by the proof of a theorem (a mistake never made by the greatest *cinéaste* of human endeavour: cf. the endings of *Scarface*, *To Have and Have Not*, *Red River*, etc.). Or again, one simply has to compare the miracle in *The Wrong Man* with the one in *Viaggio in Italia* to see the clash between two diametrically antithetical ideas, not only of Grace (in the former film, a reward for zeal in prayer; in the latter, pure deliverance lighting, within the very moment of despair, upon raw faith that is totally unaware of itself), but also of freedom, and that this preoccupation with necessity – or with logic, to use one of Rossellini's favourite terms – is carried to such lengths by these film-makers only the better to affirm the freedom of the characters and, quite simply, to make it possible: a freedom quite imposs-ible, on the other hand, in the arbitrary worlds of Cayatte or Clouzot, in which only puppets can exist. What I say of recent film-makers is also true, it seems to me, for the whole of cinema, starting with the work of F. W. Murnau; and *Sunrise* remains a perfect example of rigorous dialectical construction. In this, however, I make no claim to breaking new ground (cf., among others, Alexandre Astruc's article 'Cinéma et dialectique'). (Author's note.)

Viaggio in Italia and *The Wrong Man* are key films for *Cahiers* in this period: on *Viaggio*, as well as Rivette's 'Letter on Rossellini' and Rohmer's 'The Land of Miracles', both in this volume (Chs 26 and 27 respectively), see André Bazin, 'In Defence of Rossellini', originally published in *Cinema Nuovo*, August 1955, translated in Bazin, *What is Cinema? Vol. 2*; on *The Wrong Man*, see Godard, 'Le Cinéma et son double', *Cahiers* 72, June 1957, translated in *Godard on Godard*, Truffaut in *Films in My Life*, and Rohmer and Chabrol in *Hitchcock*.

Rivette's point about the 'classic device of the detective novel' is taken up by Tzvetan Todorov in *The Poetics of Prose*, Ithaca, NY, Cornell University Press, 1977; in his 'An Introduction to Verisimilitude', Todorov mentions *Beyond a Reasonable Doubt* while discussing the tension between revelation, or truth, and verisimilitude.

20 | Luc Moullet: 'Sam Fuller: In Marlowe's Footsteps'

('Sam Fuller – sur les brisées de Marlowe', *Cahiers du Cinéma* 93, March 1959)

Young American film directors have nothing at all to say, and Sam Fuller even less than the others. There is something he wants to do, and he does it naturally and effortlessly. That is not a shallow compliment: we have a strong aversion to would-be philosophers who get into making films in spite of what film is, and who just repeat in cinema the discoveries of the other arts, people who want to express interesting subjects with a certain artistic style. If you have something to say, say it, write it, preach it if you like, but don't come bothering us with it.

Such an *a priori* judgment may seem surprising in an article on a director who admits to having very high ambitions, and who is the complete *auteur* of almost all his films. But it is precisely those who classify him among the intelligent screenwriters who do not like *The Steel Helmet* or reject *Run of the Arrow* on his behalf or, just as possibly, defend it for quite gratuitous reasons.

Machiavelli and the cuckoo-clock

On coherence. Of fourteen films, Fuller, a former journalist, devotes one to journalism; a former crime reporter, he devotes four to melodramatic thrillers; a former soldier, five to war. His four Westerns are related to the war films, since the perpetual struggle against the elements in the course of which man recognizes his dignity, which is the definition of pioneer life in the last century, is extended into our time only in the life of the soldier: that is why 'civilian life doesn't interest me' (*Fixed Bayonets*).

In *The Dark Page*,[1] a slight crime story, cobbled together at top speed, an ambitious journalist, who has made the grade, accidentally kills his former mistress; as an act of bravado, as a game, and through professional necessity, he assigns his best reporter to the case and, as a result, he is led to commit murder after murder to avoid being found out. The problem: the portrayal – and thus the calling into question – of fascist behaviour,

145

as in *Touch of Evil*. But there, Quinlan and Vargas go hand in fist: the aesthetic dimension of the former – for fascism is beautiful – and the moral dimension of the latter – he alone has reason on his side – complement each other. Welles repudiates Quinlan, but he is Quinlan: a classic contradiction which can be traced back to the end of the Middle Ages, in the Italian Renaissance and the Elizabethan drama, and which is admirably well defined in the famous parable of the cuckoo-clock in *The Third Man*. With Fuller, it's different: abandoning the realm of the absolute, he presents us with a compromise between ethics and violence, each necessary to contain the excesses of the other. The behaviour of Adam Jones, the captain in *Hell and High Water*, the profession of soldier, of detective, even of film director, all reflect this compromise. The intrepid soldiers of *The Steel Helmet* derive the same kind of satisfaction from killing as the gangsters in *Pickup on South Street*. Only a certain initiation into the domain of relativity can provide us with a glimpse of higher realms. Rotters become saints. No one can recognize himself in them. It is for the love of a woman that the treacherous Bob Ford, the most shameful character in the whole of the Wild West saga, kills Jesse James. It is for the love of a woman that James Reavis, who has become the Baron of Arizona thanks to a monstrous conspiracy that has lasted for twenty years, confesses everything at the very moment when he has nothing more to fear, and sends himself off to prison for seven years. It is the cowardly, anti-militarist Denno who becomes the war hero (*Fixed Bayonets*). It is Skip, a pickpocket, who, thanks to a woman's love, snatches back the vital documents that Communist spies have just intercepted, and who by this act rehabilitates himself (*Pickup on South Street*). Charity Hackett, the gangsterish chief editor at Park Row, is finally brought to submission by the determination of her Democrat opponent, Phineas Mitchell, a man she has tried to bring down by every possible means; she saves him from ultimate ruin and marries him. Here, as in *Fixed Bayonets*, we find traces of the Wellesian theme of the double which becomes in *House of Bamboo* the basic framework: the identity of the investigator who is in league with the gangsters is only revealed to us in the middle of the film, and nothing before that allows us to distinguish him from any of the others. And it is the gang leader who stretches out a helping hand, who saves his life. 'Fuller, so decisive, so virile, is, paradoxically, a master of ambiguity,' says Domarchi. Here, the study of two characters gives a deeper meaning to a juxtaposition which in Welles merely reflects the strategies of a bad conscience. Quinlan and Vargas can't be compared since they are complementary; they are, ultimately, the constituent parts of a single person, the *auteur*. Here, on the other hand, Sandy and Eddie *can* be compared. That doesn't prevent Welles from being immeasurably greater than Fuller – quite the contrary. It would be a pretty safe bet, moreover, that if Welles does ever go to see *Run of the Arrow*, he will have got up and left out of exasperation before the credits come up.

146

Fuller above politics

For non-conformity, *Run of the Arrow* beats all records: immediately after the Southern defeat, the Confederate O'Meara goes off to fight with the Sioux against Northern oppression. Half convinced by Captain Clark, the Yankee liberal who shows him the futility of his hatred, and influenced by the unfortunate example of the Yankee fascist, Lieutenant Driscoll, he returns home. Fuller himself, in the *New York Times* in July 1956, was quite explicit about the meaning of this fable which, in his view, explained the difficulties faced by present-day American governments: an administration's political adversaries, at whatever moment in history, seek to hasten their revenge by allying with the country's enemies. That is open to several possible interpretations, and Fuller suggests that the alliance with the Indians after the Civil War corresponds, in terms of the Southern question, to an alliance with the most violent elements in the Black Power movement. Contrary to what has been said about Fuller, he is not in any way Manichean, even less than Brooks, since there are two types of Northerner, two types of Southerner, plus four types of Indian. *Humanité Dimanche* may well be surprised by such confusion: 'The Southerners are anti-racist, the Northerners racist, the Indians pro-American and some of the Americans pro-Indian.' When the renegades are led to contradict themselves, i.e. by having to massacre their fellow citizens, they do an about-turn: 'The end of this story can only be written by you', or, if you prefer, since the date is July 1956, the life of the United States depends on the voting paper you drop into the ballot box next November. Apparently, then, what we have here is a nationalist, reactionary, Nixonian film. Could Fuller really be the fascist, the right-wing extremist who was denounced not so long ago in the Communist press? I don't think so. He has too much the gift of ambiguity to be able to align himself exclusively with one party. Fascism is the subject of his film, but Fuller doesn't set himself up as a judge. It is purely an inward fascism he is concerned with rather than with any political consequences. That is why Meeker's and Steiger's roles are more powerfully drawn than Michael Pate's in *Something of Value*: Brooks is far too prudent to feel directly involved, whereas Fuller is in his element; he speaks from experience. And on fascism, only the point of view of someone who has been tempted is of any interest.

It is a fascism of actions rather than of intentions. For Fuller does not seem to have a good head for politics. If he claims to be of the extreme right, is that not to disguise, by a more conventional appearance, a moral and aesthetic attitude which belongs to a marginal and little respected domain?

Is Fuller anti-Communist? Not exactly. Because he confuses, partly no doubt for commercial reasons, communism and gangsterism, Communism and Nazism. He invents the representatives of Moscow, about whom he knows nothing, on the basis of what he does know, through his own experience, about Nazis and gangsters. We must not forget that he only

147

talks about what he knows. When he depicts the enemy (and in *The Steel Helmet*, *Fixed Bayonets* and *Hell and High Water*, he usually tries just to avoid doing so), it is a very abstract, conventional enemy. Only the dialogue dots the i's, and it is really unfortunate that *Pickup on South Street* and *China Gate* should remain *verboten*[2] to us for such an unjustified reason.

Morality is a question of tracking shots.[3] These few characteristics derive nothing from the way they are expressed nor from the quality of that expression, which may often undercut them. It would be just as ridiculous to take such a rich film simply as a pro-Indian declaration as it would be to take Delmer Daves for a courageous anti-racist director because there is a clause in each of his contracts which stipulates that there will be love affairs between people of different races. The unsuspecting public is taken in and he always ends up on the right side of the fence.

A modern cinema

The camera glides along to the left, looking up towards a cornfield of striking golden-yellow tones, strewn with the corpses of soldiers clothed in dark and dirty uniforms, their bodies curiously twisted up; then it pulls up to frame on Meeker, asleep on his horse, in a pitiful state. Against a background of dense black smoke, Steiger stands out, just as filthy but wearing peasant clothes. He shoots Meeker, goes to search his victim, discovers food in his pockets, squats down on the body to eat what he has found; noticing there is bread too, he takes some; he lights a cigar. Meeker begins to groan; his peace disturbed, Steiger goes to sit a bit further off. Close-up of him chewing and smoking. Then the title of the film comes up, inscribed in huge red letters on his brow and chin. This must be the first time that the credits have been projected on a man's face, and on the face of a man who is in the middle of eating. The sequence, worthy of a place in an anthology of modern cinema, reveals already some of the principal virtues of our director.

1 The poetic feeling for camera movement. For many ambitious film directors, movements of the camera are dependent on dramatic composition. Never so for Fuller, in whose work they are, fortunately, totally gratuitous: it is in terms of the emotive power of the movement that the scene is organized. At the end of *The Steel Helmet*, for example, that slow tracking of the camera as, under the passionate bursts of machine-gun fire, the enemy soldiers sink to the ground in a rhythmic musical pattern. *Fixed Bayonets* is full of very long tracking shots, in which the camera describes a complete circle, and, for good measure, of close-ups as well; springing from face to face, they too are imprinted with a fascinating rhythm.

2 A humour based on ambiguity. Here it is the contrast between Meeker's agonizing body and the starved impassiveness of Steiger. Later, in an astonishing close-up, we see a Southern peasant disgorge the whole force of his hatred of the Yankees in song. Add to that a few remarks on the

US Constitution which, in present-day terms, are quite cutting. Walking Coyote confesses that, if he hasn't tried to become the chief of his tribe, it's because he can't stand politics. Indignant that there are moves to hang him, he cries: 'Oh! what have we come to! It wasn't like that in my day! Today there's no more morality. The young massacre the old, they kill, they get drunk, they rape.' It is an outburst which would be quite at home in *Les Tricheurs*[4] or in some American sociological film, and which, put into the mouth of a Sioux in 1865, makes us snigger. Every piece of dialogue is, for Fuller, a way of amusing himself by disconcerting us; he pretends to adopt all points of view, and that's what makes his humour sublime. Every love scene (the one with the eyebrows in *House of Bamboo*, the tattooing and the slap in *Hell and High Water*, which is also a splendid send-up of polyglot commercialese) is basically a very banal idea made effective by a text full of verve and originality.

We need madmen

3 A re-creation of life which has very little to do with the version that the screen imposes on us. Rather than to the civilized Brooks, it is to *L'Atalante* that we should refer. Fuller is a coarse character: everything he does is incongruous. There is a grain of madness in him. But we really need madmen, for cinema is the most realist of all the arts; and in portraying existence, sane directors have remained faithful to traditions established over centuries by literature and painting, arts which have had to set aside even the most superficial of truths on account of their own temporally and visually limited realism. Only the insane can hope one day to create a work comparable to the living model, which will even so never attain a tenth of the truth of the original. But that's the highest bid. In Fuller we see everything that other directors deliberately excise from their films: disorder, filth, the unexplainable, the stubbly chin, and a kind of fascinating ugliness in a man's face. It was a stroke of genius to choose Rod Steiger, a short, squat, oafish character, completely lacking in stature, whose squashed-down hat hides his features whenever there is the slightest high angle shot, but whose ungainly manner and bearing confer on him the force of life itself. Our director's predilection for corpulent or plump characters may already have been noticed: Gene Evans, for example, has the starring role in four of his films. And, applying to these characters Truffaut's celebrated *auteur* theory,[5] his esteem diminishes with the number of kilos. Those slim heroes with angular profiles, John Ireland, Vincent Price, Richard Basehart, Richard Kiley, Richard Widmark, haven't the necessary weight not to be tempted into despicable acts. Man belongs to the order of the earth, and he must resemble it, in all the harshness of its beauty.

Fuller is a primitive, but an intelligent primitive, which is what gives his work such unusual resonances; the spectacle of the physical world, the spectacle of the earth, is his best source of inspiration, and if he is attached to human beings, it is only to the extent that they are themselves attached to the earth. That's why woman is often not mentioned (except in *Park Row*, *Pickup on South Street* and *Forty Guns*, where she behaves like Fullerian men; except in *Hell and High Water*, *China Gate* and again *Forty Guns*, where Fuller suggests with an insane talent the contrast between the angel and the beast, thus removing all ambivalence). That is why he is especially interested in men's physique – he is inspired a hundred times by the naked bodies of the Indians, just as he was by the naked bodies of the sailors in *Hell and High Water*; coming out of *Run of the Arrow*, one has the impression of never having seen real Indians before in a Western – and the part of the body that interests him more particularly still is the one that is constantly in contact with the ground: Fuller has a thing about feet, no doubt about that. In the foreground, at the encounter with Walking Coyote, the camera scrapes the earth, re-frames on feet, and only accidentally pulls up towards faces. And this style even becomes the foundation of the symbolic dimension of the work: the Run of the Arrow, the pivot and the title of the film, is also the run of a man in moccasins, pursuing a man without shoes (who is moreover a foot soldier, and who after meeting a certain Walking Coyote marries a certain Yellow Moccasin). The best man is the one with the strongest feet. Bloody feet, tired feet, heavy efficient feet, light feet, booted feet, with what amazing virtuosity Fuller, who had had all the time he could wish to study the question during his visit to Japan, delineates the different styles of the runners. Who better than he could film the Olympic Games in Rome next year? Buttocks have star billing too, since thirty seconds are devoted to a meticulous study of the problem of the comfort of the horseman on his saddle.

A Vigo-esque disorder

A tellurian director, a poet of the tellurial, he takes a passionate interest in the instinctive. He likes to show suffering in a way that is even more sadistic than De Mille: amputations (even the deliberate cutting off of a hand in *Hell and High Water*), the painful extraction of bullets from one's own body (*Fixed Bayonets*) or from someone else's body (*Run of the Arrow*) with great loss of blood. A defenceless kid is mown down on a corner of Park Row. Love itself does not neglect the joys of sadism (*Pickup on South Street*). After being knocked down by repeated blows of a hammer, the Jap in *Hell and High Water* complains that he hasn't been hit hard enough – as if it were just a sham. A festival of cruelties and orgies, *Run of the Arrow* ends with that splendid shot in which Meeker, who is being skinned alive, receives the *coup de grâce* in the form of a bullet right in the middle of his perspiring, bloody brow.

I have referred to Vigo, and the parallel is even more evident in *Pickup*, *Steel Helmet* and especially *Fixed Bayonets*: with a carefully worked out script and in a carefully planned shot, Fuller composes actions which have no reference to any prefabricated dramaturgy. All kinds of odd things are going on, and it is really difficult to make anything of it at all. The relationships of the soldiers between themselves, moral relationships and relationships within the frame, when all the faces are turned towards a different subject, create a whole labyrinth of meanings. And you can apply to Fuller what Rivette says about Vigo: 'He suggests an incessant improvisation of the universe, a perpetual and calm and self-assured creation of the world.'

Anti-Tati

On the formal level, we discover, for the first time in fact, that 'Fabrice at Waterloo'[6] quality to which attention has so often and so indulgently been drawn in articles on minor filmlets. The bizarre side of Fuller explains his liking for exotic settings – six of his films are situated in the Far East – mysterious pagodas (*The Steel Helmet*), statues, houses and furniture in Japanese style (*House of Bamboo*), which have as much relief, are as convincingly real, as the subway, the backyards of Chicago tenements and the houses on piles in *Pickup*. And above all, when it's a matter of evoking the complexity of modern machinery, Fuller becomes the greatest director in the world – for him, the artificial universe and the natural universe have the same characteristics: he can render admirably well the bristling, massive and mysterious aspect of firearms, of a munitions dump (*China Gate*), of a brand new office block (*House of Bamboo*), of the innards of a submarine, where the successive variations of background colouring heighten the realism and the originality, or an atomic plant (*Hell and High Water*). Nature also can provide a baroque decor: extraordinary misty woodland settings in *Steel Helmet* and snow-clad mountains in *Fixed Bayonets*.

An exception among the great colourists, he, like Joseph MacDonald,[7] prefers the intermediate shades, browns, blackish ochres, pale violets, off-whites, the colours of the earth, to the boldness of the rainbow, suggested however by the amusement park in *House of Bamboo* and the plastic forms of *Run of the Arrow*.

A film made with his feet

If, at every moment, *Fixed Bayonets* created a series of original relationships between the heroes, and chiselled faces with a consummate art, it is not at all the same with *Run of the Arrow*, in which we find these person to person confrontations only in occasional flashes. O'Meara and Driscoll, Crazy Wolf and O'Meara, Driscoll and Crazy Wolf, with their smiles out of the corner of their mouths, prefigure the joys of competing or, with their dirty looks, restrain their anger when a third party or a woman intervenes. The taste for battle, for violence, creates a feeling of complicity between the adversaries, for the sake of which one saves the other. This theme taken from *House of Bamboo* reappears several times here. Yet that only goes to make up a tiny part of the whole. Why?

While at Fox, Fuller was obliged to respect certain established practices with regard to the shooting script and the actual filming. He had to *work* within them, and that involved a great deal of care and effort. Having his own company, with its Shakespearian name,[8] six hundred miles from Hollywood, he was, on the other hand, as free as a bird. The screenplay, with its subtle correspondences, is extremely carefully worked out, but the film suffers – and benefits – from a constant lack of balance. Since Fuller likes to shoot a series of scenes that please him, rather than a complete entity, when he's free he neglects all the rest, all those obligatory transitions: he brushes them aside either during the scripting or during the shooting – hence the numerous gaps – or he loses interest in them – and his direction of actors becomes practically non-existent. *Fixed Bayonets* was disorder within order, a perfect formal synthesis of the Fullerian ethic of compromise. It was his masterpiece to the extent that madness can only really express itself through a surfeit of reason. Whereas *Run of the Arrow* is the triumph of the offhand, of the casual, of the lazy. Perhaps no director has ever gone so far in the art of throwing a film together (except the unfortunate Josef Shaftel in *The Naked Hills*). Whatever the extent of his negligence, one cannot but be fascinated by the spontaneity it brings with it. *Fixed Bayonets* is, or soon will be, a classic, whereas *Run of the Arrow* will remain a film for the bedside table. Fuller is an amateur; he is lazy, agreed. But his film *expresses* amateurism and laziness: and that is already a lot.

If the film didn't make a cent in America, that's because Fuller, who had complete responsibility, sent only a set of rushes to RKO, who cut it; Universal recut and Rank cut more still. Quite rightly, no one believed in the success of a film Sam Fuller had made with his feet, as Mrs Sarita Mann so nicely puts it: that's why the distribution got clogged up. But the cuts don't seem to have detracted much from the value of *Run of the Arrow*: it lacks above all what is never lacking in the production-line film, those sempiternal, improvised and ridiculous continuity shots.

Filming comes easy to him

What we find precious is that this animal Fuller trekked freely around Arizona for five long weeks – one of his longest shooting schedules! – with a budget of a million dollars – God knows what he did with it all! – and to bring back what? One hundred and fifty shots, which have become two hundred in the final print, linked together by impossible dissolves. And such shots! There is already nothing ordinary about his style (except in the clumsy classicism of his first piece): it's a good roughneck style! The medium close shot [*plan américain*], the perfect figure of classicism, is rare in his work, or mediocre. When he is interested in several people or objects, long shot; when it's one or two, close-up. Fuller is the poet of the close-up which, because of its elliptical nature, is always full of surprises (the beginning of *Steel Helmet*), and which gives an unexpected relief to faces or to blades of grass, accustomed in the commercial cinema to being treated with little reverence. But here, he makes even less effort: either there is talk – a lot of it, or there is action – a lot of that too; when someone is saying something interesting, he is after all hardly going to play around having it acted or using different angles to make the scene less theatrical. Clark tries to convince O'Meara of the error of his ways. A long speech. The reverse field? I'm still waiting for it. For at least four or five minutes, we see the pair of them sitting side by side without moving, exactly what the film school ABC[9] says should not happen.

This lack of effort is irritating, but such riches emerge from it! It is wrong to say that Fuller is inspired (since that means imagining the possibility that he might not be) when he films *actively*. Instinctive, a born director, he is someone to whom filming comes easy. It is enough for him just to be himself at every moment – which is something we could repeat in connection with a minor Ray piece like *The True Story of Jesse James*. His rough sketches take us by surprise and are more powerful, more revealing than a fine piece of construction. He can allow himself to mix styles: there is a completeness, a world ranging from the living desert with its clumps of spherical trees to O'Meara's delirium amid the smoke, from those burlesques filmed with an Eisenstein-like plasticity to the rigorous and Fordian composition of the distance shots of the attack on the fort. Traces of Fritz Lang were also apparent in *House of Bamboo*, in the geometrical organization of the hold-up scene, or of the billiard game, and similarly in *Pickup* (Moe's death). Even so, because of a kind of poetic homogeneity, it is always still Fuller, with its force of the instantaneous and of the unfinished.

Marlowe and Shakespeare

We accept more easily the scene – which, on reflection, has a symbolic value – in which the Yankee soldier, irritated by his syncopated calls on the harmonica, saves the young Indian mute from the quicksand at the cost of his own life, precisely because it isn't integrated into the film: thus intentions are continually being corrected by *mise en scène*. Fuller, who seemed so strongly attached to his fine ideas on America and the beauty of democratic life, contradicts himself in every frame: it is patently obvious that the customs of the Sioux inspire and please him infinitely more than the prospect of the peaceful life by the fireside so magnificently celebrated by Brooks and Hawks, as the numerous platitudes of the *mise en scène* show, a *mise en scène* which is here that of a critic, a politician, and a moralist.

Hence, in the last analysis, Fuller actually follows a path which is the opposite of Welles's, and one can say that there is a difference between them – which exists also in the realm of values – of the same order as the one between Marlowe and Shakespeare, with all the consequences that implies.

Although at the outset he rejects it, Welles manages, however, through the different forms of his art (which reveal him as both romantic and civilized) to produce the synthesis of his physical and moral aspirations, whereas Fuller, Faustian in principle and Promethean in fact, although conscious of the necessity of such a synthesis and actively searching for it, is sooner or later betrayed, when he is totally given over to himself and cannot then be artificially redeemed through the saving intervention of outside influences, by the very unambivalence in the depths of his personality.

Translated by Norman King

Notes

1 *The Dark Page*: British title of *Scandal Sheet*, director Phil Karlson, 1952.
2 *Pickup on South Street* was banned in France for its representation of the Communists, and *China Gate*, set during the Vietnamese war, for its representation of the French; *Verboten* (1958) had not yet been seen in France. When *Pickup* was finally released in France, in 1961, it was in a dubbed version called *Le Port de la drogue* (literally, 'Drug Port'), in which all reference to Communists and the smuggling of state secrets had been changed in the dubbing to a story of drug smuggling – a transformation the ease of which was taken to validate Moullet's point here about Fuller's 'abstract' depiction of the enemy. *Pickup on South Street* was reviewed by Moullet in *Cahiers* 121, July 1961, and *Verboten* also by Moullet in *Cahiers* 108, June 1960.
3 'Morality is a question of tracking shots': cf. Jean-Luc Godard's 'Tracking shots are a question of morality' in the discussion 'Hiroshima, notre amour', Ch. 6 in this volume.
4 *Les Tricheurs*, director Marcel Carné, 1958, generally taken by *Cahiers* as an attempt by the *cinéma de papa* to cash in on youth subjects thought proper to the incipient *nouvelle vague*.
5 Moullet's use of the word *théorie* rather than *politique* suggests that *Cahiers* themselves were perhaps not clear about the boundaries between the two; Moullet's use of 'theory' predates that of Sarris, who has often been taken as responsible for mistranslating the *politique des auteurs* into the *auteur* theory.
6 The reference is to Stendhal's *The Charterhouse of Parma*, in which the young *ingénu* Fabrice, full of enthusiasm for Napoleon, makes his own way to Waterloo to fight as a volunteer on the French side. The episode is narrated in a mock heroic manner: Fabrice spends more time looking for the action than participating in it, and when he does have to fight for his life it is with the retreating French.
7 Joseph MacDonald, 1906–68, US director of photography, graduating to cinematography in the 1940s; MacDonald had worked with Fuller on *Pickup on South Street*, 1952, and in colour on *Hell and High Water*, 1953, and *House of Bamboo*, 1955; MacDonald would also have been known to Moullet and *Cahiers* for his work with Nicholas Ray on *Bigger than Life*, 1956, and *The True Story of Jesse James*, 1957.
8 Fuller's production company was called Globe Enterprises. It produced *Run of*

the Arrow, 1956, and *Verboten*, 1958, both for RKO; *China Gate*, 1957, and *Forty Guns*, 1957, both for Twentieth Century-Fox; *The Crimson Kimono*, 1959, and *Underworld USA*, 1960, both for Columbia.

9 The French reads 'l'ABC idhécal', i.e. the rules taught by the Institut des Hautes Etudes Cinématographiques, commonly known as IDHEC: see Introduction to this volume, note 69.

IV | Genre

21 | Claude Chabrol: 'Evolution of the Thriller'

('Evolution du film policier', *Cahiers du Cinéma* 54, Christmas 1955)

1 In Memoriam

Success creates the fashion, which in turn shapes the genre. What corresponded to the vogue for the detective story between the two wars, in American cinema – with many poor imitations elsewhere – was the creation of a genre which rapidly gave way, predictably, to mediocrity and slovenly formulae. To begin with it generated some films that were interesting and well-made, if less than admirable: adaptations of the best-selling novels of S. S. Van Dine or Earl Derr Biggers, like the famous *Canary Murder Case*, which is unforgettable, though for reasons not directly connected with those I have mentioned (namely Louise Brooks). The tremendous success of these films prompted shrewd businessmen to manufacture an infinite number of cheap by-products, usually rehashed by some Tom, Dick or Harry, with Charlie Chan, Perry Mason, Philo Vance or Ellery Queen turning up regularly in some new adventure, and generally bearing an extraordinary resemblance to one another (in the shape of Warner Oland, Warren Williams or any other highly specialized actor), all with the purpose, I suppose, of giving their none too demanding audiences the impression that they were reading a regular Sunday comic-book.

An experience similar in every respect was the lot of those gangster films that emerged out of the very complex social, economic and political conjunctions of the 1930s. Some – the early ones – were masterpieces, based on the exploits of the famous Italian bootleggers of the Prohibition era, and were what is called 'topical'. But this topicality did not last and with it departed a fine source of inspiration. From then on, the by-products without such drawbacks as topicality had the lion's share.

Strange to say, despite a downhill course that was all too obvious even in 1935, there was virtually no merging of the two genres before 1939. The attempts at adapting the novels of Dashiell Hammett only succeeded in reducing the hero of *The Thin Man* to the proportions of a series detective who persisted, tireder, sadder, and more monotonous, until around the end of the war. Thus the state of the thriller genre – of all the thriller genres – was far from brilliant in 1940. The mystery story either visibly stood still or became impossible to transfer to the screen. Prohibition had long since been forgiven by whisky lovers, and the crime syndicate had not yet reached the public eye. The films were turning into baleful police stories, definitively condemned to tiny budgets and even smaller talents.

It was then that an unexpected rediscovery of Dashiell Hammett, the appearance of the first Chandlers and a favourable climate, suddenly gave the *tough guy* genre its aristocratic credentials,[1] and opened the doors of the studios to it once and for all. The trend in these films, from Raoul Walsh's *High Sierra* and Huston's *Maltese Falcon* onwards, continued to grow until 1948. The notion of the series underwent important modifications: if it was still a matter of exploiting a lucrative vein according to pre-established recipes, nevertheless each work was distinguishable from the others, in the best cases, by its tone or style. And if the same character appeared in several films one had to put it down to chance, or locate it in identical literary sources: no idiocy made it obligatory to identify the Marlowe of *Murder My Sweet* [UK title: *Farewell, My Lovely*] with the Marlowe of *The Lady in the Lake*. Many of these films were of high quality and often exceeded one's expectations of their directors (I have in mind Dmytryk, Hathaway or Daves). There are two reasons for this: the subjects of these films were the work of talented writers, all of them specialists in the genre, like Chandler, Burnett, Jay Dratler or Leo Rosten; and the film-makers had settled for a standard *mise en scène* that worked extremely well and was rich in visual effects, perfectly suited to a genre in which refinement seemed inappropriate.

Misfortune willed that the genre in question should carry within it the seeds of its own destruction. Built as it was on the elements of shock and surprise, it could only offer even the most imaginative of scriptwriters and the most conscientious of directors a very limited number of dramatic situations which, by force of repetition, ended up no longer producing either shock or surprise. If the *film noir* thriller – and with it the novel – managed to last eight years, it was thanks to the precise combination of two elements that were at first external: suspense[2] and reportage. There, too, the dice were loaded. Suspense, in introducing a new and infinitely dangerous instrument – anticipation – could only ring the changes on a very small number of situations, and covered up the problem without resolving it. As for reportage,[3] its multiple possibilities were stifled by the very nature of the genre, which could only preserve its most superficial features and quickly let it become dull and boring. Thus locked in the prison of its own construction, the thriller could only go round in circles, like a trapped bird unable to find a way out of its cage. Robert Montgomery's gratuitous attempts at subjective camera shots in *The Lady in the Lake*, the time-disorientation in Sam Wood's *Ivy*, Robert Florey's childish and grotesque avant-gardism in his amnesiac's story,[4] all sounded the death knell. One day Ben Hecht gave it the finishing touch, producing, from a tenth-rate novel by Eleazar Lipsky, an admirable script which was a supreme example of all the features of the detective story genre combined. As if to illustrate perfectly both the strength and the weakness of such a conception, it was Henry Hathaway, a skilled technician without an ounce of personality (author of the highest expression of the genre: the first half of *Dark Corner*), who made *Kiss of Death*, swansong of a formula, end of a recipe and the bottom of a gold mine, which at once blew up in the faces of the tycoons who had made their money but were now in trouble.

2 Nobilissima Visione

And so the film thriller is no more: the novel likewise. The source has dried up; renewal is impossible. What is left but to go beyond it? Following in the footsteps of all the other genres which created the past glory of the American cinema, the thriller, now without an existence of its own, remains a wonderful pretext.

Within civilizations – Valéry was instructive about their fate – no successes, no fashions, no genres are immortal. What remain are the works, successes or failures, but a *sincere* expression of the preoccupations and ideas of their authors. In this particular case another historical panorama is now being unveiled, offering to our eyes *One Exciting Night*, *Underworld* and *Scarface*, followed by a long bleak and empty plain: well, these few films prefigure the thriller of tomorrow.

There's no question in these films of renovating a genre, either by extending its boundaries or intellectualizing it in some way. In fact there's no question of renovation at all, simply of expression, through the telling of a not too confusing tale. Aren't the best criteria of an authentic work most often its complete lack of self-consciousness and its unquestionable necessity? So there's nothing to restrict a preference for the freshness and intelligence of that almost impenetrable imbroglio, *Out of the Past* [UK title: *Build My Gallows High*], directed by Jacques Tourneur and scripted clumsily, and utterly sincerely, by Geoffrey Homes,[5] rather than for *Dark Passage*, with its skilful construction, its judicious use of the camera in its first half, and its amusing surreal ending. But what makes the first of the two films more sincere than the other, you may ask. The very fact of its clumsiness! A film's total assimilation within a genre often means nothing more than its complete submission to it; to make a thriller, the essential and only prerequisite is that it be conceived as such and, by corollary, that it be constituted exclusively of the elements of the thriller. It is the genre that reigns over inspiration, which it holds back and locks into strict rules. Therefore it clearly takes exceptional talent to remain oneself in such a strange enterprise (that's the miracle of *The Big Sleep*), or else it takes inspiration, aspirations, and a vision of the world which are naturally in accordance with the laws of the genre (*Laura* is yet another miracle; and in a certain sense Lang and Hitchcock too).

There is no doubt that the superiority of *The Big Sleep* derives in part from the quite functional perfection achieved by director and scriptwriters; the plot of the film is a model of the thriller equation, with three unknowns (the blackmailer, the murderer, the avenger), so simple and so subtle that at first all is beyond comprehension; in fact, on a *second* viewing there is nothing easier than the unravelling of this film. The only difference between the viewer and the Marlowe-Bogart character is that the latter works it all out and understands the first time round. And so it seems this film only resembles the others in so far as it towers above them; but deep roots and firm connections link it to the body of Hawks's work. It is not just accidental that here the private eye is more intelligent and sharper than we are, and more directly than anywhere else confronted with the brutal strength of his adversaries. Beyond the shadow of a doubt, *The Big Sleep* is closer to *Scarface*, *The Thing* and even *Monkey Business* than to Robert Montgomery's *The Lady in the Lake*. It is no less true that here the function subordinates the creation, surpassed by it of course, but *definitively*, since the Hawksian treatment of the *tough guy* theme cannot be repeated without in its turn creating a dull and sterile cliché.

Things take a rather different shape in Otto Preminger's *Laura*. In this film the pure thriller element is entirely subordinate to a predetermined narrative style which in some way transmutes it. The film's inspiration, a Vera Caspary novel, is a classic detective story, or rather neo-classic – in other words based on a less stereotyped kind of realism. At any rate it is a flawless testimony to the inadequacies of a thoroughly worn-out formula. It is at the level of the characters that the displacement operates: the authors (Preminger and Jay Dratler) push them to their inevitable paroxysm, thus creating characters who are intrinsically fascinating, for whom the course they follow becomes *the only possible one*. Everything happens as if the characters had been created before the plot (it usually happens the other way round, of course), as if they themselves were constructing the plot, transposing it on to a level to which it never aspired. To accentuate this impression, Preminger thought up a new narrative technique (which moreover gave his film great historical importance): long sequences shot from a crane, following the key characters in each scene in their every move, so that these characters, *immutably* fixed in the frame (usually in close-up or in two-shot), see the world around them evolving and changing in accordance with their actions. Here was the proof that a thriller can also be beautiful and profound, that it is a question of style and conviction. Vera Caspary had written a detective story. Preminger filmed a story of characters who meant something to him. None the less *Laura* is still far from exemplary, since its success postulates a pre-existing detective story plot that fits in with the film-maker's purpose, or, more exactly, demands of the film-maker a vision that can be integrated into a given thriller theme. There again it is the director who takes the initiative and adapts to the genre. And the result, which one cannot deny is admirable, is worth infinitely more than the principle, which is no more than a half-measure.

At the same time one can easily understand that these films have constituted decisive stages in the peaceful struggle for the liberation of the genre and the shattering of its formulae; where they have not provided examples they have worked as stimulants. Thus one could see an ensemble of aggressive works, some of them failures, but often extraordinary, in any case personal and *sincere*, whose thriller theme was only a pretext or a means, but never an end in itself. Some random examples: Welles's *The Lady from Shanghai*, Nick Ray's *On Dangerous Ground* and *In a Lonely Place*,[6] Joseph Losey's *The Prowler*, Preminger's *Where the Sidewalk Ends* and *Whirlpool*, and a few others which have endowed the thriller theme with its real aristocratic credentials, films that are not subject to absurd conventions and arbitrary classifications. It is difficult at first to see any connection between *The Lady from Shanghai* and *In a Lonely Place*: the quality of this connection lies in the very difference between the two films, in the astonishing honesty, in relation to themselves, of Welles and Nicholas Ray. The wealth is in the prospectors, no longer in the mine.

There is clearly an objection possible here: all the films I've mentioned – and I've made a deliberate selection – are outstanding primarily because they set themselves miles apart from the genre, attached to it only by tenuous links that have nothing to do with their qualities. Isn't it then a little dishonest to see the future of the thriller only in the dilution of the detective story element within the films, since you only have to take things to their paradoxical conclusion to conceive of an ideal future in the suppression of this element altogether?

In reality what seems like a dilution is in fact nothing less than enrichment. All these *auteurs* have one thing in common: they no longer regard crime or any other thriller element as simply a dramatic situation that can lend itself to a range of more or less skilful variations, but see it in ontological (as with Ray, Losey or Dassin) or metaphysical (Welles, Lang or Hitchcock) terms.

It is really a matter of valorizing a theme, just as Proust tried to do with time, or Jouhandeau with homosexuality. In the realm of the cinema this can be done at the level of *mise en scène*, as with Preminger, or at the level of work done on the script with a certain kind of *mise en scène* (Hitchcock or Welles). It can also be done, dare I say it, independently, in the working out of the script. I shall take my example from this last category since its demonstration is easier on paper.

Let's look at Robert Wise's *Born to Kill*, a film that has received less than its fair share of attention. In this film, then, it's the script itself that is admirable and completely new; the weak spot is the *mise en scène*. Technically it is beyond reproach and in places quite powerful, but alas, dreadfully *ordinary* and typical of the genre, which was precisely what the film aimed to break away from and grind into dust. The script is a faithful adaptation – if, because of the time constraint, a little simplified – of a novel by someone called James Gunn. This young man wrote his book as an 'exercise in creative writing'. The University gave him the first page, and by the second, he had already eliminated all its superfluous elements, cleverly choosing as the framework for his story two well-exhausted themes of the dying genre: the woman who is more monstrous than the most monstrous man (*Deadlier Than the Male* is the original title[7]) and the old woman who turns detective in order to avenge a murdered friend. He literally explodes these themes before our eyes, through an absolutely extraordinary freedom of development and tone. Pushing each scene to its paroxysm of violence, comedy or the macabre, he succeeds in giving them all a dimension of the unexpected, the profound or the poetic and simultaneously justifying the themes chosen; for it is only through them that the characters can be pushed to their limits, that their purification can be brought about, and the style, tone and ideas justified. Over-prudent, Wise could not – or did not know how to – work in tune with this, and *Born to Kill* was by no means the masterpiece and the manifesto that it should have been.

Be that as it may, through the successes and the failures, evolution cannot be denied. Nobody, I think, would lament the passing of films like *After the Thin Man*, or more recent films like *Murder My Sweet*, on seeing new films like *In a Lonely Place* or *The Prowler*. For those who remain unconvinced of the rigour of my argument I have kept an ace up my sleeve. Better than pages of analysis, there is one film that can testify to the new truth. Enter the thriller of tomorrow, freed from everything and especially from itself, illuminating with its overpowering sunlights[8] the depths of the unspeakable. It has chosen to create itself out of the worst material to be found, the most deplorable, the most nauseous product of a genre in a state of putrefaction: a Mickey Spillane story. Robert Aldrich and A. I. Bezzerides[9] have taken this threadbare and lacklustre fabric and splendidly rewoven it into rich patterns of the most enigmatic arabesques. In *Kiss Me Deadly* the usual theme of the detective series of old is handled off-screen, and only taken up again in a whisper for the sake of the foolish: what it's really about is something more serious – images of Death, Fear, Love and Terror pass by in succession. Yet nothing is left out: the tough detective whose name we know so well, the diminutive[10] and worthless gangsters, the cops, the pretty girls in bathing suits, the platinum blonde murderess. Who would recognize them, and without embarrassment, these sinister friends of former times, now unmasked and cut down to size?

A shortage of themes, says the honest man! As if themes were not what *auteurs* make of them!

Translated by Liz Heron

Notes

1 The genre had, however, already been around for some time. It has its acknowledged origins in the magazine *Black Mask*, which was where Chandler, Hammett, Cornell Woolrich and Raoul Whitfield published their first stories. Moreover, *The Maltese Falcon* and *The Glass Key* had both been the subject of low-budget adaptations around 1933. (Author's note.)

2 It is very difficult to draw a clear line between what constitutes 'suspense' and the 'thriller'. In literature the first is closer to William Irish, the second to Chandler. In reality each has always relied very heavily on the other. (Author's note.)

3 'Reportage': Chabrol seems to be referring to the brief post-war wave of documentary-influenced thrillers associated primarily with producer Louis de Rochemont and Twentieth Century-Fox, e.g. *The House on 92nd Street*, 1945, *Boomerang*, 1947, *Call Northside 777*, *The Street with No Name* (both 1948).

4 *The Beast with Five Fingers*, 1946.

5 Pseudonym for screenwriter-novelist Daniel Mainwaring, whose novel *Build My Gallows High* was the basis for the *Out of the Past* script; in Britain the film was retitled *Build My Gallows High*.

6 It seems that Ray chooses the more esteemed authors of the genre. *On Dangerous Ground* is adapted from a fine Gerald Butler novel, *Mad with Much Heart*. As for *In a Lonely Place*, it is very freely adapted from an excellent work of the same name by Dorothy B. Hughes (the same writer who inspired *Ride the Pink Horse*). (Author's note.)

7 *Born to Kill* in fact boasts *three* titles: sometimes known as *Deadlier Than the Male*, its British title was *Lady of Deceit*.

8 'Sunlights': 'sunlight' is a technical term referring to light reaching a photographed object directly from the sun, whereas 'daylight' would include other natural light sources such as reflected light. By his choice of phrase here Chabrol seems to intend a reference to the atomic theme of *Kiss Me Deadly*, and the blinding light from the box which causes its final explosion.

9 Bezzerides is one of the better current Hollywood scriptwriters. He first came to the cinema with the adaptation of his own novel, *Thieves' Market*, for Jules Dassin (*Thieves' Highway*), and has since worked as scriptwriter or adapter on *Beneath the Twelve-Mile Reef*, *On Dangerous Ground* and other well-crafted films rich in original ideas. The character of Nick in *Kiss Me Deadly* is a typically Bezzeridean creation. To give you some idea of the physical presence of this fascinating personality, he is the one who plays Robert Ryan's second tempter (the one who tries to bribe him) at the beginning of *On Dangerous Ground*. (Author's note.)

10 Cf. note 8: Chabrol's original adjective is *atomique*, to incorporate both the atomic theme of the film and the colloquial meaning given here.

22 | André Bazin: 'Beauty of a Western'

('Beauté d'un western', *Cahiers du Cinéma* 55, January 1956)

In France the Western genre goes virtually unnoticed by the critics. I mean that if it does get talked about in the press, the reference is more or less incidental. For any and every Western you will unfailingly find three or four stock brands of criticism: 'Where are the Indians of yesteryear?'; or, 'Some good fight scenes and a fairly spectacular Indian attack fortunately allow you to forget the conventional puerility of the script'; or again, of course, 'But here the traditional framework is no more than a pretext that the film-maker has transcended to give us something much more than a Western . . .' It is glaringly obvious that the critics are on slippery ground with the Western, and have no firmer intellectual foothold than the sand of psychology or moral argument with which the writer might scatter his path. In fact, the true Western does defy criticism. Its qualities or its weaknesses are evident but not demonstrable. They reside less in the presence of the ingredients that make up the Western than in the subtle originality produced by their proportions. Analysis, therefore, can yield nothing but a crude enumeration which overlooks the essence that only taste can uncover. But try to make taste the subject of criticism! After all, an appreciation of its vulgarity or refinement presupposes love and familiarity. The evaluation of a Western shares something in common with wine-tasting. The wine-lover alone can discern the body and the bouquet, the alcohol content and the fruitiness, and all these nuances intermingled, where the uninitiated can only make a rough guess at whether it is a Burgundy or a Bordeaux. But enough of these gastronomic comparisons. It would perhaps be more to the point to say that the essential qualities of the Western come from its lyricism, and that as far as *mise en scène* is concerned what matters is not that it should sing loud, but that it should sing true. So you see Westerns praised usually for their spectacular effects or simply for the skill that the film-maker has employed in revitalizing a classic theme. Those are not necessarily qualities to be disregarded, but how much less decisive than the resonance of even the least significant scene, the timbre of its song.

Anthony Mann has this musical truth, to the highest degree. Every one of his Westerns that we have seen has been extraordinary, *The Naked Spur* in particular, which is clearly the best constructed in terms of the script. I must confess that I find myself a little irritated by the casual attitude towards the verisimilitude of his plots that is sometimes evidenced in Anthony Mann. *The Far Country* in particular had an avalanche story that was much too cumbersome for my taste. But it is obvious that there is no doubt in his mind whenever he is faced with a choice between his *mise en scène* and his script. Which accounts for my being so unperturbed by the shakiness of the adaptation in *The Man from Laramie*. Probably because in the first place it is not really so far-fetched, only obscure. It is not clear who the traitor is, nor even whether there is one at all. James Stewart has come to these parts to avenge his brother, who was killed by Indians armed with automatic rifles sold to them by a local badman. He comes up against the almost total authority of the landowner: it takes three days' ride to cross all his territory. But there is something that this all-powerful man is afraid of: his son's weak and wilful character – unchecked by a manager who is perhaps over-ambitious – and a man he sees in his dreams, who will come to destroy his hard-won patrimony. At the end he will understand that the usurper of his dreams is not the avenger from Laramie, but the manager whom he has adopted as his son. In the eyes of all the film's protagonists this is the character for whom ultimate retribution is reserved. And it could well be so. But for the audience, which is alone in witnessing certain scenes, and is consequently in the position of knowing more than James Stewart, it is the son, wrongfully exonerated by his untimely death, who is most guilty. However great the guilt of the manager, it is not so great as those who condemn him believe it to be. In any case he is not without extenuating circumstances. The harshness and patriarchal egoism of his employer give him an excuse. As the sorcerer's apprentice of the catastrophe, he did not will all the evil to which his first error condemned him. So here the classic role of the traitor is adhered to only superficially and in paradoxical fashion, since it functions as such for the protagonists alone. It is understood, of course, that these ambiguities owe nothing to psychology, they are born of the interweaving of circumstances and characters. Their subtlety is objective and aesthetic. It is engendered not by any particular psychological motivation attributed to the characters *a priori*, but by the intelligence of the narrative. Consequently the richness of this script is of quite a different kind from that of the 'super-Westerns'[1] of which *High Noon* is an example. Here the initial elements remain rigorously pure. At the beginning Anthony Mann has nothing more at his disposal than the traditional themes and devices.

There is one that he even continues to use when there is no longer any justification for it in the script. The old trapper, an out-of-luck gold prospector with only a mule to his name, bearded and philosophical, is a classic character to whom *The Naked Spur* had assigned an important role. Here he is again, but now reduced to an episodic and ornamental function. Above all he provides Anthony Mann with an excuse for a wonderful shot when the camera comes upon him alone in the middle of the landscape.

And so for the director of *The Naked Spur* man is barely separate from nature. Admittedly, right from the beginnings of the Western, landscape has been a constant basic element, but it is precisely in the function he gives it that we can recognize the vocation of the true *metteur en scène* of the Western. For Anthony Mann landscape is always stripped of its dramatically picturesque effects. None of those spectacular overhanging rocks in the deserts, nor those overwhelming contrasts designed to add effect to the script or the *mise en scène*. If the landscapes that Anthony Mann seems fond of are sometimes grandiose or wild, they are still on the scale of human feeling and action. Grass is mixed up with rocks, trees with desert, snow with pastures and clouds with the blue of the sky. This blending of elements and colours is like the token of the secret tenderness nature holds for man, even in the most arduous trials of its seasons.

In most Westerns, even in the best ones like Ford's, the landscape is an expressionist framework where human trajectories come to make their mark. In Anthony Mann it is an atmosphere. Air itself is not separate from earth and water. Like Cézanne, who wanted to paint it, Anthony Mann wants us to feel aerial space, not like a geometric container, a vacuum from one horizon to the other, but like the concrete quality of space. When his camera pans, it breathes.

Hence his extraordinary use of CinemaScope, whose format is never used as a new frame. Quite simply, like a fish in a bigger tank, the cowboy is more at home on the wide screen. If he moves across the whole field of vision it gives us twice as much pleasure, since we see him for twice as long.

For Anthony Mann contemplation is indeed the ultimate goal of the Western *mise en scène*.[2] Not that he lacks a taste for action and its violence, even its cruelty. On the contrary, he can make it explode with a dazzling suddenness, but we are well aware that it both shatters peace and aims to restore it,[3] just as the great contemplatives make the best men of action because they at once take the measure of its futility in its necessity. Anthony Mann watches his heroes struggle and suffer, with tenderness and sympathy. He finds their violence beautiful because it is human, but its dramatic outcome is of no interest to him. In *The Man from Laramie* there is a long fight with no winner.

Thus from this admirable film there emanates a wisdom of more depth than can be attributed to the organic elements of the genre alone. A kind of virile and tender serenity that is indisputably superior to the more explicit moral lessons of those films for which the critics reserve their favours because they are 'better than a Western'.

Translated by Liz Heron

Notes

1 Cf. my discussion of Bazin's essay 'Evolution of the Western' in the Introduction to this section.
2 This, alas, was the only appeal of *Strategic Air Command*. This article discusses Anthony Mann as an *auteur* of the Western, and for my part I do not judge the same talent in other areas. I thought *The Glenn Miller Story* was a disaster. I don't see anything abnormal in that. In this instance the self-same qualities went against the subject. But I do not want to open up a critical debate on this question that would take me outside the terms of my subject. (Author's note.)
3 There is less and less action in Anthony Mann's Westerns, and he seems to have set himself the ideal goal of making a film where the hero has nothing more to do than ride a horse for 120 minutes. As evidence I shall give you this outraged commentary by Jack Moffitt in the *Hollywood Reporter* on the last Anthony Mann Western, which has just come out in America: 'The only emotion inspired by *The Last Frontier* is one of pity for the actors. . . . Instead of looking for new faces the film industry would do better to look for new brains. . . . This is a Western with no action (except in the final minute) and a psychological drama with no motives.' (Author's note.)

23 | André Bazin: 'An Exemplary Western'

('Un western exemplaire', *Cahiers du Cinéma* 74, August–September 1957)

Here is a chance for me to apply what I have written about the *politique des auteurs*. My admiration for *Seven Men from Now* will not lead me to conclude that Budd Boetticher is the greatest director of Westerns – although I do not rule out this hypothesis – but simply that his film is perhaps the best Western I have seen since the war. It is only the memory of *The Naked Spur* and *The Searchers* that makes me reticent. It is in fact difficult to discern with certainty those qualities of this exceptional film which stem specifically from the *mise en scène*, from the scenario, and from the dazzling dialogue, without of course speaking of the anonymous virtues of the tradition itself which blossom freely when the conditions of production do not deny them. I confess to only having, unfortunately, too vague a memory of Boetticher's Westerns to define the role of chance or circumstance in the success of this one, a role which hardly exists, agreed, in the case of an Anthony Mann. Whatever the case, and even if *Seven Men from Now* is the result of an exceptional contingency, neverthe-less I regard this film as one of the exemplary successes of the contem-porary Western.

Let the reader excuse me if he is unable to verify my opinions; I know that I am speaking of a work which he will probably not see. Thus decree the distributors. *Seven Men from Now* has only been released in a subtitled version, in exclusivity, and in the low season, in a small cinema on the Champs-Elysées. Unless the film has been dubbed, you will not find in it the *quartiers*. It is a situation akin to that of another martyred masterpiece, John Ford's *The Searchers*, released only in a dubbed version, in midsummer.

This is because the Western continues to be the least understood of genres. For the producer and the distributor, the Western cannot be anything more than an infantile and popular film, destined to end up on television, or an ambitious superproduction with major stars. Only the box-office appeal of the actors or of the director then justifies the effort of publicity and distribution. Betwixt and between is a haphazard question of chance, and no one – the critic no more than the distributor, it must be said – draws any appreciable distinctions between the films produced under the Western label. This is how *Shane*, Paramount's ambitious super-production celebrating the cinematographic golden anniversary of Zukor, came to be greeted as a masterpiece while *Seven Men from Now*, much superior to Stevens's film, will pass unnoticed and will probably return to Warners' shelves whence it will only be brought out as a stopgap.

The fundamental problem with the contemporary Western undoubtedly consists in the dilemma between intelligence and naïvety. Today the Western cannot in most cases continue to be simple and traditional except by being vulgar and idiotic. A whole cut-price production system persists on such a basis. The fact is that, since Thomas Ince and William Hart, the cinema has evolved. A conventional and simplistic genre in terms of its primitive characteristics, the Western must, however, become adult and intelligent if it wishes to be ranked alongside films worthy of critical attention. Hence the appearance of the psychological Westerns, with their social or more or less philosophical theses: the Westerns of consequence. The apex of this evolution being precisely represented by *Shane*, a second-degree Western in which the mythology of the genre is consciously treated as the subject of the film. The beauty of the Western proceeding notably from its spontaneity and from its perfect unconsciousness of the mythology dissolved in it, like salt in the sea, this laborious distillation is an act against nature which destroys what it reveals.

But can one directly follow on today from the style of Thomas Ince while ignoring forty years of cinematographic evolution? Obviously not. *Stagecoach* undoubtedly illustrates the outer limit of a still classical equilibrium between primitive rules, the intelligence of the scenario and formal aestheticism. Beyond this point lies baroque formalism or the intellectualism of symbols, lies *High Noon*. Anthony Mann alone seems to have been able to rediscover the natural, thanks to his sincerity, but it is his *mise en scène* more than his scenarios which renders his Westerns the purest of the post-war period. Now, with all due respect to the *politique des auteurs*, the scenario is no less constitutive an element of the Western than skilful use of the horizon and the lyricism of the landscape. Moreover, my admiration for Anthony Mann has always been a little troubled by the weaknesses he was willing to tolerate in his adaptations.

Therefore the first wonder that strikes us in the case of *Seven Men from Now* has to do with the perfection of a scenario which achieves the *tour de force* of ceaselessly surprising us within the terms of a rigorously classical framework. No symbols, no philosophical backdrops, no psychological shading, nothing but ultra-conventional characters in totally familiar occupations – but an extraordinarily ingenious *mise en place* and above all a constant inventiveness in relation to details capable of renewing the interest of the situations. The hero of the film, Randolph Scott, is a sheriff hunting seven bandits who have killed his wife while stealing the Wells

Fargo coffers. It is a question of catching up with them by crossing the desert, before they cross the border with the stolen money. Another man soon becomes interested in helping him, but with a very different motive. Once the bandits are dead, he will perhaps be able to take possession of the twenty thousand dollars. Perhaps – unless the sheriff stops him, in which case he will have to kill an extra man. Thus the dramatic line is clearly drawn. The sheriff acts out of vengeance, his associate out of self-interest; in the end, the account will be settled between them. This story could make a dull and banal Western, were the scenario not built on a series of *coups de théâtre* which I will restrain myself from revealing in order to safeguard the reader's pleasure if by good fortune he should see the film. But still more than the invention of such peripeteia, it is the humour with which they are handled that seems remarkable to me. Thus, for instance, one never sees the sheriff shoot, as if he did so too fast to give the camera time to capture the reverse-field. The same comic spirit surely accounts for the heroine's dresses – too pretty or too alluring – or yet again the unexpected ellipses of the dramatic construction. Certain scenes make one smile or even laugh. But that's what is most admirable here: the humour never runs contrary to emotion and still less to a sense of admiration. No trace of parody. It supposes solely on the part of the director awareness and understanding of the springs which he sets in motion, but with no contempt or condescension. Humour is not born from a feeling of superiority, but quite the contrary, from a superabundance of admiration. When one loves to this degree the hero one creates and the situations one imagines, then and then alone can one bring into play this humorous distance which multiplies admiration through its lucidity. This kind of irony does not diminish the characters, but allows their naïvety to co-exist with intelligence. Indeed, here is one of the most intelligent Westerns I know but also the least intellectual; the most refined and the least aesthetic; the simplest and the most beautiful.

This paradoxical dialectic was possible because Budd Boetticher and his scenarist chose not to dominate their subject with paternalism or to 'enrich' it with psychological elements, but simply to push it to its logical limit and to derive all the effects from bringing situations to their completion. Emotion is born from the most abstract connections and from the most concrete kind of beauty. Realism, so imperative in historical and psychological Westerns, has no more meaning here than in the Triangle[1] films, or rather, a specific splendour arises from the fusion of extreme convention and extreme reality. Boetticher knew how to make prodigious use of the landscape, of the varied substance of the earth, of the grain and shape of the rocks. Nor do I think that the photogenic qualities of horses have been as well exploited for a very long time. For example, in Gail Russell's[2] extraordinary bathing scene where the inherent modesty of the Western is humorously pushed so far that we see only the lapping of the water in the reeds while fifty yards away Randolph Scott is grooming the horses. It is difficult to imagine simultaneously more abstraction and more transference in the matter of eroticism. I am also thinking of the white mane of the sheriff's horse, and its big yellow eye. Knowing how to use such details is surely more important in the Western than knowing how to deploy a hundred Indians in battle.

It is in fact necessary to credit this exceptional film with an altogether unusual use of colour. Served, it's true, by a colour process (WarnerColor) whose characteristics I am not familiar with, the colours of *Seven Men from Now* are uniformly transposed into the tonality of a wash-drawing whose transparency and flatness recall old stencil-colours. One could say that the conventions of colour thus come to underline those of action.

Finally, there is Randolph Scott, his face irresistibly recalling William Hart's right down to the sublime lack of expression in his blue eyes. Never a facial gesture, never the shadow of a thought or a feeling, without this impassiveness, needless to say, having anything to do with modern interiority in the style of Marlon Brando. This face expresses nothing because there is nothing to express. All motives for actions are defined here according to occupations and circumstances. This includes the love of Randolph Scott for Gail Russell, whose point of origin we know exactly (the bathing scene), and its evolution, without the hero's face betraying a sentiment. But it is inscribed in the chain of events like fate in the conjunction of the stars: essential and objective. Any subjective manifestation would then have the vulgarity of a pleonasm. We become attached no less to the characters; on the contrary, their existence is all the fuller by owing nothing to the incertitudes and ambiguities of psychology, and when, at the end of the film, Randolph Scott and Lee Marvin find themselves face to face, the heartrending to which we know ourselves condemned is moving and beautiful like tragedy.

Thus the proof of the pudding is in the eating. The Western is not condemned to justify itself by intellectualism or by spectacular effects. The intelligence we demand today may serve to refine the primitive structures of the Western and not to meditate upon them or to divert them to the advantage of interests remote from the essence of the genre.

Translated by Phillip Drummond

Notes

1 Triangle: see Jacques Rivette, 'Notes on a Revolution', Ch. 8, note 3.
2 Gail Russell: when Bazin's article was reprinted in *Qu'est-ce que le cinéma, tome III: Cinéma et sociologie*, Paris, Editions du Cerf, 1961, the name Gail Russell for the film's main actress, used in the original review, was changed to that of Janet Gaynor (and, in misprint, Gaylor). Though published after Bazin's death, his collected works – except for volume IV – had been prepared and edited by Bazin before his death. What motivated the change of actress's name is unclear: as far as we have been able to establish, the actress in question is Gail Russell.

Part Three

Italian Cinema

Introduction

Contrary to popular assumption, *Cahiers* was not more interested in, or committed to, American cinema than other cinemas: the contents of *Cahiers* simply do not support any such assumption.[1] Although it *was* primarily over responses to American cinema that *Cahiers* writers argued most among themselves and with other French critics, and although this was what marked them off most from Anglo-Saxon critics, a great deal of *Cahiers* was devoted to what in Anglo-Saxon film culture we would call 'art cinema', generally European. We might express it in this way: as *critics* involved in polemics, American cinema preoccupied them most; as *future film-makers* they were very much drawn (and not only by necessity) to European cinema.

There is in Godard's,[2] Truffaut's,[3] and Rivette's[4] writing of this period (in *Cahiers* and elsewhere) about Ingmar Bergman, for example, a recognition of the proximity between Bergman's situation as a film-maker and their own actual or potential situations, as well as a recognition of some shared attitudes to both the world and the cinema. It may seem odd that Bergman, in many ways the epitome of 'art cinema' ('difficult', intense, serious, personal, innovatory, or at least formally self-conscious), should be championed by *Cahiers* and especially by Godard ('the most original film-maker of the European cinema: Ingmar Bergman'), but the reasons for this are revealing. Truffaut emphasizes Bergman's simplicity, his exploration of essentially personal concerns, the viewer's sense 'at the start of a film that Bergman himself doesn't yet know how he'll end his story'.[5] Godard calls Bergman an 'intuitive artist' rather than a 'craftsman': 'The cinema is not a craft. It is an art. It does not mean team-work. One is always alone; on the set as before the blank page. And for Bergman, to be alone means to ask questions. And to make films means to answer them. Nothing could be more classically romantic.'[6] Bergman's own comment on this passage is apt: 'He's writing about himself.'[7]

But in the struggle for a new, or different, French cinema, the example of the Italian cinema – Fellini, Antonioni, Visconti, but especially and most consistently Rossellini – was most crucially important, particularly during the early and mid-1950s. Eric Rohmer's conclusion to his 'Rediscovering America' is that as well as loving America and American cinema, they should also love Italy and its cinema: 'It is perhaps because of its amicable if not harmonious juxtaposition of the most modern and the most ancient that Italy ought to have had the high reputation in European cinema which French cinema has enjoyed since the demise of the silent film. It is only a matter of knowing, now, how to take over.'[8] Rivette, concluding his 'Letter on Rossellini', also 1955, says: 'Here is our cinema, those of us who in our turn are preparing to make films (did I tell you, it may be soon).' This introduction and the articles which follow try to give some explanation of this relationship.

'Neo-Realism and Phenomenology' (1952) by Amédée Ayfre, a Catholic priest, forms a clear and close link with André Bazin's pre-*Cahiers* writings on neo-realism,[9] perhaps his most lastingly important work on realism and representing important shifts from the position on realism outlined in 'The Evolution of the Language of Cinema':[10] Bazin's brief note on *Umberto D* from the Cannes Festival in 1952 can serve to remind us of the general tone and stance of those writings. Ayfre draws heavily on Bazin's significant insights into the workings of, for example, *Bicycle Thieves*[11] while trying to draw out some of the underlying assumptions which Bazin does not make explicit. In turn, Bazin explicitly approved of Ayfre's formulations.[12] At many points Bazin and Ayfre are exceptionally close in their judgments, for example in their agreement on the necessity of 'fundamental ambiguity' or their approval of 'social polemic . . . but not propaganda'.[13] Ayfre's 'by giving primacy to existence over essence in all things, the method comes strangely close to what the philosophers call phenomenological description . . . Rossellini and a few others have tried . . . to go . . . to things themselves, to ask what they manifest through themselves' can be set alongside Bazin's 'Neo-realism knows only immanence. It is from appearances only, the simple appearance of beings and the world, that it knows how to deduce the ideas that it unearths. It is a phenomenology.'[14] Bazin's conclusion to his essay on *Bicycle Thieves* – 'No more actors, no more story, no more sets, which is to say that in the perfect aesthetic illusion of reality there is no more cinema'[15] – also finds strong echoes in Ayfre's essay; Bazin in turn borrowed his definition of the 'wholeness' of reality from Ayfre.[16]

Rohmer's review of *Viaggio in Italia* and Rivette's 'Letter on Rossellini' (both 1955), stimulated by the generally unsympathetic critical response to that film, indicate just how strong and central a tradition Bazin's and Ayfre's 'phenomenological realism' and its 'neutral form' was in *Cahiers* in the 1950s (this was precisely the tradition so wholly attacked by later Marxist positions[17]). Rohmer's virulently Catholic defence of 'sacred art' in relation to *Viaggio in Italia* reminds us particularly strongly of the religious base to these notions of immanence.

Rivette's long article, while recognizing the centrality of Catholicism in Rossellini, is more complex and interesting for additional reasons. The exemplary status Rivette gives Rossellini's cinema was certainly not new. As early as 1952 Godard recalls an encounter with Rohmer in which Rohmer argued that 'the real lesson of the Italian cinema has not yet been generally understood . . . I know of no film which better celebrates the traditional virtues like courage and generosity than *Rome, Open City*. Yet it is shot in a very rough and ready manner . . . French cameramen are too preoccupied with composition, but the cinema has nothing to do with painting.'[18] *Cahiers* admired the American cinema but, generally classical, popular and industrial as it was (despite the way a Nicholas Ray might be discussed[19]), it was not a cinema they could aspire to emulate. At the same time, *Cahiers* disliked the typical French films of the period for their lack of the traditional moral virtues as much as for their formal 'academicism', by which was meant both their literary quality (thus Rivette's comment that 'nothing could be less literary or novelistic' than Rossellini) and their pictorial conventions.[20] But Italian cinema represented something which new French film-makers *could* aspire to, and Rossellini in particular exemplified both moral values *Cahiers* could generally espouse and a 'modern', non-academic photographic style and non-literary narrative style which suited both their tastes and the production conditions and possibilities in France. It is this 'modernity' – stylistic and thematic – which Rivette's article seeks to define:

> For there is no doubt that these hurried films, improvised out of very slender means and filmed in a turmoil that is often apparent from the images, contain the only real portrait of our times . . . How could one fail suddenly to recognize, quintessentially sketched, ill-composed, incomplete, the semblance of our daily existence? These arbitrary groups, these absolutely theoretical collections of people eaten away by lassitude and boredom, just exactly as we know them to be, as the irrefutable accusing image of our heteroclite, dissident, discordant societies.

This, together with Rivette's sympathetic definition of Rossellini's constant theme that 'human beings are alone, and their solitude irreducible; that, except by miracle or saintliness, our ignorance of others is complete', and so on, offers pretty convincing exemplification of the typical *Cahiers* thematic proposed by John Hess.[21] But, as an *auteur*, Rossellini was interesting for other reasons, also exemplary: when Rivette expresses his 'wonder at the fact that our era, which can no longer be shocked by anything, should pretend to be scandalized because a film-maker dares to talk about himself without restraint', he is arguing for a central role for the 'personal' in art,[22] an important aspect of at least the early *nouvelle vague* films.[23] Though Rivette's conception here of *auteur* and 'creativity' is largely conventional, he makes interesting distinctions between 'isolated masters' (such as Renoir, Hawks, Lang, in their maturity) whose work is self-justifying, autonomous (and which therefore

177

cannot be learned from), and the 'exemplary' status of Rossellini's work ('everything in it is instructive, including the errors'), somehow 'shackled to time', tied to the present.[24] Knowing as we do the interesting turns that Rivette took subsequently as critic and as film-maker in the 1960s and beyond, perhaps we can in this difficult but provocative essay also see the beginnings of a concerted engagement with ideas about 'modernism'.[25]

The *Cahiers* view of the *auteur*/creator can also be assessed from the two Rossellini interview extracts, interesting for the way *Cahiers* interviewed as much as for Rossellini's views. In the *Cahiers* interview style we see a paradoxical combination of veneration (there is, almost, a definite 'truth' to be got from the director) with an interrogatory stance implying firm equality, and thus a level of detailed questioning unusual for the time.[26] *Cahiers*' questions are very directly informed by the positions associated with Bazin, and Rossellini's responses tend to confirm those positions, in both their moral (and therefore political) and their formal senses. Rossellini's manifesto-type responses, particularly in the 1959 interview, certainly inform his later, didactic television work; unsurprisingly, their general impetus closely resembles that of the *nouvelle vague* itself.

Notes

1 See also the *Cahiers* Annual Best Films Listings, in Appendix 1.

2 See, for example, in *Godard on Godard*, 'Bergmanorama' (originally published in *Cahiers* 85, July 1958), pp. 75–80, and a review of *Summer with Monika* (originally published in *Arts* 680, July 1958), pp. 84–5.

3 See, for example, in François Truffaut, *Films in My Life*, 'Bergman's Opus' (originally published in 1958), pp. 253–7.

4 See, for example, 'L'Ame au ventre', a review of *Summer Interlude* (*Sommarlek*), *Cahiers* 84, June 1958, pp. 45–7.

5 Truffaut, *op. cit.*, p. 256.

6 Godard, *op. cit.*, p. 76.

7 Ingmar Bergman, *Bergman on Bergman* (interviews with Ingmar Bergman by Stig Björkman, Torsten Manns, Jonas Sima), London, Secker & Warburg, 1973, p. 60.

8 Ch. 7 in this volume.

9 Collected in André Bazin, *What is Cinema? Vol. 2*; *Umberto D* is discussed in the essays 'De Sica: Metteur en Scène' (pp. 61–78) and '*Umberto D*: A Great Work' (pp. 79–82).

10 Reprinted in André Bazin, *What is Cinema? Vol. 1*.

11 See particularly the essays '*Bicycle Thief*' and 'De Sica: Metteur en Scène' in Bazin, *What is Cinema? Vol. 2*.

12 'In Defence of Rossellini', *ibid.*, p. 97.

13 Cf. Bazin, '*Bicycle Thief*', *ibid.*, p. 51.

14 'De Sica: Metteur en Scène', *ibid.*, pp. 64–5.

15 '*Bicycle Thief*', *ibid.*, p. 60.

16 'In Defence of Rossellini', *ibid.*, p. 97.

17 See, for example, Jean-Louis Comolli and Jean Narboni, 'Cinema/Ideology/Criticism (I)', originally published *Cahiers* 216, October 1969, translated in

Screen, vol. 12, no. 1, Spring 1971, reprinted in *Screen Reader 1* and Nichols, *Movies and Methods*.

18 Godard, *op. cit.*, p. 32.

19 See, for example, Rivette's comments on Nicholas Ray in 'Notes on a Revolution', Ch. 8 in this volume.

20 See my introduction to the section on French cinema in this volume, and particularly the comments on Truffaut's 'A Certain Tendency of the French Cinema'.

21 See Introduction to this volume.

22 Cf. François Truffaut on Becker's *Touchez pas au grisbi*, Ch. 1 in this volume, among many other examples.

23 See, for example, Jacques Rivette's 'Du côté de chez Antoine', on Truffaut's *Les 400 Coups*, *Cahiers* 95, May 1959, translated as 'Antoine's Way' in David Denby, *The 400 Blows*, New York, Grove Press, 1969.

24 Cf., in a slightly different sense, Truffaut's treatment of the Japanese film *Juvenile Passion* as exemplary, in Truffaut, *Films in My Life*, pp. 246–7.

25 Cf., for example, Rivette's contribution to the 1959 editorial discussion of *Hiroshima, mon amour*, Ch. 6 in this volume.

26 Cf. extracts from interview with Nicholas Ray, Ch. 15 in this volume.

24 | André Bazin: *Umberto D*

(from 'La Foi qui sauve: Cannes 1952',
Cahiers du Cinéma 13, June 1952)

In the work of Zavattini and De Sica *Miracle in Milan* was a parenthesis, an excursion into the world of fantasy, based on and perhaps at the service of realism but nevertheless in a perspective diverging from the one defined by *Sciuscià* (*Shoeshine*) and *Bicycle Thieves*. With *Umberto D* the scriptwriter and the director revert to total neo-realism. Zavattini's originality in Italian cinema, however, lies in his claim to go deeper into neo-realism rather than to go beyond it. A somewhat dangerous and paradoxical position after the success of *Bicycle Thieves*, so perfect that it was taken as a peak after which the authors could only go downwards again. But *Umberto D* proves that the undeniable perfection of *Bicycle Thieves* was the limit to which an aesthetic could go. That limit lay less in the total application of the laws of neo-realist narrative than in the almost miraculous balance between that revolutionary conception of the screenplay and the demands of classical narrative. Where they might have ended up with only a clever compromise, the authors reached an ideal synthesis between the rigour of tragic necessity and the accidental fluidity of everyday reality. But, for Zavattini, this success was only at the cost of sacrificing part of his aesthetic project, which we know to be to make a cinematographic spectacle from ninety minutes in the life of a man to whom nothing happens. An unrealizable project perhaps, the asymptote of an imaginary film whose relationship to reality would be like a mirror of which one would no longer know which side had the silvering, but also an aesthetic idea as fertile and inexhaustible as nature itself.

From this point of view, *Umberto D* not only endeavours to go much further than *Bicycle Thieves* but succeeds in doing so. Misunderstanding inevitably arises from the fact that the social or political actuality of the subject matter and its emotional repercussions make it appear to some as a plea for the retirement of the aged and to others as melodrama. There will always be, of course, plenty of small-scale Suares to sneer at De Sica's 'ignoble heart'. But it is clear that the real film in no sense corresponds to its plot summary. The story of Umberto D, humble retired civil servant, and his dog – assuming we can still talk about it as a 'story' – is as much in the moments when 'nothing happens' as in the dramatic sequences, like his attempted suicide. De Sica devotes more than one reel to showing us Umberto D in his room, closing the shutters, tidying a few things, looking at his tonsils, going to bed, taking his temperature. So much film for a sore throat – as much as for the suicide! And yet the sore throat does play at least a small part in the story, whereas the most beautiful sequence of the film, in which the little maid gets up, has – strictly speaking – no dramatic resonance at all: the girl gets up, potters about in the kitchen, chases away the ants, grinds the coffee . . . and all these 'unimportant' actions are recorded for us in strict temporal continuity. When I pointed out to Zavattini that this last scene sustained unfailing interest while Umberto D going to bed did not, he replied, 'You see that it is not the aesthetic principle which is at issue, only the way it is used. The more the scriptwriter turns his back on drama and spectacle, the more he intends his story to conform to the living continuity of reality, the more the choice of the minute events which form its texture becomes delicate and problematic. If I bored you with Umberto's sore throat but moved you to tears with my little heroine's coffee grinder, it only proves that in the second case I knew how to choose what I didn't know how to imagine in the first case.'

Certainly a patchy film, not as mentally satisfying as *Bicycle Thieves*, *Umberto D* at least owes its failings to its ambitions. What is successful about it is not only in the forefront of neo-realism but also at the most daring point of the invisible avant-garde which we seek to defend.

Translated by Jim Hillier

25 | Amédée Ayfre: 'Neo-Realism and Phenomenology'

('Néo Réalisme et Phénoménologie', *Cahiers du Cinéma* 17, November 1952)

'Realism' is one of those words which should never be used without a determining correlative. Does 'neo-', as applied to post-war Italian realist cinema, fit the bill? Judged in terms of the more or less universal usage it has acquired, the answer would have to be yes. But if, on the contrary, we sift through the innumerable critiques to which it has been subjected, even by artists themselves, and if we note that all those who use it do so with some reservation in the form of brackets or circumlocutions (in short, with a bad conscience), the temptation is to look for something to replace it.

But does that 'something' have to be sought retrospectively, through a process of elimination, in one of the movements classified by the 'history of aesthetics', or in the future 'in the depths of the unknown where, alone, the new is to be found'? Did neo-realism re-chart worlds already mapped in detail, or did it strike out along its own path? In other words, should the accent be on the 'realism' or on the 'neo'?

Reality and the cinema

There is no doubt that film realism has its beginnings with Lumière, a man who never imagined his invention could be anything but an instrument for reproducing the real world. But from the outset, the mere fact that he positioned his camera in a particular spot, started or stopped filming at a particular moment and recorded the world in black and white on a flat surface was enough to establish an inevitable gap between the representation and the real.

The impossibility of bridging that gap is brought out again by the strange phenomenon of Dziga Vertov. He realized that the high point of realism in film was the documentary; hence the need to shoot outside the studio, without actors or script. The ideal would have been to set a camera rolling at some crossroads. But the question then is, would what emerged from such extreme limits of realism have been a film, an *œuvre*? Or would it have been a collection of moving photographs which constituted a document of primary importance to the town planner or the sociologist, but of no great interest for those concerned with art? Vertov realized that if photographs of this kind were to be transformed into film, a particular rhythm had to be imparted to them by the editing. Thereafter, his concern with that aspect assumed such a role that he progressively lost interest in the individual elements at his disposal, retaining merely a kind of finished symphonic movement with a highly calculated tempo where the initial subject was no longer important. Thus from the starting point of the rawest kind of realism we are thrown back into abstract art. The dialectic is significant and illustrative of the inevitable dead-end to which documentary film, with its claim to passivity and its belief in its own impersonal objectivity, leads.

To avoid this dead-end, the verist movement in cinema rejected from the first any naive direct route to the real in favour of a digression via truth, i.e. via art and reason. The artist takes an event and deliberately reconstitutes it in order to give it verisimilitude. And because he knows that the 'forms' of his art must always pare down the real content, he takes care to heighten its features, either by making shadows darker still – black, intellectual verism, with all its play on the various shades of grey – or by intensifying light, which gives all the rose-tinted shades, from deepest red to palest pink, from Grémillon to Cloche, via socialist realism.

Neo-realism and phenomenology

How should 'neo-realism' be put into perspective? Should it be seen as simply a transformation of verism, or has it found an alternative way out of the documentary's dialectical impasse? To avoid arguing in the abstract, let us base the discussion on an extract which seems to all intents and purposes specifically neo-realist – the final sequence of *Germany, Year Zero*.

This film has a number of dimensions: first, documentary, the state of Germany after the war; then, psychological, social psychology that charts the ill-effects of a Nazi education, plus the individual psychology of the child. But this is where the originality begins, for the concern is in no sense with child or adolescent psychology (the cinema has plenty of that already). It is quite different, very precisely the concrete, all-embracing depiction of the human attitude of a child in a given situation. No introspection, no internal, nor very often even external dialogue, no play with facial expression. Nor, however, is there any concern with psychology in the behaviourist sense. We are well beyond psychology here and this has nothing to do with a sequence of reflexes. Rather, the issue is a human attitude in its totality, captured in a 'neutral' way by the camera. To understand the completely original element in this process, it is necessary only to grasp that at no point does the child give the impression of 'acting', or of being an actor. It is impossible to say that he 'acts' his role well or badly. He is not part of the game in that sense, just as the viewer is not involved in degrees of sympathy or antipathy. The child simply lives and exists there before us, captured in his 'existence' by the camera. For contrast, look at little Kucci in *Quelque part en Europe*, or the adolescent in *Les Dernières Vacances*, or *Le Garçon sauvage*; more often than not, they all 'act well', i.e. they give a superlative rendering of the feelings the film-maker imagines they ought to experience. In the present instance, what are the sentiments to which the child's attitude could correspond? Regret, remorse, despair, stupor? None of the labels are satisfactory, any more than their combinations, because here we are faced with the question of all-embracing human attitudes or, let us say, an existential attitude. What is at stake is the child's being as an entity; hence the child is not 'acting'.

If the foregoing is accurate, we have passed beyond psychology and, not surprisingly, ended somewhere in the area of ethics or metaphysics. We do not have to turn Rossellini into a philosopher to get there. All he has to be is a human being, depicting in its totality a human attitude. What emerges is of necessity a total sense of existence, not in the form of a thesis which the film is intended to demonstrate, or at least to illustrate and which was therefore a necessary preliminary to the conceptualization of the film, i.e. where essence preceded existence, to use a phrase which is now commonplace. On the contrary, the 'meaning' here is an integral part of the concrete attitude. Hence its ambiguity. Some see the economic disorder of a decadent society crystallizing in a child and killing him; others, the polarization of the absurd as a whole, everything 'rotten' in a world where people are superfluous. Still others see evidence of a world where God's great love can find no way through the sad and bloody play of human passions, except in the shape of a figure kneeling over a dead child. Rossellini makes no decisions. He puts the question. In the face of an existential attitude, he proposes the mystery of existence.

It is clear what distinguishes this attitude from the verist and documentary movements. This film's documentary element lays no claim to any special passive 'objectivity'; its 'neutral' presentation is never cold or impersonal. If reason and thesis play no part, there are always awareness and involvement. Social polemic there is, but not propaganda. But above all, the objective, subjective, social, etc., are never analysed as such; they are taken as a factual whole in all its inchoate fullness, a bloc in time as well as volume, and we are not spared a single second or gesture. Faced with this entity, the attitude of the viewer has to change radically. To look becomes an act because everything is called in question, answers are demanded, action required. This is a summons to freedom. It is striking to note how the film-maker places us face to face with a human event taken in its totality, but refrains from fragmentation or analysis, simply surveying it, describing it concretely and working in such a way that in the midst of watching we lose the sense of spectacle and the awareness of acting in the actors disappears. In other words, by giving primacy to existence over essence in all things, the method comes oddly close to what the philosophers call phenomenological description.

This method has undoubtedly been interpreted with a range of nuances, depending on the doctrines associated with it, but given that the artist, who is not a professional thinker, may legitimately take a little distance on things, there is no denying that Rossellini and a few others have tried, like Husserl, to go *zu den Sachen selbst*, to things themselves, to ask what they manifest through themselves.

There is, above all, their way of running an opposing course to that of analysis, of putting an end to any compartmentalized view of man and the world, ceasing to delve subtly into 'characters' and 'milieux', putting all that between brackets and in a sense attempting a total apprehension which is sequentially complete like existence in time, or like human events in which the whole mystery of the Universe is co-present. In other words, the mystery of being replaces clarity of construction.

Such a reversal of perspective, perhaps new for the cinema, was experienced by other fields of art, and the novel in particular, well before philosophers adopted the mode of expression and turned it into theory.[1]

Could it not be argued that both involve 'essays in a direct description of experience as it is, without regard to its psychological genesis or the causal explanations which the scientist, historian or sociologist may provide', a kind of 'descriptive study of a set of phenomena as they manifest themselves in time or space, as opposed to the fixed, abstract laws governing such phenomena, the transcendental realities of which they are a manifestation, or normative criticism of their legitimacy'? Now this is precisely the definition given to phenomenology by Merleau-Ponty on the one hand and, on the other, by Lalande's *Vocabulaire de la philosophie*. Obviously, the applicability of the word 'study' is open to challenge. At best, withdrawing it is basis enough for denying the works of Rossellini or Dos Passos the character of research or philosophy, something they never claimed; but perhaps it does not justify denying the aesthetic movement they represent a more accurate title than that of 'neo-realism'. Phenomenological realism, for instance.[2]

Art in phenomenological realism

Always supposing that what we are talking about is an aesthetic movement. The rejection of 'style' inherent in phenomenological realism is surely the expression of a determination to find a place outside the field of art. But to avoid arguing in a vacuum, let us look at a particular work, De Sica's *Bicycle Thieves*. Here we have a man in search of his bike who is not just a man who loves his son, a worker desperately engaged in trying to steal another bike, a man who, finally, represents the distress of the proletariat reduced to stealing the tools of its trade. He is all that and a host of other things besides, indefinable, unanalysable, precisely because primarily *he is*, and not in isolation, but surrounded by a bloc of reality which carries traces of the world – friends, church, German seminarians, Rita Hayworth on a poster. And this is in no sense merely décor, it 'exists' almost on the same level as he does.

A rejection of choice, therefore, but isn't choice what art is about? It is, but the choice is essentially one of means. In this instance the means are quite rigorous. The important thing is that the very realism of this work can only come through the use of devices much more subtle and conscious than anything attributed to the fullest kind of spontaneity. Phenomenological realism, like the method which inspires it but in a rather different sense, is also the result of a kind of parenthesis, an 'encapsulation'. Between brackets is the work, that fragment of the world which gives the viewer precisely that sense of not being present at a spectacle, even a realist spectacle. But outside the brackets there is the transcendent 'I' which is the *auteur*, the one who knows the full cost of the artistic effort required to achieve the impression of reality and to give the audience the sense that he, the *auteur*, has never set foot inside the brackets. Surely infinite art is required to organize a narrative, construct a *mise en scène*, direct actors, while giving the final impression that there are neither narrative, *mise en scène*, nor actors involved. In other words, we are dealing again with a second-stage realism, a synthesis of the documentary and verist movements. With verism came the realization that the ideal of primary realism could not be achieved by reproducing the real directly; now came the rejection of the belief that the indirect approach had to take the form of a stylization of the event. The perfect aesthetic illusion of reality can only result from ascesis of the means in which there is ultimately more art than in any of the various forms of expressionism or constructivism.

First, ascesis of the script. The concern is no longer with a script that is well-constructed according to some impeccable dramatic logic with subtle psychological counterpoints. The question is not one of architecture but of existence. If an artist merits the divine name of creator in any sphere, it is here. And he is rarely alone. Italian scriptwriting teams are famous. There has been an attempt to explain this away as a question of publicity, but its roots lie deeper, in a sense of the infinite richness of life which one man could never evoke successfully. Zavattini and De Sica worked for months on the script of *Bicycle Thieves* in order to make people believe there was no such thing.

The ascesis of the script is completed by ascesis of the *mise en scène* and actors (admirably analysed by André Bazin in his article for *Esprit*, November 1949[3]). This always calls for supplementary devices to ensure, for example, that the introduction and operation of a camera in the filming of a street scene does not cause any obvious disruption and that the worker and his son assume no more of a role than the bicycle. In phenomenological realism, art is therefore established within the very act by which it seeks to destroy itself. But it is perfectly conscious of that and indeed turns it into its claim to validity as art. The definition needs also to take account of the fact that everything is filmed in such a way as to produce the dense texture of life which, to quote a thought that predates Sartre, is the only true measure of beauty.

This is why the category of neo-realist films where the formal concerns are clear (the best example of which is *La terra trema*) cannot be brought in as an argument against the views just expressed. If they are taken as authentically phenomenological, and I believe this is true for *La terra trema* at least, they cannot be explained, like *Il Cristo proibito*, solely in terms of the conjunction between the neo-realist tendency and the great Italian tradition of the grandiose, the operatic and the baroque. Even in these films the beauty is less a function of their formal aspects than of the dense texture of life in them. The very essence of their form is the tactile quality of the subject matter, their ponderable human mass. Or to put it more precisely, what needs to be acknowledged is the masterly conjunction of the two elements, their genuine and deliberate reciprocity. It has been said that a poster must not be too beautiful or the passer-by may never get past the surface to the real point. This is not altogether so. Alongside neutral form there is a place for a translucent art, an instrumental kind of beauty which is plenitude and transparence at the same time. Like those figures which can be seen in depth or relief at will, a Vermeer painting can be a diligent lace-maker at her window or a skilful chromatic effect in blue, silver-grey and very pale orange, radiating out from a pulpy, velvety, almost fleshy surface. The same experience can come from Visconti's genuine Sicilian fishermen. The glory (in almost the theological sense of the word) he shrouds them in does not veil them but is what enables them to be seen. I know that this is dangerous ground and that the majority of other, similarly oriented films have remained trapped in their self-indulgence, but at least in this case it is impossible to avoid seeing in the formal shaping a kind of ontological humility which is to the deliberate neutralism of *Bicycle Thieves* what mysticism is to asceticism.

Human reality and its meaning

There are a number of aesthetic tendencies which may be opposed to phenomenological realism, the most appropriate being the *pièce à thèse*, the drama with a message, or its more attenuated form, the *pièce à thème*. Their constant characteristic is a certain transcendence of the work which takes the form of a particular, extrinsic end and entails a constant pursuit of the ideal of unambiguous meaning in its simplest possible form. This, even when the interpretation is subtle, is diametrically opposed to phenomenological realism with its determination not to tamper with events, nor to permeate them artificially with ideas and emotions. But the all-inclusive nature of the event takes in both the spatio-temporal reality and a relation to human consciousness which is part of its essence and is its 'meaning' or 'sense'. Because it can only be deciphered by a consciousness which is never rigidly directed to an external end, this 'sense' can

187

always be interpreted and coloured by consciousness according to its own standards and theories, i.e. its own *Weltanschauung*, exactly like the real world itself. The result is a fundamental ambiguity.

The condition, of course, is that the event has been allowed to conserve its completeness. The slightest intrusion of any treatment whereby the author tends to make his personal interpretation of the intrinsic meaning explicit compromises the whole operation. We are back with the message. This shows how far from phenomenological are those films which claim to be as existentialist as *Les Jeux sont faits* or *Les Mains sales*. Sartre clearly has a commitment in the themes (if not the message) he deals with, unlike Kafka, whom he commended for engaging in a unified situation and complete event. It is not just under the analysis of the critic that everything breaks up into problems; in order to bring them to life, the author has to be committed. To do otherwise it is probably necessary not to be a philosopher, but to have the genius of Zavattini . . . or Pagliero.

Pagliero's film, *Un Homme marche dans la ville*, is in fact a notable illustration of all that has just been said of phenomenological realism, and at the same time it offers some valuable additional dimensions. This film too describes in minute detail an all-embracing human situation and all the events, large and small, it brings together. There are no main characters for whom the rest are merely the supporting cast. They are all equally present – the big Brazilian, the presumed murderer and the corner café alike. Lives unfold side by side, sometimes enmesh, sometimes separate. The end is not really an end; one is left with the sense that everything could continue. And when the critic's eye extrapolates themes, these are so much the flesh of things that making them explicit is immediately to betray them. Since they are there, however, they need to be mentioned: the problem of the misunderstanding – the so-called murderer is innocent; the absurd – a man kills another by mistake because he takes the victim for someone else; loneliness of the gregarious kind – not one authentic communication passes between one person and another in love or hate and love is no more than the contact of skins; the child who is *de trop*, constantly pushed into the street, out of the way. The adults too suffer the nausea of existence and are in part strangers to themselves. They are all beings-for-death; the worker with the 'ugly mug' or 'the face of an undertaker', as he is often told, cannot find a job and ends up being ridiculously killed. The woman who cannot find any kind of love and gasses herself. The negro who dies of TB, killed by his working conditions. 'All men are mortal' and here no one dies of 'natural causes'. None of these people escapes his situation and in the end there is a clear sense that the boat pulling out to sea is not an escape to the 'Islands of the Blessed', but that the true murderer and the supposed one are both leaving for a new situation which will prove to be like the first. They are temporarily 'reprieved' but will never manage to extricate themselves from the situation which constantly coagulates around them.

And the formal element 'clings' strangely to these people. It can be summed up in a word: the film is 'flat'. The light has something hard and lustreless about it, not atmospheric but brittle, angular and brutal. The most gripping image, the wounded man on a stretcher ascending the steep wall that dominates the quay, is an existential metaphor of uncommon rigour and power – the 'wall' behind which there is only nothingness and death. The wall is not there to 'symbolize' the *facticity*[4] of existence, it 'is' existence itself, freezing into facticity, becoming a thing and taking on the cold permanence and blind hardness of things. There is nothing here of Carné's mists of Le Havre or the radiant light of Italian films, which each in their way evoke extra-human horizons. It is the steel screen which blots out these horizons, the wall which supports the closed doors of the human prison in which we are condemned to freedom. The total absence of music, the heavy, grating soundtrack, again underlines this aspect and prevents any evocative effect.

Thus it is an existentialist or, more precisely, Sartrian meaning that Pagliero makes us give the events he describes phenomenologically. But because he does this with a quite different sense of the demands of the work and a quite different respect for the concrete and for method, he brings a complement to the preceding analyses which is valuable in quite a different way from Sartre's own films. Since, without any obvious distortion, he ends up impressing on the audience such a clearly directed vision of the world and of man, it seems that Heidegger was right to oppose Husserl in asserting that a description of existence always and necessarily confirms the idea one has of it, since that idea is already an element, mode and factor of existence itself. It was therefore possibly a little premature to congratulate, as we just did, Rossellini, De Sica and Zavattini, for their reserve and the freedom of interpretation they allowed the audience. If their worlds seemed less marked by their vision, this was doubtless because they still hesitated in the face of choice, or because their choice was on quite a different level, up there where Gabriel Marcel's words might possibly be verified: 'All existence which does not refer to the transcendental degenerates into falsity and facticity.' It is therefore fruitless to question Pagliero's captivating depictions, and enough simply to set them at a different angle.

Phenomenological realism and the Catholic meaning of grace

This is perhaps what *Cielo sulla palude* offers. Like all the other films of the school, it constitutes a social, psychological and ethical entity. It can be seen as simply a documentary on the Pontine Marshes, for the Goretti family is presented as profoundly integrated with land, water and sky. But gradually attention is focused on the mutual attitudes of Alessandro and young Maria, without, however, causing any break with the rest of the event. The whole of life on a farm on the Pontine Marshes continues to unfold in parallel as Alessandro's attitude becomes more precise, revealing its true nature as an irresistible sexual obsession which culminates in several attempted rapes and finally the crime.

In the meantime the film shows us the girl's preparation for her first communion, then the ceremony with its always slightly fussy details, especially in countries where the old religious traditions survive. Nevertheless, the film does not conceal the sincerity and profound attention which Maria brings to the act, any more than the empty formality which it perhaps represents for some of her companions. After the crime, the injured girl is taken care of in the hospital, where she dies. The crowd sees her as a saint and prays.

These are the events as they are shown, with no pressure directing the interpretations they should be given. If, on emerging from the cinema, the viewer discovers that the girl was actually canonized, he may well find that utterly absurd. His personal set of values did not have to change for the events to hold his interest.

But for the believer, applying the religious interpretation to the intrinsic meaning of these events presents no problems. The ambiguity itself is in a sense a criterion of authenticity. The illusory area of external visions and internal voices would be far more alarming. Here everything is so profoundly marked by corporeality and so far from fantasy that it presents no problems and there is no difficulty in recognizing the finger of God. Where everything is susceptible of a natural explanation there is still room for a transcendent reality within the natural development of determinations, and indeed this is one of the characteristics of that transcendence itself.

In other words, the ambiguity is the mode of existence of the Mystery which is the safeguard of freedom. Whatever the appearances to the contrary, a Christian will have no difficulty in recognizing, from the mystical point of view, a level and a quality which is at least equal if not superior to the worlds created by Bresson.

For if the psychology in the proper sense is infinitely less elaborate, grace is no more hidden and the ambiguities are not fundamentally greater; it is in any case in the very nature of grace to be hidden and ambiguous precisely because it is the human face of the transcendent Mystery of God.

Such, it seems to me, are the possibilities and the dangers of phenomenological realism in the area of religious expression. But the bigger danger would certainly be to want to take greater care of God's interests than He does himself by trying to direct events by force and constrain the audience to read in them a meaning which is only accessible to those who discover it freely.

The gamut of meanings accessible to phenomenological realism is thus as broad as human reality itself. It rejects no *a priori*, provided these meanings remain in the order of question rather than solution, for while, like Jean Wahl, it knows that problems have a value in themselves, it believes with Pascal that they can only be resolved by stepping outside them and that the human prison is open to the sky.

Translated by Diana Matias

Notes

1 In the January 1948 issue of *Esprit*, Bazin noted that Italian realism was simply the cinematic equivalent of the American novel, which led him to dispute the influence of film on the novel noted by Claude-Edmonde Magny. Bazin concluded that it was the cinema which was twenty years behind the times. And indeed, it is a long time since painting, too, demanded an increasingly active role of the spectator. It will also be recalled that Sartre in *Qu'est-ce que la littérature?* attributed a special role to torture as creative of extreme situations in order to explain the upheaval his generation was bringing to the technique of the novel. In this context, one might raise the much criticized torture sequence in the most famous of neo-realist films, *Rome, Open City* (1945). (Author's note.)

The essay to which Ayfre refers from *Esprit*, January 1948, is Bazin's 'An Aesthetic of Reality: Neo-Realism (Cinematic Realism and the Italian School of the Liberation)', translated in Bazin, *What is Cinema? Vol. 2.*

The reference to Magny is to her *Age of the American Novel.*

2 'Metaphysical naturalism' has been proposed (Gaetan Picon, *La Table Ronde*), or *problematicismo* (Ugo Spirito, *Bianco e Nero*, July 1948), words which to me do not seem to place enough stress on the connection with a philosophy of which Breher was able to say (to Merleau-Ponty, *Bulletin de la Société Française de Philosophie*, 1947) that it had to culminate in the novel or painting. Cinema did not occur to him. Philosophers employing the phenomenological method would be the last to protest against such a label; for them 'a narrated story may signify the world with as much depth as a philosophical treatise' (Merleau-Ponty, *The Phenomenology of Perception*, XVI). (Author's note.)

3 Translated as *'Bicycle Thief'* in Bazin, *op. cit.*

4 Like the earlier *de trop*, *facticité* is used here in the Sartrian sense. For Sartre the ontological and conceptual connections between freedom and facticity are crucial and complex; briefly, facticity refers to all those 'givens' thrust upon the individual such as gender, social and economic class, etc., where the only option open is in the area of the attitudes taken to them. (Author's note.)

191

26 | Jacques Rivette: 'Letter on Rossellini'

('Lettre sur Rossellini', *Cahiers du Cinéma* 46, April 1955)

'Ordinance protects. Order reigns.'

You don't think much of Rossellini; you don't, so you tell me, like *Viaggio in Italia*; and everything seems to be in order. But no; you are not assured enough in your rejection not to sound out the opinion of Rossellinians. They provoke you, worry you, as if you weren't quite easy in your mind about your taste. What a curious attitude!

But enough of this bantering tone. Yes, I have a very special admiration for Rossellini's latest film (or rather, the latest to be released here). On what grounds? Ah, that's where it gets more difficult. I cannot invoke exaltation, emotion, joy: these are terms you will scarcely admit as evidence; but at least you will, I trust, understand them. (If not, God help you.)

To gratify you, let us change the tone yet again. Mastery, freedom, these are words you can accept; for what we have here is the film in which Rossellini affirms his mastery most clearly, and, as in all art, through the free exercise of his talents; I shall come back to this later. First I have something to say which should be of greater concern to you: if there is a modern cinema, this is it. But you still require evidence.

1 If I consider Rossellini to be the most modern of film-makers, it is not without reason; nor is it through reason, either. It seems to me impossible to see *Viaggio in Italia* without receiving direct evidence of the fact that the film opens a breach, and that all cinema, on pain of death, must pass through it. (Yes, that there is now no other hope of salvation for our miserable French cinema but a healthy transfusion of this young blood.) This is, of course, only a personal impression. And I should like forthwith to forestall a misunderstanding: for there are other films, other film-makers doubtless no less great than this; though less, how shall I put it, *exemplary*. I mean that having reached this point in their careers, their creation seems to close in on itself; what they do is of importance for, and within the

192

perspectives of, this creation. Here, undoubtedly, is the culmination of art, no longer answerable to anyone but itself and, once the experimental fumblings and explorations are past, discouraging disciples by isolating the masters: their domain dies with them, along with the laws and the methods current there. Renoir, Hawks, Lang belong here, of course, and in a certain sense, Hitchcock. *Le Carrosse d'or* may inspire muddled copies, but never a school; only presumption and ignorance make these copies possible, and the real secrets are so well hidden within the series of Chinese boxes that to unravel them would probably take as many years as Renoir's career now stretches to; they merge with the various mutations and developments undergone over thirty years by an exceptionally keen and exacting creative intelligence. In its energy and dash, the work of youth or early maturity remains a reflection of the movements of everyday life; animated by a different current, it is shackled to time and can detach itself only with difficulty. But the secret of *Le Carrosse d'or* is that of creation and the problems, the trials, the gambles it subjects itself to in order to perfect an object and give it the autonomy and the subtlety of an as yet unexplored world. What example is there here, unless that of discreet, patient work which finally effaces all traces of its passage? But what could painters or musicians ever retain from the later works of Poussin or Picasso, Mozart or Stravinsky – except a salutary despair.

There is reason to think that in a decade or so Rossellini too will attain (and acclimatize himself to) this degree of purity; he has not reached it yet – luckily, it may be said; there is still time to follow him before within him in his turn eternity. . . ,[1] while the man of action still lives in the artist.

2 Modern, I said; after a few minutes watching *Viaggio in Italia*, for instance, a name kept recurring in my mind which seems out of place here: Matisse.[2] Each image, each movement, confirmed for me the secret affinity between the painter and the film-maker. This is simpler to state than to demonstrate; I mean to try, however, though I fear that my main reasons may seem rather frivolous to you, and the rest obscure or specious.

All you need do, to start with, is look: note, throughout the first part, the predilection for large white surfaces, judiciously set off by a neat trait, an almost decorative detail; if the house is new and absolutely modern in appearance, this is of course because Rossellini is particularly attracted to contemporary things, to the most recent forms of our environment and customs; and also because it delights him visually. This may seem surprising on the part of a *realist* (and even neo-realist); for heaven's sake, why? Matisse, in my book, is a realist too: the harmonious arrangement of fluid matter, the attraction of the white page pregnant with a single sign, of virgin sands awaiting the invention of the precise trait, all this suggests to me a more genuine realism than the overstatements, the affectations, the pseudo-Russian conventionalism of *Miracle in Milan*; all this, far from muffling the film-maker's voice, gives him a new, contemporary tone that speaks to us through our freshest, most vital sensibility; all this affects the modern man in us, and in fact bears witness to the period as faithfully as the narrative does; all this in fact deals with the *honnête homme* of 1953 or 1954; this, in fact, is the theme.

3 On the canvas, a spontaneous curve circumscribes, without ever pinning down, the most brilliant of colours; a broken line, nevertheless unique, encompasses matter that is miraculously alive, as though transferred intact from its source. On the screen, a long parabola, pliant and precise, guides and controls each sequence, then punctually closes again. Think of any Rossellini film: each scene, each episode will recur in your memory not as a succession of shots and compositions, a more or less harmonious succession of more or less brilliant images, but as a vast melodic phrase, a continuous arabesque, a single implacable line which leads people inel- uctably towards the as yet unknown, embracing in its trajectory a palpitant and *definitive* universe; whether it be a fragment from *Paisà*, a *fioretto* from *St Francis* (*Francesco, guillare di dio*), a 'station' in *Europa '51*, or these films in their entirety, the symphony in three movements of *Germany, Year Zero*, the doggedly ascending scale of *The Miracle* or *Stromboli* (musical metaphors come as spontaneously as visual ones) – the indefatigable eye of the camera invariably assumes the role of the pencil, a temporal sketch is perpetuated before our eyes (but rest assured, without attempts to instruct us by using slow motion to analyse the Master's inspiration for our benefit);[3] we live through its progress until the final shading off, until it loses itself in the continuance of time just as it had loomed out of the whiteness of the canvas. For there are films which begin and end, which have a beginning and an ending, which conduct a story through from its initial premise until everything has been restored to peace and order, and there have been deaths, a marriage or a revelation; there is Hawks, Hitchcock, Murnau, Ray, Griffith. And there are the films quite unlike this, which recede into time like rivers to the sea; and which offer us only the most banal of closing images: rivers flowing, crowds, armies, shadows passing, curtains falling in perpetuity, a girl dancing till the end of time; there is Renoir and Rossellini. It is then up to us in silence, to prolong this movement that has returned to secrecy, this hidden arc that has buried itself beneath the earth again; we have not finished with it yet.

(Of course all this is arbitrary, and you are right: the first group prolong themselves too, but not quite in the same way, it seems to me; they gratify the mind, their eddies buoy us up, whereas the others burden us, weigh us down. That is what I meant to say.)

And there are the films that rejoin time through a painfully maintained immobility; that expend themselves without flinching in a perilous position on summits that seem uninhabitable; such as *The Miracle, Europa '51*.

4 Is it too soon for such enthusiasms? A little too soon, I fear; so let us return to earth and, since you wish it, talk of compositions: but this lack

of balance, this divergence from the customary centres of gravity, this apparent uncertainty which secretly shocks you so deeply, forgive me if once again I see the hand of Matisse here, his asymmetrism, the magisterial 'falseness' in composition, tranquilly eccentric, which also shocks at first glance and only subsequently reveals its secret equilibrium where values are as important as the lines, and which gives to each canvas this unobtrusive movement, just as here it yields at each moment this controlled dynamism, this profound inclination of all elements, all arcs and volumes at that instant, towards the new equilibrium, and in the following second of the new disequilibrium towards the next; and this might be learnedly described as the art of succession in composition (or rather, of successive composition) which, unlike all the static experiments that have been stifling the cinema for thirty years, seems to me to stand to reason as the only visual device legitimate for the film-maker.

5 I shall not labour the point further: any comparison soon becomes irksome, and I fear that this one has already continued too long; in any case, who will be convinced except those who see the point as soon as it is stated? But allow me just one last remark – concerning the Trait: grace and gaucheness indissolubly linked. Render tribute in either case to a youthful grace, impetuous and stiff, clumsy and yet disconcertingly at ease, that seems to me to be in the very nature of adolescence, the awkward age, where the most overwhelming, the most *effective* gestures seem to burst unexpectedly in this way from a body strained by an acute sense of embarrassment. Matisse and Rossellini affirm the freedom of the artist, but do not misunderstand me: a controlled, constructed freedom, where the initial building finally disappears beneath the sketch.

For this trait must be added which will resume all the rest: the common sense of the draft. A sketch more accurate, more detailed than any detail and the most scrupulous design, a disposition of forces more accurate than composition, these are the sort of miracles from which springs the sovereign truth of the imagination, of the governing idea which only has to put in an appearance to assume control, summarily outlined in broad essential strokes, clumsy and hurried yet epitomizing twenty fully rounded studies. For there is no doubt that these hurried films, improvised out of very slender means and filmed in a turmoil that is often apparent from the images, contain the only real portrait of our times; and these times are a draft too. How could one fail suddenly to recognize, quintessentially sketched, ill-composed, incomplete, the semblance of our daily existence? These arbitrary groups, these absolutely theoretical collections of people eaten away by lassitude and boredom, exactly as we know them to be, as the irrefutable, accusing image of our heteroclite, dissident, discordant societies. *Europa '51, Germany, Year Zero*, and this film which might be called *Italy '53*, just as *Paisà* was *Italy '44*, these are our mirror, scarcely flattering to us; let us yet hope that these times, true in their turn like these kindred films, will secretly orient themselves towards an inner order, towards a truth which will give them meaning and *in the end* justify so much disorder and flurried confusion.

6 Ah, now there is cause for misgivings: the author is showing the cloven hoof. I can hear the mutters already: coterie talk, fanaticism, intolerance. But this famous freedom, and much-vaunted freedom of expression, but more particularly the freedom to express everything of oneself, who carries it further? To the point of immodesty, comes the answering cry; for the strange thing is that people still complain, and precisely those people who are loudest in their claims for freedom (to what end? the liberation of man? I'll buy that, but from what chains? That man is free is what we are taught in the catechism, and what Rossellini quite simply shows; and his *cynicism* is the cynicism of great art). '*Viaggio in Italia* is the Essays of Montaigne,' our friend M. prettily says; this, it seems, is not a compliment; permit me to think otherwise, and to wonder at the fact that our era, which can no longer be shocked by anything, should pretend to be scandalized because a film-maker dares to talk about himself without restraint; it is true that Rossellini's films have more and more obviously become *amateur* films; home movies; *Joan of Arc at the Stake* is not a cinematic transposition of the celebrated oratorio, but simply a souvenir film of his wife's performance in it just as *The Human Voice* was primarily the record of a performance by Anna Magnani (the most curious thing is that *Joan of Arc at the Stake*, like *The Human Voice*, is a *real* film, not in the least theatrical in its appeal; but this would lead us into deep waters). Similarly, Rossellini's episode in *Siamo donne* is simply the account of a day in Ingrid Bergman's life; while *Viaggio in Italia* presents a transparent fable, and George Sanders a face barely masking that of the film-maker himself (a trifle tarnished, no doubt, but that is humility). Now he is no longer filming just his ideas, as in *Stromboli* or *Europa '51*, but the most everyday details of his life; this life, however, is 'exemplary' in the fullest sense that Goethe implied: that everything in it is instructive, including the errors; and the account of a busy afternoon in Mrs Rossellini's life is no more frivolous in this context than the long description Eckermann gives us of that beautiful day, on 1 May 1825, when he and Goethe practised archery together. So there, then, you have this country, this city; but a privileged country, an exceptional city, retaining intact innocence and faith, living squarely in the eternal; a *providential* city; and here, by the same token, is Rossellini's secret, which is to move with unremitting freedom, and one single, simple motion, through manifest eternity: the world of the incarnation; but that Rossellini's genius is possible only within Christianity is a point I shall not labour, since Maurice Schérer[4] has already argued it better than I could ever hope to do, in a magazine: *Cahiers du Cinéma*, if I remember right.

7 Such freedom, absolute, inordinate whose extreme licence never involves the sacrifice of inner rigour, is freedom won; or better yet, earned.

This notion of earning is quite new, I fear, and astonishing even though evident; so the next thing is, earned how? By virtue of meditation, of exploring an idea or an inner harmony; by virtue of sowing this predestined seed in the concrete world which is also the intellectual world ('which is the same as the spiritual world'); by virtue of persistence, which then justifies any surrender to the hazards of creation, and even urges our hapless creator to such surrender; once again the idea becomes flesh, the work of art, the truth to come, becomes the very life of the artist, who can thereafter no longer do anything that steers clear of this pole, this magnetic point. And thereafter we too, I fear, can barely leave this inner circle any more, this basic refrain that is reprised chorally: that the body is the soul, the other is myself, the object is the truth and the message; and now we are also trapped by this place where the passage from one shot to the next is perpetual and infinitely reciprocal; where Matisse's arabesques are not just invisibly linked to their hearth, do not merely *represent* it, but are the fire itself.

8 This position offers strange rewards; but grant me another detour, which like all detours will have the advantage of getting us more quickly to where I want to take you. (It is becoming obvious anyway that I am not trying to follow a coherent line of argument, but rather that I am bent on repeating the same thing in different ways; affirming it on different keyboards.) I have already spoken of Rossellini's eye, his look; I think I even made a rather hasty comparison with Matisse's tenacious pencil; it doesn't matter, one cannot stress the film-maker's eye too highly (and who can doubt that this is where his genius primarily lies?), and above all its singularity. Ah, I'm not really talking about Kino-Eye, about documentary objectivity and all that jazz; I'd like to have you feel (with your finger) more tangibly the *powers* of this look: which may not be the most subtle, which is Renoir, or the most acute, which is Hitchcock, but is the most active; and the point is not that it is concerned with some transfiguration of appearances, like Welles, or their condensation, like Murnau, but with their capture: a hunt for each and every moment, at each *perilous* moment a corporeal quest (and therefore a spiritual one; a quest for the spirit by the body), an incessant movement of seizure and pursuit which bestows on the images some indefinable quality at once of triumph and agitation: the very note, indeed, of conquest. (But perceive, I beg you, wherein the difference lies here; this is not some pagan conquest, the exploits of some infidel general; do you perceive the fraternal quality in this word, and what sort of conquest is implied, what it comprises of humility, of charity?)

9 For 'I have made a discovery': there is a television aesthetic – don't laugh, that isn't my discovery, of course – and what this aesthetic is (what it is beginning to be) I learned just recently from an article by André Bazin[5] which, like me, you read in the coloured issue of *Cahiers du Cinéma*

(definitely an excellent magazine). But this is what I realized: that Rossellini's films, though film, are also subject to this *direct* aesthetic, with all it comprises of gamble, tension, chance and providence (which in fact chiefly explains the mystery of *Joan of Arc at the Stake*, where each shot change seems to take the same risks, and induce the same anxiety, as each camera change). So there we are, because of a film this time, ensconced in the darkness, holding our breath, eyes riveted to the screen which is at last granting us such privileges: spying on our neighbour with the most appalling indiscretion, violating with impunity the physical intimacy of people who are quite unaware of being exposed to our fascinated gaze; and in consequence, to the imminent rape of their souls. But in just punishment, we must instantly suffer the anguish of anticipating, of prejudging what must come *after*; what weight time suddenly lends to each gesture; one does not know what is going to happen, when, how; one has a presentiment of the event, but without seeing it take shape; everything here is fortuitous, instantly inevitable; even the sense of *hereafter*, within the impassive web of duration. So, you say, the films of a voyeur? – or a seer.

10 Here we have a dangerous word, which has been made to mean a good many silly things, and which I don't much like using; again you're going to need a definition. But what else can one call this faculty of seeing through beings and things to the soul or the ideal they carry within them, this privilege of reaching through appearances to the doubles which engender them? (Is Rossellini a Platonist? – Why not, after all he was thinking of filming *Socrates*.[6])

Because as the screening went on, after an hour went by I wasn't thinking of Matisse any more, I'm afraid, but of Goethe: the art of associating the idea with the substance first of all in the mind, of blending it with its *object* by virtue of meditation; but he who speaks aloud of the object, through it instantly names the idea. Several conditions are necessary, of course: and not just this vital concentration, this intimate mortification of reality, which are the artist's secret and to which we have no access; and which are none of our business anyway. There is also the precision in the presentation of this object, secretly impregnated; the lucidity and the candour (Goethe's celebrated 'objective description'). This is not yet enough; this is where ordering comes into play, no, order itself, the heart of creation, the creator's design; what is modestly known in professional terms as the construction (and which has nothing to do with the assembling of shots currently in vogue; it obeys different laws); that order, in other words, which, giving precedence to each appearance according to merit, within the illusion that they are simply succeeding one another, forces the mind to conceive another law than chance for their judicious advent.

This is something narrative has known, in film or novel, since it grew up. Novelists and film-makers of long standing, Stendhal and Renoir, Hawks and Balzac, know how to make construction the secret element in their work. Yet the cinema turned its back on the essay (I employ A. M.'s[7] word), and repudiated its unfortunate guerrillas, *Intolerance*, *La Règle du jeu*, *Citizen Kane*. There was *The River*, the first didactic poem: now there is *Viaggio in Italia* which, with absolute lucidity, at last offers the cinema, hitherto condemned to narrative, the possibility of the essay.

11 For over fifty years now the essay has been the very language of modern art; it is freedom, concern, exploration, spontaneity; it has gradually – Gide, Proust, Valéry, Chardonne, Audiberti – buried the novel beneath it; since Manet and Degas it has reigned over painting, and gives it its impassioned manner, the sense of pursuit and proximity. But do you remember that rather appealing group some years ago which had chosen some number or other as their objective and never stopped clamouring for the 'liberation' of the cinema;[8] don't worry, for once it had nothing to do with the advancement of man; they simply wanted the Seventh Art to enjoy a little of that more rarefied air in which its elders were flourishing; a very proper feeling lay behind it all. It appears, however, that some of the survivors don't care at all for *Viaggio in Italia*; this seems incredible. For here is a film that comprises almost everything they prayed for: metaphysical essay, confession, log-book, intimate journal – and they failed to realize it. This is an edifying story, and I wanted to tell you the whole of it.

12 I can see only one reason for this; I fear I may be being malicious (but maliciousness, it seems, is to today's taste): this is the unhealthy fear of genius that holds sway this season. The fashion is for subtleties, refinements, the sport of smart-set kings; Rossellini is not subtle but fantastically simple. Literature is still the arbiter: anyone who can do a pastiche of Moravia has genius; ecstasies are aroused by the daubings of a Soldati, Wheeler, Fellini (we'll talk about Mr Zavattini another time); tiresome repetitions and longueurs are set down as novelistic density or the sense of time passing; dullness and drabness are the effect of psychological subtlety. Rossellini falls into this swamp like a butterfly broken on the wheel; reproving eyes are turned away from this importunate yokel.[9] And in fact nothing could be less literary or novelistic; Rossellini does not care much for narration, and still less for demonstration; what business has he with the perfidies of argumentation? Dialectic is a whore who sleeps with all odds and ends of thought, and offers herself to any sophism; and dialecticians are riff-raff. His heroes prove nothing, they act; for Francis of Assisi, saintliness is not a beautiful thought. If it so happens that Rossellini wants to defend an idea, he too has no other way to convince us than to act, to create, to film; the thesis of *Europa '51*, absurd as each new episode starts, overwhelms us five minutes later, and each sequence is above all the mystery of the incarnation of this idea; we resist the thematic development of the plot, but we capitulate before Bergman's tears, before the *evidence* of her acts and of her suffering; in each scene the

film-maker fulfils the theorist by multiplying him to the highest unknown quantity. But this time there is no longer the slightest impediment: Rossellini does not demonstrate, he shows.

And we have *seen*: that everything in Italy has meaning, that all of Italy is instructive and is part of a profound *dogmatism*, that there one suddenly finds oneself in the domain of the spirit and the soul; all this may perhaps not belong to the kingdom of pure truths, but it is certainly shown by the film to be of the kingdom of perceptible truths, which are even more true. There is no longer any question of symbols here, and we are already on the road towards the great Christian allegory. Everything now seen by this distraught woman, lost in the kingdom of grace, these statues, these lovers, these pregnant women who form for her an omnipresent, haunting cortège, and then those huddled corpses, those skulls, and finally those banners, that procession for some almost barbaric cult, everything now radiates a different light, everything reveals itself as something else; here, visible to our eyes, are beauty, love, maternity, death, God.

13 All rather outmoded notions; yet there they are, visible; all you can do is cover your eyes or kneel.

There is a moment in Mozart where the music suddenly seems to draw inspiration only from itself, from an obsession with a pure chord, all the rest being but approaches, successive explorations, and withdrawals from this supreme position where time is abolished. All art may perhaps reach fruition only through the transitory destruction of its means, and the cinema is never more great than in certain moments that transcend and abruptly suspend the drama: I am thinking of Lillian Gish feverishly spinning round, of Jannings's extraordinary passivity, the marvellous moments of tranquillity in *The River*, the night sequence in *Tabu* with its slumbers and awakenings; of all those shots which the very greatest film-makers can contrive at the heart of a Western, a thriller, a comedy, where the genre is suddenly abolished as the hero briefly takes stock of himself (and above all of those two confessions by Bergman and Anne Baxter, those two long self-flashbacks by heroines who are the exact centre and the kernel of *Under Capricorn* and *I Confess*). What am I getting at? This: nothing in Rossellini better betokens the great film-maker than those vast chords formed within his films by all the shots of eyes *looking*; whether those of the small boy turned on the ruins of Berlin, or Magnani's on the mountain in *The Miracle*, or Bergman's on the Roman suburbs, the island of Stromboli, and finally all of Italy (and each time the two shots, one of the woman looking, then her vision; and sometimes the two merged); a high note is suddenly attained which thereafter need only be held by means of tiny modulations and constant returns to the dominant (do you know Stravinsky's 1952 *Cantata*?); similarly the successive stanzas of *St Francis* are woven together on the ground bass (readable at sight) of charity. Or at the heart of the film is this moment when the characters have touched bottom and are trying to find themselves without evident

success; this vertiginous awareness of self that grips them, like the fundamental note's own delighted return to itself at the heart of a symphony.
Whence comes the greatness of *Rome, Open City*, of *Paisà*, if not from this
sudden repose in human beings, from these tranquil essays in confronting
the impossible fraternity, from this sudden lassitude which for a second
paralyses them in the very course of the action? Bergman's solitude is at
the heart of both *Stromboli* and *Europa '51*: vainly she veers, without
apparent progress; yet without knowing it she is advancing, through the
attrition of boredom and of time, which cannot resist so protracted an
effort, such a persistent concern with her moral decline, a lassitude so
unweary, so active and so impatient, which in the end will undoubtedly
surmount this wall of inertia and despair, this exile from the true kingdom.

14 Rossellini's work 'isn't much fun'; it is deeply serious, even, and turns
its back on comedy; and I imagine that Rossellini would condemn laughter
with the same Catholic virulence as Baudelaire (and Catholicism isn't
much fun either, despite its worthy apostles – *Dov'è la libertà?* should make
very curious viewing from this point of view). What is it he never tires of
saying? That human beings are alone, and their solitude irreducible; that,
except by miracle or saintliness, our ignorance of others is complete; that
only a life in God, in his love and his sacraments, only the communion
of the saints can enable us to meet, to know, to possess another being
than ourselves alone; and that one can only know and possess oneself in
God. Through all these films human destinies trace separate curves, which
intersect only by accident; face to face, men and women remain wrapped
in themselves, pursuing their obsessive monologues; delineation of the
'concentration camp world'[10] of men without God.
    Rossellini, however, is not merely Christian, but Catholic; in other
words, carnal to the point of scandal; one recalls the outrage over *The
Miracle*; but Catholicism is by vocation a scandalous religion; the fact that
our body, like Christ's, also plays its part in the divine mystery is something
hardly to everyone's taste, and in this creed which makes the presence of
the flesh one of its dogmas, there is a concrete meaning, weighty, almost
sensual, to flesh and matter that is highly repugnant to chaste spirits: their
'intellectual evolution' no longer permits them to participate in mysteries
as gross as this. In any case, Protestantism is more in fashion, especially
among sceptics and free-thinkers; here is a more intellectual religion, a
shade abstract, that instantly places the man for you: Huguenot ancestry
infallibly hints at a coat of arms. I am not likely to forget the disgusted
expressions with which, not so long ago, some spoke of Bergman's
weeping and snivelling in *Stromboli*. And it must be admitted that this
goes (Rossellini often does) to the limits of what is bearable, of what is
decently admissible, to the very brink of indelicacy. The direction of
Bergman here is totally conjugal, and based on an intimate knowledge
less of the actress than of the woman; we may also add that our little

world of cinema finds it difficult – when the couple are not man and wife[11] – to accept a notion of love like this, with nothing joyous or extravagant about it, a conception so serious and genuinely carnal (let us not hesitate to repeat the word) of a sentiment more usually disputed nowadays by either eroticism or angelism; but leave it to the Dolmancés[12] among us to take offence at the way it is presented (or even just its reflection, like a watermark, on the face of the submissive wife), as though at some obscenity quite foreign to their light, amusing – and so very modern – fancies.

15 Enough of that; but do you now understand what this freedom is: the freedom of the ardent soul, cradled by providence and grace which, never abandoning it to its tribulations, save it from perils and errors and make each *trial* redound to its glory. Rossellini has the eye of a modern, but also the spirit; he is more modern than any of us; and Catholicism is still as modern as anything.

You are weary of reading me; I am beginning to tire of writing to you, or at least my hand is; I would have liked to tell you many more things. One will suffice: the striking novelty of the acting, which here seems to be abolished, gradually killed off by a higher necessity; all flourishes, all glowing enthusiasms, all outbursts must yield to this intimate pressure which forces them to efface themselves and pass on with the same humble haste, as though in a hurry to finish and be done with it. This way of draining actors must often infuriate them, but there are times when they should be listened to, others when they should be silenced. If you want my opinion, I think that this is what acting in the cinema tomorrow will be like. Yet how we have loved the American comedies, and so many little films whose charm lay almost entirely in the bubbling inventiveness of their movements and attitudes, the spontaneous felicities of some actor, the pretty poutings and fluttering eyelashes of a smart and saucy actress; that one of the cinema's aims should be this delightful pursuit of movement and gesture was true yesterday, and even true two minutes ago, but after this film it may not be so any longer; the absence of studied effects here is superior to any successful pursuit, the resignation more beautiful than any glow of enthusiasm, the inspired simplicity loftier than the most dazzling performance by any diva. This lassitude of demeanour, this habit so deeply ingrained in every movement that the body no longer vaunts them, but rather restrains them, keeps them within itself, this is the only kind of acting we shall be able to take for a long time to come; after this taste of pungency, all sweetness is but insipid and unremembered.

16 With the appearance of *Viaggio in Italia*, all films have suddenly aged ten years; nothing is more pitiless than youth, than this unequivocal intrusion by the modern cinema, in which we can at last recognize what we were vaguely awaiting. With all due deference to recalcitrant spirits, it is *this* that shocks or troubles them, that vindicates itself today, it is in

this that truth lies in 1955. Here is our cinema, those of us who in our turn are preparing to make films (did I tell you, it may be soon); as a start I have already suggested something that intrigues you: is there to be a Rossellini school? and what will its dogmas be? I don't know if there is a school, but I do know there should be: first, to come to an understanding about the meaning of the word 'realism', which is not some rather simple scriptwriting technique, nor yet a style of *mise en scène*, but a state of mind: *that a straight line is the shortest distance between two points* (judge your De Sicas, Lattuadas and Viscontis by this yardstick). Second point: a fig for the sceptics, the rational, the judicious; irony and sarcasm have had their day; now it is time to love the cinema so much that one has little taste left for what presently passes by that name, and wants to impose a more exacting image of it. As you see, this hardly comprises a programme, but it may be enough to give you the heart to begin.

This has been a very long letter. But the lonely should be forgiven: what they write is like the love letter that goes astray. To my mind, anyway, there is no more urgent topic today.

One word more: I began with a quotation from Péguy; here is another in conclusion: *'Kantism has unsullied hands'* (shake hands, Kant and Luther, and you too, Jansen), *'but it has no hands'*.

Yours faithfully,
Jacques Rivette

Translated by Tom Milne

Notes

1 The reference is to the first line of Mallarmé's poem 'Le Tombeau d'Edgar Poe': 'Tel qu'en Lui-même enfin l'éternité le change'. (Translator's note.)

2 Cf. André Bazin: 'An Aesthetic of Reality: Neo-Realism', in *What is Cinema? Vol. 2*, p. 33.

3 *Ibid.*

4 Eric Rohmer (under his real name, Maurice Schérer): 'Génie du christianisme' (on *Europa 51*), *Cahiers du Cinéma* 25, July 1953.

5 André Bazin: 'Pour contribuer à une érotologie de la Télévision', *Cahiers du Cinéma* 42, December 1954.

6 Rossellini did, much later, make *Socrates* (1970).

7 Probably André Martin, a frequent contributor to *Cahiers* at this time. (Translator's note.)

8 A reference to the 'Objectif 49' group; see 'Six Characters in Search of *auteurs*', Ch. 2, note 4.

9 Rivette's original of this sentence reads: 'Rossellini tombe dans ce marécage comme le pavé de l'ours; on se détourne avec des moues réprobatrices de ce paysan du Danube.' The bear and the Danube peasant are references to Fables by La Fontaine. (Translator's note.)

10 The reference is to David Rousset's book, *L'Univers concentrationnaire*. (Translator's note.)

11 The adulterous affair between Rossellini and Bergman, which began during

the shooting of *Stromboli* (1949), and their subsequent child, caused an enormous press scandal which virtually exiled Bergman from Hollywood.

12 A character in De Sade's *La Philosophie dans le boudoir*. (Translator's note.)

27 | Eric Rohmer: 'The Land of Miracles'

('La Terre du Miracle', *Cahiers du Cinéma* 47, May 1955, written under his real name, Maurice Schérer)

The term 'neo-realism' has become so debased that I would hesitate to use it in relation to *Viaggio in Italia* if Rossellini hadn't in fact claimed it himself. He sees this film as embodying a 'neo-realism' that is purer and deeper than in any of his earlier films. At least that was his comment to one member of the audience at the Paris premiere. One can certainly talk about evolution in the work of the author of *Rome, Open City*. If it is true that the more recent films can only at a pinch be categorized along with all the other Italian productions – including the films of Fellini, who is his most long-standing collaborator and the closest to him in ideas – it is not true that he has denied his old loves: he has just contented himself with being out in front, condemning his rivals to staying safely where they are. With each attempt he goes through the roof at such breakneck speed that we don't even have time to adjust our instruments to measure his performance.

The public reacts in a particular way to what is new. Let's take another look at the accounts of the first exhibitions of the Impressionists or the Fauves, the first performance of *The Rite of Spring*: we hear exclamations like 'He can't paint', 'I could do as well myself', 'It's not painting, it's not music, it's not cinema'. Just as the art students of the last century forged a convention of the 'posed', so there has emerged in the darkened auditoria a convention of the *natural*. As deliberately as Manet's refusal of *chiaroscuro*, the author of *Viaggio in Italia* scorns the easy choice – of a cinematic language underlaid with fifty years of use. Before Rossellini even the most inspired and original of film-makers would feel duty-bound to use the legacy of his precursors. He was familiar with all the ways that, by some kind of conditioned reflex, particular emotional reactions could be provoked in an audience – down to the smallest gesture or movement; and he would play on those reflexes, not try to break them. He would create art, a personal work, that is, but made out of a shared cinematic substance. For Rossellini this substance does not exist. His actors do not behave like the actors in other films, except in the sense that their gestures and attitudes are common to all human beings, but they urge us to look for something else behind this behaviour, something other than what our natural role as spectators would prompt us to recognize. The old relationship between the sign and the idea is shattered: in its place there emerges a new and disconcerting one.

Such is the elevated and brand-new conception of realism that we discover here. It's not long since I praised *Stromboli* or *Europa '51* for their documentary aspects. But in its construction *Viaggio in Italia* is no closer to the documentary than it is to the melodrama or the fictional romance. Certainly no documentary camera could have recorded the experiences of this English couple in this way, or, more to the point, in this spirit. Bear in mind that even the most direct, least contrived scene is always inscribed in the convention of editing, continuity and selection, and that convention is denounced by the director with the same virulence as he displays in his attack on suspense. His direction of the actors is exact, imperious, and yet it is not at all 'acted'. The story is loose, free, full of breaks, and yet nothing could be further from the amateur. I confess my incapacity to define adequately the merits of a style so new that it defies all definition. If only in its framing and its camera movements (where even the greatest directors have achieved no innovations for a long time now) this film is unlike any others. Through its magic alone it manages to endow the screen with that third dimension so sought after for the last three years by the best technicians on both sides of the Atlantic.

I am aware of a possible objection: 'Don't attribute to supreme skill what may only be the accidental result of carelessness.' Certainly not! You don't produce literature by pulling words out of a hat, and you don't create a piece of real cinema as original as this just by wandering along the road with an 8mm camera in your hand. It is strange how everything that lacks order is like automatic writing. The greatest new eruptions can only come out of the narrowest and least discernible crack. With a simple puff of her cigarette on the slopes of Vesuvius, the heroine unleashes a thick cloud of smoke – this is how Rossellini, master magician, more than tames his material. He relies on its complicity as a musician performing in a cave would turn the echo to his advantage.

I confess that as I watched the film my thoughts went off in directions far from those of the plot itself, like someone who goes into the cinema to kill time between appointments and, with his mind more on his own concerns than those of the film, is surprised to discover himself trying to read the time on a watch that one of the actors on the screen is wearing. This kind of illusion is certainly not one that an actor would take pride in creating. I admit that I was plunged into all kinds of absurd trains of thought by things like the pattern of George Sanders's tweed jacket, how old he must be, how much he's aged since *Rebecca* or *All About Eve*, Ingrid Bergman's hairstyle, not to speak of the shape of the skulls in the catacombs or new archaeological methods – for which a more sustained tempo in the plot wouldn't have allowed time. But I noticed that even while my imagination seemed to wander, time and time again it forced me back relentlessly to the very subject of the film. In this film in which everything appears incidental, everything, even the craziest mental digressions, is essentially a part of the film. This argument will be taken for no more than it's worth. Before a work of this stature a plea of extenuating circumstances is inappropriate.

Viaggio in Italia is the story of a couple's estrangement and their subsequent reconciliation. A standard dramatic theme, and the theme also of *Sunrise*. Rossellini and Murnau are the only two film-makers who have made Nature the active element, the principal element in the story. Both, because they reject the facility of the psychological style and scorn understatement or allusion, have had the remarkable privilege of conducting us into the most secret regions of the soul. Secret? Let's make our meaning clear: not the troubled zones of the libido, but the broad daylight of consciousness. Because they refuse to illuminate the mechanics of choice, both films safeguard its freedom all the better. Thus the soul is delivered up to its own resources, and finds no higher purpose than in the recognition of order in the world. Both these films are a drama with in fact three characters; the third is God. But God does not have the same face in both. In the first a 'pre-ordained harmony' governs at one and the same time the movements of the soul and the vicissitudes of the cosmos: nature and the heart of man beat with the same pulse. The second goes beyond this order – whose magnificence it can equally reveal – and uncovers that supreme disorder that is known as the miracle.

In the course of the interview that he gave to *Cahiers* last year,[1] Rossellini talked about the 'sense of eternal life' and the 'presence of the miracle' which had been revealed to him on the soil of Naples. These two phrases are eloquent enough in themselves and will exempt me from lengthier commentary. From the museum of Naples to the catacombs, from the sulphur springs of Vesuvius to the ruins of Pompeii, we accompany the heroine along the spiritual path that leads from the platitudes of the ancients on the fragility of man to the Christian idea of immortality. And if the film succeeds – logically, you could say – through a miracle, it is because that miracle was in the order of things whose order, in the end, depends on a miracle. Such a philosophy is foreign to the art of our time. The greatest works – even those most tinged with mysticism – seem to find their inspiration in a quite opposite idea. They present a conception of man as a deity – if not entirely God – which is an enormous temptation to our pride and has almost deadened us. There is alarm over the disappearance of sacred art: what does it matter, if the cinema is taking over from the cathedrals! I will go further: what makes Catholicism so great is its extreme openness, its power infinitely to enrich itself. It is no ivy-covered temple, but an edifice whose stones increase with every century that goes by, while its unity remains unaltered. And not only through its dogmas (I'm thinking of the recently proclaimed dogma of the Assumption), but through its capacity to renew itself in life and in art, it has more and more contempt for the flimsy support of natural philosophy. By the grace of its music perhaps a Bach mass can lead us closer to God than can the majesty of the cathedrals. Is it the task of the cinema to bring into art a notion whose great riches the whole of human genius had not yet known how to uncover: the notion of the miracle?

Translated by Liz Heron

Note

1 Eric Rohmer (under his real name, Maurice Schérer) and François Truffaut: 'Entretien avec Roberto Rossellini', *Cahiers du Cinéma* 37, July 1954; extracts from this interview are translated in Ch. 28(i) below.

28 | Interviews with Roberto Rossellini

(i) Eric Rohmer and François Truffaut, 'Entretien avec Roberto Rossellini', *Cahiers du Cinéma* 37, July 1954 (extract);[1] Rohmer contributed under his real name, Maurice Schérer
(ii) Fereydoun Hoveyda and Jacques Rivette, 'Entretien avec Roberto Rossellini', *Cahiers du Cinéma* 94, April 1959 (extract)

i 1954

The message contained in the recent films of Roberto Rossellini gave rise to interpretations so diverse that a clarification by the director himself seemed to be called for. The interview that he gave us rules out any misunderstanding about the meaning of his work in moral terms. Will it win Rossellini any more admirers? That is something we could not say. But his detractors will no longer be able to accuse him of insincerity or incoherence.

One contributor to Cahiers, *Jacques Rivette, wrote recently: 'On one side there is the Italian cinema, and on the other the work of Roberto Rossellini.' What he meant was that you keep yourself apart from the neo-realist movement, under whose banner almost every one of the Italian directors would group himself . . .*
Yes, from a particular kind of neo-realism. But what is meant by the word? You know that there was a congress on neo-realism in Parma;[2] we spent a great deal of time discussing it and the term is still very vague. Most of the time it's only a label. As far as I am concerned it is primarily a moral position which gives a perspective on the world. It then becomes an aesthetic position, but its basis is moral.
The consensus is that there is a break in your work that coincides with Stromboli.
That may be true. It's difficult to be objective about oneself. In my opinion – not that I set that much store by it – there is no break at all. I think I am the same human being looking at things in the same way. But one is moved to take up other themes, interest is shifted somewhere else, you have to take other paths; you cannot go on shooting in ruined cities for ever. Too often we make the mistake of letting ourselves be hypnotized by a particular milieu, by the feel of a particular time. But life has changed, the war is over, the cities have been rebuilt. It was the story of the reconstruction that had to be told: perhaps I was not equal to it . . .
That is the theme you take up in Germany, Year Zero *and also in* Europa '51. *In both these films is there not a pessimism that was totally absent in* Rome, Open City, *but did come through in* Paisà?

I am not a pessimist: I think it's a kind of optimism to see the bad as well as the good. I was reproached with having been presumptuous in *Europa '51*; even the title shocked people. The way I meant it, it was very humble. I wanted to say with great humility what I felt about our lives today. I am a family man, so I have to be interested in everyday life. I've been just as much reproached with having given no solution, but that is a sign of humility. Anyway, if I were able to find a solution I wouldn't be making films. I would be doing something else . . .

And yet, when you propose a solution in Stromboli *the critics look askance . . .*
I haven't understood why, but it must be my fault, since I've failed to convince other people.[3]

Personally, we find rather that the Christianity of the ending gives the work its meaning.
You see it that way, but let me be the interviewer for a moment. For a few years now, the general tendency in criticism has been, not hostility, but a current of opposition to my later films. Is it because I handle subjects that the cinema won't usually approach, or because I use a style that is not cinematographic? It is not the usual language; I refuse effects, I 'feel my way' in what I think is a very personal style.

Since we like your films and feel we understand them, it is almost as difficult for us as it is for you to make sense of why some people don't like them. The unfamiliarity of your style baffled many of our colleagues to begin with; the fact is that some have had a change of heart. For instance, many of those who didn't like Europa '51 *when they saw it in Venice changed their minds when the film came out in Paris.*
It's funny to re-read what the critics said about my early films. *Rome, Open City*: 'Rossellini confuses art with reportage. The film is a piece of Grand Guignol.' In Cannes, where it was screened one afternoon, nobody noticed it; then, gradually, they began to take it seriously. They even overdid it. I remember the terrible shock I had when *Paisà* came out. I really believed in the film; it is one of the three I like best.[4] The first Italian review I set eyes on talked about 'the director's rotting brain' and went on in that vein. I don't think it possible to say anything worse about a film than what was said about *Germany, Year Zero*. Today it is referred to all the time. I find this delay very difficult to understand.

To go back to your style, what can make it bewildering is the absence of what are called 'cinema effects'. You don't emphasize the important moments, you are always not just objective, but impassive. You give the impression that everything is on the same scale, by some kind of deliberate intention.
I always try to be impassive. I find that whatever is astonishing, unusual and moving in men, it is precisely that great actions and great deeds come about in the same way, with the same resonance as normal everyday occurrences. I try to relate both with the same humility: there is a source of dramatic interest in that.

[. . .]

And Viaggio in Italia?

That is a film I like very much. It was very important for me to show Italy, Naples, that strange atmosphere which is mingled with a very real, very immediate, very deep feeling, the sense of eternal life. It is something that has completely disappeared from the world. An astonishing thing happened to Eduardo de Filippo. When he was writing his play *Napoli milionaria* he would wander round Naples to gather material. One day he heard that a Neapolitan family was putting on show a negro child that had been born to them. He went to see the show; at the door the Neapolitan husband was making people pay five lire. They went in and saw his wife, with the negro child in her arms. When de Filippo came out, since he is well known in Naples, he was asked: 'Were you satisfied, did you get a good look?' and de Filippo apparently replied: 'I'll tell you, you bastard, aren't you ashamed to charge people five lire just to see how your wife made a fool of you with a negro?' The fellow then took him to one side and told him: 'Just between the two of us, we wash the child every night!' It was a poor Neapolitan child! Since corruption existed, corruption was in demand. It was a poor family that had to live. They had made themselves fashionable!

That amazing innocence, that purity, that refusal to be contaminated, that was the miraculous thing. Do you remember in *Paisà*? – I apologize for referring to myself, but I see it as a line that is enormously important – when the negro is falling asleep, the child tells him: 'Be careful not to fall asleep or I'll steal your shoes.' The negro falls asleep and the kid steals his shoes. It's fair, it's how things are done, it's this amazing *game* that sets the boundaries of morality.

[. . .]

What role does improvisation play in your films?

In theory, I shoot according to what is planned; but I keep back some freedom for myself. I listen to the rhythm of the film. And that is perhaps what makes me obscure, I know how important it is to wait in order to reach a certain point, so I don't describe the point, but the wait, and I suddenly reach the conclusion. I really can't do it any differently, for when you have the point, the core of the thing, if you set out to enlarge this core, to put it in water, to expand it, it is no longer a core but something which has no more shape, no more meaning or emotion.

I've received Claude Mauriac's book.[5] The other evening I was reading what he had written about *Stromboli*. He says that I've put some documentary footage in the film, that was bought and edited in: like the tuna fishing sequence. That episode is certainly not documentary film; what's more, I shot it myself. I tried to reproduce that endless wait in the sun, then that dreadfully tragic moment when they kill it: that death that explodes after a wonderful, shameless, lazy, I would say benevolent wait in the sun. It was what was important, from the point of view of character. Claude Mauriac is a very careful, intelligent man; what could make a critic say such a thing? He should have got his information right to begin with.

You have a reputation for shooting without a script, and improvising all the time . . .

That's partly a myth. I carry the 'continuity' of my films in my head; and my pockets are full of notes too. Still, I must admit I have never really understood the need to have a shooting script unless it's to reassure the producers. What could be more absurd than the left-hand column: *medium shot [plan américain] – lateral travelling shot – pan and frame . . .* ? It's a bit like a novelist breaking down his book into sequences: on page 212, an imperfect subjunctive, then a complement to an indirect object . . . etc! As for the right-hand column, that is the dialogue: I don't improvise it systematically; it's written a long time in advance, and if I don't reveal it until the last moment it's because I don't want the actor, or the actress, to be too familiar with it. I also manage to keep that control of the actor by rehearsing very little and shooting fast, without too many takes. I have to be sure of the 'freshness' of the actors. I shot *Europa '51* in forty-six days and with no more than 16,000 metres of film. For *Stromboli* the figure was even lower; admittedly there were 102 shooting days but we were confined to the island, handicapped by the unpredictability of the weather and variations in the wind and sea that were too great. As far as the fishing is concerned, we waited eight days for the tuna. In short, I don't work any differently from my colleagues; I just dispense with the hypocrisy of the shooting script.

[. . .]

Translated by Liz Heron

ii 1959

[. . .] *Throughout the screening of* (India) *we felt there was a deliberate decision to minimize the story and its central message. Is it really deliberate?*

Yes, and it's more than a decision – it's a constant endeavour. In his article on *Viaggio in Italia*[6] Rivette compared me to Matisse. That made quite an impression on me, and I may say that I have become conscious of this economy. For me it represents a new endeavour, but when I manage it, then it is immeasurably exhilarating.

In your interview with Renoir and Bazin published in France-Observateur[7] *you attacked montage.*

Yes, montage is no longer necessary. Things are there – especially in this film – why manipulate them? People who make films believe that the cinema is always something of a miracle. You go into the projection room and you see something on the screen; that's astonishing in itself. And then, you can understand what the actors are saying. Even more astonishing. The technical process is always amazing: not for me, but for a lot of people. Well, it's the same thing with montage: it's a bit like the magician's hat. You put all these techniques into it and then you bring out a dove, a bunch of flowers, a carafe of water . . . you give it a stir and again you bring out a carafe of water, a dove, etc. . . . . Taken in this sense at any rate, montage is something I am averse to and that I think no longer necessary. I mean montage in the classical sense, the kind you learn as an art at IDHEC.[8] It was probably necessary in silent films. A Stroheim film couldn't exist without montage. Stroheim would try out ten solutions to see which was the most effective. At that time it was a question of constituting a genuine cinematic language, language in the sense of a vehicle, not a poetic language.

Nowadays that's no longer necessary. Of course there is an element of 'montage' in my film; it's a matter of making good use of the elements, but not a matter of language.

In the silent period what went on film had very little reality in itself. Reality was recaptured through montage.

And what is also important is that the camera today has become completely mobile. In the silent period it was totally immobile. In the early days using tracking shots was considered a piece of madness.

So your montage is not subordinate to any preconceived idea?

None at all. I have no fixed plan. What I do have, rather, is a particular speed of observation, and I work according to what I see. I always know that if the eye is drawn to see certain things, then they are the things that matter. I don't philosophize about it . . . No, really, I don't have conventional continuity in mind. I always shoot things in movement. I couldn't care less about whether I get to the end of the movement so as to fit in with the next shot. When I have shown what matters, I cut: that's enough. It is much more important to bring together what is in the image. If you look at my editing with the eye of a film-maker, I can well understand that it might jar, but I think there is no reason why you should look at it with the eye of a film-maker.

André Bazin mistrusted editing tricks. He used to say that you had to show both the man and the tiger in the same shot. Your film shows them separately.

If you want to make the story more credible, logically it is better to show them both in the same shot. But if it is credible through other means, I don't see why one should have to use a particular technique. It all depends what you want to do. I don't want to put on a spectacle. From Bazin's own point of view he was quite right. If you want to create some excitement, the excitement is of course stronger if you show the man and the tiger at the same time. But this story of mine has no need of excitement. You will remember how the episode begins: a long tracking shot in the jungle while all the time you hear the love-call of the tigers. Perhaps there wasn't even any need to see the tigers. I show them to give some emphasis.

I don't make calculations. I know what I want to say and I find the most direct way of saying it. That's all – I don't agonize over it. If it is said, the way it is said hardly matters to me. You assure me that my film gives the impression of a choice made in advance. No, things are not 'chosen', but the ideas are solid. Some kind of choice has doubtless been made, but about the idea. What matters are the ideas, not the images. You only have to have very clear ideas and you find the image that most directly expresses them.

That is essentially your article of faith as a film-maker.
Yes, there are a thousand other ways of expressing ideas besides film; like writing, if I were a writer. The only advantage of film is that you can include ten different things at the same time in one frame. You don't have to be analytical on film – while at the same time you are.
Then can we put to you the other side of the question we asked earlier? Why not just a documentary, like Flaherty?
What mattered to me was man. I have tried to express the soul, the light that is inside these men, their reality in its absolute intimacy and uniqueness, attached to an individual with all the meaning of the things that are around him. For the things that are around him have a meaning, since there is someone who looks at them, or at least this meaning becomes unique by virtue of someone looking at them: the hero of each episode who is also the narrator. If I had made a strict documentary I would have had to forsake what went on inside, in the hearts of these men. And besides, to push documentary to its limits, I think it was also necessary to look at the hearts of these men.
That is, in short, a return to early neo-realism?
Yes, that's right.
But can we ask you yet again, why India? Do you think that what you did in India could be done just as well in Brazil, and even in France or Italy?
Yes. I ought even to tell you that my whole Indian project was for me a kind of study for a project on a bigger scale that I have already started.

I think that every cultural medium has become sterile because of the fact that the search for man as he really is has been completely abandoned. We are now being given stereotyped men, ersatz feelings, of love, death, sexuality, morality. We deal with false problems, because we live immersed in a civilization whose banner is optimism. Everything is going fine . . . except for a few little things. That's how pseudo-problems have been constructed. For example – and this is one of the clichés that irritate me most – the youth problem. Youth has always been and will always be a problem. It is not a problem specific to this century.
[. . .]
So today they set up pseudo-problems as the target and forget the real problems of mankind. And what are the real problems? First, we have to get to know human beings as they really are, we have to begin with an act of deep humility and try to get close to men, see them as they are, with objectivity, without preconceptions, without moral arguments, at least to begin with. Personally I have a very deep respect for human beings. The most dreadful man is still worthy of respect. What matters is to discover the reasons why he is dreadful. I don't let myself make condemnations.

With the world now shrunk so small, we go on not knowing one another at all. We don't know our neighbours, we don't know the people on the Left Bank, we don't know the Swiss! Today, when we live on top of one another, it is extremely important that we start getting to know one another, because it is only from the basis of a very deep knowledge of men, and through truly analysing them, without any prejudice, without wanting to prove anything, from that tenderness and affection that can be kindled towards another individual, that we shall perhaps find a solution to the problems that present themselves now, and which, even technically, are different from those that arose before our time.

Perhaps that takes us a bit off the point, but I want to say what my moral concerns are. Abstract art has become official art. I can understand an abstract artist, but I cannot understand how abstract art can have become official art, since it is genuinely the least intelligible kind of art. Phenomena like that don't come about for no reason. The reason? It's the attempt to forget man as much as possible. In modern society and throughout the world, except probably in Asia, man has become a cog in a huge, monstrous machine.

He has become a slave. And the entire history of mankind consists of passages from slavery to freedom. There has always been a point where slavery prevailed, and then freedom got the upper hand again – very seldom, or for very short periods, since liberty had hardly been achieved when slavery was again established. In the modern world a new slavery has been created – the slavery of ideas. And it's being done by every means available, from the detective story to the radio, the cinema, etc. Also through the fact that techniques are so highly developed and that the knowledge possible at any deep level, in a restricted area, if it is to be effective in social terms, prevents man from having other areas of knowledge. I don't remember who it was said: 'We live in the century of vertical invasion by the Barbarians.' In other words, we have an extreme deepening of knowledge in one direction and enormous ignorance in any other.

Since I have been making films, I have heard people say that films have to be made for an audience with the average mental age of a child of twelve. It is true that the cinema (I am speaking in general), like the radio, television, or any form of mass entertainment, brings about a kind of cretinization in adults, and, on the other hand, immensely speeds up the development of children. That's the source of the lack of equilibrium to be seen in the modern world: it comes from the impossibility of understanding one another.

[. . .]

Well, what is there to stop us from making the effort to go and see men everywhere, to start to tell others about them, show that the world is full of friends – not full of enemies, even if some are enemies. The tiger, suddenly, by some accident, becomes a man-eater. But he is not one by nature. Cars too are man-eaters, since every day fifteen people die on the roads of France. Yet you cannot hate the car because there are accidents.

Well now, what about the cinema? What function can it have? The function of putting mankind face to face with things and realities as they are, and making other men and other problems known to them.

[. . .]

The project I am talking about has to be advanced in every possible way. My endeavour may be ridiculous, futile, unsuccessful, but at any rate I've started making programmes for television.[9] Through television, I was able not only to provide the image, but to say and explain particular things. In that way I have tried to add to the knowledge of a world which is very close to us, and yet numbers four hundred million people. Four hundred million people, that's quite a lot. It's a sixth of the human race, and we ought to know it.

Perhaps my television programme will be able to help people understand my film. The film is less technical, less documentary, less explanatory, less didactic, and since it perceives a country through emotions rather than through statistics, it doubtless offers the possibility of an even greater insight. That, I think, is what is important, and what I intend to do in the future. That is why, with some friends, I have tried to initiate a similar project in France.

Do you want to shoot those films yourself?

Most of all I want to get them made. Starting off with the research and the documentation, and then going on to the dramatic themes, but in order to represent things as they are, to remain on the terrain of honesty. Yes, the cinema has to teach men to know, and to recognize, one another, instead of continuing to tell the same old story. It's all variations on the same theme. Everything there is to know about robbery we know. We know everything there is to know about hold-ups. Everything there is to know about sex: not as it really is, of course, but we do know all its surrounding areas. But what does death mean now? What does life mean? What does pain mean? Everything has lost its real meaning. I repeat, we need to try and see things again as they are, not in some plastic form, but in real substance. There is no doubt that that's the solution. Then, perhaps, we shall be able to begin to have a sense of direction.

Translated by Liz Heron

Notes

1 An additional extract from this interview, concerning the origins of *Europa '51*, is translated in Don Ranvaud, *Roberto Rossellini*, London, British Film Institute, 1981, p. 15.

2 The congress, held in December 1953, was fully reported in *Cahiers* in articles by Jean-Louis Tallenay and Jules Gritti, *Cahiers du Cinéma* 41, December 1954.

3 Rossellini expanded on his response to the attacks on *Stromboli* in part III of three articles on his own work published later in *Cahiers*: 'Dix ans de cinéma' I, *Cahiers du Cinéma* 50, August–September 1955; II, *Cahiers du Cinéma* 52, November 1955; III, *Cahiers du Cinéma* 55, January 1956; translated in David Overbey, *Springtime in Italy: A Reader on Neo-Realism*, London, Talisman, 1978, with the passages on *Stromboli*, pp. 104–10, partially reprinted in Ranvaud, *op. cit.*

4 The other two being *St Francis (Francesco, giullare di dio)* and *Europa '51*. (Interviewers' note.)

5 Claude Mauriac, *L'Amour du cinéma*, Paris, Editions Albin Michel, 1954, pp. 108–13.
6 Jacques Rivette, 'Letter on Rossellini', Ch. 26 above.
7 Translated (slightly abridged) as 'Cinema and Television: Jean Renoir and Roberto Rossellini interviewed by André Bazin', *Sight and Sound*, vol. 28, no. 1, Winter 1958–9, pp. 26–30.
8 L'Institut des Hautes Etudes Cinématographiques: see Introduction, note 69. Cf. François Truffaut's review of *Juvenile Passion*, *Cahiers du Cinéma* 83, May 1958, translated in Truffaut, *Films in My Life*, p. 247.
9 Rossellini had already made a series of films on India, *L'India vista da Rossellini*, for Italian television; between 1964 and his death in 1977 almost all Rossellini's films were made for Italian and/or French television; for details, see Ranvaud, *op. cit.*, pp. 24–36.

Part Four

Polemics

Criticism

Introduction

For most of its history, *Cahiers* has been nothing if not polemical. Most of the material collected in this volume must be considered explicitly or implicitly polemical, often passionate, arguments for one kind of film, or one conception of cinema, as opposed to another, and one of the clearest consistencies over the nine years of articles printed in this volume is the writers' pleasure in delighting and outraging their readers (although Bazin's earnest seriousness sometimes gets the better of him and comes out as moderation). But we should not let the evident love of polemic obscure the fact that serious tasks were being undertaken: upsetting established values, re-writing film history, re-thinking popular, commercial cinema. Although many of the articles presented in other sections of this volume would have justified space under 'Polemics' (and similarly most of the pieces here could appear in other sections – Domarchi's and Bazin's lengthy articles, for example, relate primarily to American cinema), all the articles in this section do, nevertheless, seek both to argue vividly, and to generalize, about the specific nature of cinema, about critical responsibility, about the relationship of cinema to social reality. In so doing they all need to begin to elaborate 'theory' (that is, a general conceptual context within which to make sense of the particular concrete instance) and to consider the 'specificity' of cinema – in short, to consider (to take the title of Bazin's collected texts) 'What is cinema?' Presented and introduced separately are three short articles about CinemaScope, intended as a small case study in polemic.

Pierre Kast occupied a Marxist, anti-clerical position considerably to the left of most *Cahiers* opinion, and his early article 'Flattering the Fuzz' is written very much from a position of hostility to the *status quo* in both society and film industry. Although Truffaut and others would have shared Kast's views about the film industry, Kast's views about, for example, French colonialism were by no means generally shared at *Cahiers*, which proved not very active in opposition to the Algerian war. Kast argues that in the cinema 'good will on its own is more often than not totally useless' and that the system or institution of cinema (its 'apparatus', as Brecht put it in relation to theatre[1]) and its conventions work to ratify 'the state of the world as it is'. Given the political-economic situation of cinema, Kast argues for the greater scope for radical social critique indirectly, through the use of the 'parable' mode, rather than well-intentioned, socially conscious, but necessarily hopelessly compromised 'leftist' or 'liberal' films. A number of points here link Kast to more general *Cahiers* positions – particularly his perception of the *possibilities* in American cinema (recalling in particular Rohmer on violence and morality[2]) as opposed to the *closed* nature of French cinema,[3] and his polemic against the well-intentioned.[4] At the same time Kast's political clarity and ideological sophistication might have recommended him to *Positif*, *Cahiers'* rival journal and much more committed to left-liberal politics. If he continued to write for *Cahiers*, then this can be explained partly by *Positif*'s continuing greater commitment to both 'good intentions' and the possibilities for 'personal' expression within cinema.

Although Kast may have been in many ways isolated at this time, the position he sketches out here was very important and significantly informs a lot of later *Cahiers* work (which, however, by not following Kast's political line or commitments, effectively depoliticized Kast's thesis). The process of 'reading' which Kast implies, which may sound banal today, was not so banal at the time. Nor, indeed, ten years later, when the positions adopted by *Sight and Sound*[5] implied a refusal to read American cinema in this way, and even as intelligent (and Marxist-schooled) a critic as Geoffrey Nowell-Smith could drive himself into considerable confusions and contortions trying to cope with this problem.[6] *Twenty* years later the concept of 'reading' (*lecture*) – a necessary process of ideological decipherment below a surface 'naturalized' by visual pleasure and narrative flow – now thoroughly 'laundered' and theorized in Marxist terms, becomes *Cahiers'* major strategy.[7]

Taken together, Kast's article and Jean Domarchi's 'Knife in the Wound' provide clear enough evidence that there was an awareness of Marxism at *Cahiers* well before 1968. Where Kast represented an actively Marxist position very often in conflict with other *Cahiers* writers and editors,[8] Domarchi, a professor of philosophy, wrote from a more detached position well founded in Hegelian philosophy (though his article is also firmly grounded in the time of its writing: 1956, the anti-Stalinist 'thaw', Khrushchev, crisis in the French Communist Party). Domarchi's thesis can be considered, nevertheless, within the same broad perspective as Kast's in the sense that both pose themselves against well-intentioned cinema with 'social content' – a cinema often treated with indulgence by 'Stalinists' and liberals alike – and in favour of the less direct but more radical critique they perceive in some Hollywood cinema, and both therefore raise (without resolving) questions about decipherment, about audience readings. Undoubtedly, Domarchi, in his concern with the dialectical nature of art and its symbolic reproduction of contradictions, with 'the *mediations* through which one passes from the real world (defined by *particular* relations of production and/or a *particular* condition of the forces of production) into the imaginary world of the novelist, painter or film-maker', anticipates post-1968 *Cahiers* concerns more emphatically and theoretically than Kast. But the examples which both Kast and Domarchi discuss would fall clearly into the category of 'films which seem at first sight to belong firmly within the ideology and to be completely under its sway, but which turn out to be so only in an ambiguous way' in the classification established by Jean-Louis Comolli and Jean Narboni in their 'Cinema/Ideology/Criticism' editorial in 1969.[9]

Domarchi's article, and the position it expresses, was precisely the kind of thing likely to be dismissed as extremist, intellectually pretentious or just plain nutty by the Anglo-Saxon critical establishment of the time – and, of course, precisely the kind of thing likely to excite those enervated by English empiricism and 'good taste'. However, as Bazin's article on the *politique des auteurs* makes clear, there were strong voices within *Cahiers* (although Bazin became increasingly isolated in some of his positions) arguing against views like Domarchi's and, in its broader thrust, 'extreme' authorship positions. Bazin had engaged in the authorship battle before,[10] 'clarifying' *Cahiers*' editorial position following a special issue on Hitchcock[11] and the 'fuss' it had caused. There Bazin argued both a different view than the 'young Turks' (Rohmer, Truffaut, Rivette, Chabrol, all of whom were now regular contributors but none of whom was on the editorial group) about Hollywood cinema in general, regretting its 'ideological sterilization',[12] and a broad agreement with the value they placed on *mise en scène* as 'to a large extent the very stuff of the film, an organization of beings and things which is its own meaning unto itself – moral meaning as well as the aesthetic'.[13] Though in this important later article Bazin continued a broad sympathy with the *auteur* principle, he also continued to insist upon a different perspective which makes it difficult to place him unproblematically alongside Truffaut and Rivette (which Edward Buscombe tends to do, despite seeing the differences[14]). It may be that Bazin's sympathies prevent him from following through the implications he undoubtedly perceived in the cruder *auteur* positions. Neither Bazin's clarity about the development of nineteenth-century Romanticism ('there can be no definitive criticism of genius or talent which does not first take into consideration the social determinism, the historical combination of circumstances, and the technical background which to a large extent determine it') nor his insistence on cinema 'as an art which is both popular and industrial' find much support in most *Cahiers* writing at this time: Bazin was, for example, one of the few important *Cahiers* critics to write intelligently about genre. Indeed, any real sense of social determinants on cinema was to become progressively lost in *Cahiers* over the next few years.[15] In many ways, Bazin's different perspectives were more important for developments outside *Cahiers* and outside France: his comments about the 'vitality' of the Hollywood tradition look forward, for example, to Robin Wood's work on Hawks,[16] and Anglo-Saxon work on genre[17] owes a good deal to Bazin's tenacious commitment to the concept.

Bazin's increasing isolation in the two years before his death in November 1958 is dramatized vividly in his response to Luc Moullet's comment on Kurosawa's *Living*, and in Rivette's indirect rejoinder on Mizoguchi's *Ugetsu Monogatari*. The tension developing in 1957–8 and coming out into the open in 1958–9 – evident in these short exchanges, and also in Moullet's article on Fuller[18] – was basically between Bazin's commitment to a *mise en scène* at the service of liberal-humanist subject matter and treatment[19] and an opposing tendency interested not at all in liberal-humanist good intentions and concerned only with *mise en scène* as the essence of cinema. Rivette's article seeks, rather imperiously, to put an end to the Moullet–Bazin argument (generally as well as specifically) in entirely predictable terms which minimize (without absolutely rejecting)[20] Bazin's consistent emphasis on context and tradition, and value Mizoguchi as a 'personal genius' communicating through the universal language of *mise en scène*. Imposing 'the sense of a specific language and world, answerable only to him', Mizoguchi is taken to create a world which is universal because individual – and one which, one might add, in its movement towards 'reconciliation', as Rivette puts it, is noticeably similar ideologically to the thematic 'world' of *Cahiers*' other favoured *auteurs*.

Taken to further 'extremes', the enshrinement of *mise en scène* – usually as felicities of directorial invention within mainstream American cinema, audacities within classicism, as it were – threw up the distinctly illiberal, anti-humanist 'MacMahonist' tendency (so called after the Paris cinema which specialized in showing popular American cinema) and the 'notorious' figure of Michel Mourlet. Less than a year after Bazin's death, *Cahiers* (then edited by Jacques Doniol-Valcroze and Eric Rohmer) published its first major article by Mourlet with an editorial note dissociating *Cahiers* from the article's 'extreme' position and, extraordinarily, printing the whole article in italics! Justly notorious, the article (whose main points of reference were Losey, Fuller, Lang, Walsh, Cottafavi, Preminger, Don Weis), contained material such as this:

The curtains open. The house goes dark. A rectangle of light presently vibrates before our eyes. Soon it is invaded by gestures and sounds. Here we are absorbed by that unreal space and time. More or less absorbed. The mysterious energy which sustains with varying felicities the swirl of shadow and light and their foam of sounds is called *mise en scène*. It is on *mise en scène* that our attention is set, which organizes a universe, which covers the screen – *mise en scène*, and nothing else. Like the shimmer of the notes of a piano piece. Like the flow of words of a poem. Like the harmonies and discords of the colours of a painting. From a subject, from a story, from 'themes', and even from the final draft of the script, there spurts forth a world of which the least one can ask is that it does not render vain the effort which gave it birth. The placing of the actors and the objects, their displacements within the frame, should express everything, as one sees in the supreme perfection of the two latest Fritz Lang films, *The Tiger of Eschnapur* and *The Indian Tomb*.[21]

Bazin's increasing critical isolation should not obscure the extent to which his earlier work on realism had become *Cahiers* orthodoxy.[22] Bazin's assumptions about the nature of film, his thinking about transparency and narrative, are present in some force in formulations such as Alexandre Astruc's 'the cinema assumes a certain trust in the world just as it is' in his essay 'What is *mise en scène*?'. The question of the specificity of cinema, around the idea of *mise en scène*, had exercised *Cahiers* for a long time: Rivette, for example, asks himself the same question in his 1954 article on *Angel Face*[23] (and answers it – 'What is cinema, if not the *play* of actor and actress, of hero and set, of word and face, of hand and object?'). Some of this concern had stemmed from earlier work by Astruc himself, whose celebrated 1948 article, 'The Birth of a New Avant-Garde: *la Caméra stylo*',[24] had argued that 'the fundamental problem of the cinema is how to express thought' and abstraction, proposing *mise en scène* as the means for their expression, and vitally influencing work in both the *Revue du Cinéma* and *Cahiers*. Extending the earlier article, which had wanted film to be an 'artistic' medium (that is, subject to individual artistic control and 'as flexible and subtle as written language'), 'What is *mise en scène*?' is concerned primarily to draw distinctions between film and novel, focusing, again, on *mise en scène* as the specifically cinematic. At the same time, one senses that Astruc's argument here – in its somewhat mystical stance on *mise en scène*, in the centrality it accords violence, even in its choice of Mizoguchi as primary reference point, as the summit of cinema – also genuflects to those more recent developments at *Cahiers* associated with the 'MacMahonists'. Thus, the cycle of critical influences comes full circle.

Notes

1 See Bertolt Brecht, 'The Modern Theatre is the Epic Theatre', in John Willett (ed.), *Brecht on Theatre*, New York, Hill & Wang, 1964.

2 Eric Rohmer, 'Rediscovering America', *Cahiers* 54, Christmas 1955, Ch. 7 in this volume.

3 Cf. François Truffaut, 'A Certain Tendency of the French Cinema', originally published in *Cahiers* 31, January 1954, translated in *Cahiers du Cinéma in English*, no. 1, 1966, reprinted in Nichols, *Movies and Methods*.

4 Cf., for example, Claude Chabrol, 'Les Petits Sujets', *Cahiers* 100, October 1959, translated as 'Big Subjects, Little Subjects' in *Movie* 1, June 1962, and as 'Little Themes' in Graham, *New Wave*.

5 See, for example, Richard Roud, 'The French Line', *Sight and Sound*, vol. 29, no. 4, Autumn 1960.

6 Geoffrey Nowell-Smith, 'Movie and Myth', *Sight and Sound*, vol. 32, no. 2, Spring 1963.

7 See, for example, the Editors of *Cahiers du Cinéma*, 'John Ford's *Young Mr.*

Lincoln', originally published in *Cahiers* 223, August 1970, translated in *Screen*, vol. 13, no. 3, Autumn 1972, reprinted in *Screen Reader 1* and Nichols, *Movies and Methods*.

8 See, for example, Kast's polemic against Truffaut's 'dogmatism' about *The Wild One*, and his own respect for the film in the terms offered by 'Flattering the Fuzz', in *Cahiers* 36, June 1954.

9 Jean-Louis Comolli and Jean Narboni, 'Cinema/Ideology/Criticism (1)', originally published in *Cahiers* 216, October 1969, translated in *Screen*, vol. 12, no. 1, Spring 1971, reprinted in *Screen Reader 1* and Nichols, *Movies and Methods*.

10 André Bazin, 'Comment peut-on être Hitchcocko-Hawksien?', *Cahiers* 44, February 1955.

11 *Cahiers* 39, October 1954.

12 Bazin, *op. cit.*, p. 18.

13 *Ibid*.

14 Edward Buscombe, 'Ideas of Authorship', *Screen*, vol. 14, no. 3, Autumn 1973, reprinted in Caughie, *Theories of Authorship*.

15 See, for example, Fereydoun Hoveyda, 'Les Taches du soleil', *Cahiers* 110, August 1960.

16 Robin Wood, *Howard Hawks*, see particularly introduction, pp. 7–16.

17 See, for example, Jim Kitses, *Horizons West*, London, Secker & Warburg, 1969, and Colin McArthur, *Underworld USA*, London, Secker & Warburg, 1972.

18 Luc Moullet, 'Sam Fuller: In Marlowe's Footsteps', *Cahiers* 93, March 1959, Ch. 20 in this volume.

19 Cf. the 'revolutionary humanism' Bazin claimed for Italian neo-realism, in 'The Evolution of the Language of Cinema' in Bazin, *What is Cinema? Vol. 1*.

20 Robin Wood expresses a similar view in the introductory paragraph of his essay on *Ugetsu Monogatari* and *Sansho Dayu*, 'The Ghost Princess and the Seaweed Gatherer' in Wood, *Personal Views*, London, Gordon Fraser, 1976.

21 Michel Mourlet, 'Sur un art ignoré', *Cahiers* 98, August 1959, p. 27.

22 See, for example, Fereydoun Hoveyda on *Les 400 coups*, 'The First Person Plural', Ch. 4 in this volume.

23 Jacques Rivette, 'The Essential', *Cahiers* 32, February 1954, Ch. 17 in this volume.

24 Originally published in *L'Ecran Français*, no. 144, 1948, translated in Graham, *New Wave*.

29 | Pierre Kast: 'Flattering the Fuzz: Some Remarks on Dandyism and the Practice of Cinema'

('Des confitures pour un gendarme: remarques sur le dandysme et l'exercice du cinéma', *Cahiers du Cinéma* 2, May 1951)

The official soothsayers of ancient Rome could not pass each other in the street without smiling: film people are rarely endowed with a similar sense of humour. The assertion that cinema was a species of manifestation of an artist's creative genius, made in the face of all the evidence, was doubtless pretty daring once. On the other hand, it ought to be made clear that it gave rise to a deplorable confusing of the possibilities of expression in the cinema and the conditions under which films are made. The notion that all you need to make a film is inspiration, is one great joke.

To state yet again that the cinema is a function of social and economic necessity may perhaps be so obvious that it almost need not be said, but it nevertheless does not diminish the advantage of a clear-sighted view of the situation it gives rise to. The opinion of the public's taste formed by the haruspices who control distribution quite obviously represents a force far more powerful than any discussion of styles or movements within the creative process.

The fact that up to now no film-maker has thought of diverting that minimal part of his earnings that could be spent on making five or ten minutes of film just for himself, even if it turned out to be the purest pornography, gives rise to a great deal of thought. I am well aware that those who do not use their income to construct a public persona use it to distract themselves from their role as mercenaries with deep-sea fishing, women, drinking or travelling abroad. I am equally aware that the myth of cinema without cash represents a challenge and also that amateur cinema provides ample proof of this and that the final aim of cinema is not to get lost on the periphery.

The major problem is acquiring the wherewithal, and the restrictions implied by this have absolutely nothing in common with the kind of formal constraints imposed by the fugue, say, or the heroic couplet.

Apart from a few extremely rare cases of private patronage or cunning the potential *auteur* of a film is compelled to fit into a system of production with aims totally alien to his own. The choice of subject and the choice of means are never under his control in any real sense. For all that, he is not entirely restricted. There is a tiny margin of freedom left to him provided he is completely aware of the real state of affairs.

Obviously, I am not talking here about those who accept both the society we have to put up with and the production system prevailing at present. In the better cases, their natural virtuosity and what it is customary to call their technical ability find ways of revealing themselves in an amiable, clean-limbed and entertaining optimism which only adds – if that is at all possible – to the confusion that envelops these problems.

The worst kind of conventional film will be transformed into a detailed observation of the behaviour patterns of the lower classes in Paris, for instance, and there will be solemn discussions about the painstaking realism informing some bromide story about a couple of workers.

It is pretty generally acknowledged that there can be no likelihood of agreement about the essentials of a subject between the maker of a film and those controlling the commercial machinery of production without the film-maker being obliged to make a great many concessions on the meaning of what he wants to say if he chooses straightforward expression of ideas. Can anyone imagine, for instance, a film being made nowadays about the methods used by the police which does not end up one way or another as an apologia for those methods? It is greatly to the credit of several makers of *film noirs* in America such as *The Maltese Falcon, Murder, My Sweet* and *The Asphalt Jungle* that they dared to transform the detective proceeding by ingenious deduction into a predator who thrives on black-mail, shadowing suspects, informers and brutality. It was still a matter of adapting a novel, but at the same time they used it as a vehicle for something totally different. In any case, the reaction was inevitable. This kind of film has more or less ceased to be made for quite a time now. The cops and robbers detective film remains brutal, but now the cop is a good family man while in his own home: in *Naked City* it is the devoted little wife herself who helps him on with his shoulder holster before he sets off to work which in his case means killing a thief.

In just the same way it is obvious that any subject the least bit contro-versial, i.e. with some relevance to contemporary life, cannot even be contemplated without these same concessions being implicit. The best intentions run the risk of blowing up in the face of an unsuspecting film-maker who fails to set about his task with complete and utter caution. The condition of the working classes in France, for instance, undoubtedly provides the starting point for innumerable startling films. Dmytryk, concentrating on one particular aspect of related problems, unemployment and class structure, was able to make a very tough and yet at the same time very romantic film about the life led by Italian immigrant building workers in the United States.[1] My guess is that the exotic nature of the subject enabled the film to slip through. Dmytryk's great skill lay first and foremost in his being able to avoid any kind of scoring of points and to confining himself to statement, pure and simple, in his scenario.

Conversely, a French film featuring the life of miners ends up by completely reversing the brave and sincere intentions which were uppermost in the mind of the film-maker while he was making it, precisely because he lacked the necessary sense of perspective and was unable to keep within the kind of limits Dmytryk imposed upon himself. It has long been recognized that good will on its own is more often than not totally useless. The notion of the makers of the film in question, that they were going to make something wholesome and healthy, will be viewed by an audience so accommodating that each and every member of it can genuinely accept the proposition that a miner's life is not *that* terrible when all is said and done. But just look where the desire to avoid possible morbidity can lead: to saying the opposite of what was intended – at least one hopes this is the case. Taking a desire to show the conditions of the miners as your starting point you finish up not so very far from the message – 'Sign up, sign on in the forces overseas' – of the recruiting posters stuck up outside every police station. The managers of the mines have hearts of gold and behave like fathers of the regiment and sonny will dig coal just like daddy did.

In spite of everything, this edifying and wishy-washy portrait was turned down flat by the distributors – which just goes to show that compromise for the sake of compromise doesn't pay off in the long run.

Dandyism can be defined as the rejection of all mystification imposed from outside. Moreover, you can see that when it comes to putting a film together, if you play the game according to the rules set down by the bosses who run the system you can end up on the same side: every upbeat ending, for example, ratifies the state of the world as it is and becomes part and parcel of the machinery for providing reassurance and comfort that the cinema has itself become. Refusal to be a party to this mechanism, rejection of the principle of a good evening's entertainment at the pictures which is the main motive force, can itself constitute a kind of dandyism and moreover may well represent its contemporary form. The film-maker who thinks that under the present production system it is possible to express himself is not only labouring under an enormous delusion but also, no matter how pure his intentions, protecting and defending the mystificatory deceptions which the cinema ladles out so generously to the audience.

It is quite obvious that there is no way of making the films one would like to make about the army of French colonialism. Even inside France it is impossible to make a film which would relate to the French parliamentary and electoral system in the way that *Mr. Smith Goes to Washington* relates to the American system, even though that came to the reassuring conclusion that if the wicked do become powerful it is an exception to the rule that the good win in the end. Our own delightful French system has reached such a stage of timidity, blindness and concealed police coercion that we cannot even imagine making a film about the French colonial empire – our great-grandfathers' Morocco or the Madagascar our uncle from the colonies controlled – which even approaches a film like *Pinky* and similar films, for all their slyly underhand racialism. Straightforward vindication apart, there isn't a hope of saying a thing.

What is so obviously true about the French political system and the French empire is, in practical terms, true of every aspect of existence. Every year in France there are as many abortions as there are live births. It is as clear as crystal that it is totally impossible to make a film about this situation – not even a conformist film. Or take the French prison system whose principal glories are the huge central jails like Poissy, Fontevrault, etc. Who could imagine for a second that you could say about them even as much as *The Big House* said about Sing Sing, let alone the countless other American films starting with *Sullivan's Travels* which, often unintentionally, cast a disturbing light on the repressive system of civilized Christian society in the Western world.

To demonstrate how true all this is seems so easy that I hesitate to go on giving examples. In practical terms an impassable barrier of *de facto* censorship comes down on every attempt at direct expression of contemporary problems. You may think I am exaggerating. If only I were. The system for producing films today is such that as a final instance I let my imagination sketch the reactions of distributors faced with a project which concerns nothing more alarming than bringing on to the screen a naive pastoral novel – amazingly popular amongst provincials and pretty absurd in any case – namely Zola's *La Faute de l'Abbé Mouret*: Grade 5 rating from the Catholic film board, forbidden to minors, etc. I have deliberately refrained from mentioning George Bataille's marvellous novel, *L'Abbé C*, a sort of inspired, laicized, erotic mirror-image of the *Journal d'un curé de campagne*.

There are some professional film-makers working in the cinema today who, with an amazing puritanical sectarianism, are obsessed by the concept of a healthy cinematographic optimism which unfortunately, in my opinion, totally denies the very view they uphold. We are faced here with intellectual short-sightedness in its most extreme form. A strange conditioned reflex leads to the stuffing of all manifestations of violence higgledy-piggledy into the same bag labelled 'morbid'. Their entire reasoning is indubitably based on the engagingly simple-minded yet unexpected notion that in spite of everything there still remains some kind of freedom of choice as far as subject matter is concerned. It is true enough that you are free to choose Fernandel, Bourvil or the jolly lower classes of Paris, not really wicked, certainly foul-mouthed and yet so very, very droll.

Under these conditions, the parable is a powerful weapon when it is employed to banish current taboos or to destroy conventional illusions about the legitimacy or the permanent nature of society as we know it. Thus *The Lady from Shanghai*, *Monsieur Verdoux* and *Kind Hearts and*

Coronets are both the best examples of the use of parable and the most significant films to launch an offensive on society that have been made in recent years. Resorting to English humour allowed people who felt themselves under suspicion partly to avoid the blows aimed at them.

Clearly, these films were helped by an extremely vigorous English literary tradition: at the very least Swift and Samuel Butler stand in direct relation to them. The *Modest Proposal* or the pamphlet inviting settlers to colonize Erewhon as the Indies or the French colonies were colonized, for example, explain and make acceptable to the public Chaplin's comedy of murder or Robert Hamer's treatise on social ascent by means of rationally planned homicide. It is not so much a question of joking or some kind of macabre humour. The *Néant* cabaret approach where larky trippers from the provinces quaff lemonade from pottery skulls is completely different. The violent or hypocritically amused reactions provoked by these three films are very revealing on this score.

The Lady from Shanghai is clearly based on the juxtaposition within the same film of a detective thriller and an ice-cold, calculated parody of itself: the bad guys are shown sniggering in the foreground with just a little too much conviction. It is also the most violent blow delivered so far to the archetypal female myth in the American cinema. The greatness of the final sequence has been discussed hundreds of times. When the male and female leads cannot get married, they die rapturously in each other's arms: you take your choice between a happy ending and a daring one. For Mike the sailor to leave the vamp to die alone and wretched is clean against all the rules. Orson Welles should indeed be admired for standing on its head every single value normally advanced by the traditional detective thriller precisely because of the unbelievable stupidity and implausible confusion of the plot. But John Huston and Dmytryk have done the same thing. The poetic value of *The Lady from Shanghai* which in my opinion raises it way above other *films noirs* about gangsters derives from the parable of the shark fight which suddenly lets this very divided and ambivalent film make sense. The parable expands the meaning of the film and completely transforms it. The sea covered with the blood of the sharks which are devouring one another not only gives the film itself a deeper meaning but is also, because it is executed in a uniquely icy and imperturbable fashion that permits the use of that appalling expression, a comment on our times.

Only André Gide, to the best of my knowledge, has examined the aesthetic implications of that familiar scriptural saying to the effect that he who would save his life must lose it. Its applicability to the present circumstances in the making and distributing of films is exceedingly strange: because it is impossible to bear witness to really essential factors in contemporary existence, anyone wanting to do so in spite of everything ends up by being obliged to abandon his point of view – thus in the most unexpected way a confused and slapdash detective film, badly finished, baroque in form, is able to state more than any amount of choruses on the lines of let-us-work-together-brothers-our-time-has-come.

The main drawback of André Bazin's article on *Monsieur Verdoux* in the *Revue du Cinéma*[2] is that it is altogether too comprehensive. Yet at least he dealt justly with what is beyond a shadow of doubt Chaplin's most important film. But the article discourages any reflection; at least on the part of the supporters – not in fact so very numerous – of perhaps the richest and most important work in the entire history of cinema.

Sunday schools have done a great deal to debase the currency of parables because so much time is spent trying to render their meaning in simple everyday language, draining the lily of the field and the eye of the needle of their true meaning. The noises made by officially approved critics, and Bazin's reservations about the very basis of *Monsieur Verdoux*'s deepest meaning, form a part of this confirmation class approach. It would seem that the social content of the film is, in plain language, puerile: after all, we know, don't we, that society isn't perfect and that crime and industry are closely linked? What is more, the ideas of Mr Chaplin are a bit of a letdown after the vitality of Charlie's knockabout comedy.

It seems to me that a similar transposition into another medium of Kafka's 'In the Penal Settlement' or 'Investigations of a Terrier' would in all likelihood fail to convey the essence of Kafka's ideas about penology or *Angst*. The tremendous importance of *Monsieur Verdoux* derives precisely from the analogy to be made between it and Kafka's or Swift's universe: some long-serving critical wheelhorse based his chief criticism of the film on the fact that the Paris it showed bore no resemblance whatsoever to the real Paris. As if Verdoux were proposing to inhabit any realm other than Erewhon or Lilliput.

Kind Hearts and Coronets fared scarcely any better. A theme which was, broadly speaking, very close to that of *Verdoux* and a marvellous elegance of form allowed scope for ambivalence. All very amusing. Meanwhile the film has been crushed by its own success as comedy. The fact that no French film has ever treated our own brave light infantry officers as the British film treated admirals, which would be roughly the equivalent in military terms, or that no *curé* has ever, fortunately, undergone anything approximating to the sermon or prison chaplain sequences, should have given rise to the suspicion that this film is neither so macabre nor so humorous nor so screamingly funny as it appeared. What it was all about in fact was, just like *Verdoux*, one of the cruellest and most savage attacks made on our society and its structures because it brings into question the very right to exist. The films considered 'social', such as *The Grapes of Wrath* and the like, are forced by the distribution set-up to portray the exceptional, the dreadful and appalling even, thereby implicitly justifying what is not in fact exceptional at all – ordinary national and domestic virtues. Neither Ford nor Capra, not even the much more misleading Sturges, has questioned the society in which he lives, merely its deviations or excesses. Michèle Vian's excellent article in *Les Temps modernes* about

Intruder in the Dust has shed light in the same way on the implicit racialism in an approach that is totally and innocently soothing and reformist even though it attacks only the superficial manifestations of such a deep-rooted canker in society.

Not to put too fine a point on it, it seems that in an age like the present, one of the most oppressed by tyrannies, mystification, taboos and anxious imperatives, no willingness to express this social reality in the cinema by direct means is possible without causing the film-makers' own good intentions to turn against them.

In other words, it seems that those conveying the message are scarcely able to do more than lodge themselves in the defensive outworks of the very society they wish to attack or accuse.

The best example of this idiotic state of affairs is the wave of optimism which uplifts, admittedly rather feebly, a handful of naive *cinéastes*, enabling them to believe in decency, hope and virtue.

In complementary fashion, those who are in no way claiming to convey a message have, by a strange coincidence, caused the foundations of the social edifice they didn't give a damn about preserving or not, but merely depicted, to totter in the most violent way imaginable.

Valéry's *Faire sans croire* and his address to the French Academy are the application of an identical point of view to a social career. Valéry treats social success and a career as a successful writer in exactly the same way that Verdoux treats his business and Louis Mazzini in *Kind Hearts and Coronets* treats his noble lineage. In this respect the characters represent the contemporary version of the dandy's disdain and lucidity when confronted with social, sentimental and other categories of phenomenon.

Neither Welles nor Chaplin nor Robert Hamer is any more free in his period than was Swift in Augustan England or Butler in the late Victorian era. No doubt it could be argued that the approach via parables is not necessarily the only one untainted by hypocrisy or blindness in literature, despite the fact that Raymond Queneau's *The Bark-tree* and *Saint Glinglin*, for instance, seem to me to be greatly in advance of the lyrical imprecations of all the others who fancy themselves as prophets.

But where cinema is concerned, where the burden of social and economic restrictions crush even the slightest impulse to mount a serious attack on existing social taboos, the same approach via parables is the only one that makes no concessions on absolute essentials to the machinery of distribution, that safeguards itself from a society which believes itself to be divinely ordained.

I have no wish to say or even to believe that this is the only approach possible. I have absolutely no taste or capacity for playing at prophets or indulging in profundities. It is merely that I find the enormous fuss made about a few films of the *Antoine et Antoinette* variety of the recent past, or unrealistic charades like the latest Duvivier, quite unbalanced and infuriating.

I am glad that it was none other than Engels who defined the function of the novelist as fulfilling his task perfectly when by faithfully representing real social relations he destroys conventional illusions about the nature of those relations, shatters the optimism of bourgeois society, and obliges others to call into question the permanent nature of the existing order even when he does not directly indicate any solution or openly take sides.

Translated by Diana Matias

Notes

1 *Give Us This Day*, dir. Edward Dmytryk (GB, 1949).
2 'Le mythe de *M. Verdoux*', *Revue du Cinéma*, no. 9, January 1948; translated as 'The Myth of Monsieur Verdoux' in André Bazin, *What is Cinema? Vol. 2*.

('Le Fer dans la plaie', *Cahiers du Cinéma* 63, October 1956)

'Should Kafka be burned?' You may perhaps remember the enquiry conducted by the weekly *Action* (now defunct) on the pernicious role of the author of *Metamorphosis* in contemporary literature. The participants vied with each other in denouncing the 'noxious' influence of his work, its 'petit-bourgeois' and 'counter-revolutionary' significance and its destructive nihilism. The sole aim of the case brought against him was to relegate him (along with Dostoevsky and a few others) to that hell where the 'enemies' of the people are roasting. Kafka, symbol of bourgeois decadence, had to die a second time. All this took place something over ten years ago, unless I am mistaken. The auto-da-fé has been burning a long time. Kafka is still very much alive. Meanwhile the world has been shaken by a great event, Khrushchev's denunciation of 'Stalinist tyranny'. A new character, far more fascinating than the heroes of Soviet novels, has come into being, the kind of monster we have lost touch with since classical times, a sort of Probus combining the duplicity of Tiberius, the black humour of Nero, the exhibitionism of Commodus and the ferocity of Constantine. Yes, Stalin was all that, and yet how good it had been to bow down to him. You could no more look into his face than at the sun, for he was God on earth, father and shepherd of the nations. He was the one who knew, whose word was law. Could it really be necessary to obey this new order and renounce 'heaven on earth'? As well ask an opium addict to give up his drug without warning. Stalin provided Communist intellectuals with an admirable excuse. In him their guilty consciences found a saviour. Under his aegis, they could be washed clean of the original sin of uselessness and, spirits assuaged, be transformed into the infinitely pliable bureaucrat. Why give up the pleasure of expiating an essential curse? Surely it could not be necessary to abandon, on a word of command, the height of sensual pleasure which is the will to total self-abasement.

Marxist and Stalinist criticism

Why the foregoing exordium? What have Stalin and Kafka to do with a journal like the present one? For a time I believed that the de-Stalinization offensive would circulate a breath of fresh air through the Communist press and blow away the stifling, sterile miasma of conformism. I thought that our Catholics-in-reverse (i.e. the Communist intellectuals) would be converted to the spirit of criticism and adopt an attitude to the products of bourgeois civilization closer to the spirit of dialectical materialism itself, and therefore free of religiosity. When you have at your disposal a method of reflection as effective as Marxism, what need is there to denigrate and reject all that does not carry the stamp of strictest orthodoxy? Why not indulge in the luxury of equanimity? Alas, I was disappointed. Far from leading to a more flexible ideology, the famous Khrushchev speech was followed by an even greater hardening of the line. As proof, I need only note Garaudy's accession to the Communist Party's Bureau Politique. Not a cause for surprise. The spirit of orthodoxy and intolerance triumphs because no member of the Stalinist intelligentsia has taken Marx's historical dialectical materialism seriously. They are no doubt perfect Communists; they are certainly execrable Marxists. It is no use bending the knee to Marx's portrait without a knowledge of the profound sources which animate works like *The Poverty of Philosophy* and *Capital*. I defy anyone to cite a single piece of art or film criticism undertaken from a genuinely dialectical materialist standpoint; I can, however, produce evidence of the reactionary spirit which animates our Stalinists, especially in the cinema, where a radical absence of dialectical materialist thinking is only too evident.

It is not enough to decry an American film because it is *American* (while indulging in a small exception to the rule every ten years or so) in order to produce a piece of Marxist criticism. Any more than it is enough to praise to the skies the latest Yves Allégret or Le Chanois. Still less to exalt all Soviet films because they are *Soviet*.

I would even go so far as to say that there is more chance of remaining true to the real spirit of Marxism in the reverse attitude, and indeed the latest American films offer too good an example for me not to grab them in passing. I want no cries of 'Paradox' or accusations of illogicality. I have, once again, too many examples in the forefront of my mind to be bothered by sarcasm or pitying smiles. For a Marxist, many American films are manna from heaven, and if they did not exist we would have to invent them. I am even sure that Marx would have paid tribute to *The Barefoot Contessa*, as he did in his time to *La Comédie humaine*, and that one of Anthony Mann's Westerns would have fascinated him as much as Eugène Sue's *Les Mystères de Paris*. Our Stalinists, however, prefer to ban American cinema, as they banned Kafka, in the name of proletarian optimism. But Hawks, Mankiewicz, Aldrich, Welles, Hitchcock, Minnelli and Lang are far more representative of the contradictions of the capitalist system than Biberman or, in this country, Daquin or Allégret. This is what I mean to try and show in the course of this article, but first the mechanism of Stalinist film criticism needs to be analysed.

Stalinist critics use a *ne varietur* schema, based on the following three postulates:

1. The 'manichean' postulate. What is Soviet is good, what is American is bad. Note nevertheless one deliberate distortion of the postulate: French cinema, although bourgeois, has the right to every kind of accommodation.
2. The sociological premise. The sole valid criterion for the appreciation of a film is its *social* content. Good is that which exalts the work and struggle of the working class, that which describes (in a moving and instructive way) the daily life of workers. Good too is that which denounces the decay of the propertied class. Bad is all the rest (i.e. it stands accused of formalism in the name of revolutionary realism). The value of a film is thus determined in terms of its *class content*.
3. The political postulate (the most important of the three). Good is all that corresponds to the Party line, bad all that deviates from it or ignores it. Aesthetic judgment is therefore subordinated to the simple criterion of tactical expediency; hence the placing on the Index of a film which does not help the Party in the struggle against the bourgeoisie and the education of the working class.

Optimism, realism, moralism, opportunism. These then are the four articles of Stalinist criticism. It is all too easy to demonstrate the inconsistency of this new 'poetics'. There is first of all a contradiction between postulates 1 and 2. Praising a Soviet film at all costs means rejecting a class viewpoint, since certain films of the Stalinist era were apologias for Tsarist generals in the name of a patriotic ideal and ridiculed France and the French Revolution (I have in mind a certain *Suvarov* of odious memory). On the other hand, condemning an American film on principle means closing off the possibility of defining its class content, which is no less present for being implicit in form. But this is to anticipate the argument. There is also a contradiction between postulates 2 and 3 because the revolutionary realism of such a film may not coincide at all with the political objectives of the moment. Nor, moreover, does it need to. In the present state of affairs, I see no possibility of (a) proof of the validity of these postulates except on the basis of blind acceptance; (b) compliance with one which does not *ipso facto* overrule the other two.

Revolutionary realism

What is serious here is not the adherence to some critical imperative, but the condemnation to perpetual inconsistency. Since the appeal to authority is based on an aesthetic view of class, it would be well to define social class once and for all. Now Marx himself, as we know, hesitated between a bipartite definition of class (capitalists or proletarians) and a tripartite one (capitalists, proletarians and landowners). It is impossible to argue seriously in terms of class content without a clear and distinct idea of social class. Hence the difficulties that arise whenever the attempt is made to define revolutionary realism. The most frequent definition of this central concept in the Marxist aesthetic is not gleamingly precise. In its terms, any work which described a proletarian struggle against capitalist or feudal exploiters would conform to revolutionary realism. And the works of Eisenstein and Pudovkin are, justifiably, cited . . . in order the better to pour scorn on the American cinema.

I have a strong sense that at the bottom of all this there may be a serious ambiguity. The very term 'revolutionary realism' is a contradiction, since realism presupposes, precisely, an objectivity in the way of seeing and describing which revolution excludes. A revolutionary artist *chooses* the proletarian cause and rejects the lucid equanimity of a realist narrator. If he is successful, his work (film, painting, poem, it does not matter which) takes its rightful place in the *epic genre*. But since when has an epic work laid claim to realism, except in accuracy of detail? The reader is struck by the clinical rigour with which Homer describes the wounds of the combatants in the *Iliad*. Does that therefore entitle us to call Homer a realist? He is no more so than Eisenstein, and when I see *Alexander Nevsky* or *Ivan the Terrible* (and even more, *Battleship Potemkin*) I would not dream of treating him as a realist.

The lark mirror[1]

We know Saint-Réal's famous definition of the novel, later taken up by Stendhal, as 'a looking-glass borne down a road'. It could be applied to the whole realist aesthetic, responding closely to that impartial exactness I mentioned a moment ago, and to the refusal to speak for or against something or someone. If we accept this definition, where do we find the work to which it would correspond exactly? I doubt whether Stendhal, Balzac or Flaubert, who are so modish with the progressives, wrote novels which fulfil this programme. As a looking-glass, realism is of the lark mirror kind, a myth which, very fortunately, writers have been careful not to take too literally. No writer or film-maker worthy of the name can be faithful to it except superficially, since the essence of realism is alien to art. The realist programme in all its rigour, as defined by Saint-Réal, would end up presenting the reader with a job lot of sundry kinds of *behaviour*, the explanation of which would be left to him. Angling the mirror this way or that is not allowed, and if moralists, writers or film-makers have so far found the odds stacked against them (even though they are consciously or unconsciously among the privileged), it is hard to see how a revolutionary artist, whose work postulates *the destruction of an entire world*, is to achieve it.

Realism in art does not exist, unless it is understood in a clearly limited sense (one may, for instance, speak of the realism of ideas, psychological realism, or the realism of local colour). But I doubt whether our aestheticians take this as meant for them. True, they laud the films of Autant-Lara, Allégret or Grémillon, whose realism is limited to the least risky acceptance of its meaning, but I assume that this is simply the expression of a political expediency. In any case, they betray the ideal they mean to defend by praising such products. I am well aware that what I am saying runs counter to a profound tendency in the workers' movement on every occasion that it has taken a position on questions of art; it is obsessed with the need to find, everywhere and always, the proletarian condition in the work of art. I fully believe that the description of a worker's life or the activity of a factory is not incompatible with art. Since the sixteenth century, painting has offered innumerable proofs of this, tirelessly showing the humble and the disinherited of all kinds. But in the case in point, the question is a purely theoretical realism, since what is ugly in life becomes beautiful when it is contemplated in a gallery or a room. The fidelity and precision of the painter conspire to place his painting at the extreme opposite of reality.

This is the case with Albrecht Dürer's hare. Who would dream of going into raptures over a real hare and who does not marvel at Dürer's painting, or the crab by the same artist? The fact that a watercolour can denaturalize reality to the point of making us admire what in nature is the object of pure indifference if not disgust is the paradox of 'realist' art, in fact the mystery of art full stop. I would therefore say to our Stalinist aestheticians, depict workers as much as you like, but what you will offer is a simple *duplicatum* of reality; there is small chance that art will benefit. In cinema as elsewhere, the antinomy between the real and the dream, between reality and truth, is the inexhaustible source of all artistic creation.

I wrote earlier that the very notion of revolutionary realism is a contradiction. I have no hesitation in adding that there is not only a contradiction between the terms (i.e. between realism and revolution), but within the concept of realism itself (because it only exists in a *partial* way in art, and only on condition that it denies itself). In its genuine sense (i.e. Saint-Réal) it excludes the artistic world (objectivity is a quality alien to art); in its limited sense (the one in which it is usually understood by literary or art critics), it tends towards contradiction. The artist must therefore be sufficiently aware of these contradictions to overcome them and thus, as Hegel said, to be 'within the element of Truth'.

The sin of abstraction

I imagine the preceding exposition is enough to convey the idea that it is impossible to approach the questions of aesthetics properly, except by forging a dialectical mentality. The use of such notions as 'revolutionary realism', 'mass art', 'proletarian optimism' is not forbidden, provided that their deceptive and illusory side is made clear. As soon as one or other of these notions is examined more closely, a mass of contradictions comes to light, which should make us sceptical as far as the common usage of these terms is concerned. I could go further. To speak of the class content of a novel or film is to show that one is totally estranged from the very spirit of dialectics and above all from historical materialist dialectics. It is in fact the arbitrary isolation of one element of reality to the detriment of all the rest. To neglect the complexity of a work in order to focus on its class content alone is precisely to refuse to analyse the contradictory forces which brought it into being. What is left of Dostoevsky's *Devils*, for instance (that 'repugnant but masterful work', to quote Lenin), if you limit yourself to determining its class content? You discover that it is bound up with a counter-revolutionary ideology without realizing that it illustrates the conflicts which divided members of the Russian intelligentsia in the 1860s as Dostoevsky lived them. It is of little consequence that the novelist resolves the opposition between science and faith in favour of the latter. What interests Marxists is the conflict itself, and behind it the internal contradictions of the Tsarist society it reflects, in what is undoubtedly a truncated but singularly revealing way. Again, limiting oneself to simple class content is to commit the sin (unpardonable in a Marxist) of *abstraction*. Art, in fact, because it lives on conflicts, tensions, irreducible oppositions, contradictory aspirations, is dialectical in its very essence. I would be the last to deny that these tensions reflect and *reproduce symbolically* the contradictions of society and that they depend in part on the class conflicts which riddle that society. What I ask of our Stalinists is that in order to do justice to the thought they lay claim to and betray so deliberately, they should (as they never do) determine the *mediations* through which one passes from the real world (defined by *particular* relations of production and/or a *particular* condition of the forces of production) into the imaginary world of the novelist, painter or film-maker.

These mediations are complex, I agree, but it is their analysis which allows a demonstration of the extent to which Balzac's *Splendeurs et misères des courtisanes* is both the alienated and authentic reproduction of French society under the July Monarchy, and also the expression of a tragedy which greatly surpasses the material and social conditions which governed bourgeois France in the time of Louis Philippe. The tragedy is that of alienation, and it would be possible to say, for example, without exaggeration, that the whole *Comédie humaine* is a phenomenology of the alienated conscience. These words, borrowed from philosophical jargon, should not make the reader nervous, for they cover fairly simple realities and characterize them in a useful way. I shall, moreover, give a necessarily summary and therefore unfaithful explanation of them, and if I make an issue of it, it is solely to support my argument (according to which the American cinema throughout warrants a dialectical reflection), not in order to transform *Cahiers* into an addendum to the *Revue de métaphysique et de morale* or the *Revue internationale de philosophie*.

'The long hard road'

It is to Hegel that we owe the introduction of alienation into the philosophical vocabulary. It is probably a familiar fact that in *The Phenomenology of Mind* Hegel sought to describe the 'long hard road' which consciousness has to travel before it reaches Absolute Knowledge. Before it arrives, it takes on a series of 'forms' or 'moments', each form actualizing a type of experience in which, every time, the consciousness discovers that what it took for truth was simply illusion. It is therefore necessary to pass beyond the abstract moment where the consciousness of self seeks to accede to an inaccessible ideal, on to the level of *mind* where the *world* as the *actualization of Reason* is no longer opposed to the consciousness of self.[2] The first moment of a properly historical phenomenology would be the *immediate mind*, or 'the world of ethical freedom', where the 'identity of self and substance' is actualized, i.e. identity of singularness (the self as an ethical nature) and the universal (substance as universal essence). But this moment cannot persist and the Greek city which incarnated it historically is rent by scission between human law (the universal) and divine law (the singular). It is not possible to reconcile political and social laws with those of the family and rituals for the dead. Creon as defender of civil order, the expression of the common will of the citizenry, is opposed by Antigone, who represents the rights of the clan. The tragedy is thus born of the conflict of laws against laws, and that conflict is irresolvable. The Greek city for Hegel, as for Goethe and Hölderlin, represented a harmonious world which, to use Goethe's expression, had 'to be discovered with the eyes of the soul' ('Das Land der Griechen mit der Seele suchen').

For Hegel in any case that harmony could only be ephemeral, and it is precisely in Greek tragedy (Sophocles and Aeschylus) that the contradictions of the classical Greek world conceived as 'immediate mind' are expressed. The primary world of the mind is thus succeeded by the world of *alienation* and *culture*, a torn and divided world in which mind becomes a stranger to itself. The moment of *implicit* opposition when the self expresses itself in a naive and contradictory manner as the singularness and the universalness of ethical life, is succeeded by the moment when the self alienates its immediate certainty and through that alienation becomes substance. At the same time, however, that substance becomes strange to it. While the self has, through civilization, acceded to the Universal, the very *content* of that universal substance progressively eludes it. The ethical life with which it coincided in a spontaneous and naive way appears, now that it has been appropriated, to be a very opaque reality. The world has become the 'negativity of the consciousness of self'. In alienating its natural being, the self has become not only strange to the world it has appropriated, but strange to itself.

Let us now try to put into ordinary language what Hegel expresses in the language of philosophy. In denying the state of nature and civilizing himself, man has undoubtedly acquired greater power, but the world he believes he dominates eludes him; it transforms itself into an *objective* reality, external to those who conceived it and therefore oppressive. The State and Wealth, which are products of human activity, become so many strange and hostile realities, entities which are literally indifferent. The State and Wealth define two moments of a dialectic which is precisely that of the alienated consciousness. The nobleman who would once have considered it an honour to serve the State, expects only material advantages, pensions and titles, from the moment that the State becomes universal and abstract. The sentiment of honour is replaced by flattery because there is no other way of obtaining these advantages than by paying court to the king. *The noble consciousness is opposed to the base consciousness. In exchanging honour for money, consciousness appropriates the State*, since it is the very essence of State power to recompense its servants and reward its functionaries. But in so doing, it denies the State, since it retains only a material appearance, *money*. The power of the State is thus succeeded by the power of money, obeisance to the sovereign by submission to wealth. In alienating itself in money and through flattery, consciousness renders the State strange, incorporating its substance into itself, but reducing its universal and abstract meaning into a simple singular 'me' (Absolute Monarch), relegated to the level of being purely a dispenser of favours. In one movement, consciousness alienates itself into a thing, money, the negation of the State, and into the anonymity of economic life. Wealth now becomes the universal, transforming human relations into *objective* and abstract relations, links between object and object, supply and demand.

Supply and demand

Marx was very familiar with this dialectic of alienation and culture. He provided, moreover, a masterly commentary on *The Phenomenology of Mind* in his *1844 Manuscripts*. However, it seemed to him that Hegel had not worked through the effective transcending of bourgeois alienation. In Hegel the transcending is purely speculative, absolute knowledge, which suppresses alienation only ideologically and is therefore itself alienation. For Marx it was not possible to overcome the world of wealth by a purely mental process, even if that process were the 'pure knowledge of self by the self'. The reason being that the dialectic of Wealth and the State is not the expression of a consciousness of self, but the *ideal* reproduction of a real dialectic – that of a commercial society and, more particularly, capitalist society. Thus Marx replaces the notion of idealist alienation (*Entfremdung*) with the materialist notion of reification (*Verdinglichung*). In capitalist society, personal relations become relations between objects, buyers and sellers. Everything is exchangeable, at a price – love, intelligence, dignity, etc. The feudal society's code of submission and honour gives way to the law of supply and demand of capitalist society. This is the reign of the fetishization of commodity and again of universal abstraction, and clearly, if history is envisaged no longer as the history of the mind, but as the real history of relations of production and exchange, the only way real alienation (reification) can be overcome is by destroying those relations through concrete action (revolution) and not ideally, through absolute knowledge.

Marx's dialectical and historical materialism thus consisted in envisaging human history as the natural history of material relations of production, consumption and exchange. The Hegelian phenomenology which described the future as 'the Calvary of history, without which the mind would be solitude within life' is replaced by the exploitation of man by man which can only be ended by a classless society. But the development of this perpetual oppression and the struggle against it can only be understood dialectically. The capitalist world being the world of absolute and universal abstraction, the dialectic of mind must be replaced by the dialectic of capital, and the metamorphosis of capital has to be studied as Hegel studied the metamorphosis of mind. Hence the esoteric and abstract nature of *Capital*, as enigmatic and rambling to the uninitiated reader as Hegel's *Phenomenology*.

Hollywood, the microcosm

If the reader has had the patience to follow me this far (which I would not dare to presume) I can now say what for me constitutes the essential originality of the great American directors. *They have been more or less consciously obsessed by the 'reified' nature of American society.* They have all more or less tried to bring on to the screen the fall of American man. They have therefore brought to the surface the mystificatory aspect of the American way of life and violently denounced the fetishization of money. They have shown us man hunted and besieged by the demands of success, profit, social climbing, and the need to defend the advantage acquired. The nostalgia for purity or authenticity (let's use the word, despite the dubious use Montherlant made of it) which stirs the greatest of them is only the inverse of that passionate or ironic critique of the extremely commercialized American consciousness.

And I will add that it is at moments when their subject seems furthest from any social preoccupation that the critique goes furthest, touching the sensitive nerve of the new Leviathan which is American capitalist society.

If proof is needed, first place goes to a whole group of films which have Hollywood as a direct or general concern: *The Bad and the Beautiful*, Minnelli; *A Star is Born*, Cukor; *The Barefoot Contessa*, Mankiewicz; *The Big Knife*, Robert Aldrich; a major part of Welles's work, *Citizen Kane*, *The Lady from Shanghai*; Hawks's *Monkey Business* and *Gentlemen Prefer Blondes*; Fritz Lang's *While the City Sleeps*; and Hitchcock's especially extraordinary *Strangers on a Train*. These films all deal with the same subject – the impossibility in the present state of things of an effective and genuine morality, or, if you like, the *incompatibility of morality* (other than that of the police) and capitalist society. If the Hollywood un-American Activities investigation had had any sense, it would have been the directors just named who would have lost their right to work, not those doubtless admirable but infinitely less dangerous directors like Dassin, Losey or Berry.

Alongside such destroyers, who would certainly not have escaped the fires of the Inquisition, how innocuous seem Kazan, Stevens and Benedek, not to mention Daniel Mann.

I think it is worth going into some detail. It is not chance that has so often made Hollywood and its activities the object of study by film directors. First, for a very obvious reason. These directors know what they are talking about, they know better than anyone the often unenviable position of the film-maker in the Hollywood hierarchy (cf. Harry Dawes in *The Barefoot Contessa*). They have had the time to take to pieces a society which seems to be heading towards a caste-system. Hence their total lack of indulgence and the cruelty evident in their portrayal, all the more implacable for denying itself excess and exaggeration.

Second, because Hollywood is a microcosm which reproduces, magnified many times over, the defects of American society. It is capitalism to the nth degree, a monstrous excrescence of that 'air-conditioned nightmare' which Henry Miller mentions when talking about America. Minnelli himself, the 'precious' Minnelli, must have had an attack of rage which translated itself into *The Bad and the Beautiful*, that much-neglected film whose meaning I understood so belatedly. The subject is, it will be remembered, a producer who ends up exhausting his entire circle with his demands, his way of treating the closest and most valued collaborators as objects, in terms of their usefulness of the moment. Is he to blame? Yes and no, but it soon becomes clear that we are not being given a non-committal answer. He is undoubtedly just as hard on himself, he is a 'promoter' in the full meaning of the term, a discoverer, and in this sense to be admired, but Minnelli lets a doubt hang over the fate awaiting him (we never know whether or not he is recalled to Hollywood after his exile), possibly because his responsibility is very attenuated. It seems clear, and this is implicit in the incisiveness of Minnelli's portrayal, that the system is responsible and that after all the producer is only applying the *inhuman rules of the game* which reach beyond Hollywood to involve the whole of America. Minnelli, as admirable moralist, denounces the essential artificiality of Hollywood circles and, a fact for which I am most grateful to him, does so with delicacy and a lightness of touch. Who would have thought that Minnelli (and he would no doubt be astounded to hear it) would link up with the existential philosopher Martin Heidegger who, in *Being and Time*, describes the existence of the 'one', i.e. the individual to whom any authenticity is alien. The Stalinists will roar; what, Heidegger, the fascist! Forgetting that in this instance Heidegger is purely and simply translating the accounts of Hegel and Marx into his 'existential analysis'.

The denunciation of artificiality is found at its bitterest in *The Big Knife* and *Kiss Me Deadly* (Aldrich), on which I will be forgiven for being brief. I would simply note that in certain characters, alienation or reification reaches the point where common respect for the life of another has *no meaning* for them. They settle the death of a defenceless person quite calmly, without turning a hair. These are perfectly respectable people. Smiley Coy, the producer's public relations man, soberly decides on the death of a starlet whose indiscretions risk affecting the reputation of an actor whose box-office appeal brings the company considerable profit. We are well inside a world ruled by buying and selling. And yet Mr Smiley Coy was a major in the US Air Force and – an important detail – is received by the famous composer of *Showboat* and *Roberta*, Jerome Kern. In other words, he is as unlikely as Caesar's wife to invite suspicion.

Cukor's *A Star is Born* seems to be about something different, the life of a couple. In fact it poses the question of the saleability of the star. After all, it matters little that the eccentricities of the actor Norman Maine lead to his inevitable downfall. What counts is that he is less and less effective, brings in less and less money. He becomes a dead weight and then, no quarter! The fact that the rise of his wife Vicky Lester brings him face to face with his decline and that rejection of her pity, even love, leads him to suicide is only part of what the film is about. It is also about the destruction of all personal life, an analysis of the star system as the principal destroyer of any human relationship. It is about *the annihilation of the person to the exclusive benefit of appearance*.

The actor, like the financier or the press magnate, is *for others*. He may rejoice in this (like Orson Welles's Charlie Kane) or deplore it, it makes no difference. He exists solely for the look of the other. He is the fleshly symbol of the omnipotence of money alienated in the anonymous look of the crowd and in which the crowd in its turn is alienated. This reciprocal alienation replaces concrete personal relations with objective relations – the star is the *object* of a cult, the financier the *object* of hatred, the politician the *object* of disgust, and as such they belong to the crowd, which is free to weigh them up at its leisure and free to change its initial evaluation.

From Marx to Minnelli

It is in a different light again that Mankiewicz tackles *All about Eve* and above all *The Barefoot Contessa*. The latter is one of the few films to escape condemnation from the Stalinists, but I fear the reasons for their praise are not the right ones. As in *Five Fingers*, Mankiewicz offers a theme which allows for endless variations and lends itself very precisely to a dialectical formulation. Behind the plot of the film, one gets the sense that what interested Mankiewicz was *the conflict between reality and appearance*. The Contessa dies because she believed in a reality which was itself only apparent in order to escape the artificiality of her existence as a star: the fairy stories about her disinherited childhood to which she clings desperately have no more foundation than the vain existence she has had since she achieved fame. She meets a (quite real) Prince Charming, of course, but that good-looking young man symbolizes sterility and impotence. Her sexual unconventionality (she sleeps with lower-class men) is doubtless a kind of rejection of the artificiality, but it is also the symptom of a radical maladjustment, a lack of ability to face up to the present. Her death is the logical result of her cowardice, or rather of a certain very feminine and very charming irresponsibility. Where, then, is the truth? Not in the fairy stories of little girls who never grow up, nor in society life. It lies in a certain disenchanted lucidity engagingly represented by Harry Dawes, the Contessa's former director. It also lies in work and precisely in films (such as those Mankiewicz makes as an independent director) which give a clearer view of reality than the two-a-penny films (of Gregory LaCava perhaps) which the adorable Contessa loved too well. Vargas, the Contessa Torlato-Favrini, victim of bad cinema, just as noxious as society life, because just as artificial. The moral of this admirable film is extremely severe: the road to authenticity is very hard, Harry Dawes stumbled along it, Maria Vargas was unable to follow it through to the end. (Harry Dawes leaving Maria's grave to go back to his work in the last shot of the film illustrates this perfectly.) There might have been a risk, with a theme as difficult as the conflict between reality and appearance, that the treatment would tend to be rather dry. This is not so, because the variations grafted on to it are of a high quality. In the brilliant dialogue Mankiewicz opposes two ideas, two attitudes to wealth, the hoarding mentality as against the prodigal and ostentatious mentality.

The insistence with which the most important film-makers of the young generation describe the different modes of the alienated consciousness is found in older film-makers like Hawks (I mention as a reminder the role of Marilyn Monroe in *Gentlemen Prefer Blondes*).

In Hitchcock, the question is broached within a dialectic of the criminal consciousness, an existential dialectic which only assumes its meaning by reference to American capitalist society. The criminal can only affirm himself through a negation of the other, because he cannot realize himself within *universal values, which no longer exist since the system has long since destroyed them.* Fear of the police, which may make the mediocre pause to reflect, does not hold back the out-of-the-ordinary individuals who literally fascinate Hitchcock as much as they repel him.

Perhaps it will be admitted that the road which leads from Marx to Minnelli, Mankiewicz and others is shorter than it seems. And why condemn film-makers who bear witness to a serious crisis in the American economy's system of purely material values? I agree that the only solutions they offer are escapist. It is nevertheless true that we have yet to see such lucid and serious testimonies of the decay of our own culture.

Translated by Diana Matias

Notes

1 A 'lark mirror' (*miroir aux alouettes*) is a decoy for larks in the form of a curved piece of wood set with small mirrors, mounted on a spindle and twined by a string. (Translator's note.)
2 Hegel has just analysed the ultimate forms of the empirical consciousness in which it discovers itself as reason. The Self of the chapter on the Mind is the subject engaged in a historical community and alienation is the loss of the subject in the object. (Author's note.)

31 André Bazin: 'On the *politique des auteurs*'

('De la politique des auteurs', *Cahiers du Cinéma* 70, April 1957)

Goethe? Shakespeare? Everything they put their name to is supposed to be good, and people rack their brains to find beauty in the silliest little thing they bungled. All great talents, like Goethe, Shakespeare, Beethoven, Michelangelo, created not only beautiful works, but things that were less than mediocre, quite simply awful. (Tolstoy, *Diary 1895–99*)

I realize my task is fraught with difficulties. *Cahiers du Cinéma* is thought to practise the *politique des auteurs*. This opinion may perhaps not be justified by the entire output of articles, but it has been true of the majority, especially for the last two years. It would be useless and hypocritical to point to a few scraps of evidence to the contrary, and claim that our magazine is a harmless collection of wishywashy reviews.

Nevertheless, our readers must have noticed that this critical standpoint – whether implicit or explicit – has not been adopted with equal enthusiasm by all the regular contributors to *Cahiers*, and that there might exist serious differences in our admiration, or rather in the degree of our admiration. And yet the truth is that the most enthusiastic among us nearly always win the day. Eric Rohmer put his finger on the reason in his reply to a reader in *Cahiers* 63: when opinions differ on an important film, we generally prefer to let the person who likes it most write about it.[1] It follows that the strictest adherents of the *politique des auteurs* get the best of it in the end, for, rightly or wrongly, they always see in their favourite directors the manifestation of the same specific qualities. So it is that Hitchcock, Renoir, Rossellini, Lang, Hawks, or Nicholas Ray, to judge from the pages of *Cahiers*, appear as almost infallible directors who could never make a bad film.

I would like to avoid a misunderstanding from the start. I beg to differ with those of my colleagues who are the most firmly convinced that the *politique des auteurs* is well founded, but this in no way compromises the general policy of the magazine. Whatever our differences of opinion about films or directors, our common likes and dislikes are numerous enough and strong enough to bind us together; and although I do not see the role of the *auteur* in the cinema in the same way as François Truffaut or Eric Rohmer for example, it does not stop me believing to a certain extent in the concept of the *auteur* and very often sharing their opinions, although not always their passionate loves. I fall in with them more reluctantly in the case of their hostile reactions; often they are very harsh with films I find defensible – and I do so precisely because I find that the work transcends the director (they dispute this phenomenon, which they consider to be a critical contradiction). In other words, almost our only difference concerns the relationship between the work and its creator. I have never been sorry that one of my colleagues has stuck up for such and such director, although I have not always agreed about the qualities of the film under examination. Finally, I would like to add that although it seems to me that the *politique des auteurs* has led its supporters to make a number of mistakes, its total results have been fertile enough to justify them in the face of their critics. It is very rare that the arguments drawn upon to attack them do not make me rush to their defence.

So it is within these limits, which, if you like, are those of a family quarrel, that I would like to tackle what seems to me to represent not so much a critical mistranslation as a critical 'false nuance of meaning'. My point of departure is an article by my friend Jean Domarchi on Vincente Minnelli's *Lust for Life*,[2] which tells the story of Van Gogh. His praise was very intelligent and sober, but it struck me that such an article should not have been published in a review which, only one month previously, had allowed Eric Rohmer to demolish John Huston.[3] The relentless harshness of the latter, and the indulgent admiration of the former, can only be explained by the fact that Minnelli is one of Domarchi's favourites and that Huston is not a *Cahiers auteur*. This partiality is a good thing, up to a certain point, as it leads us to stick up for a film that illustrates certain facets of American culture just as much as the personal talent of Vincente Minnelli. I could get Domarchi caught up in a contradiction, by pointing out to him that he ought to have sacrificed Minnelli in favour of Renoir, since it was the shooting of *Lust for Life* that forced the director of *French Cancan* to give up his own project on Van Gogh. Can Domarchi claim that a *Van Gogh* by Renoir would not have brought more prestige to the *politique des auteurs* than a film by Minnelli? What was needed was a painter's son, and what we got was a director of filmed ballets!

But whatever the case, this example is only a pretext. Many a time I have felt uneasy at the subtlety of an argument, which was completely unable to camouflage the naïveté of the assumption whereby, for example, the intentions and the coherence of a deliberate and well thought out film are read into some little 'B' feature.

And of course as soon as you state that the film-maker and his films are one, there can be no minor films, as the worst of them will always be in the image of their creator. But let's see what the facts of the matter are. In order to do so, we must go right back to the beginning.

Of course, the *politique des auteurs* is the application to the cinema of a notion that is widely accepted in the individual arts. François Truffaut likes to quote Giraudoux's remark: 'There are no works, there are only *auteurs*' – a polemical sally which seems to me of limited significance. The opposite statement could just as well be set as an exam question. The two formulae, like the maxims of La Rochefoucauld and Chamfort, would simply reverse their proportion of truth and error. As for Eric Rohmer, he states (or rather asserts) that in art it is the *auteurs*, and not the works, that remain; and the programmes of film societies would seem to support this critical truth.

But one should note that Rohmer's argument does not go nearly as far as Giraudoux's aphorism, for, if *auteurs* remain, it is not necessarily because of their production as a whole. There is no lack of examples to prove that the contrary is true. Maybe Voltaire's name is more important than his bibliography, but now that he has been put in perspective it is not so much his *Dictionnaire philosophique* that counts nowadays as his Voltairean wit, a certain *style* of thinking and writing. But today where are we to find the principle and the example? In his abundant and atrocious writings for the theatre? Or in the slim volume of short stories? And what about Beaumarchais? Are we to go looking in *La Mère coupable*?

In any case, the authors of that period were apparently themselves aware of the relativity of their worth, since they willingly disowned their works, and sometimes did not mind even being the subject of lampoons whose quality they took as a compliment. For them, almost the only thing that mattered was the work itself, whether their own or another's, and it was only at the end of the eighteenth century, with Beaumarchais in fact, that the concept of the *auteur* finally crystallized legally, with his royalties, duties and responsibilities. Of course I am making allowances for historical and social contingencies; political and moral censorship has made anonymity sometimes inevitable and always excusable. But surely the anonymity of the writings of the French Resistance in no way lessened the dignity or responsibility of the writer. It was only in the nineteenth century that copying or plagiarism really began to be considered a professional breach that disqualified its perpetrator.

The same is true of painting. Although nowadays any old splash of paint can be valued according to its measurements and the celebrity of the signature, the objective quality of the work itself was formerly held in much higher esteem. Proof of this is to be found in the difficulty there is in authenticating a lot of old pictures. What emerged from a studio might simply be the work of a pupil, and we are now unable to *prove* anything one way or the other. If one goes back even further, one has to take into consideration the anonymous works that have come down to us as the products not of an artist, but of an art, not of a man, but of a society.

I can see how I will be rebutted. We should not objectify our ignorance or let it crystallize into a reality. All these works of art, the Venus de Milo as well as the Negro mask, did in fact have an *auteur*; and the whole of modern historical science is tending to fill in the gaps and give names to these works of art. But did one really have to wait for such erudite addenda before being able to admire and enjoy them? Biographical criticism is but one of many possible critical dimensions – people are still arguing about the identity of Shakespeare or Molière.

But that's just the point! People *are* arguing. So their identity is not a matter of complete indifference. The evolution of Western art towards greater personalization should definitely be considered as a step forward, as a refinement of culture, but only as long as this individualization remains only a final perfection and does not claim to *define* culture. At this point, we should remember that irrefutable commonplace we learnt at school: the individual transcends society, but society is also and above all *within* him. So there can be no definitive criticism of genius or talent which does not first take into consideration the social determinism, the historical combination of circumstances, and the technical background which to a large extent determine it. That is why the anonymity of a work of art is a handicap that impinges only very slightly on our understanding of it. In any case, much depends on the particular branch of art in question, the style adopted, and the sociological context. Negro art does not suffer by remaining anonymous – although of course it is unfortunate that we know so little about the societies that gave birth to it.

But *The Man Who Knew Too Much*, *Europa 51*, and *Bigger Than Life* are contemporary with the paintings of Picasso, Matisse, and Singier! Does it follow that one should see in them the same degree of individualization? I for one do not think so.

If you will excuse yet another commonplace, the cinema is an art which is both popular and industrial. These conditions, which are necessary to its existence, in no way constitute a collection of hindrances – no more than in architecture – they rather represent a group of positive and negative circumstances which have to be reckoned with. And this is especially true of the American cinema, which the theoreticians of the *politique des auteurs* admire so much. What makes Hollywood so much better than anything else in the world is not only the quality of certain directors, but also the vitality and, in a certain sense, the excellence of a tradition. Hollywood's superiority is only incidentally technical; it lies much more in what one might call the American cinematic genius, something which should be analysed, then defined, by a sociological approach to its production. The American cinema has been able, in an extraordinarily competent way, to show American society just as it wanted to see itself; but not at all passively, as a simple act of satisfaction and escape, but dynamically, i.e. by participating with the means at its disposal in the building of this society. What is so admirable in the American cinema is that it cannot help being spontaneous. Although the fruit of free enterprise and capitalism – and harbouring their active or still only virtual defects – it is in a way the truest and most realistic cinema of all because it does not shrink from depicting even the contradictions of that society. Domarchi himself, who has demonstrated the point very clearly in a penetrating and well-documented analysis,[4] exempts me from developing this argument.

But it follows that every director is swept along by this powerful surge; naturally his artistic course has to be plotted according to the currents – it is not as if he were sailing as his fancy took him on the calm waters of a lake.

In fact it is not even true of the most individual artistic disciplines that genius is free and always self-dependent. And what is genius anyway if not a certain combination of unquestionably personal talents, a gift from the fairies, and a moment in history? Genius is an H-bomb. The fission of uranium triggers off the fusion of hydrogen pulp. But a sun cannot be born from the disintegration of an individual alone unless this disintegration has repercussions on the art that surrounds it. Whence the paradox of Rimbaud's life. His poetic flash in the pan suddenly died out and Rimbaud the adventurer became more and more distant like a star, still glowing but heading towards extinction. Probably Rimbaud did not change at all. There was simply nothing left to feed the flames that had reduced the whole of literature to ashes. Generally, the rhythm of this combustion in the cycles of great art is usually greater than the lifespan of a man. Literature's step is measured in centuries. It will be said that genius foreshadows that which comes after it. This is true, but only dialectically. For one could also say that every age has the geniuses it needs in order to define, repudiate and transcend itself. Consequently, Voltaire was a horrible playwright when he thought he was Racine's successor and a story-teller of genius when he made the parable a vehicle for the ideas which were going to shatter the eighteenth century.

And even without having to use as examples the utter failures which had their causes almost entirely in the sociology of art, creative psychology alone could easily account for a lot of patchiness even in the best authors. *Notre-Dame-de-Paris* is pretty slight compared with *La Légende des siècles*, *Salammbô* does not come up to *Madame Bovary*, or *Corydon* to *Le Journal des faux-monnayeurs*. There is no point in quibbling about these examples, there will always be others to suit everyone's taste. Surely one can accept the permanence of talent without confusing it with some kind of artistic infallibility or immunity against making mistakes, which could only be divine attributes. But God, as Sartre has already pointed out, is not an artist! Were one to attribute to creative man, in the face of all psychological probability, an unflagging richness of inspiration, one would have to admit that this inspiration always comes up against a whole complex of particular circumstances which make the result, in the cinema, a thousand times more chancy than in painting or in literature.

Inversely, there is no reason why there should not exist – and sometimes there do – flashes in the pan in the work of otherwise mediocre filmmakers. Results of a fortunate combination of circumstances in which there is a precarious moment of balance between talent and milieu, these fleeting brilliancies do not prove all that much about personal creative qualities; they are not, however, intrinsically inferior to others – and probably would not seem so if the critics had not begun by reading the signature at the bottom of the painting.

Well, what is true of literature is even truer of the cinema, to the extent that this art, the last to come on to the scene, accelerates and multiplies the evolutionary factors that are common to all the others. In fifty years the cinema, which started with the crudest forms of spectacle (primitive but not inferior), has had to cover the same ground as the play or the novel and is often on the same level as they are. Within this same period, its technical development has been of a kind that cannot compare with that of any traditional art within a comparable period (except perhaps architecture, another industrial art). Under such conditions, it is hardly surprising that the genius will burn himself out ten times as fast, and that a director who suffers no loss of ability may cease to be swept along by the wave. This was the case with Stroheim, Abel Gance and Orson Welles. We are now beginning to see things in enough perspective to notice a curious phenomenon: a film-maker can, within his own lifetime, be refloated by the following wave. This is true of Abel Gance or Stroheim, whose modernity is all the more apparent nowadays. I am fully aware that this only goes to prove their quality of *auteur*, but their eclipse still cannot be entirely explained away by the contradictions of capitalism or the stupidity of producers. If one keeps a sense of proportion, one sees that the same thing has happened to men of genius in the cinema as would have happened to a 120-year-old Racine writing Racinian plays in the middle of the eighteenth century. Would his tragedies have been better than Voltaire's? The answer is by no means clear-cut; but I bet they would not have been.

One can justifiably point to Chaplin, Renoir or Clair. But each of them was endowed with further gifts that have little to do with genius and which were precisely the ones that enabled them to adapt themselves to the predicament of film production. Of course, the case of Chaplin was unique since, as both *auteur* and producer, he has been able to be both the cinema and its evolution.

It follows, then, according to the most basic laws of the psychology of creation, that, as the objective factors of genius are much more likely to modify themselves in the cinema than in any other art, a rapid maladjustment between the film-maker and the cinema can occur, and this can abruptly affect the quality of his films as a result. Of course I admire *Confidential Report*, and I can see the same qualities in it as I see in *Citizen Kane*. But *Citizen Kane* opened up a new era of American cinema, and *Confidential Report* is a film of only secondary importance.

But let's pause a moment on this assertion – it may, I feel, allow us to get to the heart of the matter. I think that not only would the supporters of the *politique des auteurs* refuse to agree that *Confidential Report* is an inferior film to *Citizen Kane*;[5] they would be more eager to claim the contrary, and I can well see how they would go about it. As *Confidential Report* is Welles's sixth film, one can assume that a certain amount of progress has already been made. Not only did the Welles of 1953 have more experience of himself and of his art than in 1941, but however great was the freedom he was able to obtain in Hollywood *Citizen Kane* cannot help remaining to a certain extent an RKO product. The film would never have seen the light of day without the co-operation of some superb technicians and their just as admirable technical apparatus. Gregg Toland, to mention only one, was more than a little responsible for the final result. On the other hand, *Confidential Report* is completely the work of Welles. Until it can be proved to the contrary, it will be considered *a priori* a superior film because it is more personal and because Welles's personality can only have matured as he grew older.

As far as this question is concerned, I can only agree with my young firebrands when they state that age as such cannot diminish the talent of a film-maker, and react violently to that critical prejudice which consists in always finding the works of a young or mature film-maker superior to the films of an old man. It has been said that *Monsieur Verdoux* was not up to *The Gold Rush*; people have criticized *The River* and *Carrosse d'or*, saying they miss the good old days of *La Règle du jeu*. Eric Rohmer has found an excellent answer to this: 'The history of art offers no example, as far as I know, of an authentic genius who has gone through a period of true decline at the end of his career; this should encourage us rather to detect, beneath what seems to be clumsy or bald, the traces of that desire for simplicity that characterizes the "last manner" of painters such as Titian, Rembrandt, Matisse or Bonnard, composers such as Beethoven and Stravinsky . . .' (*Cahiers* 8, 'Renoir Américain'). What kind of absurd discrimination has decided that film-makers alone are victims of a senility that other artists are protected from? There do remain the exceptional cases of dotage, but they are much rarer than is sometimes supposed. When Baudelaire was paralysed and unable to utter anything other than his 'cré nom', was he any less Baudelairean? Robert Mallet tells us how Valéry Larbaud, Joyce's translator into French, struggling against paralysis after twenty years of immobility and silence, had managed to build up for himself a vocabulary of twenty simple words. With these, he was still able to bring out some extraordinarily shrewd literary judgments. In fact, the few exceptions one could mention only go to prove the rule. A great talent matures but does not grow old. There is no reason why this law of artistic psychology should not also be valid for the cinema. Criticism that is based implicitly on the hypothesis of senility cannot hold water. It is rather the opposite postulate that ought to be stated: we should say that when we think we can discern a decline it is our own critical sense that is at fault, since an impoverishment of inspiration is a very unlikely phenomenon. From this point of view, the bias of the *politique des auteurs* is very fruitful, and I will stick up for them against the naïveté, the foolishness even, of the prejudices they are fighting.

But, always remembering this, one has nevertheless to accept that certain indisputable 'greats' have suffered an eclipse or a loss of their powers. I think what I have already said in this article may point to the reason for this. The drama does not reside in the growing old of men but in that of the cinema: those who do not know how to grow old *with* it will be overtaken by its evolution. This is why it has been possible for there to have been a series of failures leading to complete catastrophe without it being necessary to suppose that the genius of yesterday has become an imbecile. Once again, it is simply a question of the appearance of a clash between the subjective inspiration of the creator and the objective situation of the cinema, and this is what the *politique des auteurs* refuses to see. To its supporters *Confidential Report* is a more important film than *Citizen Kane* because they justifiably see more of Orson Welles in it. In other words, all they want to retain in the equation *auteur* plus *subject* = *work* is the *auteur*, while the subject is reduced to zero. Some of them will pretend to grant me that, all things being equal as far as the *auteur* is concerned, a good subject is naturally better than a bad one, but the more outspoken and foolhardy among them will admit that it very much looks as if they prefer small 'B' films, where the banality of the scenario leaves more room for the personal contribution of the author.

Of course I will be challenged on the very concept of *auteur*. I admit that the equation I just used was artificial, just as much so, in fact, as the distinction one learnt at school between form and content. To benefit from the *politique des auteurs* one first has to be worthy of it, and as it happens this school of criticism claims to distinguish between true *auteurs* and directors, even talented ones: Nicholas Ray is an *auteur*, Huston is supposed to be only a director; Bresson and Rossellini are *auteurs*, Clément is only a great director, and so on. So this conception of the author is not compatible with the *auteur*/subject distinction, because it is of greater importance to find out if a director is worthy of entering the select group of *auteurs* than it is to judge how well he has used his material. To a certain extent at least, the *auteur* is a subject to himself; whatever the scenario, he always tells the same story, or, in case the word 'story' is confusing, let's say he has the same attitude and passes the same moral judgments on the action and on the characters. Jacques Rivette has said that an *auteur* is someone who speaks in the first person. It's a good definition; let's adopt it.

The *politique des auteurs* consists, in short, of choosing the personal factor in artistic creation as a standard of reference, and then assuming that it continues and even progresses from one film to the next. It is recognized that there do exist certain important films of quality that escape this test, but these will systematically be considered inferior to those in which the personal stamp of the *auteur*, however run-of-the-mill the scenario, can be perceived even minutely.

It is far from being my intention to deny the positive attitude and methodological qualities of this bias. First of all, it has the great merit of treating the cinema as an adult art and of reacting against the impressionistic relativism that still reigns over the majority of film reviews. I admit that the explicit or admitted pretension of a critic to reconsider the production of a film-maker with every new film in the light of his judgment has something presumptuous about it that recalls Ubu. I am also quite willing to admit that if one is human one cannot help doing this, and, short of giving up the whole idea of actually criticizing, one might as well take as a starting point the feelings, pleasant or unpleasant, one feels personally when in contact with a film. Okay, but only on condition that these first impressions are kept in their proper place. We have to take them into consideration, but we should not use them as a basis. In other words, every critical act should consist of referring the film in question to a scale of values, but this reference is not merely a matter of intelligence; the sureness of one's judgment arises also, or perhaps even first of all (in the chronological sense of the word), from a general impression experienced during a film. I feel there are two symmetrical heresies, which are (a) objectively applying to a film a critical all-purpose yardstick, and (b) considering it sufficient simply to state one's pleasure or disgust. The first denies the role of taste, the second presupposes the superiority of the critic's taste over that of the author. Coldness . . . or presumption!

What I like about the *politique des auteurs* is that it reacts against the impressionist approach while retaining the best of it. In fact the scale of values it proposes is not ideological. Its starting-point is an appreciation largely composed of taste and sensibility: it has to discern the contribution of the artist as such, quite apart from the qualities of the subject or the technique: i.e. the man behind the style. But once one has made this distinction, this kind of criticism is doomed to beg the question, for it assumes at the start of its analysis that the film is automatically good as it has been made by an *auteur*. And so the yardstick applied to the film is the aesthetic portrait of the film-maker deduced from his previous films. This is all right so long as there has been no mistake about promoting this film-maker to the status of *auteur*. For it is objectively speaking safer to trust in the genius of the artist than in one's own critical intelligence. And this is where the *politique des auteurs* falls in line with the system of 'criticism by beauty'; in other words, when one is dealing with a genius, it is always a good method to presuppose that a supposed weakness in a work of art is nothing other than a beauty that one has not yet managed to understand. But as I have shown, this method had its limitations even in traditionally individualistic arts such as literature, and all the more so in the cinema where the sociological and historical cross-currents are countless. By giving such importance to 'B' films, the *politique des auteurs* recognizes and confirms this dependence *a contrario*.

Another point is that as the criteria of the *politique des auteurs* are very difficult to formulate the whole thing becomes highly hazardous. It is significant that our finest writers on *Cahiers* have been practising it for three or four years now and have yet to produce the main corpus of its theory. Nor is one particularly likely to forget how Rivette suggested we should admire Hawks: 'The evidence on the screen is proof of Hawks's genius: you only have to watch *Monkey Business* to know that it is a brilliant film. Some people refuse to admit this, however; they refuse to be satisfied by proof. There can't be any other reason why they don't recognize it . . .'[6] You can see the danger: an aesthetic personality cult.

But that is not the main point, at least to the extent that the *politique des auteurs* is practised by people of taste who know how to watch their step. It is its negative side that seems the most serious to me. It is unfortunate to praise a film that in no way deserves it, but the dangers are less far-reaching than when a worthwhile film is rejected because its director has made nothing good up to that point. I am not denying that the champions of the *politique des auteurs* discover or encourage a budding talent when they get the chance. But they do systematically look down on anything in a film that comes from a common fund and which can sometimes be entirely admirable, just as it can be utterly detestable. Thus, a certain kind of popular American culture lies at the basis of Minnelli's *Lust for Life*, but another more spontaneous kind of culture is also the principle of American comedy, the Western, and the gangster film. And its influence here is beneficial, for it is this that gives these cinematic genres their vigour and richness, resulting as they do from an artistic evolution that has always been in wonderfully close harmony with its public. And so one can read a review in *Cahiers* of a Western by Anthony Mann (and God knows I like Anthony Mann's Westerns!)[7] as if it were not above all a Western, i.e. a whole collection of conventions in the script, the acting, and the direction. I know very well that in a film magazine one may be permitted to skip such mundane details; but they should at least be implied, whereas what in fact happens is that their existence is glossed over rather sheepishly, as though they were a rather ridiculous necessity that it would be incongruous to mention. In any case, they will look down on, or treat condescendingly, any Western by a director who is not yet approved, even if it is as round and smooth as an egg. Well, what is *Stagecoach* if not an ultra-classical Western in which the art of Ford consists simply of raising characters and situations to an absolute degree of perfection;[8] and while sitting on the Censorship Committee I have seen some admirable Westerns, more or less anonymous and off the beaten track, but displaying a wonderful knowledge of the conventions of the genre and respecting the style from beginning to end.

Paradoxically, the supporters of the *politique des auteurs* admire the American cinema, where the restrictions of production are heavier than anywhere else. It is also true that it is the country where the greatest technical possibilities are offered to the director. But the one does not cancel out the other. I do however admit that freedom is greater in Hollywood than it is said to be, as long as one knows how to detect its manifestations, and I will go so far as to say that the tradition of genres is a base of operations for creative freedom. The American cinema is a classical art, but why not then admire in it what is most admirable, i.e. not only the talent of this or that film-maker, but the genius of the system, the richness of its ever-vigorous tradition, and its fertility when it comes into contact with new elements – as has been proved, if proof there need be, in such films as *An American in Paris*, *The Seven Year Itch* and *Bus Stop*. True, Logan is lucky enough to be considered an *auteur*, or at least a budding *auteur*. But then when *Picnic* or *Bus Stop* get good reviews the praise does not go to what seems to me to be the essential point, i.e. the social truth, which of course is not offered as a goal that suffices in itself but is integrated into a style of cinematic narration just as pre-war America was integrated into American comedy.

To conclude: the *politique des auteurs* seems to me to hold and defend an essential critical truth that the cinema needs more than the other arts, precisely because an act of true artistic creation is more uncertain and vulnerable in the cinema than elsewhere. But its exclusive practice leads to another danger: the negation of the film to the benefit of praise of its *auteur*. I have tried to show why mediocre *auteurs* can, by accident, make admirable films, and how, conversely, a genius can fall victim to an equally accidental sterility. I feel that this useful and fruitful approach, quite apart from its polemical value, should be complemented by other approaches to the cinematic phenomenon which will restore to a film its quality as a work of art. This does not mean one has to deny the role of the *auteur*, but simply give him back the preposition without which the noun *auteur* remains but a halting concept. *Auteur*, yes, but what *of*?

Translated by Peter Graham

Notes

1 Eric Rohmer, 'Les Lecteurs des *Cahiers* et la politique des auteurs', *Cahiers* 63, October 1956, pp. 54–8.
2 Jean Domarchi, 'Monsieur Vincent', *Cahiers* 68, February 1957, pp. 44–6.
3 Eric Rohmer, 'Leçon d'un échec: à propos de *Moby Dick*', *Cahiers* 67, January 1957, pp. 23–8.
4 Jean Domarchi, 'Le Fer dans la plaie', *Cahiers* 63, October 1956, pp. 18–28, translated in this volume as 'Knife in the Wound' (Ch. 30).
5 Cf. Eric Rohmer, 'Une Fable du XXe siècle' (on *Confidential Report*), *Cahiers* 61, July 1956, pp. 37–40; cf. *Cahiers*' 'All-Time Best Films' in Appendix 1 in this volume.
6 Jacques Rivette, 'Génie de Howard Hawks', *Cahiers* 23, May 1953, pp. 16–23, translated in this volume as 'The Genius of Howard Hawks' (Ch. 16).
7 Cf. André Bazin, 'Beauté d'un western' (on Mann's *The Man from Laramie*), *Cahiers* 55, January 1956, pp. 33–6, translated in this volume as 'Beauty of a Western' (Ch. 22).
8 Cf. André Bazin, 'Evolution du Western', *Cahiers* 54, Christmas 1955, pp. 22–6,

translated as 'Evolution of the Western' in André Bazin, *What is Cinema? Vol. 2*, reprinted in Nichols, *Movies and Methods*.

Luc Moullet, André Bazin, Jacques Rivette: Exchanges about Kurosawa and Mizoguchi

Luc Moullet: on Kurosawa's *Living*

(from 'Petit journal du cinéma' report on Cinémathèque, *Cahiers du Cinéma* 68, February 1957)

Setting up a Kurosawa retrospective was an excellent idea: of his work we in France knew only *Rashomon*, *The Seven Samurai* and *Record of a Living Being* (*Ikimono no kiroku*). *Drunken Angel* (*Yoidore tenshi*, 1948) and *Living* (*Ikiru*, 1952) were preceded by a flattering reputation which had increased our impatience. Well, in the event it's a total disaster, which is a bit difficult to account for. *Drunken Angel* never rises above the level of mediocrity and is completely lacking in interest: its aesthetic pretensions, especially in the dream sequence and the hero's death scene, surpass in their grotesqueness anything even the European cinema has produced. But *Living* is the ultimate in absurdity. We know it is the story of a broken-down old civil servant, suffering from cancer and trying to achieve something before he dies. Struggling against all the bureaucratic red tape, he succeeds in establishing the idea of a public park for the kids in a poor district of Tokyo. He dies the day it is opened. Up to this point it is all quite innocuous. But the film is nearly two and a half hours long, and for the last five reels we are treated to . . . an absolutely flabbergasting funeral meal. Here the director's misanthropy goes to such extremes that it quickly turns against him. As for the ending with the swing, confronted by such a piece of idiocy and affectation the audience is left speechless. The real Japanese cinema is elsewhere.

Translated by Liz Heron

André Bazin: on Kurosawa's *Living*

(from 'Petit journal du cinéma', *Cahiers du Cinéma* 69, March 1957)

What had put our friend Moullet so out of humour when he penned that note for the last 'Petit Journal' column on the Kurosawa retrospective at the Cinémathèque? Since he was the only one to go and see it, no one could contradict him, and all the more so as at *Cahiers* the director of *Rashomon* is somewhat the victim of a prejudice which works to the advantage of the tender, musical Mizoguchi. I shall return to this opposition later, and for the moment shall only point out that the Cinémathèque's interesting initiative should, precisely, have allowed us to revise our opinion of Kurosawa, who was quite inadequately known in France by only two films: *Rashomon* and *The Seven Samurai*.

But there is, in fact, no doubt that these two productions both attest to an extremely skilful and deliberate Westernism. This concern is very well explained and analysed in the outstanding little book by Shinobu and Marcel Giuglaris (*Le Cinéma japonais, 1896–1955*, Paris, Editions du Cerf, 1956). Kurosawa Akira, who belongs to a relatively young generation (he was born in 1910, while Mizoguchi has just died aged fifty-eight), is practically a post-war director. He is evidently very much influenced by Western cinema of the thirties, and perhaps even more by American films than by neo-realism. His admiration for John Ford, Fritz Lang and Chaplin in particular is clear enough. But this is not a passive influence. What matters for him is not just absorbing it; his intention is to use it to transmit back to us an image of Japanese tradition and culture that we can assimilate visually and mentally. He succeeds in doing this so well with *Rashomon* that this film can truly be said to have opened the gates of the West to the Japanese cinema. But in its wake came many other films – notably Mizoguchi's – which have revealed to us a production which, if not more authentic, is at any rate more characteristic and more pure. From then on ingratitude came easily; and just as it has been the done thing to condemn the snobbery of exoticism in the glamour of the Japanese cinema, in Kurosawa it is his reverse exoticism that has been attacked, in other words his compromises with the rhetoric of Western cinema. These compromises were even more in evidence in *The Seven Samurai*, which, at a secondary level, was a John Ford Western on a feudal theme.

I do not know whether it was this ensemble of critical prejudices – which I myself shared in part – that blinded Moullet as he watched the films screened at the Cinémathèque, but the fact remains that, for one of them at least, I am obliged to bring to bear a radically different testimony.

This is in relation to *Living*, which Moullet coolly describes as the ultimate in absurdity, while I find it the most beautiful, most accomplished and most moving Japanese film that it has ever been my lot to see, at any rate among the productions of the modern cycle.

But first of all I want to point out that here the script is in fact a contemporary one and that this immediacy radically modifies the disturbing problem of influences. Without any doubt, for a multitude of profound reasons, *Living* is a specifically Japanese film, but what is striking about this work and what one cannot fail to be aware of is the universal value of its message. To be more precise, *Living* is Japanese in the same way that *M* was German or *Citizen Kane* American. There is no need for any mental translation from one mode of culture to another for both the specific inspiration and the general meaning to be simultaneously clearly legible. The international character of *Living* is not geographical but geological; its source is at the depth of the subterranean moral stratum where Kurosawa knew it was to be found. But since he is also dealing with men of our time, contemporaries with whom a face-to-face encounter is only hours away by plane, Kurosawa is also within his rights to draw, now and then, on international film rhetoric, just as James Joyce drew on the vocabulary of many languages in order to re-invent English, an English that could be said to be already translated and yet untranslatable.

And this is perhaps why in 1952 *Living* could be ranked first among the ten best national films by the Japanese critics, whose reservations about Samurai films for festivals – and notably *Rashomon* – are known. So that I wonder whether, instead of regarding Kurosawa's cosmopolitanism as a commercial compromise, albeit of superior quality, we should not rather see it from now on as a dialectical progression pointing the way forward for the Japanese cinema. When it comes to my personal taste, I still perhaps prefer Mizoguchi's style, like the pure Japanese music of his inspiration, but I surrender before the breadth of intellectual, moral and aesthetic perspectives opened up by a film like *Living*, which is suffused with values that are incomparably more important, in its script just as much as in its form.

I won't come back to Moullet's little résumé which, after all, is no more unfaithful to the film's subject than can be helped when it is taken out of the context in which it was made. But I shall draw your attention to the fact that there is in a sense an inversion of the Faust theme. What the old doctor desires is to rediscover his youth so that he can live his life evilly. The hero of *Living* knows he is condemned and quite innocently tries to find how, in the few months he has left, he can know the life that has been unknown to him. If he discovers that the simplest thing is, as a public official, to do the good deed that is within his power, it is not that good tempts him more than evil, but because a young, simple creature has revealed to him the meaning of the most modest creation. Unwittingly, and unknown to everyone, this old fellow becomes a saint, because it is the shortest route from himself to life.

One can see all the pitfalls such a theme might hold: sentimentality, melodrama, moralism, social problem. All these dangers are more than avoided: they are transcended, and this is thanks to narrative structures of an intelligence that left me open-mouthed with astonishment. What Moullet calls 'the interminable funeral', which in fact takes up nearly half the film, is an unbelievably bold piece of story-telling. For a whole hour we watch and listen to friends, relatives and colleagues who have come to the funeral, as they talk about the dead man. All the while drinking rice wine and nibbling little cakes. Of course, these conversations are intercut with flashbacks which gradually reveal to us what the hero did before his death, and thereby his true personality. But each of these flashbacks is quite short, and they in no way reduce the guests' discussion to a mere device of presentation. Thus the substance of the film is just as much in the present as in the past, and the narrative tension derives from the convergence which is progressively drawn between the secret truth of the reality evoked and the understanding of it which the observers gradually acquire. At the end, they have at last understood the dead man's secret: he knew he was to die and had sacrificed the last days of his life to an exemplary task. But by then too they are all drunk, and this truth exalts only very worthy drunkards who will have forgotten it tomorrow.

There is a lot more to be said about *Living* – notably about the role of time in the story, which is so different from Western dramatic conventions with their artificial symmetries, yet without a single minute that could be considered gratuitous. This composition is only more skilful and more delicate. But it is truly to be hoped that some French distributor will be wise enough before long to offer this masterpiece to the public, and we will then have the opportunity to return to it.

Translated by Liz Heron

Jacques Rivette: 'Mizoguchi Viewed from Here'

('Mizoguchi vu d'ici', *Cahiers du Cinéma* 81, March 1958)

How does one talk about Mizoguchi without falling into a double trap: the jargon of the specialist or that of the humanist? It may be that his films owe something to the tradition or the spirit of Nô or Kabuki; but then who is to teach us the deep meaning of those traditions, and is it not a case of trying to explain the unknown by the unknowable? What is beyond doubt is that Mizoguchi's art is based on the play of personal genius within the context of a dramatic tradition. But will wanting to approach it in terms of the national culture and to find in it above all such great universal values make us any the wiser? That men are men wherever they may be is something we might have predicted; to be surprised by it only tells us something about ourselves.

But these films – which tell us, in an alien tongue, stories that are completely foreign to our customs and way of life – do talk to us in a familiar language. What language? The only one to which a film-maker should lay claim when all is said and done: the language of *mise en scène*. For modern artists did not discover African fetishes through a conversion to idols, but because those unusual objects moved them as sculptures. If music is a universal idiom, so too is *mise en scène*: it is this language, and not Japanese, that has to be learned to understand 'Mizoguchi'. A language held in common, but here brought to a degree of purity that our Western cinema has known only rarely.

Some will object: why retrieve only Mizoguchi from those hazardous probings that are our visions of Japanese cinema? But is Japanese cinema all that foreign to us anyway? It is in a language close to it, but not the same, that other film-makers speak to us: exoticism accounts sufficiently for the superficial tone that separates a Tadashi Imai (*Darkness at Noon/ Mahiru no ankoku*) from a Cayatte, a Heinosuke Gosho (*Where Chimneys are Seen/Entotsu ni mieru basho*) from a Becker, a Mikio Naruse (*Mother/O-kasan*) from a Le Chanois, a Teinosuke Kinugasa (*Gate of Hell/Jigokumon*) from a Christian-Jaque, indeed a Satoru Yamamura (*The Crab-canning Factory/*

Kanikosen) from a Raymond Bernard. We may perhaps leave out Kaneto Shindo (*Children of Hiroshima/Genbaku no ko*) and Keisuke Kinoshita (*She Was Like a Wild Chrysanthemum/Nogiku no gotoki kimi nariki*); the unfamiliarity of their inflexions, however, owes more to preciosity than to the impulse of a personal voice. It is, in short, the best-indexed language of Western cinema: the classic case being Kurosawa, passing from European classics to contemporary 'adventure' films with the peevish and humourless affectation of an Autant-Lara. Moreover, just compare his Samurai films with the historical films of Mizoguchi, where one would search in vain for any trace of a duel or for the smallest grunt (those 'picturesque' qualities that made for the facile success of *The Seven Samurai*, of which we may now rightly ask whether it was especially aimed at the export market), and where an acute sense of the past is achieved by means of a disconcerting and almost Rossellinian simplicity.

Enough of comparisons: the little Kurosawa–Mizoguchi game has had its day. Let the latest champions of Kurosawa withdraw from the match; one can only compare what is comparable and equal in ambition. Mizoguchi alone imposes the sense of a specific language and world, answerable only to him.

Mizoguchi charms us because in the first place he makes no effort to charm us, and never makes any concession to the viewer. Alone, it seems, of all the Japanese film-makers to stay within his own traditions (*Yang Kwei-Fei* is part of the national repertoire by the same token as our *Cid*), he is also the only one who can thus lay claim to true universality, which is that of the individual.

His is the world of the irremediable; but in it, destiny is not at the same moment fate: neither Fate nor the Furies. There is no submissive acceptance, but the road to reconciliation; what do the stories of the ten films we now know matter? Everything in them takes place in a pure time which is that of the eternal present: there, past and future time often mingle their waters, one and the same meditation on duration runs through them all; all end with the serene joy of one who has conquered the illusory phenomena of perspectives. The only suspense is that irrepressible line rising towards a certain level of ecstasy, the 'correspondence' of those final notes, those harmonies held without end, which are never completed, but expire with the breath of the musician.

Everything finally comes together in that search for the central place, where appearances, and what we call 'nature' (or shame, or death), are reconciled with man, a quest like that of German high Romanticism, and that of a Rilke, an Eliot; one which is also that of the camera – placed always at the exact point so that the slightest shift inflects all the lines of space, and upturns the secret face of the world and of its gods.

An art of modulation.

Translated by Liz Heron

33 | Alexandre Astruc: 'What is *mise en scène*?'

('Qu'est-ce que la mise en scène?', *Cahiers du Cinéma* 100, October 1959)

One doesn't need to have made a lot of films to realize that there is no such thing as *mise en scène*, that actors can do quite well without it and that any chief cameraman knows how to position the camera to get the appropriate shot, that the continuity between shots takes care of itself, etc. Mizoguchi and Ophuls obviously understood this very quickly and then moved on to what really interested them. . . . Watching how people act? . . . Not exactly. It could more aptly be described as presenting them, watching how they act and at the same time what makes them act.

The difference between the cinema and anything else – including the novel – is, primarily, the impossibility of telling a lie, and secondly the absolute certainty, shared by the spectator and the author alike, that on the screen everything will be resolved with time. If the director – the film-maker – actually intervenes anywhere in the making of the film it is essentially here. He runs a course between two realities: the image through which he observes the world and the duration within which the resolution comes.

Within which he does not, however, destroy: the slow erosion of truth which is the art of a Proust and which explodes in someone like Faulkner presupposes the novel written in words, the fragments of eternity. While it may hold and fix the real, it does so only at the cost of an unceasing effort of decomposition and destruction of forms, a relentless advance and assault on a vocabulary whose debris is carried drifting in the current.

The camera fixes; it does not transcend, it looks. One has to be naive to imagine that the systematic use of an 18.5 lens will make things any different from what they are. In exchange, it never lies. What is caught by the lens is the movement of the body – an immediate revelation, like all that is physical: the dance, a woman's look, the change of rhythm in a walk, beauty, truth, etc.

The cinema assumes a certain trust in the world just as it is. Even in the midst of ugliness and poverty; it uncovers that strange and cruel tenderness, that terrible sweetness of *Hiroshima*, where some rapid tracking shots in the heart of a city, and the voice of a woman, are enough to dissipate so many horrors and to bring about a change in the landscape so that, quite naturally, it becomes organized into a human perspective, and some strange seductive force makes it seem that, quite naturally, all that is still an expectation here will some day be completely fulfilled.

One of the most beautiful films in the world has been made by an old Japanese director, the author of some hundred or so films, with, I am certain, no other desire than properly to practise his craft. It takes only five minutes for *Ugetsu monogatari* to demonstrate clearly the meaning of *mise en scène* – for some at any rate: a certain way of extending states of mind into movements of the body. It is a song, a rhythm, a dance. Mizoguchi is well aware that what is expressed in physical violence cannot be made to lie. It is not character, it is not self-knowledge, but that irresistible movement that casts itself ever forward along the same paths, in the pursuit of fulfilment – or destruction. I imagine that what interests him – after so many films – is no longer even this spectacle itself, but the impossibility of turning away and ceasing to contemplate it. It is possible that a writer writes to free himself – for a director it is never quite that. In the tenderness or in the horror of the universe that he exploits he has to meet what one might call a kind of willingness or complicity, but which for the artist is never anything but the source of the greatness that obsesses him and which he believes he can reveal.

Then what happens to technique? It ceases to be a way of showing – or of concealing. Style is not simply a means of making beautiful what is ugly, and vice versa. Not one director in the world will trust photography if the limits of his ambition go beyond competing with picture postcards. Or even the development of an awareness: tracking shots are not notes, or references at the foot of a page. I rather think that the only function of technique is to generate that mysterious distance between the author and his characters — whose fluctuations and mad races through the forest seem to be accompanied by the movements of the camera with such fidelity.

Seem: for the strength and the greatness of this universe which reappears in film after film comes from the author's constant domination of its elements. He bends them – not perhaps to his own vision – Mizoguchi is a film director, not a novelist – but to a certain need to draw back from them, wisdom or the will to wisdom. So the tragic poem draws its force from the apparent insensitivity and coldness of the artist, who seems to have taken up his position, camera in hand, at the bend in the river; surveying the plain from where the actors in the drama will emerge.

The exquisite and moving sweetness of *Ugetsu monogatari* consists, as in some Westerns, in that irrevocable slowness that urges on, maybe through violence and anger, a handful of individuals whose destiny is insignificant.

But Mizoguchi knows very well that ultimately it matters little whether his films end well, just as he does not worry whether the strongest bonds

267

between himself and his characters are those of tenderness or of contempt. He is like the voyeur who sees pleasure reflected in the face of the one he watches, even though he is well aware that it is more than this reflection that he seeks: perhaps it is quite simply the wearying confirmation of something that he has always known but cannot resist making sure of.

So I see *mise en scène* as a means of making the spectacle one's own – but then what artist doesn't know that what is seen matters less, not than the way of seeing, but than a particular way of needing to see and to show.

Between the canvas and the figures that obsess him, what the hand of the painter brings is not a different manner of looking, but a new dimension. A Manet painting is not 'nature observed by a particular temperament', it is a thoroughfare for an aesthetic will, as irreducible to themes as it is to the secret motivations of the artist, which perhaps sustain but never exhaust it. *Mise en scène* isn't necessarily the will to give a new meaning to the world, but nine times out of ten it is built on the secret certainty of holding some fragment of truth, first about man, and then about the work of art – indissolubly linked. Mizoguchi uses violence, rapacity or sexual desire to express on the screen what he can release only on condition that he meets those elements. But it would be absurd to say that violence is the subject of his films. If he needs it, it is like the alcoholic's need to drink: not to become drunk, but to feed his drunkenness. With him, as with the great masters of the screen, it is never the plot, nor the form, nor even the effect that matters, nor even the possibility of placing frenzied characters within an extreme situation: Mizoguchi, like all Orientals, scorns psychology and verisimilitude. He needs violence as the key that will open the door to another world. But as in Baroque painting, the rain of the storm lashing on to those grimacing faces and those crippled bodies is the harbinger of calm. Beyond desire and violence, the world of the Japanese director, like the world of Murnau, lets the veil of indifference descend once more, through which, in a cinema that could be described as 'exotic', metaphysics makes a sudden intrusion.

Is there in the end such a difference between a Japanese film-maker, master enough of his craft to be offered a seven-year Hollywood contract – a man who is in fact very much like one's idea of a monthly salaried engineer – and a late nineteenth-century *poète maudit*? Baudelaire's opium and Mizoguchi's craft have the same role in the end: they are pretexts, like Proust's asthma or his homosexuality, like the yellow that intoxicated Van Gogh – but who would say that yellow was even the subject of Van Gogh's paintings, or their purpose? The artist seeks where he thinks to find his conditions of creation: the director in the studio, in the brothel, in the museum. . . .

The world of an artist is not the one that conditions him, but the one which he needs in order to create and to transform perpetually into something that will obsess him even more than that by which he is obsessed.

The obsession of the artist is artistic creation.

Translated by Liz Heron

II | Dossier – CinemaScope

Introduction

CinemaScope, introduced in 1953, was enthusiastically received by popular audiences but met with a rather negative response from the 'serious' critical establishments in many countries, not least Britain. *Sight and Sound* noted that it 'received more unsolicited manuscripts on Cinema-Scope and the widescreen movement than on any other subject, and all have expressed, in varying degrees, distrust and dislike'.[1] As the enthusiastic articles by Truffaut, Rohmer and Rivette reprinted here make clear, the response at *Cahiers* was very different, though Rohmer and Rivette both refer to much critical response in France which echoed that of *Sight and Sound*. The sharp contrast between the two journals merits some brief comment.

The fundamental distrust of Hollywood felt by *Sight and Sound* – for example, Walter Lassally: 'with the emphasis on novelty, noise and spectacle, the cinema is on its way to returning to its birthplace, the fairground'[2] – can be contrasted with Truffaut's response, in which a recognition of the essentially commercial nature of Hollywood ('where . . . not even ten metres of film are shot without a dozen gentlemen giving their opinions eight times over and doing a recalculation of the finances') and disappointment at the mediocrity of the first films made in CinemaScope are only preliminaries to the real question since, as Rivette argues, 'money puts colour and sound on offer, but who imposes them, if not the film-maker, in his desire to take up the challenge that they present to his imagination?'

Basic attitudes to film aesthetics and film history are at stake here. When Truffaut, Rohmer and Rivette refer to attitudes to the coming of sound, and to a certain extent colour, they adopt a distinctly Bazinian view of film history and aesthetics, as developed in Bazin's essay on film language.[3] Rivette's idea that 'sound remedied a defect' in cinema is a precise reprise of Bazin's thesis that, for example, *Greed* and *The Passion of Joan of Arc* were 'virtually sound films' and that sound was a 'natural extension' of the silent film aesthetic exemplified by film-makers like

270

Stroheim, Murnau, Flaherty or Dreyer 'precisely because its aesthetic conception was not bound up with editing'.[4] Bazin opposed 'directors who believed in the image' (that is, those relying on both editing and 'plasticity' – sets, lighting, framing, etc.) with 'those who believed in reality',[5] and this is very much the aesthetic espoused here by both Rohmer ('no more will we speak of framing or lighting; instead, we will talk about landscapes and light') and Rivette ('Freed from framing (and slavery to plasticity) . . . freed from editing, now sacrificed to a simple succession of takes or fragments of cinema, and to the play of breaks – this at last is our cinema'). The supposed approximation to the perception of physical reality which Bazin had welcomed in deep focus, and these writers welcome in wide-screen and colour, is precisely what Richard Kohler's article on 'The Big Screens' in *Sight and Sound* refuses, on the basis that it involves the 'sacrifice' of most of the 'interpretative characteristics of the cinema' – lighting, framing and so on.[6]

In this stark opposition we have, indeed, what Rivette calls 'two ideas of the cinema, two fundamentally opposed and irreconcilable ways of loving and understanding it'. Against the defenders of what Rivette calls 'everything that habit has endowed with the illusion of the irreplaceable . . . art defined by divine right as silent, narrow, and black and white', these three *Cahiers* critics argue that CinemaScope (and colour) are not more appropriate to some subjects than to others, that nothing has been lost, but rather a good deal gained, at least once CinemaScope became a normal part of the technology at the film-makers' disposal.

Bazin himself, though like Truffaut disappointed by *The Robe*, was enthusiastic on the theoretical level and saw that CinemaScope, 'better than depth of field, definitively destroys montage as a major element of cinematographic discourse. Montage, in which people have wanted wrongly to see the essence of cinema, is in fact . . . condemning the director to the breaking up of reality. From this point of view, Cinema-Scope inscribes itself in the logical progression of the evolution of the cinema over the last fifteen years, from *La Règle du jeu* to *The Best Years of Our Lives*, from *Citizen Kane* to *Europa '51*.'[7]

Cinerama came late to France, but it too was received seriously by *Cahiers*. Bazin related Cinerama to his earlier theses about deep focus, arguing that earlier images were 'impotent in rendering space, limiting themselves to translating it by the geometrical symbolism of perspective', while Cinerama's 146° angle of vision more or less equalled our natural angle of vision, noting that one is 'physiologically unable to synthesize all the elements of the image: one must exercise one's look, not only by turning one's eyes but by moving one's head', thus contributing, as Bazin had argued deep focus did, to 'the "participation" of the spectator'.[8] Richard Kohler's *Sight and Sound* article had steadfastly resisted the loss of 'that "aesthetic distance" vital to all art': 'by assaulting the spectator on the "actual" plane of consciousness, the enveloping screen in fact makes him physically too much a part of the scene'.[9] By contrast, Rohmer begins his article by stating that he likes 'to be enveloped in the spectacle' and Truffaut's 'full view' requires getting close to the screen.

Leaving aside the ultimate validity of Bazin's theses about realism in film, in retrospect it seems clear that on the question of CinemaScope *Cahiers* was right and *Sight and Sound* was wrong. The differing responses of the two journals go a long way to explaining why in the 1950s *Cahiers* seemed stimulating and progressive while *Sight and Sound* seemed academic and conservative. Kohler's contention that 'a very wide horizontal screen emphasizes scenic display but can be of little use in suggesting ideas or the course of human relationships'[10] looks intellectually ludicrously threadbare today, while *Cahiers'* predictions about the aesthetic future of widescreen proved fundamentally correct.

Notes

1 'The Big Screens', *Sight and Sound*, vol. 24, no. 3, January–March 1955, p. 120.
2 Walter Lassally, 'The Big Screens (2)', *Sight and Sound, op. cit.*, p. 124.
3 André Bazin, 'The Evolution of the Language of Cinema', in Bazin, *What is Cinema? Vol. 1*.
4 *Ibid.*, p. 38.
5 *Ibid.*, p. 24.
6 Richard Kohler, 'The Big Screens (1)', *Sight and Sound, op. cit.*, p. 121.
7 André Bazin, 'Fin du montage', *Cahiers* 31, January 1954, p. 43.
8 André Bazin, 'Un peu tard (Place au Cinérama)', *Cahiers* 48, pp. 46–7.
9 Kohler, *op. cit.*, p. 120.
10 *Ibid.*, p. 122.

34 | François Truffaut: 'A Full View'

('En avoir plein la vue', *Cahiers du Cinéma*
25, July 1953)

If he had been with us that morning, our greatly missed friend Jean-George Auriol[1] would have been the first to express his enthusiasm; he was the one who always said, as he took his place in the front row of the stalls: 'When you're at the cinema you have to make sure you get a full view.

Admirable sentiment, admirable maxim, completely justifying Cinema-Scope. The more one goes to cinemas, the more one feels the need to get close to the screen in order to mitigate the hateful critical objectivity induced by habit that turns us into a blasé audience and therefore a bad audience.

Here we have the closeness, still refused by some, coming to us of its own accord, demolishing the arbitrary boundaries of the screen and replacing them with the almost ideal – with panoramic vision.

The journalists' mistake was a grave one (and there is no need to look elsewhere for the reasons why some people were misled). It was to concentrate all the publicity for CinemaScope on the three-dimensional effect, which was in fact non-existent and which would not have interested us in the slightest. With the wide screen the cinema of its own account reinvents the bas-relief, the essential medium of sculptural narrative, and in the same way gives 'depth' a primacy over 'relief', which, as we have seen in the recent 3-D films that need polaroid glasses, points in the direction of an affectation with nothing to offer us but a vision of the world that is naively monstrous and totally unrealistic. André Bazin's hypothesis that 'the screen is a mask' (analogous to Sartre's 'to speak is to move words through silence') is still pertinent to CinemaScope. The cinema remains a window on the world, but hasn't modern architecture bricked up the old vertical window and opened up the window-wall, the glass-panelled bay, whose shape is oblong (blocks of flats, Le Corbusier, *Rope*, etc. . . . .)? It's worth reminding ourselves that the cinema is a visual art and our natural vision is panoramic: our eyes are one beside the other, not one on top of the other – they complement one another along the horizontal axis and are no use at all to each other along the vertical.

All the questions raised when one starts thinking about CinemaScope – the survival of the close-up, the effectiveness of camera movements, etc. – are dissipated and all at once resolved before the *fait accompli*. The close-ups of Victor Mature in *The Robe* leave us with no doubt in our minds: the soft focus effect is there around the faces as in *Notorious*; a long scene with Lauren Bacall assures us that the two-shot is alive and well and becoming even more interesting.

Every work is in one way or another the story of a man's progress, and in CinemaScope he will go far.

It is pleasant to think of the films one likes and to conclude that the extended length of the apartment in *Rope*, the cars in *Europa '51* and the turning wheels of *Le Carrosse d'or* would all gain additional fascination.

Certainly – the extracts that have been shown prove it – the first films made in CinemaScope will be mediocre. How could the most inspired production manager or the most inventive director improvise the smallest original detail on a set where – with all the money in Hollywood at stake – not even ten metres of film is shot without a dozen gentlemen giving their opinions eight times over and making a recalculation of the finances?

We shall have to wait for the shooting of a film in CinemaScope to be as natural an occurrence as an ordinary flat black and white film before directors can enjoy the same kind of freedom. We must recognize that if CinemaScope is a commercial REVOLUTION it is also an aesthetic EVOLUTION. If you agree that every stage of perfection must of necessity be an effective increase in realism, then CinemaScope is a stage in that perfection, the most important one since the introduction of sound.

We are entering the age of wide vision. We will turn to the cinema and we will have 'a full view'.

Translated by Liz Heron

Note

1 Jean-George Auriol, b. 1907, d. 1950 in a car accident; founder and editor of the journal *Revue du Cinéma* 1928–32 and 1946–9, when several critics associated later with *Cahiers du Cinéma* wrote for it. See Introduction to this volume for further comment.

35 | Jacques Rivette: 'The Age of *metteurs en scène*'

('L'Age des metteurs en scène', *Cahiers du Cinéma* 31, January 1954)

How does one become a Persian? Even more, how does one accept CinemaScope? Such is my feeling on the subject that I do not entertain the slightest reservation, let alone the possibility of rejecting it. At the very least the anamorphic lens will have this initial advantage: it will finally have drawn a clearly defined boundary between two schools and even two ideas of the cinema, two fundamentally opposed and irreconcilable ways of loving and understanding it. I see only one difference, but it is an important one: it is no longer to do with geography, but with history. Many a plea to hold back change will be swept away to join the nostalgic longings for the days of the silents, the lamentations for black and white – and those who make such pleas too, if they are not careful.

Let's be frank. The advent of CinemaScope is a matter of quite a different order from the start of the talkies, on the level of aesthetics, that is: for the talkies only confirmed an established fact, remedied a defect, proved the truth of Griffith, Murnau and Stroheim against, you might say, Chaplin or Eisenstein. It's a deaf man indeed who is not pursued by the memory of Lillian Gish's clear, sparkling voice, or the nuances of the authoritative tones in which Lil Dagover parried Tartuffe, or the strangled cries of Fay Wray; and the only thing Lubitsch's brilliant conversationalists lacked in *Lady Windermere's Fan* was speech – no, not even that, just voices.

Much more then than the *coup d'état* of sound, it seems to me that the history of the cinema has its turning point in the irresistible infiltration of colour. CinemaScope is, more than anything else, the crowning moment and the consecration of this long process; from now on they go hand in hand, both pursuing the same objective. I make no claim to express it in just a few words; but it is no longer from the shadow of things that the film-maker will draw substance, but from their most alive and striking forms. He now has to create with what is most concrete, most weighty in them, and if he wishes to carry them, always *unique*, towards the abstract, it will not be at the expense of the individual and the singular. It looks as

275

if any hint of syntactical or literary algebra has had its day and, however much it may displease the pedants, the cinema is not a language.

And without wishing to upset too many people I must say that when I am in front of the CinemaScope screen I experience no regret for the old screen, nor do I give it the slightest thought. Yet I already yearn for CinemaScope whenever I am faced with an ordinary screen. Watching *The Naked Spur* again the other day in the front row of a cinema which in fact has a reasonably big screen, throughout the film I never shook off the oppressive sensation of narrowness, of an intolerable appropriation of the edges where there is room for air to circulate, of the most artificial limits that can be imposed on the eye or the mind. What justifies CinemaScope in the first place is our desire for it, which goes beyond the simple role of the spectator.

There's no doubt, however, that the bitterness of the critics is justified: they like to see what they already know; they allow of no beauty as yet unclassified. For them beauty is classical, and they spend the greater part of their time lamenting what is gone; what agonies to be forever denied the satisfaction of those tedious close-ups, that framing so compliantly subject to the laws of the golden number, everything that habit has endowed with the illusion of the irreplaceable. But how can it fail to fire the imagination – the idea of what is yet to come, but is promised to us, the knowledge of all that can now happen; in these new expanses what harm can come to that close-up, whose every artifice we know so well, whose every inflexion is so predictable? Art lives not necessarily in what is new, but in what is discovered; that is what unbends the most stubborn and emboldens the most timid.

I don't want to base an argument on my own personal taste. For example, that these new proportions inspire in me the idea of elegance above all, and that they satisfy intellectually as much as visually; nor will I linger over a description of the new viewpoint offered to the spectator, and the talk scarcely seems to be about what is the essential – that is, the fact that visual range is not extended at the expense of closeness; the anamorphic lens is the real triumph of the wide-angle, the mark of true film-makers. But since it is generally felt that CinemaScope is primarily a problem of *mise en scène*, let's talk about that.

Admittedly, *The Robe* is no masterpiece (though it's still better than Alan Crosland's 1927 film). If certain documentary images are superior, it is because it is in the logic of things that the genius of the machine bursts out in advance of the creators' genius. Lumière will always have more charm than Méliès, as will the raw use of the invention rather than the later, somewhat over-ingenious applications made by its manipulators. I'm thinking specifically of some of Negulesco's shots in the film we saw at the Rex – they seemed to accumulate rhetorical precautions to justify a process whose very evidence is the trump card: precautions that give rise either to suspicion or to a feeling of redundancy. Yes, I think that in practice I still prefer the total absence of research and ideas of a Koster, who seems hardly bothered by CinemaScope and who proves thereby, no doubt quite involuntarily, that in effect everything is possible. Here we have an example of how a *mise en scène* which is conventional to the point of parody, and stupid in places, acquires an added dimension simply through the anamorphic lens – breadth and nothing more – and manages to sum up a certain style, one that is still ambiguous and confused, but indisputable. What will it be like with the added ingredient of talent? I can't see how anything should have to be sacrificed to the new lens in any way imaginable. I see rather what each aspect of *mise en scène* will gain in effectiveness, in beauty, and in breadth – truly and spiritually as well as visibly.

For this is the bone of contention: our critics acknowledge the process, but they want to limit the damage, or else to restrict it to the level of a curiosity or an attraction that does not trespass on art (with art defined by divine right as silent, narrow, and black and white), to channel it into certain genres and, I dare say, keep it confined to location filming (yet how can you see *Rope* again without immediately recognizing the most inspired insight into the cinema of tomorrow?). These arguments are not new by any means, but two years after they were first heard there were no more silent films and colour was only a matter of months away. For it's the directors who decide, who alone know how to distinguish between what increases their powers and what limits them – and the critics follow. They even soon discover and acclaim what had heralded the new technique. *La Passion de Jeanne d'Arc* has many parallels in our time. It won't be long before they are claiming that our best recent films – and no doubt all the great films in the history of the cinema – contain within them either an appeal to CinemaScope or nostalgia for it, that so many pans, lateral tracking shots, careful arrangements of characters over the surface of the screen (*Le Carrosse d'or*) had perhaps a meaning – even if it were simply that of breadth.

No, I'm not going to attempt to describe this cinema – not what it will be an hour from now, far less tomorrow. I am making a statement: CinemaScope, Abel Gance's triple screen, Cinerama – whatever; they are always that same desire to break out of the antiquated frame and, more than that, the desire for the kind of sudden opening-out of the screen that is like the blossoming of a Japanese paper flower plunged in running water. The search for depth is out of date; that is what condemns 3–D more surely than all the technical imperfections. What new problems could it hope to offer directors today? After so many years of depth, what novelty, what challenge is there? Money puts colour and sound on offer, but who imposes them, if not the film-maker, in his desire to take up the challenge that they present to his imagination, letting himself become involved, then discovering, sometimes in spite of himself, the new dimensions of his art? Is challenge too slim a criterion? But what was Michelangelo's fresco technique or Bach's fugue technique if not the compulsion to invent an answer to some vexing question (and I'll say nothing of the infinite challenges of technique and construction – often subtle to the point of seeming trivial – which all artists secretly impose on themselves, and which will never be known to the public). Yes, there is the essential element of art; 'the study of beauty is a duel . . .'

It seems that the history of *mise en scène* is inseparable from the frenzied exploration of that narrow corridor of space that would always close in on the eye of the film-maker as soon as he looked through the lens (what was the widest wide angle compared with the impatience of that look which could take in all the breadth and space of a scene in a lightning glance?), but inseparable also from the obsession, running secretly through the work of the greatest directors, with the spreading out of that *mise en scène* on the screen, the desire for a perfect perpendicular in relation to the spectator's look. From *Birth of a Nation* to *Le Carrosse d'or*, from the Murnau of *Tabu* to the Lang of *Rancho Notorious*, this extreme use of the breadth of the screen, the physical separation of the characters, empty spaces distended by fear or desire, like lateral movements, all seem to me to be – much more than depth – the language of true film-makers, and the sign of maturity and mastery. Look at how Renoir has moved on from *Madame Bovary* or *La Règle du jeu* to *Diary of a Chambermaid* and *The River*. If, as Bresson has said, the cinema is the art of connections, then the first are those of confrontations, looks, distances, and their variations, which in depth are indiscernible with any precision, or even more confused. The use of depth, where the distorted perspective imposes on the protagonists an often arbitrary variation in scale, dominated by disproportions, incongruities, ridicule, is surely allied to a sense of the absurd; while the use of breadth surely goes with intelligence, equilibrium, lucidity, and – by the very openness of its relationships – with morality. Isn't that an aspect of the eternal conflict between the baroque and the classical? And wouldn't great *mise en scène*, like great painting, be flat, hinting at depth through slits rather than gaps?

The future opens up these questions, and others more to do with the everyday practice of the film-maker. Must we expect the theatre to teach us the lessons of a drama as vast as the universe? Of course, but at the same time the cinema would only lose itself if it gave up the search for an exact and clearly articulated mode of writing of its own, the obsession with an abstract figure, of which the work of the theatre is ignorant, subject as it is to the logic of drama, the explaining of situations, the showing of the scene. What can we hope will come from great painting except simply a bold example, equally governed by mural display and the theatre? Freed from framing (and slavery to plasticity), now abolished in favour of the lens; freed from editing, now sacrificed to a simple succession of takes or fragments of cinema, and to the play of breaks – this at last is our cinema, now forced to look for its real problems.

I am exaggerating a little. *The Robe* clearly shows how CinemaScope gives weight to everything, even if left to itself. Henry Koster changes shots, regulates the camera movements according to plan, without any significant miscalculation, and still encounters happy accidents, unexpected successes. A thousand details, a thousand tricks that will soon wear thin, are none the less proof that things will not stop there. In the end it will be necessary to embark on the search for a new breadth of expression and attitude; above all, a contemporary breadth of expression which will stand out on this flat backdrop. The director will learn how he can sometimes claim the whole surface of the screen, mobilize it with his own enthusiasm, play a game that is both closed and infinite – or how he can shift the poles of the story to their opposites, create zones of silence, areas of immobility, the provoking hiatus, the skilful break. Quickly wearying of chandeliers and vases brought into the edges of the image for the 'balance' of the close-ups, he will discover the beauty of the void, of free, open spaces swept by the wind; he will know how to lay bare the image, how to be no longer afraid of gaps or disequilibrium, and how to multiply his transgressions against plasticity in order to obey the truths of the cinema.

He will not waste time: genius is first distinguished from talent by its haste to make use of the new, to discover with it, go beyond its time, and to create from its material. For us the history of Technicolor is synonymous with films of Jean Renoir, Alfred Hitchcock, Howard Hawks or Fritz Lang. We should not complain – we already know one early inspired use of CinemaScope: that short by Hawks on one of Marilyn's songs – three minutes of total cinema.

For forty years the masters have shown the way. We can't reject their example, we must fulfil it. Yes, ours will be the generation of Cinema-Scope, the generation of *metteurs en scène*, at last worthy of the name, as they move the creatures of our mind on the infinite stage of the universe.

Translated by Liz Heron

36 | Eric Rohmer: 'The Cardinal Virtues of CinemaScope'

('Vertus cardinales du Cinémascope',
Cahiers du Cinéma 31, January 1954, written
under his real name, Maurice Schérer)

It is primarily a medical point. In putting a premium on the back rows, the mass of cinemagoers show a devotion to health rather than aesthetics, to the point where fanatics have trouble persuading the usherette to take them down to the front. I like to be enveloped in the spectacle, but I do suffer from too close a proximity to the quivering screen. This is not the least of the reasons why I had no hesitation in welcoming the Chrétien process.[1]

Many of my colleagues are worried about the break-up of the proportions of the image. I am not going to reply by pointing out that such a format is as familiar to painters as the old proportions, shaky since the reduction of 1930. It is not by trimming a photograph that you convey any idea of the panoramic screen to people who have never seen it. It is not the frame that is modified, but the conditions of viewing. I will go further and say that in everything that goes beyond the old limits, and is slightly distorted by perspective, there will probably be nothing – be it actors, objects, even sets – that the old screen would not have shown us. My objection to the traditional frame was that it made us squash everything (which is why I have always preferred lenses of short focal length). To hell with this tyranny, this niggardly stranglehold that only the great film-makers have managed to loosen, by what magic I do not know! CinemaScope finally brings to our art the only palpable element it lacked: air, the divine ether of the poets.

No, it is not quite the three-dimensional we are aiming at. The polaroid process would rather compress space. Anyway, I can't stand it. I have, however, unfailingly wished that the brutality of technical invention might deliver us, once and for all, from the superstition of the beautiful image: 'Cinema is the silent close-up', to quote the response of one of our more experienced critics to Jacques Doniol-Valcroze in a recently broadcast radio debate. It pains me to be the one to shake up these fixed ideas. In all naïveté I believed that many of the sounder ideas of the 'Objectif 49' group[2] had made some headway in France, and their best work since those days – generally done in Hollywood, alas – continues to demonstrate the validity of those ideas. There was potential CinemaScope in *La Règle du jeu*, *The Magnificent Ambersons* and *Rope*. But not just because these films endorsed the long take. It is their spatial continuity that matters most to me. Certain poor bits of sequential cutting break it up while some of the most fragmented cuts can still preserve it. I am not aware that montage effects are henceforth to be condemned. The new process brings more than it takes away. Fluidity of movement or the entry of a detail into the general scene operates with no less facility.

By distancing, rather than bringing one closer, isn't CinemaScope condemning one of the most famous discoveries of the art of the screen? Moreover, does it not nullify what is called the 'close-up style', even as by the same token it reinforces its effectiveness by making it an exception, as in the good old days of Griffith? What is the difference between the theatre and the cinema? I rather think it is that the latter can vary the size of its actors at will. All the more need for this trick of the lens to be wished for and agreed to by the spectator. I would speculate that, with the majority of films currently made, this is very seldom how it is.

But what's wrong with that? The wide screen will certainly be preferred for the 'big spectacular'. I myself was too passionate a defender of intimate cinema to be accused of bias. Contact with nature, Nature on a grand scale, can reveal our inner being to us as well as the secrecy of the monk's cell. A return one might say, the eternal return, to the primary aesthetic. The films of Murnau, Griffith and Gance are sometimes considered location films. Let's look at them again. Are they any less profound? In any case, the familiarity of tone of numerous recent works is more than I can bear. One quickly tires of the ingenuous. For a while now I've been looking for more grandeur, more breadth of expression, more fresco, less miniature.

They say that new art demands new themes. It is inappropriate to assume the role of prophet: I will simply say that those films I have really liked would lose nothing by the new technique – and with their editing technique unchanged. As for mediocre films, they gain by it. *The Robe*, of course, is not a very good example. Without stipulating a masterpiece, I would have preferred something like *Niagara*. Hathaway's direction would have found favour in my eyes if it had done no more than show the famous waterfalls even better than it did. Six out of every ten films made will be shot almost entirely on location. Let's get some fresh air for a while. There's plenty of time for us to lock ourselves indoors.

Above all, let us rejoice that the advent of CinemaScope also means the definitive arrival of colour. What fallacies abound there too! Not to speak of all the nostalgics who miss their cherished lighting effects, and their even more cherished back lighting. The call was for colour that would be expressive, by which I mean stylized, schematic. I recognize the need for an initial selection of tones – strangely, all wrong in *The Robe* – but with certain precautions the most vivid colours, like those found in nature, should run no risk of clashing. Expressive colour should be something not judged according to the criteria of the painter. I can think of no better example than *Niagara* itself. Its colour is alive, it speaks, even if it is a shade on the vulgar side. But this shrillness is about something new, and I find it very exciting. It only has to be harnessed now. It's not true that Technicolor, Eastman, or any of the other processes are better suited to the themes of antiquity or the fantastic. In modern life they reveal an iridescence that has become imperceptible to the human eye after a hundred years of responding to a world put together by photography. I very much like that Parisian view by Ichac[3] that begins the programme. Colour reinforces belief in reality. It can only be treated realistically.

Thus a cinema bereft of all the prestige with which the aesthetes embellished it; but forms of prestige as mediocre as the words used to describe them are ugly. And so no longer will we speak of framing or lighting; instead, we will talk about landscapes and light. The whole vocabulary of poetry begs to be admitted into our writing. Let's put that awful technical terminology out of our heads.

And think of national pride – what a beautiful parade ground to show it off! It is our invention, and while we have not known how or been able to take the lead, we can still close the gap. It is said that in the years to come fewer films will be made. This means that the films that are made will have to be more ambitious and perfected. That way they will have more impact in foreign cinemas equipped to handle them. In this way French art, formerly so scorned in America, will have the opportunity to make itself known and, I hope, loved.

In the debate mentioned above Pierre Kast, my old enemy, claimed to equate the avant-garde with the simple desire to 'demystify', to undermine some kind of social conformity. For my part, I would be more inclined to see in all works of art throughout history a sincere, nay naive, conservatism. The essence of art is to respect, not destroy: but the glass through which it invites us to look is constantly altered. The cinema is indebted to a technician for its existence. Let technique have the first word if not the last. This art form is moving infinitely faster than all the others. We should be glad that change is already here, before we start feeling that we have had enough of the old ways. It is the pulsating inner force that must be heeded, not suspect imperatives, imported from somewhere else.

Let us be rid of trifling regrets. If the cinema, as you conceived of it, seems betrayed, beware lest that conception itself one day appear as an even greater betrayal. As for those who find their ideas confirmed by the new development, they would indeed be ungracious if they did not hail it triumphantly. The notion of the avant-garde has given us too many bad films. I've thought it right to question it in the past. Let me now take responsibility for it and give it its true meaning. There will be a time for other quarrels. But in this year of 1954 now beginning, the avant-garde first and foremost is CinemaScope.

Translated by Liz Heron

Notes

1 Henri Chrétien, 1879–1956, French inventor who developed, after 1925, an anamorphic lens process, patented as Hypergonar; the patent was sold in 1952 to Twentieth Century-Fox, who used it as the basis for their CinemaScope system.
2 'Objectif 49': see 'Six Characters in Search of *auteurs*', Ch. 2, note 4.
3 Marcel Ichac, b. 1906, French documentary film-maker specializing in mountaineering photography; evidently Ichac had made a documentary short which was included in the first CinemaScope programme.

Appendix 1

Cahiers du Cinéma Annual Best Films
Listings 1955–9

Despite the element of play which invites their being frowned upon, annual best films lists often have a polemical edge which can function as a useful indicator of broadly shared tastes and values. Certainly this was the case with *Cahiers* and in publishing the lists we have in mind Peter Wollen's comment, listing his 'pantheon' directors, that 'it is only by the publication, comparison and discussion of rankings that individual, subjective taste can be transcended and some degree of general validity established'.[1] Although individual top ten lists, from which these composite lists were made up, were often more indicative of the tastes or polemics of individual critics or film-makers, these composite lists were more representative of *Cahiers* as a whole.

Individual top ten lists were contributed by regular critics (varying slightly over the years, of course) such as André Bazin, Charles Bitsch, Claude Chabrol, Jean Domarchi, Jacques Doniol-Valcroze, Jean-Luc Godard, Pierre Kast, Louis Marcorelles, Jacques Rivette, Eric Rohmer, François Truffaut and, later, Jean Douchet, Fereydoun Hoveyda, Luc Moullet. These were always supplemented by invited contributions from long-time associated film-makers and occasional *Cahiers* contributors like Roger Leenhardt, Alexandre Astruc and Pierre Braunberger, critics from other journals or newspapers like Claude Mauriac and Jean de Baroncelli, historian-critics and occasional *Cahiers* contributors like Georges Sadoul, Henri Agel and Jean Mitry, and friendly young film-makers like Jacques Demy, Agnès Varda, Alain Resnais (from the so-called 'Left Bank' group of the 'Nouvelle Vague'). As *Cahiers* put it, these were not exactly '*Cahiers* lists' nor lists representative of all critics. The choice of contributors corresponded to 'the desire to reach a certain objectivity by including in it several tendencies but excluding those which were frankly anti-*Cahiers*. A list of friends, then, but often disagreeing with us . . . and among themselves'.[2]

This leavening of the tastes of those critics most often associated with *Cahiers* makes the lists perhaps less astonishing than the disbelief and outrage they tended to excite in Britain[3] might lead us to expect. Even so, there are plenty of films – particularly, of course, American films – highly valued in these lists but hardly imaginable on similar lists in Britain at the time. Nevertheless, note should be taken of the evident importance attached to the work of film-makers who *would* have been valued in Britain and the USA – Bergman, Fellini, Visconti, Dreyer, Renoir, Bresson, Buñuel, Mizoguchi, and so on.

Regular composite listings began only in February 1956, for 1955's films, but also included is a listing from *Cahiers* 10 (March 1952) relating to 1951's best films. The lengths of the annual lists vary, usually according to *Cahiers'* assessment of the 'richness' of the year in question. The titles used here for non-English language films are those in most common use in Britain and the USA.

1951 (Cahiers 10, March 1952)
1 *The River* (Jean Renoir, USA-India, 1951)
2 *Le Journal d'un curé de campagne* (Robert Bresson, France, 1951)
3 *Miracle in Milan* (Vittorio De Sica, Italy, 1950)
4 *Los Olvidados* (Luis Buñuel, Mexico, 1950)
5 *All about Eve* (Joseph L. Mankiewicz, USA, 1950)
6 *Miss Julie* (Alf Sjöberg, Sweden, 1951)
7 *Cronaca di un amore* (Michelangelo Antonioni, Italy, 1950)
8 *Sunset Boulevard* (Billy Wilder, USA, 1950)
9 *Edouard et Caroline* (Jacques Becker, France, 1951)
10 *Francesco giullare di dio* (Roberto Rossellini, Italy, 1949)
11 *Les Miracles n'ont lieu qu'une fois* (Yves Allégret, France, 1951)
12 *Il Cristo proibito* (Curzio Malaparte, Italy, 1950)
13 *A Walk in the Sun* (Lewis Milestone, USA, 1946)
14 *Give Us This Day* (Edward Dmytryk, GB, 1949)
15 *La Course de taureaux* (Pierre Braunberger, France, 1951)

1955 (Cahiers 56, February 1956)
1 *Viaggio in Italia* (Roberto Rossellini, Italy, 1953)
2 *Ordet* (Carl Dreyer, Denmark, 1955)
3 *The Big Knife* (Robert Aldrich, USA, 1955)
4 *Lola Montès* (Max Ophuls, France, 1955)
5 *Rear Window* (Alfred Hitchcock, USA, 1954)
6 *Les Mauvaises Rencontres* (Alexandre Astruc, France, 1955)
7 *La Strada* (Federico Fellini, Italy, 1954)
8 *The Barefoot Contessa* (Joseph L. Mankiewicz, USA, 1954)
9 *Johnny Guitar* (Nicholas Ray, USA, 1954)
10 *Kiss Me Deadly* (Robert Aldrich, USA, 1955)
11 *Death of a Cyclist* (Juan A. Bardem, Spain, 1954)
12 *To Catch a Thief* (Alfred Hitchcock, USA, 1954)
13 *Du rififi chez les hommes* (Rififi) (Jules Dassin, France, 1955)
14 *Salt of the Earth* (Herbert J. Biberman, USA–Mexico, 1953)
15 *Raices* (Benito Alazraki, Mexico, 1955)
16 *Apache* (Robert Aldrich, USA, 1954)
17 *French Cancan* (Jean Renoir, France, 1955)
18 *Blackboard Jungle* (Richard Brooks, USA, 1955)
19 *Lo Sceicco bianco* (Federico Fellini, Italy, 1952)
20 *Lourdes et ses miracles* (Georges Rouquier, France, 1955)

1956 (Cahiers 68, February 1957)
1 *Un Condamné à mort s'est échappé* (Robert Bresson, France, 1956)
2 *Eléna et les hommes* (Jean Renoir, France, 1956)

3 *Rebel Without a Cause* (Nicholas Ray, USA, 1955)
4 *Confidential Report/Mr Arkadin* (Orson Welles, Spain–France, 1956)
5 *Senso* (Luchino Visconti, Italy, 1953)
6 *Smiles of a Summer Night* (Ingmar Bergman, Sweden, 1955)
7 *Il Bidone* (Federico Fellini, Italy, 1955)
8 *L'Amore* (Roberto Rossellini, Italy, 1948)
9 *Picnic* (Joshua Logan, USA, 1954)
10 *La Paura* (Roberto Rossellini, Italy, 1955)
11 *While the City Sleeps* (Fritz Lang, USA, 1955)
   It's Always Fair Weather (Stanley Donen–Gene Kelly, USA, 1955)
13 *Bus Stop* (Joshua Logan, USA, 1956)
   The Man Who Knew Too Much (Alfred Hitchcock, USA, 1956)
   La Traversée de Paris (Claude Autant-Lara, France, 1956)
   'hors concours': *Nuit et brouillard* (Alain Resnais, France, 1955)

1957 (Cahiers 80, February 1958)
 1 *A King in New York* (Charles Chaplin, GB, 1957)
 2 *Will Success Spoil Rock Hunter?* (GB: *Oh! For a Man*) (Frank Tashlin, USA, 1957)
 3 *Le Notti di Cabiria* (Federico Fellini, Italy, 1957)
 4 *The Wrong Man* (Alfred Hitchcock, USA, 1957)
 5 *The Criminal Life of Archibaldo de la Cruz* (Luis Buñuel, Mexico, 1955)
 6 *Sawdust and Tinsel* (Ingmar Bergman, Sweden, 1953)
 7 *Bigger than Life* (Nicholas Ray, USA, 1956)
 8 *The Girl Can't Help It* (Frank Tashlin, USA, 1956)
 9 *Beyond a Reasonable Doubt* (Fritz Lang, USA, 1956)
10 *Twelve Angry Men* (Sidney Lumet, USA, 1957)
11 *A Face in the Crowd* (Elia Kazan, USA, 1957)
12 *Bitter Victory* (Nicholas Ray, USA, 1957)
13 *La Casa del angel* (Leopoldo Torre-Nilsson, Argentina, 1957)
14 *The Bridge on the River Kwai* (David Lean, GB, 1957)
15 *Sait-on jamais . . .* (Roger Vadim, France, 1957)
   Chikamatsu monogatari (Kenji Mizoguchi, Japan, 1955)
17 *Porte des Lilas* (René Clair, France, 1957)
18 *Written on the Wind* (Douglas Sirk, USA, 1957)
   Hollywood or Bust (Frank Tashlin, USA, 1956)
20 *Toro* (Carlos Velo, Mexico, 1956)

1958 (Cahiers 93, March 1959)
 1 *Touch of Evil* (Orson Welles, USA, 1958)
 2 *The Seventh Seal* (Ingmar Bergman, Sweden, 1956)
 3 *White Nights* (Luchino Visconti, Italy, 1957)
 4 *Il Grido* (Michelangelo Antonioni, Italy, 1957)
 5 *Bonjour Tristesse* (Otto Preminger, USA, 1957)
 6 *Journey into Autumn* (Ingmar Bergman, Sweden, 1955)
 7 *Une Vie* (Alexandre Astruc, France, 1958)
 8 *Mon Oncle* (Jacques Tati, France, 1958)
 9 *The Quiet American* (Joseph L. Mankiewicz, USA, 1957)
10 *Summer Interlude* (Ingmar Bergman, Sweden, 1950)
11 *Les Girls* (George Cukor, USA, 1957)
12 *Les Amants* (Louis Malle, France, 1958)

13 *Kanal* (Andrzej Wajda, Poland, 1957)
14 *Montparnasse 19* (Jacques Becker, France, 1958)
15 *Waiting Women* (Ingmar Bergman, Sweden, 1952)

1959 (Cahiers 105, March 1960)
  1 *Ugetsu monogatari* (Kenji Mizoguchi, Japan, 1953)
  2 *Hiroshima mon amour* (Alain Resnais, France, 1959)
  3 *Ivan the Terrible* (Sergei M. Eisenstein, USSR, 1958)
  4 *Pickpocket* (Robert Bresson, France, 1959)
  5 *Les 400 Coups* (François Truffaut, France, 1959)
  6 *Rio Bravo* (Howard Hawks, USA, 1959)
  7 *Wild Strawberries* (Ingmar Bergman, Sweden, 1959)
  8 *Vertigo* (Alfred Hitchcock, USA, 1958)
  9 *Yang kwei fei* (Kenji Mizoguchi, Japan, 1955)
 10 *The Tiger of Eschnapur* (Fritz Lang, West Germany, 1958)
 11 *Moi, un noir* (Jean Rouch, France, 1959)
 12 *Anatomy of a Murder* (Otto Preminger, USA, 1959)
 13 *Le Déjeuner sur l'herbe* (Jean Renoir, France, 1959)
 14 *La Tête contre les murs* (Georges Franju, France, 1959)
 15 *Il Generale della Rovere* (Roberto Rossellini, Italy, 1959)
 16 *Run of the Arrow* (Samuel Fuller, USA, 1957)
 17 *Les Cousins* (Claude Chabrol, France, 1959)
 18 *I Soliti ignoti* (Mario Monicelli, Italy, 1958)
 19 *Rally Round the Flag, Boys* (Leo McCarey, USA, 1959)
 20 *Deux hommes dans Manhattan* (Jean-Pierre Melville, France, 1959)
 21 *Wind Across the Everglades* (Nicholas Ray, USA, 1958)

All-Time Best Films
Following the 'Confrontation des Meilleurs Films de Tous les Temps', Brussels, 1958, *Cahiers du Cinéma* published its own 'all-time best' listing (Cahiers 90, December 1958). Several points recommend printing the list here. First, the voters (André Bazin, Claude Beylie, Charles Bitsch, Claude Chabrol, Philippe Demonsablon, Jean Domarchi, Jacques Doniol Valcroze, Jean Douchet, Claude Gauteur, Jean-Luc Godard, Fereydoun Hoveyda, Louis Marcorelles, André Martin, Luc Moullet, Jacques Rivette, Eric Rohmer, François Truffaut) were effectively the *Cahiers* 'team' at that time. The listing gives little indication of the supposed extremism of *Cahiers* in this period. In particular, the common identification of *Cahiers* with American cinema clearly cannot be sustained by the list. Second, not surprisingly given *Cahiers*' commitments, the list is effectively a list of *auteurs*. The first round of vote-casting had been on authors, the second on individual works (i.e. the 1–12 ranking here is really of directors). These first twelve had been followed in the first round by (13) Ophuls, (14) Lang, (15) Hawks, Keaton, (17) Bergman, (18) Nicholas Ray, (19) Norman McLaren, Flaherty, (21) Buñuel, Clair, (23) Visconti, Dovzhenko.
  1 *Sunrise* (F. W. Murnau, USA, 1927)
  2 *La Règle du jeu* (Jean Renoir, France, 1939)
  3 *Viaggio in Italia* (Roberto Rossellini, Italy, 1953)
  4 *Ivan the Terrible* (Sergei M. Eisenstein, USSR, 1945/1958)
  5 *Birth of a Nation* (D. W. Griffith, USA, 1915)
  6 *Confidential Report/Mr. Arkadin* (Orson Welles, Spain–France, 1956)

7 *Ordet* (Carl Dreyer, Denmark, 1955)
8 *Ugetsu monogatari* (Kenji Mizoguchi, Japan, 1953)
9 *L'Atalante* (Jean Vigo, France, 1934)
10 *The Wedding March* (Erich von Stroheim, USA, 1927)
11 *Under Capricorn* (Alfred Hitchcock, GB, 1949)
12 *Monsieur Verdoux* (Charles Chaplin, USA, 1947)

Notes

1 Peter Wollen, *Signs and Meaning*, p. 166.
2 *Cahiers* 67, January 1957, p. 2.
3 See, for example, Richard Roud: 'The French Line', *Sight and Sound*, vol. 29, no. 4, Autumn 1960, pp. 166–71.

Appendix 2

Guide to *Cahiers du Cinéma* Nos 1–102, April 1951–December 1959, in English translation

There is no comprehensive record of material from *Cahiers du Cinéma* which has been translated into English. This appendix offers, both for further reading and as a research resource, a tentative listing of such material which is nevertheless as comprehensive as it has been possible to make it. The editor would welcome information on additional entries from readers.

Book and journal references are given in full in each entry except for a few books which are cited frequently and therefore given in abbreviated form in the entries. Full details of these books are as follows:

Bazin, André, *What is Cinema? Volume 1* (Essays selected and translated by Hugh Gray, foreword by Jean Renoir), Berkeley, University of California Press, 1967; selected from Bazin, *Qu'est-ce que le cinéma? tome 1: Ontologie et langage* and *tome 2: Le Cinéma et les autres arts*, Paris, Editions du Cerf, 1958, 1959.

Bazin, André, *What is Cinema? Volume 2* (Essays selected and translated by Hugh Gray, foreword by François Truffaut), Berkeley, University of California Press, 1971; selected from Bazin, *Qu'est-ce que le cinéma? tome 3: Cinéma et sociologie* and *tome 4: Une esthétique de la Réalité: le néo-réalisme*, Paris, Editions du Cerf, 1961, 1962.

Bazin, André, *Jean Renoir* (Edited with an introduction by François Truffaut), New York, Simon & Schuster, 1973; London, W. H. Allen, 1974; originally published as Bazin, *Jean Renoir* (Avant-propos de Jean Renoir, Présentation de François Truffaut), Paris, Editions Champ Libre, 1971.

Braudy, Leo, and Dickstein, Morris (eds), *Great Film Directors: A Critical Anthology*, New York, Oxford University Press, 1978.

Caughie, John (ed.), *Theories of Authorship*, London, Routledge & Kegan Paul, 1981 (BFI Readers in Film Studies series).

Godard, Jean-Luc, *Godard on Godard: Critical Writings by Jean-Luc Godard* (ed. Jean Narboni and Tom Milne, trans. Tom Milne, with an introduction by Richard Roud), London, Secker & Warburg; New York, Viking, 1972 (Cinema Two series); originally published as *Jean-Luc Godard par Jean-Luc Godard*, Paris, Editions Pierre Belfond, 1968.

Graham, Peter (ed.), *The New Wave* (Critical landmarks selected and translated by

Peter Graham), London, Secker & Warburg; New York, Doubleday, 1968 (Cinema One series).

Nichols, Bill (ed.), *Movies and Methods: An Anthology*, Berkeley, University of California Press, 1976.

Sarris, Andrew (ed.), *Interviews with Film Directors*, New York, Bobbs-Merrill, 1967.

Truffaut, François, *The Films in My Life* (translated by Leonard Mayhew), New York, Simon & Schuster, 1978; London, Allen Lane, 1980; originally published as Truffaut, *Les Films de ma vie*, Paris, Flammarion, 1975.

ARANDA, J.-F.
'La Passion selon Buñuel' in *Cahiers* 93 (March 1959)
trans. as 'The Passion According to Buñuel' in Buñuel, L., *The Exterminating Angel/Nazarin/Los Olvidados*, London, Lorrimer, 1972.

ASTRUC, Alexandre
'Le Feu et la glace' (on Murnau) in *Cahiers* 18 (December 1952)
trans. as 'Fire and Ice' in *Cahiers du Cinéma in English*, no. 1 (1966).

'Qu'est-ce que la mise en scène?' in *Cahiers* 100 (October 1959)
trans. as 'What is Mise-en-Scène?' in *Film Culture*, no. 22–3 (Summer 1961), and *Cahiers du Cinéma in English*, no. 1 (1966); also translated in this volume (Ch. 33).

AUBIER, Dominique
'Mythologie de La Strada' in *Cahiers* 49 (July 1955)
trans. as 'Cosmic Vision and Metaphysical Instinct' in Salachas, G. (ed.), *Federico Fellini*, New York, Crown, 1969.

BAZIN, André
'Pour en finir avec la profondeur de champ' in *Cahiers* 1 (April 1951)
incorporated into 'Evolution of the Language of Cinema' in Bazin, *What is Cinema? Vol. 1*, and, in a different translation as 'The Evolution of Film Language', in Graham, *New Wave*.

'La Stylistique de Robert Bresson' in *Cahiers* 3 (June 1951)
trans. as 'Le Journal d'un curé de campagne and the Stylistics of Robert Bresson' in Bazin, *What is Cinema? Vol. 1*, reprinted in Braudy and Dickstein, *Great Film Directors*, and in Ayfre, A., *et al.*, *The Films of Robert Bresson*, London, Studio Vista, 1969; New York, Praeger, 1970.

'Renoir Français' in *Cahiers* 8 (January 1952)
trans. as 'French Renoir' in Bazin, *Jean Renoir*, reprinted in Braudy and Dickstein, *Great Film Directors*; extracts trans. as 'Evolution of Jean Renoir' and 'The Camera and the Screen' in Leprohon, P., *Jean Renoir*, New York, Crown, 1971.

'Othello' (review from Cannes 1952) in *Cahiers* 13 (June 1952)
trans. as 'Review of Othello' in Eckert, C. (ed.), *Focus on Shakespearian Films*, Englewood Cliffs, NJ, Prentice-Hall, 1972.

'Le Réel et l'imaginaire' (on *Crin Blanc*) in *Cahiers* 25 (July 1953)
incorporated into 'Virtues and Limitations of Montage' in Bazin, *What is Cinema? Vol. 1*.

'Entretien avec Luis Buñuel' (with Jacques Doniol-Valcroze) in *Cahiers* 36 (June 1954) trans. (abridged) as 'Conversation with Buñuel' in *Sight and Sound*, vol. 24, no. 4, Spring 1955.

'Hitchcock contre Hitchcock' in *Cahiers* 39 (October 1954)
trans. as 'Hitchcock versus Hitchcock' in *Cahiers du Cinéma in English*, no. 2 (1966), reprinted in LaValley, Albert J. (ed.), *Focus on Hitchcock*, Englewood Cliffs, NJ, Prentice-Hall, 1972.

'Comment peut-on être Hitchcocko-Hawksien?' in *Cahiers* 44 (February 1955)
trans. (extract) in Caughie, *Theories of Authorship*.

'Evolution du Western' in *Cahiers* 54 (Christmas 1955)
trans. as 'Evolution of the Western' in Bazin, *What is Cinema? Vol. 2*, reprinted in Nichols, *Movies and Methods*.

'Montage interdit' in *Cahiers* 65 (December 1956)
trans. as 'Forbidden Montage' in *Film Culture*, no. 22–3, Summer 1961, and incorporated into 'The Virtues and Limitations of Montage' in Bazin, *What is Cinema? Vol. 1*.

'En marge de "L'Erotisme au Cinéma" ' in *Cahiers* 70 (April 1957)
trans. as 'Marginal Notes on "Eroticism in the Cinema" ' in Bazin, *What is Cinema? Vol. 2*.

'De la politique des auteurs' in *Cahiers* 70 (April 1957)
trans. as 'La Politique des Auteurs' in Graham, *New Wave*, reprinted in this volume (Ch. 31), and as 'On the Politique des Auteurs' in *Cahiers du Cinéma in English*, no. 1 (1966); extract trans. in Caughie, *Theories of Authorship*.

'Cabiria ou le voyage au bout du néo-réalisme' in *Cahiers* 76 (November 1957)
trans. as 'Cabiria: The Voyage to the End of Neo-Realism' in Bazin, *What is Cinema? Vol. 2*, and as 'Beyond Neo-Realism' in Salachas, G. (ed.), *Federico Fellini*, New York, Crown, 1969.

'Bio-filmographie de Jean Renoir' in *Cahiers* 78 (December 1957) (notes by Bazin on *Une vie sans joie, ou Catherine, La Petite marchande d'allumettes, La P'tite Lili, The Diary of a Chambermaid*)
trans. in Bazin, *Jean Renoir* (which also includes Bazin on *La Fille de l'eau, Tire au flanc, Le Tournoi, Le Bled*, material which did not appear in *Cahiers* 78).

Closely related material: see contemporaneous but non-*Cahiers* writings translated in *What is Cinema? Vols 1 and 2*, Bazin, André, *Orson Welles, A Critical View*, London, Elm Tree Books, 1978, and Williams, Christopher, *Realism and the Cinema*, London, Routledge & Kegan Paul, 1980 (for the essay 'William Wyler, or the Jansenist of *mise en scène*').

BECKER, Jacques
'Entretien avec Howard Hawks' (with Jacques Rivette and François Truffaut) in *Cahiers* 56 (February 1956)
trans. in Sarris, *Interviews with Film Directors*.

BÉRANGER, Jean
'Rencontre avec Ingmar Bergman' in *Cahiers* 88 (October 1958)
trans. in Steene, B. (ed.), *Focus on The Seventh Seal*, Englewood Cliffs, NJ, Prentice-Hall, 1972.

BERGMAN, Ingmar
'Qu'est-ce que "faire des films"?' in *Cahiers* 61 (July 1956)
trans. as 'What is Film-Making?' in Geduld, H. M. (ed.), *Film-Makers on Film-Making*, Bloomington, Indiana University Press, 1967, and as 'What is Making Films?' in Sarris, *Interviews with Film Directors*.

'Rencontre avec Ingmar Bergman' (by Jean Béranger) in *Cahiers* 88 (October 1958)
trans. in Steene, B. (ed.), *Focus on The Seventh Seal*, Englewood Cliffs, NJ, Prentice-Hall, 1972.

BUNUEL, Luis
'Entretien avec Luis Buñuel' (by André Bazin and Jacques Doniol-Valcroze) in *Cahiers* 36 (June 1954)
trans. (abridged) as 'Conversation with Buñuel' in *Sight and Sound*, vol. 24, no. 4, Spring 1955.

CHABROL, Claude
'Hitchcock devant le mal' in *Cahiers* 39 (October 1954)
trans. as 'Hitchcock Confronts Evil' in *Cahiers du Cinéma in English*, no. 2, 1966.

'Les Petits Sujets' in *Cahiers* 100 (October 1959)
trans. as 'Big Subjects, Little Subjects' in *Movie*, no. 1, June 1962, and as 'Little Themes' in Graham, *New Wave*.

Closely related material: see Rohmer, Eric and Chabrol, Claude, *Hitchcock, The First Forty-Four Films*, New York, Frederick Ungar, 1979, originally published Paris, 1957, and incorporating material close to work published on Hitchcock by Rohmer and Chabrol in *Cahiers*.

COCTEAU, Jean
'Hommages à Renoir' (Petit Journal du Cinéma) in *Cahiers* 82 (April 1958)
trans. as 'Family Resemblance' in Leprohon, P., *Jean Renoir*, New York, Crown, 1971.

COLPI, Henri
'Dégradation d'un art: le montage' (A propos du montage I) in *Cahiers* 65 (December 1956)
trans. as 'Debasement of the Art of Montage' in *Film Culture*, no. 22–3, Summer 1961, and in *Cahiers du Cinéma in English*, no. 3, 1966.

DE GIVRAY, Claude
'Bio-filmographie de Jean Renoir' in *Cahiers* 78 (December 1957) (notes by de Givray on *La Chienne*, *Les Bas-fonds*, *La Bête humaine*)
trans. in Bazin, *Jean Renoir*.

DEMONSABLON, Philippe
'La Hautaine Dialectique de Fritz Lang' in *Cahiers* 99 (September 1959)
trans. as 'The Imperious Dialectic of Fritz Lang' in Jenkins, S. (ed.), *Fritz Lang: The Image and the Look*, London, British Film Institute, 1981.

DOMARCHI, Jean
'Entretien avec Luchino Visconti' (with Jacques Doniol-Valcroze) in *Cahiers* 93 (March 1959)

trans. as 'Visconti Interviewed' in *Sight and Sound*, vol. 28, nos 3–4, Summer–Autumn 1959.

'Les Secrets d'Eisenstein' in *Cahiers* 96 (June 1959)
trans. as 'The Old and the New' in Moussinac, L. (ed.), *Sergei Eisenstein*, New York, Crown, 1969.

DONIOL-VALCROZE, Jacques
'Entretien avec Luis Buñuel' (with André Bazin) in *Cahiers* 36 (June 1954)
trans. (abridged) as 'Conversation with Buñuel' in *Sight and Sound*, vol. 24, no. 4, Spring 1955.

'Bio-filmographie de Jean Renoir' in *Cahiers* 78 (December 1957) (note by Doniol-Valcroze on *Une Partie de campagne*)
trans. in Bazin, *Jean Renoir*.

'Entretien avec Luchino Visconti' (with Jean Domarchi) in *Cahiers* 93 (March 1959)
trans. as 'Visconti Interviewed' in *Sight and Sound*, vol. 28, nos 3–4, Summer–Autumn 1959.

'Cannes 1959' (note on *Les 400 Coups*) in *Cahiers* 96 (June 1959)
trans. as 'Report from Cannes' in Denby, D. (ed.), *The 400 Blows*, New York, Grove Press, 1969.

EISENSTEIN, Sergei M.
'L'Unité organique et le pathétique dans la composition du "Cuirassé Potemkine" ' in *Cahiers* 82 (April 1958)
trans. as 'Organic Unity and Pathos in the Composition of *Potemkin*' in *Cahiers du Cinéma in English*, no. 3, 1966, reprinted in Sarris, *Interviews with Film Directors*; translation from original Russian in Eisenstein, S. M., *Notes of a Film Director*, London, Lawrence & Wishart, 1959, reprinted in Eisenstein, S.M., *Battleship Potemkin*, London, Lorrimer, 1968.

FELLINI, Federico
'Les Femmes libres de Magliano' in *Cahiers* 68 (February 1957)
trans. as 'The Free Women of Magliano' in Salachas, G. (ed.), *Federico Fellini*, New York, Crown, 1969.

FORD, John
'Rencontre avec John Ford' (by Jean Mitry) in *Cahiers* 45 (March 1955)
trans. in Sarris, *Interviews with Film Directors*.

FRANJU, Georges
'Le Style de Fritz Lang' in *Cahiers* 101 (November 1959)
trans. as 'The Style of Fritz Lang' in Braudy and Dickstein, *Great Film Directors*.

GODARD, Jean-Luc
Review of *No Sad Songs for Me* (under pseudonym Hans Lucas) in *Cahiers* 10 (March 1952)
trans. as 'No Sad Songs for Me' in *Godard on Godard*.

'Suprématie du sujet' (on *Strangers on a Train*) (under pseudonym Hans Lucas) in *Cahiers* 10 (March 1952) trans. as 'Strangers on a Train' in *Godard on Godard*.

'Défense et illustration du découpage classique' (under pseudonym Hans Lucas) in *Cahiers* 15 (September 1952)
trans. as 'Defence and Illustration of Classical Construction' in *Godard on Godard*.

'Mirliflores et Bécassines' (on *Artists and Models* and *The Lieutenant Wore Skirts*) in *Cahiers* 62 (August–September 1956)
trans. as 'The Lieutenant Wore Skirts and Artists and Models' in *Godard on Godard*.

'Le Chemin des écoliers' (on *The Man Who Knew Too Much*) in *Cahiers* 64 (November 1956)
trans. as 'The Man Who Knew Too Much' in *Godard on Godard*.

'Montage, mon beau souci' (A Propos du montage II) in *Cahiers* 65 (December 1956)
trans. as 'Montage My Fine Care' in *Godard on Godard*, also in Mussman, T. (ed.), *Jean-Luc Godard: A Critical Anthology*, New York, E. P. Dutton, 1968, in *Film Culture*, Summer 1961, and in *Cahiers du Cinéma in English*, no. 3, 1966.

'Futur, présent, passé' (on *Magirama*) in *Cahiers* 67 (January 1957)
trans. as 'Future, Present, Past: Magirama' in *Godard on Godard*.

'Rien que le cinéma' (on *Hot Blood*) in *Cahiers* 68 (February 1957)
trans. as 'Hot Blood' in *Godard on Godard*, reprinted in this volume (Ch. 13).

'Au petit trot' (on *Courte-Tête*) in *Cahiers* 70 (April 1957)
trans. as 'Courte-Tête' in *Godard on Godard*.

'Soixante Metteurs en Scène Francais' in *Cahiers* 71 (May 1957) (notes by Godard on Robert Bresson, Norbert Carbonn(e)aux, Roger Leenhardt, Jacques Tati)
trans. as 'Dictionary of French Film-Makers' in *Godard on Godard*.

'Le Cinéma et son double' (on *The Wrong Man*) in *Cahiers* 72 (June 1957)
trans. as 'The Wrong Man' in *Godard on Godard*.

'Des preuves suffisantes' (on *Sait-on jamais?*) in *Cahiers* 73 (July 1957)
trans. as 'Sait-on jamais?' in *Godard on Godard*, reprinted in this volume (Ch. 3).

'Hollywood ou mourir' (on *Hollywood or Bust*) in *Cahiers* 73 (July 1957)
trans. as 'Hollywood or Bust' in *Godard on Godard*.

'Le Cinéaste bien-aimé' (on *The True Story of Jesse James*) in *Cahiers* 74 (August–September 1957)
trans. as 'The True Story of Jesse James' in *Godard on Godard*.

'Photos d'août-septembre' (note on *Will Success Spoil Rock Hunter?*, UK title *Oh for a Man*) in *Cahiers* 74 (August–September 1957)
trans. as 'Will Success Spoil Rock Hunter?' in *Godard on Godard*.

'Petit Journal du Cinéma: Signal' (note on *Forty Guns*) in *Cahiers* 76 (November 1957)
trans. as 'Forty Guns' in *Godard on Godard*, reprinted in Will, D., and Wollen, P. (eds), *Samuel Fuller*, Edinburgh, Edinburgh Film Festival, 1969.

'Bio-filmographie de Jean Renoir' in *Cahiers* 78 (Christmas 1957) (notes by Godard on *La Nuit du carrefour*, *Swamp Water*, *Eléna et les hommes*)
trans. as 'Jean Renoir' in *Godard on Godard*, also in Bazin, *Jean Renoir*.

'Au délà des étoiles' (on *Bitter Victory*) in *Cahiers* 79 (January 1958)
trans. as 'Bitter Victory' in *Godard on Godard*, reprinted in this volume (Ch. 14).

'Un Bon Devoir' (on *The Killing*) in *Cahiers* 80 (February 1958)
trans. as 'The Killing' in *Godard on Godard*.

'Rétrospective Ophuls' in *Cahiers* 81 (March 1958) (note by Godard on *Caught*)
trans. as 'Caught' in *Godard on Godard*.

'Une Bonne Copie' (on *The Wayward Bus*) in *Cahiers* 81 (March 1958)
trans. as 'The Wayward Bus' in *Godard on Godard*.

'Esotérisme farfelu' (on *Le Temps des œufs durs*) in *Cahiers* 82 (April 1958)
trans. as 'Le Temps des Œufs Durs' in *Godard on Godard*.

'Sympathique' (on *Rafles sur la ville*) in *Cahiers* 82 (April 1958)
trans. as 'Rafles sur la ville' in *Godard on Godard*.

'Saut dans le vide' (on *Montparnasse 19*) in *Cahiers* 83 (May 1958)
trans. as 'Montparnasse 19' in *Godard on Godard*.

'Malraux mauvais français?' in *Cahiers* 83 (May 1958)
trans. as 'Malraux a Discredit to France?' in *Godard on Godard*.

'Bergmanorama' in *Cahiers* 85 (July 1958)
trans. as 'Bergmanorama' in *Godard on Godard*, also trans. in *Cahiers du Cinéma in English*, no. 1, 1966.

'Une Fille nommée Durance' (on *L'Eau vive*) in *Cahiers* 85 (July 1958)
trans. as 'L'Eau Vive' in *Godard on Godard*.

'Voyez comme on danse' (on *The Pajama Game*) in *Cahiers* 85 (July 1958)
trans. as 'The Pajama Game' in *Godard on Godard*.

'Travail à la chaîne' (on *The Long Hot Summer*) in *Cahiers* 85 (July 1958)
trans. as 'The Long Hot Summer' in *Godard on Godard*.

'Télégramme de Berlin' (as Hans Lucas) in *Cahiers* 86 (August 1958)
trans. as 'Telegram from Berlin' in *Godard on Godard*.

'Ailleurs' (on *Une Vie*) in *Cahiers* 89 (November 1958)
trans. as 'Une Vie' in *Godard on Godard*, and as 'Review of Astruc's *Une Vie*' in Graham, *New Wave*.

'La Photo du Mois' (note on *Les Cousins*) in *Cahiers* 89 (November 1958)
trans. as 'Les Cousins' in *Godard on Godard*.

'Georges Franju' in *Cahiers* 90 (December 1958)
trans. as 'Georges Franju' in *Godard on Godard*.

'Chacun son Tours' (on the Tours Film Festival) in *Cahiers* 92 (February 1959)
trans. as 'Take Your Own Tours' in *Godard on Godard*.

'Super Mann' (on *Man of the West*) in *Cahiers* 92 (February 1959)
trans. as 'Man of the West' in *Godard on Godard*.

'La Photo du Mois' (note on *Les 400 Coups*) in *Cahiers* 92 (February 1959)
trans. as 'Les 400 Coups' in *Godard on Godard*, reprinted in this volume (Ch. 4), and as 'Photo of the Month' in Denby, D. (ed.), *The 400 Blows*, New York, Grove Press, 1969.

'Le Conquérant solitaire' (on *Le Rendez-vous du Diable*) in *Cahiers* 93 (March 1959)
trans. as 'Le Rendez-vous du Diable' in *Godard on Godard*.

'Dura lex' (on *La Loi*) in *Cahiers* 93 (March 1959)
trans. as 'La Loi' in *Godard on Godard*.

'La Photo du Mois' (note on *La Ligne de mire*) in *Cahiers* 93 (March 1959)
trans. as 'La Ligne de Mire' in *Godard on Godard*.

'L'Afrique vous parle de la fin et des moyens' (on *Moi, un noir*) in *Cahiers* 94 (April 1959)
trans. as 'Africa Speaks of the End and the Means' in *Godard on Godard*.

'Des larmes et de la vitesse' (on *A Time to Love and a Time to Die*) in *Cahiers* 94 (April 1959)
trans. as 'A Time to Love and a Time to Die' in *Godard on Godard*, and as 'Tears and Speed' in *Screen*, vol. 12, no. 2, Summer 1971.

'Petit Journal du Cinema: Boris Barnett' in *Cahiers* 94 (April 1959)
trans. as 'Boris Barnett' in *Godard on Godard*.

'Une Loi obscure' (on *La Tête contre les murs*) in *Cahiers* 95 (May 1959)
trans. as 'La Tête contre les murs' in *Godard on Godard*.

'Le Passe-temps retrouvé' (on *The Perfect Furlough*, UK title *Strictly for Pleasure*) in *Cahiers* 95 (May 1959)
trans. as 'The Perfect Furlough' in *Godard on Godard*.

'Cannes 1959' (note on *India*) in *Cahiers* 96 (June 1959)
trans. as 'India' in *Godard on Godard*.

'Franc-tireur' (on *Tarawa Beachhead*) in *Cahiers* 96 (June 1959)
trans. as 'Tarawa Beachhead' in *Godard on Godard*.

'Le Brésil vu de Billancourt' (on *Orfeu Negro*) in *Cahiers* 97 (July 1959)
trans. as 'Orfeu Negro' in *Godard on Godard*.

'Une Femme est une femme: scénario' in *Cahiers* 98 (August 1959)
trans. as 'Une Femme est une Femme' in *Godard on Godard*, also in *Cahiers du Cinéma in English*, no. 12, 1967, and in Mussman, T. (ed.), *Jean-Luc Godard: A Critical Anthology*, New York, E. P. Dutton, 1968.

See also Godard's personal annual 'Ten Best' lists for 1956 (*Cahiers* 67, January 1957), 1957 (*Cahiers* 79, January 1958), 1958 (*Cahiers* 92, February 1959), 1959 (*Cahiers* 104, February 1960).

Closely related material: see contemporaneous but non-*Cahiers* writing collected in *Godard on Godard*.

HAWKS, Howard
'Entretien avec Howard Hawks' (by Jacques Becker, Jacques Rivette, François Truffaut) in *Cahiers* 56 (February 1956)
trans. in Sarris, *Interviews with Film Directors*.

KAST, Pierre
'Des confitures pour un gendarme' in *Cahiers* 2 (May 1951)
trans. (extract) in Caughie, *Theories of Authorship*; trans. in full in this volume (Ch. 29).

'Défense de jouer avec les allumettes' (on *The Day the Earth Stood Still*) in *Cahiers* 12 (May 1952)
trans. as 'Don't Play with Fire' in Johnson, W. (ed.), *Focus on the Science Fiction Film*, Englewood Cliffs, NJ, Prentice-Hall, 1972.

LEENHARDT, Roger
'Ambiguïté du cinéma' in *Cahiers* 100 (October 1959)
trans. as 'Ambiguity of the Cinema' in *Cahiers du Cinéma in English*, no. 1, 1966.

MARCORELLES, Louis
'Bio-filmographie de Jean Renoir' in *Cahiers* 78 (December 1957) (note by Marcorelles on *Salute to France*)
trans. in Bazin, *Jean Renoir*.

'Ford of the Movies' in *Cahiers* 86 (August 1958)
trans. as 'Ford of the Movies' in Caughie, *Theories of Authorship*.

MITRY, Jean
'Rencontre avec John Ford' in *Cahiers* 45 (March 1955)
trans. in Sarris, *Interviews with Film Directors*.

MONOD, Roland
'En travaillant avec Robert Bresson' in *Cahiers* 64 (November 1956)
trans. (abridged) as 'Working with Bresson' in *Sight and Sound*, vol. 27, no. 1, Summer 1957.

MOULLET, Luc
'Sainte Janet' (on *Jet Pilot*) in *Cahiers* 86 (August 1958)
trans. as 'Saint Janet' in Baxter, P. (ed.), *Sternberg*, London, British Film Institute, 1980

'Sam Fuller sur les brisées de Marlowe' in *Cahiers* 93 (March 1959)
trans. (extract) in Caughie, *Theories of Authorship*; trans. in full in this volume (Ch. 20).

MOURLET, Michel
'Trajectoire de Fritz Lang' in *Cahiers* 99 (September 1959)
trans. as 'Fritz Lang's Trajectory' in Jenkins, S. (ed.), *Fritz Lang: The Image and the Look*, London, British Film Institute, 1981.

OPHULS, Max
'Entretien avec Max Ophuls' (by Jacques Rivette, François Truffaut) in *Cahiers* 72 (June 1957)
trans. as 'Interview with Max Ophuls' in Willemen, P. (ed.), *Ophuls*, London, British Film Institute, 1978.

'Mon expérience' in *Cahiers* 81 (March 1958)
trans. as 'My Experience' in *Cahiers du Cinéma in English*, no. 1, 1966, reprinted in Sarris, *Interviews with Film Directors*.

RENOIR, Jean
'On me demande . . .' in *Cahiers* 8 (January 1952)
trans. as 'Personal Notes' in *Sight and Sound*, vol. 21, no. 4, April–June 1952, and

(extract) as 'The Profession of Director' in Leprohon, P., *Jean Renoir*, New York, Crown, 1971.

'Entretien avec Jean Renoir' (by Jacques Rivette, François Truffaut) in *Cahiers* 34 and 35 (April and May 1954)
trans. (abridged) as 'Renoir in America' in *Sight and Sound*, vol. 24, no. 1, July–September 1954.

'Nouvel entretien avec Jean Renoir' (by Jacques Rivette, François Truffaut) in *Cahiers* 78 (Christmas 1957)
trans. (extracts) as 'Reality and Magic', 'The Uses of Art' and 'Preparing for Shooting' in Leprohon, P., *Jean Renoir*, New York, Crown, 1971.

RIVETTE, Jacques
'Génie de Howard Hawks' in *Cahiers* 23 (May 1953)
trans. as 'The Genius of Howard Hawks' in *Movie*, no. 5, December 1962 (abridged), modified translation (complete) in McBride, J. (ed.), *Focus on Howard Hawks*, Englewood Cliffs, NJ, Prentice-Hall, 1972, reprinted in Braudy and Dickstein, *Great Film Directors*, and in this volume (Ch. 16).

'Entretien avec Jean Renoir' (with François Truffaut) in *Cahiers* 34 and 35 (April and May 1954)
trans. (abridged) as 'Renoir in America' in *Sight and Sound*, vol. 24, no. 1, July–September 1954.

'Lettre sur Rossellini' in *Cahiers* 46 (April 1955)
trans. as 'Letter on Rossellini' in Rosenbaum, J. (ed.), *Rivette: Texts and Interviews*, London, British Film Institute, 1977; reprinted in this volume (Ch. 26).

'Notes sur une révolution' in *Cahiers* 54 (Christmas 1955)
trans. (extract) in Caughie, *Theories of Authorship*; trans. in full in this volume (Ch. 8).

'Entretien avec Howard Hawks' (with Jacques Becker, François Truffaut) in *Cahiers* 56 (February 1956)
trans. in Sarris, *Interviews with Film Directors*.

'Entretien avec Max Ophuls' (with François Truffaut) in *Cahiers* 72 (June 1957)
trans. as 'Interview with Max Ophuls' in Willemen, P. (ed.), *Ophuls*, London, British Film Institute, 1978.

'La Main' (on *Beyond a Reasonable Doubt*) in *Cahiers* 76 (November 1957)
trans. as 'The Hand' in Rosenbaum, J. (ed.), *Rivette: Texts and Interviews*, London, British Film Institute, 1977; reprinted in this volume (Ch. 19).

'Bio-filmographie de Jean Renoir' in *Cahiers* 78 (Christmas 1958) (notes by Rivette on *Le Bled*, *Le Petit Chaperon rouge*, *La Tosca*, *The Woman on the Beach*, *The River*, *French Cancan*)
trans. in Bazin, *Jean Renoir*.

'Que Viva Eisenstein' in *Cahiers* 79 (January 1958)
trans. as 'Que Viva Eisenstein' in Moussinac, L. (ed.), *Sergei Eisenstein*, New York, Crown, 1969.

'Du côté de chez Antoine' (on *Les 400 Coups*) in *Cahiers* 95 (May 1959) trans. as 'Antoine's Way' in Denby, D. (ed.), *The 400 Blows*, New York, Grove Press, 1969.

ROHMER, Eric
'Renoir Américain' (under his real name Maurice Schérer) in *Cahiers* 8 (January 1952)
trans. (extract) as 'American Renoir' in Caughie, *Theories of Authorship.*

'Entretien avec Roberto Rossellini' (under his real name Maurice Schérer, with François Truffaut) in *Cahiers* 37 (July 1954)
trans. in *Film Culture*, no. 2, vol. 1, March–April 1955, reprinted in Sarris, *Interviews with Film Directors*; extracts also in this volume (Ch. 28).

'A qui la faute?' (under his real name Maurice Schérer) in *Cahiers* 39 (October 1954)
trans. (extract) in Caughie, *Theories of Authorship.*

'Le Celluloïd et le marbre II: le siècle des peintres' in *Cahiers* 49 (July 1955)
trans. as 'Celluloid and Marble II (The Century of Painters)' in Williams, C. (ed.), *Realism and the Cinema*, London, Routledge & Kegan Paul, 1980.

'Le Celluloïd et le marbre III: de la métaphore' in *Cahiers* 51 (October 1955)
trans. as 'Celluloid and Marble III (On Metaphor)' in Williams, C. (ed.), *Realism and the Cinema*, London, Routledge & Kegan Paul, 1980.

'Bio-filmographie de Jean Renoir' in *Cahiers* 78 (December 1957) (notes by Rohmer on *Boudu sauvé des eaux*, *Madame Bovary*, *The Southerner*, *Le Carrosse d'or*)
trans. in Bazin, *Jean Renoir.*

Closely related material: see Rohmer, Eric, and Chabrol, Claude, *Hitchcock, The First Forty-Four Films*, New York, Frederick Ungar, 1979, originally published Paris, 1957, and incorporating material close to work published on Hitchcock by Rohmer and Chabrol in *Cahiers.*

ROSSELLINI, Roberto
'Entretien avec Roberto Rossellini' (by Eric Rohmer, under his real name Maurice Schérer, and François Truffaut) in *Cahiers* 37 (July 1954)
trans. in *Film Culture*, no. 2, vol. 1, March–April 1955, reprinted in Sarris, *Interviews with Film Directors*; extracts also in this volume (Ch. 28).

'Dix ans de cinéma I–III' in *Cahiers* 50, 52 and 53 (August–September and November 1955, and January 1956)
trans. as '10 Years of Cinema I–III' in Overbey, D. (ed.), *Springtime in Italy*, London, Talisman, 1978.

TRUFFAUT, François
'Notes sur d'autres films' (on *Dr Cyclops*) in *Cahiers* 25 (July 1953)
trans. as 'Dr Cyclops' in Johnson, W. (ed.), *Focus on the Science Fiction Film*, Englewood Cliffs, NJ, Prentice-Hall, 1972.

'Du mépris considéré' (on *Stalag 17*) in *Cahiers* 28 (November 1953)
trans. (of version close to original) as 'Stalag 17' in Truffaut, *Films in My Life.*

'Une Certaine Tendance du cinéma français' in *Cahiers* 31 (January 1954)
trans. as 'A Certain Tendency of the French cinema' in *Cahiers du Cinéma in English*, no. 1, 1966, reprinted in Nichols, *Movies and Methods*; extract reprinted in Caughie, *Theories of Authorship.*

'Aimer Fritz Lang' (on *The Big Heat*) in *Cahiers* 31 (January 1954)
trans. as 'Loving Fritz Lang' in Braudy and Dickstein, *Great Film Directors*.

'Les Truands sont fatigués' (on *Touchez pas au grisbi*) in *Cahiers* 34 (April 1954)
trans. (of version close to original) as 'Touchez pas au grisbi' in Truffaut, *Films in My Life*; trans. of original in this volume (Ch. 1).

'Entretien avec Jean Renoir' (with Jacques Rivette) in *Cahiers* 34 and 35 (April and May 1954)
trans. (abridged) as 'Renoir in America' in *Sight and Sound*, vol. 24, no. 1, July–September 1954.

'Entretien avec Roberto Rossellini' (with Eric Rohmer, under his real name Maurice Schérer) in *Cahiers* 37 (July 1954)
trans. in *Film Culture*, no. 2, vol. 1, March–April 1955, reprinted in Sarris, *Interviews with Film Directors*; extracts also in this volume (Ch. 28).

'Un Trousseau de fausses clés' (on Hitchcock) in *Cahiers* 39 (October 1954)
trans. as 'Skeleton Keys' in *Film Culture*, no. 32, Spring 1964, reprinted in *Cahiers du Cinéma in English*, no. 2, 1966.

'L'Admirable Certitude' (on *Johnny Guitar*) (under pseudonym Robert Lachenay) in *Cahiers* 46 (April 1955)
trans. (of version of original) as 'Johnny Guitar' in Truffaut, *Films in My Life*; trans. of original in this volume (Ch. 11).

'Abel Gance, désordre et génie' (on *La Tour de Nesle*) (under pseudonym Robert Lachenay) in *Cahiers* 47 (May 1955)
trans. as 'La Tour de Nesle' in Truffaut, *Films in My Life*.

'Le Derby des psaumes' (on *Vera Cruz*) in *Cahiers* 48 (June 1955)
trans. as 'Vera Cruz' in Truffaut, *Films in My Life*.

'La Comtesse était Beyle' (on *The Barefoot Contessa*) in *Cahiers* 49 (July 1955)
trans. (of version of original) as 'The Barefoot Contessa' in Truffaut, *Films in My Life*.

'Portrait d'Humphrey Bogart' (under pseudonym Robert Lachenay) in *Cahiers* 52 (November 1955)
trans. (of revised version of original) as 'Portrait of Humphrey Bogart' in Truffaut, *Films in My Life*.

'Lola au bûcher' (on *Lola Montès*) in *Cahiers* 55 (January 1956)
trans. (of version of original) as 'Lola Montès' in Truffaut, *Films in My Life*.

'Entretien avec Howard Hawks' (with Jacques Becker, Jacques Rivette) in *Cahiers* 56 (February 1956)
trans. in Sarris, *Interviews with Film Directors*.

'La Main de Marilyn' (on *The Seven Year Itch*) (under pseudonym Robert Lachenay) in *Cahiers* 57 (March 1956)
trans. (of version close to original) as 'The Seven Year Itch' in Truffaut, *Films in My Life*.

'L'Attraction des sexes' (on *Baby Doll*) in *Cahiers* 67 (January 1957)
trans. (of version of original) as 'Baby Doll' in Truffaut, *Films in My Life*.

'Entretien avec Max Ophuls' (with Jacques Rivette) in *Cahiers* 72 (June 1957)
trans. as 'Interview with Max Ophuls' in Willemen, P. (ed.), *Ophuls*, London, British Film Institute, 1978.

'Parlons-en!' (on *Twelve Angry Men*) in *Cahiers* 77 (December 1957)
trans. as 'Twelve Angry Men' in Truffaut, *Films in My Life*.

'Bio-filmographie de Jean Renoir' in *Cahiers* 78 (Christmas 1957) (notes by Truffaut on *Nana*, *Charleston*, *Marquitta*, *Tire au flanc*, *Toni*, *Le Crime de Monsieur Lange*, *La Vie est à nous*, *La Grande Illusion*, *La Marseillaise*, *La Règle du jeu*, *This Land is Mine*)
trans. in Bazin, *Jean Renoir*.

'Photo du Mois: Les avions font l'amour dans *Jet Pilot* de Sternberg' in *Cahiers* 80 (February 1958)
trans. (of version of original) as 'Jet Pilot' in Truffaut, *Films in My Life*.

'Si jeunes et des Japonais' (on *Juvenile Passion*) in *Cahiers* 83 (May 1958)
trans. as 'Juvenile Passion' in Truffaut, *Films in My Life*.

'Il faisait bon vivre' (on Bazin) in *Cahiers* 91 (January 1959)
trans. as 'It was good to be alive' in *New York Film Bulletin*, vol. 3, no. 3 (no. 44), n.d., reprinted in Denby, D. (ed.), *The 400 Blows*, New York, Grove Press, 1969.

Closely related material: see contemporaneous (though often revised) but non-*Cahiers* writing collected in Truffaut, *Films in My Life*; François Truffaut (with the collaboration of Helen G. Scott), *Hitchcock*, New York, Simon & Schuster, 1967; London, Secker & Warburg, 1968 (originally published as *Le Cinéma selon Hitchcock*, Paris, 1966) strongly reflects Truffaut's work on Hitchcock in the 1950s.

VISCONTI, Luchino
'Entretien avec Luchino Visconti' (by Jacques Doniol-Valcroze and Jean Domarchi) in *Cahiers* 93 (March 1959)
trans. as 'Visconti Interviewed' in *Sight and Sound*, vol. 28, nos 3–4, Summer–Autumn 1959.

Appendix 3

Cahiers du Cinéma in the 1960s and 1970s

This volume of material from *Cahiers du Cinéma* covers the period 1951–9. Forthcoming volumes will select material from 1960 through to the mid-1970s.

Volume 2: 1960–8
By 1959 *Cahiers* was well established as the major influence in French film criticism. Its polemical positions on American cinema, in particular, had begun to generate enormous controversy in critical circles both in France and elsewhere, notably in Britain. At the same time, there is little doubt that this controversy would not have received the attention it did had the films of the French 'New Wave' not dominated critical attention as extensively as they did in the period from 1958 to the early 1960s. Although by no means all the new French film-makers came from the ranks of *Cahiers* critics, enough important ones – Truffaut, Godard, Chabrol, later Rivette and Rohmer – did, and the prestige won by their films forced even critics hostile to *Cahiers* criticism to take their critical interests and judgments seriously. Thus, Richard Roud:

> I wonder how many English critics would have included (in their lists of ten best films of the year) Hitchcock's *Vertigo*, Samuel Fuller's *Run of the Arrow*, Douglas Sirk's *A Time to Love and a Time to Die*, or Nicholas Ray's *Wind Across the Everglades*. One's first reaction might be to conclude that these men must be very foolish. And indeed, until a year or two ago, one might have got away with it. But today it would be difficult, I think, to maintain that film-makers like Alain Resnais, François Truffaut, Claude Chabrol, Jean-Luc Godard, Pierre Kast and Jean-Pierre Melville are fools.[1]

The combination of prestige and controversy brought the circulation of *Cahiers* from around 3,000 in the early and mid-1950s to around 12,000 in the early 1960s and to a peak of over 13,000 in the mid- and late 1960s.

A great deal of the supposed critical 'excess' of *Cahiers* belongs to the early 1960s, when Eric Rohmer was largely responsible for editorial policy. It was an excess marked by the growing influence of a group of critics, often identified as 'MacMahonists', after the MacMahon cinema which specialized in American movies, but pulling along with them others on the journal, including Rohmer himself, and shifting the central focus of criticism to an almost abstract conception of *mise en scène* and to a group of newly acclaimed *auteurs*, among whom figures like Joseph Losey, Raoul Walsh, Fritz Lang, Otto Preminger and Italian epic director Vittorio Cottafavi were pre-eminent. Perhaps out of modesty, but nevertheless surprisingly, relatively little was written about the French New Wave in the early 1960s. Certainly, the interest in European cinema, and particularly Italian cinema, which had been so important in the 1950s now seemed in decline. There is little doubt that these directions of *Cahiers* worried some of its earlier editorial leaders who continued to be associated with the journal. Jacques Doniol-Valcroze and Pierre Kast, for example, both Left or liberal, were concerned about its increasing 'apoliticism', if not its drift to the Right. Godard was arguing in 1962 that no new ideas were coming out of *Cahiers*: 'There is no longer any position to defend . . . Now that everyone is agreed, there isn't so much to say. The thing that made *Cahiers* was its position in the front line of battle.'[2] Jacques Rivette and Michel Delahaye wanted to see more discussion in *Cahiers* of 'new cinema', new cultural theories, politics – directions which Rohmer did not find very sympathetic. In 1963, as a result of these dissatisfactions, an editorial committee was imposed on Rohmer, who was soon after replaced as chief editor by Rivette, who remained there in the period 1963–5.

To be fair, the early 1960s were not in fact as narrow as this account implies. The contents of Volume 2 show that alongside the 'extremist' work on American cinema, there was a growing interest in quite different areas, such as the influence of Bertolt Brecht's work on film-making and film criticism and the developments in *cinéma-vérité* and direct cinema. Such new directions were given considerable impetus, however, in the mid-1960s, with the very conscious encouragement of an interest in current theoretical work in areas like anthropology and linguistics which were relevant to film – represented in Volume 2 by an interview with Roland Barthes. Probably most important was the development of a polemic for a 'new cinema' and for a conscious politicisation of criticism. Inevitably, these new directions involved a reassessment of the stance *Cahiers* had taken to American cinema in the past, as well as a recognition that American cinema itself was undergoing significant changes. Certainly, overall, one needs to think of *Cahiers* in this period as beginning to question assumptions which had been fundamental to its earlier views on American cinema: questions about the concept of authorship, questions about the ideological function of American cinema. To be clear, this was not a *rejection* of American cinema, rather a *re-thinking* in the context of a more rigorously political and theoretical critical practice

Volume 3: 1969–1972

These more rigorously political and theoretical positions are, of course, those generally associated with *Cahiers* in the *post*-1968 period, but it would be wrong to see the events of 1968 as a sudden turning point: very clearly, the journal was already moving in these directions from the mid-1960s onwards. Paradoxically, *Cahiers* changed owner-publisher in the mid-1960s and was redesigned to look more 'popular', just at the time it was beginning to become less 'popular' in the areas of cinema it valued and hence less 'popular' in appeal. During the short but very intense period covered by Volume 3, *Cahiers* lost readers and went through ownership crises, ending the period with a very austere cover design and a new financial structure.

If the critical identity of *Cahiers* had been clear and influential in the late 1950s, then less distinct in the 1960s, it now became, in the post-1968 period, once again polemical and a source of enormous influence and controversy. This time, however, the polemics – more political, more theoretical – had less widespread appeal: whereas the critical controversies around authorship and American cinema and *mise en scène* in the late 1950s subsequently entered, in however crude or partial a form, writing about film generally – in newspaper reviewing, for example – the theoretical work of *Cahiers* in the 1969–72 period had its effects in the narrower field of serious film writing and film teaching.

Those effects were, however, very radical. They had to do, essentially, with the elaboration of a 'politics of cinema' in the wake of the events of May 1968[3] and the upheaval they caused within left wing politics in France and, within those politics, radical thinking about the function of culture and cultural work. The crucial areas of debate became those embodied in the title of a celebrated 1969 *Cahiers* editorial: 'Cinema/Ideology/Criticism'.[4] Central to this debate was the concept of 'dominant ideology', formulated by philosopher Louis Althusser in his re-reading of Marx, and the manner in which such a dominant ideology was carried in cinema. As Volume 3 puts it, part of what was involved was a definitive break with the 'idealist' representational aesthetic of realism associated with André Bazin, so central to *Cahiers*' past, and its replacement with an aesthetic based on 'montage' and its association with dialectical materialism, in particular its relationship to Eisenstein and the Soviet cinema of the 1920s, which became a major area for 'rediscovery' by *Cahiers* in this period.

The nature and function of criticism itself also became central: what was the status of the 'scientific' criticism *Cahiers* wished to practise, with its borrowings from the post-Freudian psychoanalytic work of Jacques Lacan, in relation to the spectator as 'subject', and from grammatologist Jacques Derrida, in relation to the process of 'reading'? As well as a rediscovery of Soviet cinema, this period also produced sustained work in the 're-reading' of French and American cinema of the past, in analysis of the new cinema of film-makers such as Miklos Jancsó and Jean-Marie Straub and Danièle Huillet, and in systematic ideological analysis of contemporary 'political' films, such as those by Costa-Gavras.

Volume 4: The Later 1970s
The *Cahiers* project in the later 1970s very much continues and extends the political and theoretical positions elaborated in the post-1968 period, in particular questions around the place of the spectator, from the psychoanalytic work of Lacan, and questions around politics and history arising out of the work of Michel Foucault. The continuing overall commitment to understanding the operation of bourgeois cinema, through systematic re-reading of both films and film history, criticism and theory, was complemented by a commitment to exploring alternatives to bourgeois cinema, whether the deconstructed European cinema of Godard, Straub-Huillet and others or, increasingly important in this period, the 'anti-imperialist' cinema in, for example, Algeria, Palestine, China, Chile. To some extent there was also a re-focusing on French cinema, as *Cahiers* had done in the 1950s, prior to the New Wave, and on the way in which a genuinely 'national' French cinema needed to be understood and generated. In these senses, questions about cinema and cultural struggle remained at the head of the *Cahiers* agenda: what could a radical film journal contribute to political struggle on the cultural front?

Notes

1 Richard Roud, 'The French Line', *Sight and Sound*, vol. 29, no. 4, Autumn 1960, p. 167.
2 Interview with Jean-Luc Godard, *Cahiers* 138, December 1962; trans. in Tom Milne (ed.), *Godard on Godard*, London, Secker & Warburg; New York, Viking, 1972, p. 195.
3 For an account of the events of May 1968, see Sylvia Harvey, *May 68 and Film Culture*, London, British Film Institute, 1978.
4 Jean-Louis Comolli and Jean Narboni, 'Cinema/Ideology/Criticism', *Cahiers* 216, October 1969; trans. in *Screen*, vol. 12, no. 1, Spring 1971, reprinted in Bill Nichols (ed.), *Movies and Methods*, Berkeley, University of California Press, 1976, and in *Screen Reader 1*, London, Society for Education in Film and Television, 1977.

Index of Names and Film Titles

307